THE SYRIAN DESERT

The United States
THE MACMILLAN COMPANY, NEW YORK

Australia and New Zealand
THE OXFORD UNIVERSITY PRESS, MELBOURNE

Canada
THE MACMILLAN COMPANY OF CANADA, TORONTO

South Africa
THE OXFORD UNIVERSITY PRESS, CAPE TOWN

India and Burma
MACMILLAN AND COMPANY LIMITED
BOMBAY   CALCUTTA   MADRAS

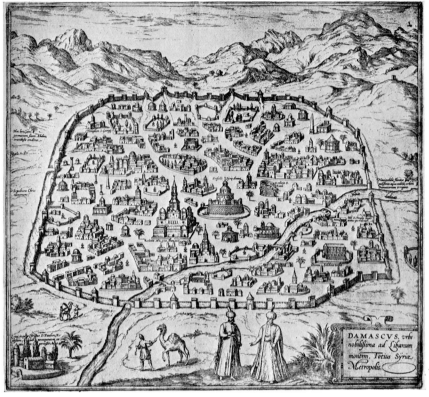

DAMASCUS IN THE SIXTEENTH CENTURY

British Museum

THE SYRIAN DESERT

Caravans, Travel and Exploration

by

CHRISTINA PHELPS GRANT

M.A., PH.D.

WITH SIXTEEN PLATES
AND FOUR MAPS

A. & C. BLACK LTD

4, 5 & 6 SOHO SQUARE, LONDON W.1

1937

MADE IN GREAT BRITAIN
PRINTED BY R. & R. CLARK, LIMITED, EDINBURGH

CONTENTS

CHAPTER I
THE SYRIAN DESERT AND ITS INHABITANTS

CHAPTER II
CHANNELS OF ANCIENT AND MEDIEVAL TRADE

CHAPTER III
TRAVELLERS AND EXPLORERS OF THE SYRIAN DESERT

CHAPTER IV
THE MERCHANT CARAVANS

CONTENTS

CHAPTER V

EIGHTEENTH-CENTURY TRAVEL ACROSS THE DESERT

CHAPTER VI

PRIVATE CARAVANS OF THE GREAT DESERT ROUTE

CHAPTER VII

THE GREAT "HAJJ" CARAVANS

CHAPTER VIII

ELEVEN CENTURIES OF POSTAL SERVICE

CHAPTER IX
THE ERA OF MECHANICAL TRANSPORT

APPENDICES

ILLUSTRATIONS

MAPS

ACKNOWLEDGMENTS

THE writer of any outline such as the following must obviously and inevitably be indebted to a great many people. The nature of this indebtedness is indicated below, but its full extent can only be realized by the author.

My first and most heartfelt thanks are due to Professor Eileen Power of the London School of Economics and Political Science. She has been the good and guiding genius of this book from the first to the last page. Although herself busy with innumerable things, Miss Power has never been too rushed to read typescript, suggest improvements in the text, and give much-needed advice and help in the matter of publication.

No less sincere is my gratitude to Mr Douglas Carruthers, who, out of his far greater knowledge of the subject in general and his own desert experiences in particular, has read and amended for me a number of sections of the text. Mr Carruthers has also, with great kindness, advised in the important matter of maps and photographs.

During four years spent in the Near East, I was assisted in my researches by a number of kindly and interested people. Sir Harold Satow, then H.B.M.'s Consul-General at Beyrout, enabled me to obtain a great deal of information relating to communications, both past and present, between Syria and Irak. President Bayard Dodge of the American University of Beyrout aided me in a variety of ways, as did Professor J. S. Crawford and Professor Assad Rustum of the same University. In the field of archaeology, I was privileged to have a most illuminating interview with the Reverend Father Antoine Poidebard of the University of St. Joseph, Beyrout; as also with Monsieur Daniel Schlumberger of the *Service des Antiquités*. The former was then engaged upon making aerial surveys of the Northern Syrian Desert, and the latter was excavating in Palmyra. Mr Norman Nairn was of the

greatest assistance in helping me to collect material for the section
on motor transport; and in addition to giving me a good deal
of personal and private information concerning the Nairn Transport Company, he also introduced me to a number of other
helpful people in Beyrout, Damascus and Baghdad, including—
in particular—Mr Francis A. Kettaneh of the Eastern Transport
Company. While in Egypt, two of the late King Fuad's Ministers,
namely, H. E. Hassan Anis Pasha (then Controller of Civil
Aviation) and H. E. Ahmed Mohammed Hassanein Bey (then
First Chamberlain), gave me some interesting sidelights on
personalities, and on some of the practical aspects of desert exploration. From Hajji Selim Sawwaf of Damascus a good deal
of information was obtained for the chapter on the Great Hajj
caravans. Last, but in nowise least, were numerous officers of the
Royal Air Force stations at Amman, Baghdad and Heliopolis,
and various pilots of Imperial Airways Limited, all of whom
contributed odds and ends of relevant information.

In London was done the greater part of the historical searching
for this study. It would be difficult for me to acknowledge
adequately the extent of my indebtedness to the Staffs of the
British Museum, the Royal Geographical Society and the London
Institute of Historical Research. Every member of these institu-
tions whom I had occasion to consult was kindness and considera-
tion personified. I owe most especial thanks to Mr A. I. Ellis,
Deputy Keeper and Superintendent of the Reading Room of the
British Museum; Mr Sidney Smith, Keeper of the Department of
Egyptian and Assyrian Antiquities; Mr E. W. O'F. Lynam,
Assistant Keeper of the Department of Printed Books, Maps,
Charts and Plans; Mr A. S. Fulton, Assistant Keeper of the
Department of Oriental Printed Books and Manuscripts; Pro-
fessor Albert F. Pollard and Mr Guy Parsloe of the Institute of
Historical Research; and Mr W. D. Woodrow of the Royal
Geographical Society. I am also obliged to the Librarians of the
India Office and the Record Office for their assistance during my
occasional use of the manuscripts in these archives.

Finally, there are a few individuals each one of whom granted

me a single interview: namely, Sir Arnold Wilson, the late
Colonel T. E. Lawrence, Major C. G. Lynam, Mr R. V. Vernon
of the Colonial Office, Professor H. A. R. Gibb of the School of
Oriental Studies (University of London), Professor W. L.
Westermann of Columbia University (in New York), Professor
W. R. Taylor of the University of Toronto and Professor
Arnold Toynbee of the Royal Institute of International Affairs,
London. Their helpfulness, one and all, can most emphatically
not be gauged by the length of my conversations with each of the
above-named gentlemen.

There is, of course, one patient individual who has counselled
and advised, read and re-read, corrected and amended manuscript
and typescript; one who, in addition to all these labours, has also
prepared the data for the two principal maps. Namely, Mr Alan
Fraser Grant. For the painstaking effort of the ultimate proof-
reading, I am indebted also to the timely assistance of Miss Mary
Grant and Mr John Cook.

To each and every one of the above-mentioned, I would
tender my profound gratitude for all they have done, and for
what of interest there may be in the following pages.

CHRISTINA PHELPS GRANT

LONDON, 1936

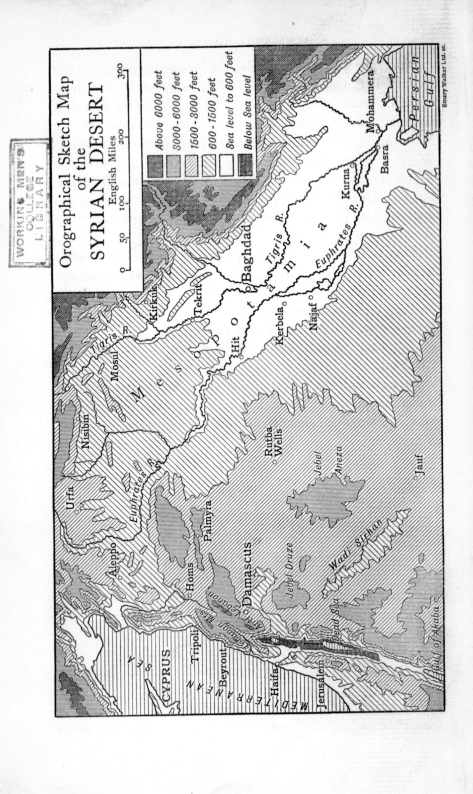

Orographical Sketch Map
of the
SYRIAN DESERT

English Miles

0   50   100   200   300

Above 6000 feet
3000 - 6000 feet
1500 - 3000 feet
600 - 1500 feet
Sea level to 600 feet
Below Sea level

Emery Walker Ltd. sc.

Persian Guf

Mohammera

Basra

Kurna

Euphrates R.

Tigris R.

Baghdad

Tekrit

Kirkuk

Kerbela

Najaf

Hit

Tigris R.

Mosul

M   e   s   o   p   o   t   a   m   i   a

Nisibin

Urfa

Euphrates R.

Aleppo

Rutba Wells

Jebel Aneza

Jauf

Homs

Palmyra

Damascus

Jebel Druze

Wadi Sirhan

Anti Lebanon Mts.

Tripoli

Beyrout

Haifa

Jerusalem

Dead Sea

Gulf of Akaba

CYPRUS

M E D I T E R R A N E A N   S E A

THE SYRIAN DESERT

CHAPTER I

THE SYRIAN DESERT AND ITS INHABITANTS

I

PROLOGUE

In recent years the cartographical face of the Syrian Desert has become increasingly familiar to the general reader. The press, post-War writers of near-eastern reminiscences, and various students of the mandate system (as it has been applied in Syria, Palestine and Irak) have all contributed to arouse interest in this relatively small and arid plateau.

Certain deserts divide countries and their civilizations, inexorably; others unite them. The Syrian Desert is one of those which unites adjacent lands; and during the last twenty years, the uniting of those lands has acquired a new importance. Since the Great War, the desert regions have been the scene of a mechanical revolution; medieval methods of transport have suddenly, almost magically, given place to the most advanced exponents of modern transport. For more than three thousand years the trade routes of this desert have linked the eastern seaboard of the Mediterranean with Mesopotamia; they have fostered cultural and religious, as well as commercial exchanges between the Near and the Middle East. Furthermore, until the opening of the Suez Canal, the Syrian Desert was almost universally recognized as a short-cut between the Occident and the Orient. For a brief period after 1869, however, the desert highways were first neglected, and then forgotten.

Camel caravans could have no place in the development of modern transport systems. Trans-desert railways were visualized, but all plans for such were vetoed. The desert was not considered a potentially modern link for the purpose of connecting the West with the East. Instead, the building of a "Berlin to Baghdad" railway was undertaken; but before its completion the Great War intervened. During and after the War, armoured cars were used in certain parts of the Syrian Desert, and its arid plains were found to be suitable for motor transport. Also, Royal Air Force machines flew from Cairo to Baghdad, after the beginning of 1921, thus inducing a new awareness of this ancient short-cut to the East.

During 1923–24 popular interest was stimulated by the opening of a trans-desert motor route between Damascus and Baghdad. The exploits of the Nairn Transport Company, the development of a desert mail and of various passenger motor services, the alarms and excursions of the Druze rebellion (in 1925–26) increasingly focused attention upon the new motor highways. Thereafter, the public imagination was further stirred by the opening of imperial air routes. First Imperial Airways, next the French Air Orient, then the Dutch "K.L.M." flew the desert from Gaza, Galilee and Damascus to Baghdad and Basra. Most recently of all, two great pipe-lines have been laid across this desert, through which oil is pumped from Kirkuk to Tripoli and to Haifa. Sketch-maps in the daily papers have made us familiar with the course of motor tracks and pipe-lines, and with the outlines of the great space which they all traverse: an expanse long empty of any permanent human habitation except the ancient city of Palmyra and its neighbouring mud villages. Today, in the emptiness, there stands the rest-house and fort at Rutba Wells, and nine pumping-stations of the Iraq Petroleum Company.

So rapid and many-sided a development of transport services does more than stir the imagination; it stirs the curiosity as well. One becomes intrigued by the story of desert travel as a whole, and by the experiences of previous desert travellers. There grows a desire to learn something about the ancient and medieval methods of transport which have been so completely transformed within the past thirteen years. Former conditions of desert travel, its peculiarities, the nature of its hardships and all related problems have acquired an especial and comparative significance of their own. Hurried voyagers who cross the modern desert track between Damascus and Baghdad are tempted to compare previous varieties of caravans with their own convoys; and to wonder how merchants used to go about their business: how they conducted their affairs and carried on their trading ventures under more primitive conditions. Similarly, a modern traveller who looks upon the ruins of Palmyra, Jerash or any other caravan city, feels inclined to ask questions about its origin and place in caravan life, and its role in desert history. It is hoped that this book, which is a condensed summary of caravan life and desert travellers, may give a partial answer to the unvoiced questions of the historically curious. There is no chapter included in this survey which could not be indefinitely expanded and elaborated; each one is in itself a potential book; so that the sum of these chapters is, obviously, no more than an outline of the methods and conditions of travel in the desert regions, from Roman times to the present day.

This book has another, a secondary purpose. It is intended as an introduction to the classics of desert travel—those to come, as well as those already written and appreciated. Taken collectively, the following chapters are meant to serve as a background for the adventures and experiences of all who, for whatever reason, have travelled in and across the waste spaces which intervene between Mesopotamia and the Mediterranean. Some desert travellers have been men, and even women, of great reputation, such as Ibn Battuta, Pietro della Valle, Huber, the Blunts, Colonel Chesney and Gertrude Bell. Others, like Burckhardt, Doughty and T. E. Lawrence, never crossed the Syrian Desert; but they made an intimate study of its south-western territory. Still others, less famous, have voyaged thither for various reasons; and these have become known, indirectly, through the writings of fellow travellers, or else their own meagre writings have been found scattered among the greater travel collections (such as Hakluyt and Purchas), or the lesser compilations (such as Ray and Murray). The vast majority of travellers, however, have been individually unknown; nameless because of their numbers. Merchants, Mohammedan pilgrims, soldiers and civil servants, couriers and dispatch-bearers have all played their part, as well as explorers and men of science. Their private concerns are no longer—if they ever were—of general interest; but the manner of their voyaging will always stir the curiosity of those who are interested in desert travel. In order to create a common setting for travellers of the Syrian Desert, down the ages, their various narratives have been taken into account and welded into a single story. Many of these men lived or travelled in the desert during different epochs of its history, so the elements of contrast, as well as those of similarity in their respective periods, have necessarily been noted. Moreover, with the exception of Alois Musil, no one of them ever attempted to traverse the whole of this arid region; so that it has been possible to paint only a collective picture of the desert as seen through their eyes.

Geographically speaking, the Syrian Desert is the shortest highway between the Orient and the Occident. This means that Syria, Palestine and Mesopotamia have automatically become intellectual and commercial middlemen between these two geographical extremes. Immemorially, also, it has served as a bridge between the successive civilizations which have centred in the Near and Middle East. Of course, *the highway* is collective in its meaning. It must be understood to include each and every one of the numerous caravan tracks that cross the desert, by all of which the contacts between east and west have been maintained.

In modern times the desert has become a subject of interest in itself, over and above its use as a highway. Before the nineteenth century, Europeans journeyed across it from necessity; since then, many have travelled in it from curiosity, and to advance some one of the branches of human knowledge. Various geographers, geologists, zoologists, botanists, archaeologists and ethnologists have found food for thought therein, and material for study.

Greece, Rome and Byzantium have left their traces in this desert: temples and caravan cities as well as route-markings. Ruined palaces, castles and the remains of ancient fortifications in mid-desert testify, similarly, to the occupation of early Arab princes, Lakhmid and Ghassanid, and to the rule of medieval Saracens. Primitive Safaitic inscriptions furnish clues to the later Arabic scripts; and modern Arab nomads preserve ancient customs in their age-old surroundings. Thus the Syrian Desert has an inherent interest of its own, apart from the travel to which it has perennially given rise.

Before embarking upon a description of any one of the various phases of desert life and travel, some preliminary remarks must be made. A few words are needed concerning the nature—geological and otherwise—of the Syrian Desert; concerning its history also, and its boundaries in successive historical periods. Something must likewise be said on the subject of the migratory inhabitants of these waste spaces; the principal Beduin tribes; the general characteristics of both the settled Arab and the nomad; and their beasts of burden. The reader who desires to know what sources of information are at his disposal, concerning trade, travel and transportation across the Syrian Desert, will find a selected bibliography at the end of the book. Lastly, a special appendix (No. 1) is devoted to an explanation of the writer's personal system of Arabic transliteration, and to a discussion of the phonetic rendering of certain words and place-names. This note on transliteration is of peculiar importance, because of the unique character of the Arabic language and its many dialects. It needs more than a paragraph to make clear the difficulties which confront anyone who tries to follow or establish a consistent phonetic system, amidst the chaos of existing and conflicting systems. Nevertheless, some understanding of the problem is an essential and prerequisite part of any discussion of the various regions where Arabic is spoken. For the greater convenience of the reader, this note on transliteration is followed (on pp. 302-315) by a short glossary of the Arabic words which occur in the text; and by a separate glossary of geographical names.

2

GEOGRAPHY OF THE SYRIAN DESERT

The aspect of the Syrian Desert is a great surprise to many travellers; because the word desert is apt to conjure up a picture of golden sands blown into dunes, only less mobile than the sea. Whereas the traversible part of this particular desert is flat in appearance, like a vast undulating plain; and the warmth of its colours astonishes even those who have become accustomed to their variety. The plain is in part gravel-strewn; in part sand-covered; and in part hard caked with whitish, glittering dried mud. Then, after first getting used to the sight of a plain, the traveller is again surprised to find any number of green plants scattered thinly over most of its surface. These plants are small and aromatic; gray-green, tinged with red; and they grow on all the desert lowlands. On the north and west desert hills are etched along the sky-line; to the east and south deeply-cut wadis, or dry water-courses, indent the plain's surface. The rocky hills of sand and limestone give changing colours to the desert plain. At mid-day, these are fused into a yellow-tinted gray by the sun's glare; but early in the morning, and late in the afternoon, they run the gamut of a rainbow in which lustrous reds and violets predominate.

In order to understand the peculiar significance of the Syrian Desert routes, and the reason why they have always made so convenient a short-cut to the east, one must consider the geological nature of the desert: its divisions and limitations, as well as its points of vantage. To do this one is also forced to take into account Arabia, which intervenes between Africa and Asia. The southern fringes of this great peninsula, famed as the "incense lands", are Oman, Mahra, Hadramaut and Yemen. The principal town of Oman is Muscat, so well known in the seventeenth century; and the fleetest dromedaries, or riding-camels, of all Arabia are bred by the Beduin of Mahra. The interior of the peninsula, which stretches across more than ten degrees of latitude, is divided into three parts. There is a southern desert of reddish sand, the "Empty Quarter" (*el-Rub el-Khali*) formerly held to be impassable; a central plateau, the great highland called Nejd, which is a relatively healthful and fertile country (especially in the Kasim district, which is traversed by the *Wadi er-Rumma*); and a northern mountainous area, the *Jebel Shammar* region, which forms the southern rampart of another vast sand-wilderness. This northern desert, similar to that south of Nejd, is called the *Nefud*, an Arabic word signifying high sand dunes; its dune crests vary in height from 150 feet on the north and north-east to 600 feet on the south-west. East of the Nefud are long fingers of ridged sands, called the *Dahana*, which taper off (toward the Persian Gulf) into desert country of the smooth, stony type. The northern limits of Arabia may be said to coincide, roughly, with the thirtieth degree of latitude.[1]

Until the nineteenth century, the interior of Arabia was never penetrated by Europeans. But a few westerners had made tentative excursions through some of Arabia's coastal lands, especially those which border the Red Sea, from Sinai in the north to Aden at the southern tip of the peninsula; and the Hejaz, which contains the Holy Cities of Mecca and Medina, had been frequented by Moslems of every sect and nationality. On the eastern, or Persian Gulf side, Oman is divided from Kuwait (in southern Irak) by the Hasa,

---

[1] Some students of these regions insist that *Jebel Shammar*, as the frontier of Nejd, should also form the northern boundary of Arabia; but the *Nefud* and *Dahana* sands form, with equal emphasis, the southern frontier of the Syrian Desert; and their only parallel are the sands of the *Rub el-Khali* in Southern Arabia. The 700 miles which separate the sands of the *Rub el-Khali* and the *Nefud* are actually crossed by sand stretches of the southern *Dahana*. Carl Ritter, in the famous map of Arabia which he published in 1852—which was the first modern map to distinguish between the deserts of Arabia and of Syria—places the Jauf-Sakaka oases on the southern edge of the "Badiet e' Scham" (or Syrian Desert). Fifty years later D. G. Hogarth, the great student of Arabia, led the way in asserting that the thirtieth parallel was the logical boundary between Arabia and the Syrian Desert.

For a description of the great sand-filled depression—the 30,000 square miles of sand-barrier—which is the Nefud, see chap. v of Mr Douglas Carruthers' *Arabian Adventure* (1935), pp. 114-130.

with its ancient port of Gerrha and the pearl fisheries of the Bahrein Islands. The best known towns of central Arabia are Riyadh, the capital of southern Nejd; Hayil, the capital of northern Nejd; and Tayma, near the south-western border of the Nefud.

Geologically speaking, the Syrian Desert is a continuation of the Arabian plateau. It may be thought of as a triangle whose base rests on the thirtieth parallel of latitude, and whose apex projects itself north-westward towards Asia Minor—to where the fertile lands of Syria and Mesopotamia converge (see map, p. xvi). The shortest side of this desert triangle is on the west, where it is bounded by the Sinai Peninsula, the Dead Sea and Jordan valleys, and the Anti-Lebanon Mountains of Syria. In the north, the city of Aleppo is—to all intents and purposes—at the apex of the triangle, because the plain which extends from this city to the Taurus Mountains is now under cultivation. The third side of the triangle stretches south-east from Aleppo, and is bounded by the river Euphrates. Near its mouth, at the south-eastern angle of the triangle, the Euphrates is joined by the Tigris, and the two great rivers—known in their conjunction as the *Shatt el-Arab*—empty into the Persian Gulf.

These rivers have not always joined as they do today. Between the seventh and the fifteenth centuries, the main stream of the Euphrates (called *el-Frat* by the Arabs) held to a more westerly course, from just above Babylon; and just below Kufa (or Meshed Ali) it discharged its waters into what was called the "Great Swamp". Some time after the eighteenth century, the "Great Swamp" (the lower part of which is now a lake) drained into an estuary that passed the site of Medieval Basra, and emptied into the Persian Gulf at Abadan. At some unknown time between the middle of the fifteenth and the middle of the seventeenth centuries the Tigris changed to its present eastern bed; and the head-waters of the Persian Gulf gradually receded. Abadan now lies some twenty miles up the estuary. Since the eighteenth century, the Euphrates has flowed through a more easterly bed to the ancient lagoons of the Tigris, in what used to be the "Great Swamp". Today, the *Frat* joins the Tigris at Kurna, and their joint stream becomes the *Shatt el-Arab*. The records describing the changes of these two great rivers are not altogether satisfactory, and leave considerable gaps of time to the imagination; but at least the original changes appear to have been caused by a great flood that occurred in A.D. 629. It is interesting to note that the modern course of the Tigris, since the seventeenth century, is apparently the same as the channel which the Tigris followed in pre-Islamic days.

The Syrian Desert plateau is between two and three thousand feet above sea-level. In the south, the highlands of *Jebel Aneza* rise to an altitude of 3300 feet; in the west, *Jebel Druze* does the same; and in the north, a chain of sand and limestone hills, 3000 feet above sea-level, stretch diagonally north-east across the desert, from Damascus to Palmyra and thence to the Euphrates (north of Deir ez-Zor). There is also a range of low hills, the *Jebel Melossa*, which run south-east from the salt marshes of Palmyra. These are the only important exceptions to the general flatness of the plateau, although the occasional isolated mountain, called *jebel* by the Arabs, or hill, called *tell*, raise their heads above the plains. *Jebel Tenf*, a landmark near the modern Damascus motor route, is one of these. On the limestone plateau east of *Jebel Aneza*, sinter cones have been found which suggest extinct geysers. From the vicinity of Palmyra a volcanic zone extends southwards into Arabia, as far as Mecca. Even in historical times there have been eruptions, the most recent of which was recorded in 1256. Naturally enough, earthquakes have also occurred; and to this cause must be attributed the ruins of the caravan cities and walled towns, those in the desert (like Palmyra and Resafa) as well as those on its edge (like Jerash and Umm el-Jemal). In the neighbourhood of Aleppo there are patches of low-lying waste land, with an altitude of only 1000 feet, much of which is composed of crystallized salt marshes, known as *sebkha*. Eastwards from Palmyra there lies a broad belt of similar low-lying land, also containing a wide *sebkha*. East of Rutba Wells the hard surface of the desert is dotted with mud-flats—some of which are bituminous. Since the whole desert plateau declines gradually toward the Euphrates valley, sloping from north and west to south and east, its altitude naturally decreases until, near Basra, it approximates sea-level.

This great triangle of land has not always gone under the name of the Syrian Desert. Ptolemy, for example, divided it, like Gaul, into three parts. He named its south-western third "Arabia Petraea", after the then flourishing caravan city of Petra; the central and south-eastern portions he named "Arabia Deserta", and all the rest—which had been lavishly Romanized—he called Syria. Thus was the Desert of Syria triply-named (by Occidentals) until the seventeenth century, as may be seen in the various maps of these lands which were made by the distinguished French geographer Sanson. In the Ottoman period, Arabia was held to embrace all three of these regions, and the northern limit of "Turkish Arabia" was the so-called fertile crescent which connected Damascus with the Euphrates. This designation was as convenient as it was necessary, because the Porte never had more than a nominal control over its Arabian "subjects", and was never able to collect taxes from any desert nomads. Today the frontiers of Syria, Irak, Trans-Jordan and "Sa'udi Arabia" all meet in the Syrian Desert, and have artificially divided it once more into several new sections.[1]

---

[1] Beazley has shown, in *The Dawn of Modern Geography*, how hazy were European conceptions of *Arabia Deserta* and *Syria Deserta* during the Middle Ages. Take, for example, Burchard of Mount Sion, who was a pilgrim traveller in the Levant in the second half of the thirteenth century. He vaguely applied the name "Greater Syria" to all the regions between Egypt and the Tigris, and he conceived of Arabia as extending northward to the Jordan. Other and later medieval concepts, when comprehensible at all, appear to reproduce the Ptolemaic system, with its triple division of the Syrian Desert.

Nicolas Sanson was a very distinguished French geographer and engineer; Louis XIII was a pupil of his, and later—after Richelieu had appointed him geographer to the king—Louis XIII paid his former teacher a state visit. Sanson's maps of the Near and Middle East are representative of the most advanced geographical knowledge of his time; and they illustrate the prevailing European ignorance of that part of the world. Maps of his dated 1652 show that he relied principally upon Ptolemy; in detail they are inconsistent. A general map pushes Arabia as far north as the plains of Aleppo; a more specific one reproduces the Ptolemaic divisions. Syria and its deserts he designates as follows: "Barraab ou Arabie Petrée"; "Beriara ou Arabie Deserte"; "Sourie ou

ROMAN RUINS AT JERASH

Photograph by the author

The Arabs of the Syrian Desert have their own name for this nomad's-land. By them it is called the *Badia*, which signifies waste or open country—the untilled or empty regions where no permanent habitations exist. But the *Badia* is not necessarily desert country; parts of it are potentially capable of cultivation. Sometimes the Beduin distinguish between the *Badiet esh-Shem* and the *Badiet el-Irak*, the waste lands of Syria and of Irak respectively; but not always. Incidentally, since the Saracen period, Arabs have called Syria by the name of *esh-Shem*—for rather an interesting reason. The word *shem* is a contraction of the Arabic word meaning left, or left-hand. Now Syria is on the left hand of all Mohammedans who look toward Mecca, when they are in the west, or on the Mediterranean sea-board. According to the same reasoning, the *Hejaz* (meaning middle or centre) is where Mecca is situated; and the country to the right of the *Hejaz* is called *Yemen*, which is a derivative of the Arabic word which means right, or right-hand.

For our purposes it is both permissible and logical to think of the Syrian Desert, this plateau some 2000 feet in elevation, as a geographical unit; which unit resolves itself into two principal component parts. In the eighteenth century, English travellers christened the southern part, which is quadrilateral in shape, the *Great Desert*; and they called the northern part, a triangle which is

Soristan"—according to Ptolemy's triple division. Palmyra, under the name of "Fayd ou Tamoz", is correctly placed in "Sourie", though too far to the east of Damascus; but the one or two other key towns are placed differently on his various maps. "Sukana" (Sukhna) is consistently located close to Anna, but on one map Anna is more or less where it belongs, whereas on another it is placed near "Retsafa" (Resafa), and the great bend of the Euphrates is straightened out of recognition.

The only clue to the origin of the name Beriara is the name of a hamlet west of Palmyra: el-Beida, which is alternatively called Beriarac by some French archaeologists. To confuse the name of a village with that of a district whose limits might be only vaguely ascertainable is far-fetched, but not entirely improbable.

C. Raymond Beazley (1897–1906), vol. iii, p. 385. Le Sr. d'Abbeville Sanson, *Geographe Ordinaire du Roy*, "L'Asie"; "En plusieurs cartes nouvelles, et exactes; et en Divers Traictes de Geographie, et d'Histoire". Paris, 1652. Philips' *Historical Atlas* (1927), maps, Nos. 2, 32, 40 and 82. R. Dussaud, article in *Syria* (1929), vol. x, p. 54 and map.

set within the larger triangle of the whole, the *Little Desert*. It is the southern, or *Great Desert* which divides, and the northern, or *Little Desert* which connects the fertile lands of the Mediterranean seaboard with the equally fertile valley of Mesopotamia.

Most early Arab geographers (including el-Bekri) called the whole of the *Great Desert* by the name of *as-Samawa*. It extends, roughly, from the thirtieth to the thirty-third parallel of latitude; and it divides itself into three natural parts, each of which has distinctive physical features of its own. The *Hauran*, on the northwest, includes *Jebel Druze* (formerly known as *Jebel Hauran*) and some of the worst of the lava country; the *Hamad* is a central strip of stony, waterless desert, dominated by the heights of *Jebel Aneza*; and the *Wadian*, which slopes down towards the Euphrates, is a network of wadis whose sands are alternately loose and hard-packed. *Jebel Aneza* is the great watershed of the Syrian Desert; in its foothills the larger wadis have their rise. The Wadi Hauran, for instance, slopes from the summit of *Jebel Aneza* to the Euphrates, for a distance of about 300 miles; in places it is 200 feet deep and as much as a mile wide. After a winter rain this wadi, like all the other dry water-courses of the desert, is temporarily flooded. More than two degrees south of *Jebel Aneza* lies the large sandstone depression (sometimes called the "Juba Depression") which contains the Jauf-Sakaka oases. Between Trans-Jordan and this group of oases extends (for more than 200 miles) that other unique depression known as the Wadi Sirhan. *As-Samawa*, or the *Great Desert*, coincides (for all practical purposes) with Musil's "Arabia Deserta"—which thus recalls, but is not identical with, the "Arabia Deserta" of Ptolemy. The nature of its terrain will be described more fully in the next chapter, where the origins and courses of certain ancient trade routes are discussed.

The *Little Desert*, called the *Shamiya* by the Beduin, is conspicuously different from *ás-Samawa*; and it is the only easily traversible part of the Syrian Desert. It has been spoken of as triangular in shape, and its apex, like that of the greater desert triangle, is the narrow strip of semi-arable land between Aleppo and the westernmost bend of the river Euphrates. The broad base of this triangle corresponds, roughly, to the thirty-third parallel of latitude. It rests on the northern fringes of the *Hauran* and the *Hamad*, so the common frontier of the *Great* and the *Little* deserts is a broad strip of excessively hard, stony and barren desert; and this is completely waterless, except for Rutba[1] and the other ancient wells of the Wadi Hauran. The peculiar flatness of the Little Desert has already been commented upon. Actually, it has often been called arid steppe land rather than desert. During the winter there is a rainfall of from three to five inches, so that—in spring—patches of the desert are thinly covered with a kind of tall feathery grass; and all the year round most of the plain is sparsely covered with camel thorn, and a variety of gray-green aromatic plants. Water is near the surface in every wadi or depression; natural springs (*'ain*), and wells or dug-out springs (*bir*) occur frequently; also the less reliable water-holes (*maurid*). In the low-lands, mud-flats are numerous as well as salt marshes (*sebkha*), but these are dry and hard-caked, except just after a winter rain. In many places the surface is hard and relatively smooth, so that it is adapted to the use of any sort of travel—camels and motor cars alike. Sand-dune formation is unknown (except near the banks of the Euphrates), and patches of soft sand are rare. It is small wonder that many tribes migrate northwards every summer, in order to pasture their flocks and their camels in this comparatively fertile and well-watered region; or that the black tents of certain nomad tribes are to be seen there the whole year round.

There are only two serious obstacles to transport in this steppe land. For one thing, numerous wadis on its eastern edge slope down to the Euphrates; several of these, notably Wadi Hauran and Wadi Suab, are difficult to cross. For another, there is the range of desert hills (previously mentioned) which crosses the great plain diagonally, from the neighbourhood of Damascus to

[1] A group of half a dozen Roman wells are situated about 500 yards W.N.W. of the Iraki fort at Rutba. They are all well constructed, stone-lined (at least at the top) and between forty and fifty feet deep. The well-tops are flush with the ground, and the stone-work at their mouths is deeply scored by the friction of the ropes.

the Euphrates, just north of Deir ez-Zor. Between Palmyra and the river, this hilly divide is rather broad, rocky and irregularly spread out; but from Palmyra to Dumeir (near Damascus) the highland narrows into a single range of mountains called *Jebel Rawak*. There are of course mountain passes, leading from the north-western to the south-eastern parts of this plain; and these have naturally predetermined the course of its various routes. Palmyra, situated on the eastern mountain slopes, commands the most strategically important of these passes; which was the reason for the commercial supremacy of this famous caravan city during so many centuries of its history. For this reason, Musil and certain noted French archaeologists, Dussaud and Poidebard in particular, have named the *Little Desert* "Palmyrena". The region has an essential and effective unity which is rendered the more striking by the fact that the whole of its territory was once within the frontiers of the Roman Empire. Today, whenever the *Little Desert* is distinguished from the Syrian Desert as a whole, it is most commonly called Palmyrena. Nevertheless, whenever the southern and the northern parts of the Syrian Desert have to be contrasted or compared, the writer prefers to use the older and more distinctive designations of the *Great* and the *Little* deserts.

The wild animal life which supports itself on the Syrian Desert is quite varied—considering the general aridity of the region. Gazelles and hares are plentiful, especially in the *Little Desert*; so also are the scavengers: vultures, hyaenas and a variety of jackal. Ostriches used also to be plentiful, but are now found only in the *Great Desert*. Wild asses (or "onagers"), once numerous throughout the Syrian Desert, disappeared therefrom during the eighteenth century; and the Arabian oryx antelope—described by Tenreiro (in 1528) under the name of "wild cow"—must have retreated southward, into Arabia, even before then. Douglas Carruthers, who hunted the oryx in 1909, found that rarest of antelopes only in the north-western part of the Great Nefud, and just to the south-west of the Wadi Sirhan. Foxes are not uncommon in the Syrian Desert; and the jerboa, or desert rat—often described by travellers after the sixteenth century—is seen occasionally. This animal is larger than a rat, sandy-white in colour, and is constructed like a kangaroo. A seventeenth-century traveller (M. Carré) claims to have killed a crocodile in a salt marsh between Taiyiba and Aleppo, and it is possible that he did see and kill what may have been a so-called "relict survivor" from a crocodile colony of an earlier age. Travellers, as late as the end of the eighteenth century, reported seeing lions and tigers near the Euphrates. Tigers have never existed within the historical period in the Syrian Desert; but lions have been seen (and killed) along the whole length of the Euphrates, from Birejik to Basra, at least as late as the middle of the nineteenth century—although they are now wholly extinct in the river valley. Wolves are the only large animals to be met with in the wilderness today. Game birds, the bustard and a species of small partridge are still hunted in the *Little Desert*. Lastly, there are several kinds of harmless snakes and insects, including locusts; and there are scorpions—particularly the black scorpions—whose sting is poisonous.

Three kinds of domesticated animals can also find enough food in the desert to keep them alive. Camels, the single-humped pack-camels from north-eastern Arabia and the Hasa, and the fast riding-camels or dromedaries (also single-humped) from Oman and Mahra; both kinds have been used on the desert, and have been bred to sell, since the ninth century B.C. They live on camel-thorn and any other green plants which they can find; and they are able to go from four to ten days without water, according to the season of the year (that is, they need less water in cool weather, and when their "green" food contains some moisture). When camels are working and heavily freighted, their owners often supplement their grazing food by giving them barley "cakes" or little balls of a kind of dough, and sometimes even dates. The two-humped Bactrian camels were once tried in the *Little Desert*, before those from Arabia were imported; but, though surer-footed in the rainy season than the single-humped camels, they did not long withstand the heat of summer. Horses, which the nomads breed chiefly for their own use (rather than for sale), are able to live in the desert; but they require relatively careful treatment. They must have more food, and that of better quality, than camels need; and they must be watered much more often and more regularly— usually once in every twenty-four hours at the least. Many nomad tribes perform all their raiding sorties on horse-back; their shaykhs always own either a mare or a stallion; and a brood mare is the most valued possession of any Beduin family. Sometimes several families will own such a mare in common. Desert-bred asses are also used; but—though hardier—they are valued less highly than horses, and are of less use than camels.

3

BEDUIN TRIBES, THEIR ORIGINS AND ORGANIZATION

The human inhabitants of the Syrian Desert have always been Arabs. From time immemorial Arabian tribes have left their native Arabia and pushed northward into the *Badia*. These migra- tions have been prompted by various conditions. A succession of bad seasons in northern Arabia, extremes of drought or famine, the pressure of an increasing and therefore expanding population in Nejd or even more remotely in Yemen, have all had their share in stimulating tribal movements. The least change in their physical surroundings disturbs the ever-precarious equilibrium of Arab tribes. Therefore, since there are no political frontiers, in the European sense of the word, and because the *Great Desert* is easy of access, infiltration from Arabia is not only possible, it is in- evitable. An Arabian tribe, having once wedged itself into the *Badia*, must either exterminate or expel the majority of whatever tribes may happen to be already in occupation of the inner Syrian Desert. The newcomers, accordingly, displace its inhabitants gradually, or else push them northwards—by force of arms.

Occasionally there is a religious motive for tribal migrations, especially when they occur on a large scale. This was the case in the seventh century, after the death of Mohammed, when Arabian tribes (called Saracens by the Byzantines) invaded not the desert only, but the settled districts of Syria and Mesopotamia as well.

A recrudescence of this spirit, another *jehad*, or holy war against Unbelievers, occurred in the second half of the eighteenth century, but with a difference. The Wahhabis, a "fundamentalist", puritanically-minded sect of southern Nejd, inspired by Mohammed ibn Abd el-Wahhab and led by Abd el-Aziz ibn Sa'ud of Dariya, founded the first Wahhabi state. In order to cleanse and reform Islam, the Wahhabis conquered and converted the whole of central Arabia. Then they sacked Kerbela and occupied Mecca; and finally, under the third ibn Sa'ud, they raided the Middle Euphrates and Syria—carrying their campaigns (between 1803 and 1808) to the very outskirts of Basra, Damascus and Aleppo. Not until the Turks became sufficiently alarmed to send an army against them, were the Wahhabis driven back into central Arabia. First Tusun and his father, Mohammed Ali Pasha of Egypt, led an expedition against the Wahhabi Empire; later Ibrahim Pasha (the adopted son of Mohammed Ali) invaded Nejd, sacked Dariya, and captured the Sa'udi leader in 1818. After the evacuation of Nejd by Ibrahim Pasha, a few (ephemeral) Turkish and Egyptian garrisons were left behind, to guarantee the enforced peace in Arabia. Thus the Wahhabis, unlike the Saracens, did not long continue in occupation of the Syrian Desert. However, Wahhabism did not die: it lay dormant; and Riyadh became the capital of a reviving Wahhabi state. Another outbreak was threatened in this twentieth century. During the World War and the difficult period that followed the inauguration of the Mandate system in the Near East, Abd el-Aziz of Riyadh, a descendant and namesake of Abd el-Aziz I, made himself King Ibn Sa'ud of a united (central) Arabia. After 1928 he added the Hejaz to his kingdom; his nomad armies occupied most of the *Hamad*, as far north as Syria; and the Wahhabis raided into Trans-Jordan and Irak, upon more than one occasion. Sir Gilbert Clayton's mission eventually forced a compromise upon Ibn Sa'ud, and he gave up most of the land that he had annexed in the *Hamad*. Nevertheless, "Sa'udi Arabia" still projects itself into the Syrian Desert, and includes all the territory that belonged, before 1913, to the Rashids of Hayil and Jauf.

Several of the most powerful tribes of the Syrian Desert have

2

continued to live partly in Arabia. Certain sections of the Aneza and (more particularly) of the Shammar tribes live in northern Arabia in the winter, and migrate northwards through the Syrian Desert in the early spring. They travel leisurely across the *Great Desert*, and do not reach the *Little Desert* until the summer-time, after water and pasturage has become too scarce in the more southerly regions. When on the move, tribes generally do not camp in one place for more than two nights at a time. Other sections of these same tribes, on the other hand, confine their migrations to wandering to and fro between the *Great* and the *Little* deserts. Other tribes again, who live nearer the desert frontiers, the outer fringes of cultivation, have less need to migrate. Those on the borders of Syria or Mesopotamia, or near the oases and waterholes of the Wadi Sirhan, do not wander far. Their *dira*, or tribal orbit, is relatively small, because their means of subsistence is relatively great.

To nomads, the term Arab means "the people"—all the people of all the tribes, both east and west. Arabs of the Syrian Desert may be divided into two principal groups. There are the Beduin, or nomads, whose tribes range the waste spaces of the desert; and there are the settled Arabs, originally nomads, who have anchored themselves in such parts of the desert and its fringes as are tillable. The nomads derive their name, Beduin, from the *Badia*, the great waste wilderness which they roam. A single nomad of the Syrian Desert is called a "Bedu", and the plural of the word is "Bedawi". Beduin (literally Bedui) is a collective, dual or impersonal form of the noun, which is a case much used in colloquial Arabic.

When first westerners heard of the Beduin, Arab kingdoms were also in existence, on the frontiers of the civilized states. In the *Little Desert* there was the ancient caravan centre of Tadmor, which was an Arab kingdom long before its greater Palmyrene days. Further south, the Nabataeans, first mentioned in Roman sources in 312 B.C., founded a kingdom which became the caravan empire of Petra. They were, supposedly, the heirs of the Lihyanites, who had succeeded the Sabaeans in north-western Arabia, and—more remotely still—the Minaeans of the first millennium B.C.

After the Roman period, the Byzantine Empire held its

BYZANTINE RUINS AT RESAFA

Photograph by the author

southern and Syrian frontiers—against both the Beduin and the Iranians—with the help of the Ghassanid princes. From the end of the fifth century until the invasion of the Saracens in the seventh, the Ghassanids—whose tribe had come originally from the Yemen, by way of the Hejaz—ruled over a kingdom which included Phoenicia (as far north as the Lebanon Mountains), Palestine and the Jordan valley, the *Hauran* and the *Little Desert* (as far north as Resafa). They were subsidized by the Byzantine emperors; and Justinian appointed the Ghassanid ruler "lord over all the Arab tribes in Syria". He also made the Arab prince next in rank to himself, by conferring upon him the titles *Phylarch* and *Patricius*. The Iranians, on their side, were protected by the Kingdom of the Lakhmids. The Lakhmid kings were vassals of the Iranians, and had been installed by the latter—about A.D. 300—on the ancient Babylonian–Arabian frontier, as outposts against the Beduin. The realm of the "Lakhmids of Hira" extended south and west of seventh-century Kufa, which was near the still later site of Meshed Ali; and, in contrast to the Ghassanid princes, these kings had a fixed residence. Also of South Arabian stock, the Lakhmids were the natural enemies of the Ghassanids; but they were inferior to them, culturally speaking, because they had not had their rivals' close contact with Byzantine civilization.

During the seventh century, both the Ghassanid and the Lakhmid kingdoms were destroyed by the newly Mohammedanized tribes of northern and western Arabia. These proselytizing hordes filled the *Badia* to overflowing, and then pushed further north, west and east in their triumphal progress. The descendants of the conquerors, known to Europeans as Saracens, inhabited the *Badia* and its borderlands throughout the Middle Ages.[1] The centre of

---

[1] The word Saracen has an interesting history. The original Saracens were Arabs belonging to a small tribe of the Sinai Peninsula. Their district was known to Ptolemy as *Sarakene*. Later, *Saraka* was defined by Stephanus Byzantinus as "a district beyond the Nabataeans". In the third century A.D. the tribesmen of Saraka (or Sarakene) grew relatively powerful, incorporated all the smaller tribes in their vicinity, and disturbed the Roman frontier. Gradually, among Byzantine writers, the term Saracen came to be used synonymously with Arabian.

After the founding of the Arabian Empire by the successors of the Prophet

Islamic civilization and political power shifted, in the middle of the seventh century, from Medina to Damascus; and a century later it shifted again, to Baghdad. Then, five centuries later, after the sack of Baghdad in 1258, Cairo inherited the power and the prestige of Islam. During these successive changes, however, and even under the Mamluk Sultans of Egypt, the shaykhs of the Syrian Desert managed to maintain their practical, if not their theoretical independence; an independence which they had arrogated to themselves when first they occupied the *Badia* in the seventh century.

In the early Saracen period, the *Little Desert* was exceedingly popular as a health and holiday resort; and it was much used by the Omayyad Caliphs and their retainers. The wind-blown highlands were considered very healthful, as compared with crowded cities; and the excellent hunting which the desert afforded gave varied sport to the Caliph and his court. The Saracens built summer palaces and royal hunting-lodges in the *Badia*, as the Palmyrenes had done before them. In addition, the wide-open spaces had another, very special use. They were well suited to be a training-ground for young princes and nobles, where they might learn the arts of war and of the chase.

When, in the sixteenth century, the *Badia* came under the nominal rule of the sultans of the Ottoman Empire, there was scarcely any change in the status of its inhabitants. The Beduin never paid taxes to the Turkish government, and they were very rarely intimidated by Turkish troops, whether spahis or janissaries. Always the Beduin have looked upon the *Badia* as their own territory; and they possess its lands in the truest sense, for only Arabs could live in it year in and year out. It is this belief, this confidence in their ownership of the waste lands, that has led them to

Mohammed, in the seventh century, the Byzantines called all the Moslem subjects of the Caliph by the name of Saracens. During the Crusades, the word Saracen was transmitted to Western Europe through the medium of the Byzantines.

Modern Arabs, strangely enough, do not know the name, either as applied to a small tribe or as a collective name for the tribes of North Arabia. Cf. *The Encyclopaedia of Islam*, article on the Saracens.

resist the encroachments of all outsiders; that has caused them to refuse to pay taxes to the Ottoman or any other government; and that has encouraged them to levy tolls (at the point of the sword) upon all caravans, commercial or otherwise, which have crossed the *Badia*. Even modern motor caravans, for their own safety, had to subsidize the Beduin for a number of years; and few Beduin have as yet been genuinely reconciled to the laying of the Iraq Petroleum Company's pipe-line. When the line was being laid they demonstrated their resentment, time and again, by mutilating or even stealing sections of the pipe. It must be admitted that, in some people's eyes, this interference with the pipe-line was merely an instance of their mischievous or wantonly destructive disposition.

In the seventeenth century a great tribal change occurred. Arabs of a kindred stock, from the Shammar district in Nejd, swept northwards into the Syrian Desert. They displaced and drove out to the desert frontiers its existing Saracen occupants. Before the end of the same century the *Badia* was invaded by another tribe of Nejd Arabs, called the Aneza. During a century and a half of inter-tribal warfare, they in their turn established their supremacy in the *Great* and the *Little* deserts, and drove many of the Shammar tribes across the Euphrates—where the latter settled in Mesopotamia. From the early nineteenth century to the present day, the Aneza has been the principal and ruling tribe in the Syrian Desert. Moreover, throughout the Ottoman period, they remained politically—if not economically—independent of the Turks.

The subdivisions of the Aneza are numerous. When they were listed by the Blunts, in 1879, there were nine Aneza tribes, each one of which was composed of minor sections or clans. Of all these, the Rualla was then, and is today, the largest and most powerful. The size of a tribe is reckoned according to the number of its tents, and the Rualla tents were accounted 12,000 in the nineteenth century; and their camels numbered 150,000. Today the Rualla are said by Raswan to number 35,000, with only 7000 tents; although their camels have increased to the approximate

number of 350,000. Many other tribes also range the *Badia*, north, west and east of the Aneza. A few of them, like the Moali—in the neighbourhood of Aleppo—are allies, or else tributaries of the Aneza. Others are entirely independent, like the Sherarat of the Wadi Sirhan. Others again have become more or less settled, like the Montefik Arabs between Hilla and Basra.[1]

Reference has already been made to the seasonal migrations of the Beduin, which they undertake for the purpose of procuring adequate food and water for themselves and their animals. As everyone knows, the Beduin live by breeding and raising camels to sell. Each tribe has its own allotted district, or *dira*, in the *Badia*. The extent of every *dira* depends upon its available water supplies and the nature of its scattered pastures; because each district must, in normal years, be capable of supporting the herds of camels of a given tribe, and of supplying the tribal households with water as well. The extreme scantiness of desert pasturage, and the inadequacy of water sources make it impossible for any large tribe to live as a unit; so every tribe splits up into sub-tribes. These resemble Scottish clans; and each clan lives unto itself alone. As has been well said, these clans wander each apart in their own

---

[1] There is a species of "Gipsy" tribe called the Suluba, which comes under none of these categories. They are supposedly of Indian origin; at least they are not "pure" Arab. Like the Aneza, the Suluba inhabit the inner Syrian Desert, and range from Nejd in the south to northern Palmyrena. But unlike the Aneza and other Beduin tribes, they possess no camels, preferring to breed asses for sale along the desert frontier. They follow the herds of gazelle, in their seasonal migrations, and hunt these animals for food. The Suluba are noted for the work they do as tinkers, smiths and workers in wood. Less recently, the name Suluba was spelled Sleb, Sleyb, Solubba and Suleib.

For information concerning these and other tribes of the Syrian Desert, see Lady Anne Blunt, *The Bedouins of the Euphrates* (1879), notably vol. ii, chap. xxiv, especially pp. 187-193. Charles M. Doughty, *Travels in Arabia Deserta* (preferably ed. of 1933), *passim.* J. L. Burckhardt, *Notes on the Bedouins and Wahabys* (1831), especially i, pp. 1-32; ii. pp. 1-50. Burckhardt's information, though interesting, is a century out of date; and some of his "notes", such as those concerning the habits and locations of certain tribes, is therefore inaccurate.

For more modern material, see Ct. Victor Müller, *En Syrie avec les Bédouins. Les Tribus du désert* (1931). Carl Raswan, *Black Tents of Arabia* (1935).

cycles, within the orbit of the tribal whole. Fighting occurs among the Beduin, spontaneously, whenever years of drought force a tribe, or some one of its clans, to seek water or pasturage outside of its customary cycle or the tribal orbit. Such fighting engenders blood-feuds, and blood-feuds are transmitted from generation to generation. The Beduin press upon one another, as they do upon the semi-fertile frontiers of the states which surround their *Badia*. This pressure is more acute in years of drought; but at all times, in every year, the tribesmen are impoverished, restless, and in a state of chronic flux and instability.

They are a hardy people, these Arab nomads, whose trade is hunting and fighting as well as the breeding of camels and horses. Frequently also they are bandits. Faced with the arduous conditions of life on the desert, only the very fit are able to survive at all. As Mohammedans they are trained to endure want and privation; their religion and their environment equally force them to live abstemiously. Doubtless the Prophet considered the physical as well as the spiritual needs of his people, and laid down his rules accordingly. It is true that the modern Beduin are neither deeply nor fanatically religious, excepting always the Wahhabis; but the force of religious custom is strong among them. In fact, custom and tradition is the nomad's only law. A certain English traveller, while crossing from Aleppo to Basra, once remarked upon the great fatigues of desert travel. He expressed surprise that the Arabs themselves could endure it, year in and year out. "They are certainly in many respects so very like their camels," said he, "that Providence seems to have equally designed them for the desert. I have observed them to walk and work all day, watch at night, and repeat their labour next day without any sign of fatigue, and have likewise remarked that, like unto their beasts, when food and water have been plenty their chops were never still, but can in proportion to their strength go as long without either." [1] Nevertheless, and in spite of their hardiness, a daily existence of

[1] William Beawes (1745). Quoted from the edition of his narrative which is printed in No. LXIII, Second Series, of the Hakluyt Society's publications, London (1929), p. 30.

unremitting hardship shortens the lives of the Beduin; so that neither the old nor the accidentally infirm can hope to outlive their strength. Consequently they usually die young, in comparison with Europeans.

Each Beduin tribe governs itself along quasi democratic lines. The group council of its shaykhs in assembly—of whom the principal shaykh or *saiyid* is but *primus inter pares*—decides all important matters, whether of war and peace, of justice, raids and blood-feuds. The *saiyid*, or lord of a tribe, is the chosen leader of his tribesmen. In theory, the dignity is not hereditary; but actually, the son of an able leader automatically fills his father's place, unless he is personally disqualified through physical or mental weakness. Shaykhs are seniors, or men of authority, because they are proven leaders, or else the heads (often the very young heads) of a powerful family; not because they are venerable with age. The office of iudge (*el-kadi*) is the one dignity that is hereditary; and that is because a thorough knowledge of the Moslem or Koranic Law and of tribal customs is requisite; and this knowledge is most satisfactorily handed down from a father to his son.

The reader must look elsewhere for interesting descriptions of Beduin customs. There is, unfortunately, no place in this survey for the minutiae of tribal organization, or for the details of clan councils and the less formal coffee-gatherings, where all family and tribal matters are discussed.

Those who desire insight into their daily and precarious lives should turn to the narratives of such travellers as have lived amongst them, and of these, one can learn more about the Arabs in Doughty's *Arabia Deserta* than in any other one book. It is only where Beduin character is influenced by certain aspects of commercial life; or when either religious fanaticism or the greed which grows out of enforced abstemiousness affects their treatment of foreigners, that Arabs and their characteristics enter into this story of travel and commerce and trade-routes.

On the commercial side the Beduin are surprisingly flexible. Their extreme independence of spirit, coupled with a necessarily narrow outlook on the world, might have been expected to make them unadaptable to new ideas or to a changing environment. But the reverse is the case—within the limits of their natural poverty. They have proved susceptible from the first to such innovations as coffee and tobacco, cottons and coarse cloths—for their wearing apparel—and firearms. The most recent instance of their suggestibility is provided by motor cars. Many Beduin shaykhs own (or are in debt for) cars which they have learned to drive—although they have not yet learned to take care of them; and the Rualla even organize and carry out most of their raids with motor cars. During the drought of 1932, Beduin tribesmen actually came into the settled districts between Palmyra and Damascus and hired Chevrolet lorries to carry skins of water out to their thirsting herds. They are, in fact, modernizing themselves as much as such a process is compatible with the conditions of nomadic life.

In spite of their adaptability as consumers, however, the Beduin have never taken part in commerce on a large scale. Even the Agail Arabs, whose activities will be described in the chapter on desert commerce, were in the habit only of providing camels for the trading caravans, and of defending these *en route*, against the attacks of marauding nomads. For this purpose the Agails hired out the services of themselves and their camels; but they never became merchants on their own account. Other Beduin tribes, that had no personal connection with commercial caravans, levied transit tolls. They habitually exacted money payments (*khifara*) from the merchants of such caravans, in exchange for a guarantee of immunity. This custom has been called blackmail; and in the old meaning of the word—"tribute exacted by freebooters for protection and immunity"—the term was fair enough (even though the Beduin are not freebooters in the ordinary sense at all); but the word blackmail is misleading, and should be avoided, because of its modern connotation. In addition to this system of tribute-collecting, there was another time-honoured institution— still in existence today—which has long brought a certain amount of profit to desert-dwellers. All townspeople who travelled in the Syrian Desert were under the necessity of establishing the bond of "brotherhood" (*el-khuwa*, or *el-ukhuwa*) with the Beduin whose *diras* they expected to traverse. This could be done in person, or vicariously and for a sum of money. But the intricacies of the *Akhwan* system and its bearing on desert commerce will be more fully explained hereinafter. Even among the Beduin themselves, weaker tribes have had to purchase protection from stronger tribes by the payment of a brotherhood tax.

On the other hand, and by way of contrast to the nomads, there are the settled Arabs, both fellaheen and those who reside in towns. These are collectively called the *Hadar*: an *Hadari* in the singular, and the *Hadariyeen* in the plural. It is noteworthy that the common Arabic adverb for here, is *hadar*; and it is significant that the word *hadarah* connotes culture and civilization. Actually, the settled Arabs are in a state of transition, and have acquired none of the virtues implicit in this word; but they have the right to be optimistic. There are several kinds of *Hadariyeen*. Some are riverain Arabs, who cultivate the fertile banks of the Euphrates. Others are the occupants of desert villages, such as the oases of Sukhna and Taiyiba; or else the inhabitants of towns which border on the desert, such as Hama and Homs. Some of them, of course, have even drifted into the larger cities, such as Damascus, Aleppo or Basra—but these quickly deteriorate, both morally and physically. Others again have built themselves compact settlements in the vicinity of a big city: such as the "bee-hive" villages to the south and east of Aleppo.

The *Hadariyeen* are naturally less hardy, less independent and less courageous than the *Bedawi*. Worst of all, they are far less trustworthy. All travellers—from the Middle Ages to the present day—unite in condemning them. This is particularly true of the so-called riverain Arabs. One reason for the moral inferiority of the riverain Arabs is their lack of any tribal cohesion. Soon after tribes settled on the river-banks, they broke up into sections even smaller than clans; and each household grew selfishly individualistic. As tillers of the soil they had no occasion to unite, for fighting purposes, under a few responsible shaykhs; so they grew gradually intolerant of any form of tribal discipline. Eventually tribal shaykhs, unable to enforce their authority, gave place to village shaykhs; and the latter were unable to maintain any effective control over their own villagers. A village, as a unit, could not openly take part in raiding enterprises, for fear of retaliation; neither could it (after the middle of the sixteenth century) afford to flout Turkish government officials, lest Turkish "justice" and reprisals be visited upon the whole village. So such *Hadariyeen* as were impelled to plunder, had to undertake their robberies singly, or secretly—usually by treacherous means. Each caravan which passed within easy reach of a settlement of riverain Arabs, and each boat that descended the Euphrates, was the potential prey of the *Hadariyeen* of that settlement. It was a temptation not often to be resisted. Riverain Arabs acquired a bad name for thieving and murder; and knowledge of their own evil reputation encouraged them in their treacheries—in that they had no good name to preserve.

Between the predatory Arabs of the Euphrates, and the nomads of the *Badia*, the moral gap is wide, and was noted by the earliest desert travellers. Pietro della Valle, who referred to the Beduin as "Deserticolae", claimed that those who wandered "about the Fields with black tents" were the noblest Arabs of them all. No subsequent travellers have ever disagreed with della Valle on this point. Generally speaking, the Beduin have a natural courtesy and dignity, and rigid standards of their own, which they are careful to uphold. They also observe the laws of hospitality, and keep any contract which they have freely made.

Since the Great War, conditions are thought to have changed. It is believed by many who are familiar with the desert and its ways that traditional laws of hospitality and courtesy are no longer observed with customary strictness; that the word and good faith of even a Beduin shaykh is not invariably to be trusted; and that tribal representatives (*rafeeks*) can no longer guarantee security even among their own tribesmen. British gold (so liberally distributed during the War) is partially blamed for this breakdown of their morale; and the possession of firearms which the Beduin were enabled both to buy and to seize. Nevertheless, there are still any number of tribes that have not been spoiled by their contact with Europeans; and travellers on the desert, under ordinary circumstances, still feel quite safe and secure from bodily harm. The Beduin have acquired a new respect for Europeans and Englishmen, and a realization of the meaning of *pax Britannica*, which helps to offset the ill-effects of their incipient westernization.

After 1918 several army officers were murdered in the mandated territories, and this shook the faith of many who had formerly believed in the proverbial chivalry of the Arabs. But distrust of the Beduin is not justifiable on this score, because no one of these officers, nor any other kind of traveller for that matter, has been murdered in the Syrian Desert. Colonel G. E. Leachman was the victim of the most famous of these tragedies. But he was killed in Mesopotamia, east of Felluja, not in the Syrian Desert. The supposedly authentic account of his death, which was witnessed only by Arabs, is as follows. Colonel Leachman had driven to Khan Muktar (in his capacity of Chief Political Officer in charge of northern Mesopotamia) to interview Shaykh Dhari of the Zoba section of the Dulaim—in an attempt to talk him out of joining in a revolt that had been planned by all the riverain Arabs of southern Irak. Most of the Dulaim, whose tribal centre is at Ramadi, have ceased to be nomads; and the Zoba, which is permanently settled within fifteen miles of Baghdad, is their most easterly section. Shaykh Dhari refused his co-operation, and declined to carry out an order; so Leachman, intending to browbeat him, pulled the Shaykh's beard. Instantly Dhari's son and several other Zoba Arabs shot down Colonel Leachman and the two men—his driver and his bearer—who were with him. The Arabs were all outraged by this treachery, for Leachman was a guest of the Zoba at the time of the interview. This was the only known case of a similar breach of hospitality. It is significant to note that all sections of the Dulaim refused, on this account, to rise or to join in any revolt against the government of Irak. At all events, the murder of so important a Political Officer in August 1920, so soon after the Armistice, gives no real indication of Arab standards of honour and chivalry in an era of comparative peace and order. Anyone who travels in times of political unrest incurs unpredictable risks.

Travellers' opinions of the Beduin have varied, but those who have known them most intimately have liked them, and trusted to their chivalry. In the eighteenth century, Europeans who crossed the Syrian Desert were, for the most part, well treated by the Arabs of their own caravans, and unmolested by the Beduin. This fact led to a revision of western opinion concerning them. Before then, between the sixteenth and the middle of the eighteenth centuries, there had been a misconception of their characters, owing to great tribal conflicts and the chronic warfare between Arab and Turk. But in a relatively more peaceful epoch, after 1750, Europeans came to see that the Beduin were not the terrifying bandits which they had once appeared. Crossing the desert proved to be a safer matter than travelling in parts of the Continent that were off the beaten track. A few travellers, nevertheless, persisted in holding the old opinions; Bartholomew Plaisted for one, and—to a lesser extent—John Carmichael. Plaisted maintained that Arabs would "stop at nothing to enrich themselves", and that every Arab was brought up from infancy to the "trade of robbery", and would cut anyone's throat for ten piastres. He, obviously, made no distinction between the *Hadar* and the Beduin. On the other hand, a majority of travellers after them (Plaisted and Carmichael were among the first to use the Great Desert Route during the eighteenth century) [1] commented upon the hospitality of the Beduin, and praised them for their kindness, and for the honourable way in which they fulfilled their promises to foreigners. Colonel James Capper and Lieutenant William Heude were particularly eulogistic in these respects, and both of them dedicated several pages of their narratives to proving their statements, in the hope of inducing other contemporary Englishmen to revise their inherited prejudices against the desert Arabs. More than twenty years before they journeyed in the Syrian Desert, before even

---

[1] In the eighteenth century the so-called "Great Desert Route" connected Aleppo with Basra. It crossed the *Little Desert* diagonally, and skirted the eastern edge of the *Great Desert*. Cf. pp. 44 and 171.

Plaisted made the crossing, William Beawes had stated that he found the Arabs not in the least exorbitant in their demands for services rendered. He also remarked that there was "infinitely" more hospitality to be found among the Beduin than among "much politer peoples"! Beawes' observations are still true today, among such Arabs as have not been spoiled by their contacts with Europeans.

Most modern travellers concur in holding a favourable opinion of the Beduin, especially explorers who have spent many months either living amongst or travelling with one or more of the *Great Desert* tribes: notably Charles Doughty, and Mr Wilfrid Blunt and his wife (Lady Anne Blunt) in the later nineteenth century; Gertrude Bell, Alois Musil and Douglas Carruthers in the twentieth century. T. E. Lawrence, who lived amongst the Arabs of the west on an equally intimate but rather different footing, confirms this prejudice in favour of the Beduin. In one case only did Arabs signally fail in their treatment of foreign explorers. This exception was Charles Huber, whom they murdered in 1884; but this tragedy occurred in the *Tehama* (or coastal plain) of the fanatical Hejaz, not in the Syrian Desert. The murder was committed (theoretically for plunder) by the *rafeeks* of Huber's own escort, but—according to Hogarth—he was known to have fallen out with the Ateiba tribe, and it is therefore quite possible that he had incurred a blood-feud. The only narrow escape which Doughty had, in his two years of wandering, was also in the *Tehama*—near Mecca. His travels in the *Great Desert*, central Arabia and the Hejaz, immediately preceded those of Huber.

In striking contrast to these incidents in the Hejaz stands the experience of Gertrude Bell. It speaks more than well for the chivalry of the Arabs that an Englishwoman—unescorted by any man of her own race—should have been able to travel widely, not only through the Syrian Desert, but also in Nejd and in north-western Arabia. Time and again she tested in every way the loyalty of her Arab escorts; and not once, but many times she trusted herself alone among her Beduin "friends". Her trust was never betrayed. She even ventured into the outlawed regions of *Jebel*

Druze (scorning the "protection" of Turkish escorts, and defying official warnings and prohibitions), and returned to praise its hospitable inhabitants.

Doughty, who journeyed amongst the Beduin as a *Hakim* (or physician), has shown them to be very like wilful, fickle, precocious children; many of whom are likeable, some of whom are not. The pages of his *Travels in Arabia Deserta* reflect their narrow-mindedness, their selfishness and their cruelty; but his narrative also reflects their spontaneous generosities and their warm-hearted hospitality. The Beduin live from day to day, from hand to mouth, in a state of perpetual and irremediable poverty; their self-contained communities are unimaginably cut off from contact with the changing world outside; their inheritance is the barren desert, and the personal freedom with which this very barrenness has endowed them. But they are care-free, because they are fatalists; and reckless, because they have nothing to lose. Their moods are alternately quiescent—to the point of apathy—and passionately intense—to the point of fierceness.

There is a lesson to be learned from this portrayal of Beduin character. It would seem that their treatment of foreigners depends largely upon the foreigners' treatment of them. They respond in kind to trust and courtesy and kindliness, as they do to the reverse. So that a stranger, even an unbeliever, may go freely and safely amongst them, if he bear these things in mind.

CHAPTER II

CHANNELS OF ANCIENT AND MEDIEVAL TRADE

I

SYRIAN DESERT ROUTES

THOSE who would picture the journeys of caravan travellers must begin by visualizing the highways of which they made use. To do this, two things must be constantly borne in mind: available routes, and the original reasons for selecting them. Before the twentieth century there was only·one method of crossing the Syrian Desert, and that was by camel caravan. Today, of course, "ships of the desert" can be understood to designate motor cars as well as camels; but in the history of desert transport this is the latest phase, and has no bearing whatever on the original problem. Until the twentieth century, only those parts of the desert might be crossed which could be negotiated by camels heavily laden; and water had, of necessity, to be within three or four calculable days of any large caravan. One might say here, parenthetically, that mail couriers, because they travelled alone and as fast as possible, were always less dependent upon formal routes than any other type of desert traveller. In accordance with that attribute of genius which is described as the capacity for taking infinite pains, those who crossed the desert by its various and arid ways not only took infinite pains, but endured the same for countless monotonous days. The desert has ever and impartially imposed the same arduous conditions upon all those who thrust themselves into its inhospitable terrain: an inescapable routine of privation, repetition, and almost incredible slow deliberation.

A cinema film purporting to show the development of desert transport or the evolution of its arteries of trade would—if true to

3

history—be a slow-motion picture, giving almost identical views for each century under review; because the physical features of this particular plateau are such that they, and not man's convenience, have necessarily dictated the paths which should be followed by armies, trade caravans, Mohammedan pilgrims, mail couriers and all other miscellaneous travellers. And because these physical characteristics have always been more or less the same, the highways of the Syrian Desert have accordingly changed but little, and the principal trade routes of the first century B.C. practically coincide with those of the nineteenth century A.D. Only political cataclysms, drastic enough to shift the centres of economic power and divert the main channels of trade, have been able to displace one group of routes by another. Thus some of them fell— from time to time—into temporary disuse; whereas others were resurrected to bear unusually heavy traffic. And because a desert route has never required the laying of a formal road-bed, the practicable highways are all immemorially old, and their use—at any given time—has only varied with the trade requirements of the period in question. In a few rare cases only has the life of a desert road ever depended upon its upkeep. The Romans paved, in part at least, two or three of their most important roads; and certain routes, not otherwise practicable, they rendered so temporarily, by sinking wells in districts which were inadequately supplied with natural sources of water. In like manner the Saracens rendered practicable the potential highways leading from Lower Mesopotamia to central and north-western Arabia. As long as these wells were kept clean and in repair, and guarded from mutilation, such routes could be kept open. But when the wells were neglected, the highways which they had sustained gradually relapsed into their former untraversible state.

The one thing to consider, then, in looking for a clue to permanent trans-desert routes is this: what are now, and what always have been the natural, obvious paths whereby travellers would seek to cross from one side of the desert to the other. Or, in other words, what were the routes that the caravan leaders of any age considered the most direct, the safest and the best suited for supplying the needs of a caravan. An answer to this question will help to place any ancient or medieval highways which cannot be easily traced from written records. Thus, for example, although we have but little detailed or specific information from Latin texts and inscriptions concerning Roman trans-desert routes, all of the important ones have been exactly located, from end to end. Men with constructive imaginations, knowing the genius of the Roman for utilizing every potential military road or avenue of productive trade within imperial boundaries, have known where to look for the remains of long-unused roads. And searching, often laborious, has brought to light here a fort, there a well, elsewhere paving or milestones. In similar fashion, a search for Nabataean inscriptions has revealed much to illumine an earlier period for which our accounts are even more vague and fragmentary. In Jauf, for instance, which has been identified with the ancient Dumat el-Jandel, or Adumu, Nabataean inscriptions have been found which indicate that the ancient route from Petra, through Maan and the oasis of Jafar, was in use at least as early as the Phoenician period.

With respect to the northern routes, Père Poidebard (in collaboration with the French Army Air Force) has made a series of aerial surveys which have established the authenticity of the Palmyrene trans-desert highways—notably of the track between Palmyra and Hit, with its branch to Dura-Europos. Landmarks and contours picked up thus from the air have led to the discovery of the lost parts of certain routes, which were known to have existed either from Arab tradition or else from Roman remains. One hundred and twenty kilometres, for example, of the Palmyra-Hit road was untraceable from the ground, having been obscured by drifting sand and the growth of camel-thorn; this was found by Père Poidebard, in March 1930, in a French army aeroplane, which was reconnoitring to find traces of the southernmost (Syrian) outposts of the Roman boundary or *limes*.

Similarly, even before the finding of the Palmyra-Hit road, Group-Captain Rees of the Royal Air Force had found traces of an ancient road across the lava country, when he was patrolling the Amman-Rutba section of the air mail route. He found that the

western section of the ancient caravan route between Azrak and
Baghdad was lined with the remains of Roman or pre-Roman
stone buildings and watch-towers. This was a track that could
have been used by small caravans in the winter months; its
caravans doubtless made use of the wells of Rutba. The Roman road
which connected Palmyra with the Wadi Sirhan intersected with
this trans-desert route at Azrak. The Roman roads of the Hauran
radiated from Bosra eski-Shem, and two of them went eastward,
through Salkhad, to the lava country. They were laid straight and
were well marked with milestones; and though unpaved, were
piled at the sides with pebbles and stones—just as were parts of the
highway between Palmyra and Hit.

Bearing in mind these things, one can profitably turn to physical
maps of these regions for further illumination. The Syrian Desert,
for purposes of communication, is divided into three main zones
or areas: a southern zone (the southernmost part of the *Great
Desert*), which is closely bound up with Arabia; a central one which
is almost impassable (the *Hamad*); and a northern zone (Palmyrena
or the *Little Desert*), liberally criss-crossed by routes which have
connected the Mediterranean with Mesopotamia from time immemorial.

In the south, a group of oases, of which Jauf is the most important, form a convenient centre for the intersection of four
principal highways. Jauf, just below the thirtieth parallel, is at the
south-eastern end of a great depression called the Wadi Sirhan.
This depression slants south-eastwards from Trans-Jordan to
central Arabia, thus affording direct communication between the
Mediterranean and central Arabia. The Wadi Sirhan is much too
large to be considered as analogous to the dry-river type of wadi.
It is very wide, over two hundred miles long, and is dotted with
oases; the eastern side of this valley bottom furnishes plentiful and
perennial supplies of water which, though salt or brackish to the
taste, is nevertheless acceptable to Arabs and their pack animals.
At the north-western end of the Wadi is Kasr Azrak—once a
Roman outpost—whence roads connect, through Amman and
Bosra, with Palestine and southern Syria. By this route, within the

AZRAK. THE FORT

AZRAK. THE CASTLE

R.A.F. official photographs : Crown copyright reserved

last ninety years, the explorers Wallin, Palgrave, Guarmani, Blunt, Huber, Aylmer and Butler and Musil have all found their way to or from Jauf. Another road, intermittently in use through the centuries, gives direct communication between this mid-desert city and southern Palestine, or Egypt, by way of the ancient caravan city of Petra. A track goes east from Petra, through Maan and Jafar, and follows an imaginary line to the oasis of Jauf, which almost coincides with the thirtieth parallel of latitude. But except during the days of Petra's commercial glory, trade has often been diverted northwards to Azrak, to follow the course of the Wadi Sirhan; or else southwards to join the principal Arabian routes through trade centres such as Tayma and Hayil. From Jauf, one route curves north-east to Najaf (or Meshed Ali) and Kerbela, towards Baghdad; and a second principal route goes more directly eastwards to Basra, for Lower Mesopotamia. And from Sakaka, Kara and the other oases in the neighbourhood of Jauf, various routes penetrate to the hub cities of central Arabia, to the Hejaz (for southern Arabia and Africa) and to the Arabian coastal towns on the Persian Gulf.

It is a question as to whether there were any direct trade connections at all between Jauf and the Persian Gulf, or Lower Mesopotamia, before the Mohammedan era. Mr Sidney Smith, the great student of Assyrian and Babylonian inscriptions, states that there is absolutely no inscriptional evidence whatever to show that, in pre-Mohammedan days, any trading was done between Jauf and north-western Arabia on the one hand, and Lower Mesopotamia on the other. The only known references to these routes go to prove that (on the rare occasions when they were used by individuals and small caravans) they were thought to be exceptionally dangerous highways. In other words, that merchant caravans would never have trusted themselves to these potential routes until such time as they were provided with adequately supplied and fortified watering stations. This was first accomplished under the Abbasid Caliphs of Baghdad, in the eighth and ninth centuries A.D. And from that period dates our first documentary evidence to prove that Jauf and the north-western Arabian cities were directly connected with Lower Mesopotamia. Of course, this is only negative evidence, and several modern authorities hold the opposite view; but unless positive proof is forthcoming to show that commerce was actually carried on by way of some southern Mesopotamian trade route, Mr Smith's theory seems—at least to the writer—the most logical one.[1]

The importance of these southernmost routes of the Syrian Desert is due to the fact that they pass between two barren tracts of land, neither of which is traversable for purposes of trade. Jauf is on the northern fringe of the *Nefud*, a region of deep drifting sands, in dune formation; a surface which is very treacherous for laden camels; and in addition, water is chronically scarce there at all seasons of the year. North of Jauf is a wide strip of almost waterless desert, which is rocky and mountainous, and contains patches of volcanic ground bestrewn with extinct craters, solidified lava flows, and great basalt boulders. The *Harra* or lava country is invariably shunned by caravan leaders because its flint-covered surface is peculiarly hard on the feet of camels.

El-Hamad is an Arabic word signifying hard, barren desert; and both hard and barren is this central tableland, crowned by *Jebel Aneza*, which divides the lowlands of the Euphrates from the *Hauran* and the Wadi Sirhan. Furthermore, the lava country of the *Hauran* extends eastwards for more than sixty miles. So that, actually, there are no practicable routes which cross the desert between the thirtieth and the thirty-third degrees of latitude. This is not to say that the *Hamad* has never been crossed by single travellers and small caravans. Alois Musil circumnavigated *Jebel Aneza* in 1909; and twenty years later Eldon Rutter travelled diagonally south-eastwards, between Wadi Sirhan and the heights of *Jebel Aneza*. Major Holt, while making his surveys for the Air Mail Route and the railway (in 1921 and 1922; see p. 289), ex-

---

[1] It is, however, believed by some authorities (*e.g.* Professor W. R. Taylor of the University of Toronto) that the Lakhmids of Hira had begun to develop these trade routes (between southern Mesopotamia and north-western Arabia) in the Byzantine Period; and therefore that the Saracens—after defeating the Sasanians in the seventh century—merely improved caravan highways which had been used by the Sasanian Iranians and their vassals, the Lakhmid Arabs.

plored the territory north, east and west of *Jebel Aneza*, though he used Ford cars for the purpose instead of camels. Other sections of the *Hamad* were explored by individuals at various times; and it is known that several fugitives, seeking to escape from either Mesopotamia or Trans-Jordan, have crossed within these latitudes —between the seventh century A.D. and the present day. During the periodically rainy years, when the *Hamad* is dotted with many fresh-water pools (see p. 52), it is always a feasible matter for a small caravan to make the journey by the track which was explored by Group-Captain Rees. But this has no bearing on commerce, or on the feasibility of establishing any permanent system of regular com-munication. Merchant caravans have always crossed the desert either just to the north of the *Great Desert* or else just to the south of it.

The most frequently used part of the Syrian Desert is Palmyrena. It is almost impossible to enumerate the routes transecting this *Little Desert*, because its surface is so smooth and level, relatively speaking, that caravans can conveniently cross almost any part of it; and water is never far to seek. In order to avoid confusion, it would be better to specify only the most important of these highways.

Between the Euphrates and the inland cities of Syria there are three major groups of desert tracks: those which connect Damas-cus, Palmyra and Aleppo with various points on the river.

The most southerly highway (not counting the modern motor route) is that between Damascus and Kubaisa, called the *Darb es-Sa'i*, or road of the courier, because it was used exclusively by those who travelled fast and hard. It is almost a straight road from Damas-cus by way of Dumeir, Bir Melossa and Muheiwir to Kubaisa, where it branches to the riverain towns of Hit and Ramadi. This road has always been impracticable for large caravans because it lies too far south of Palmyrena—too close to the waterless area of the *Hamad*. The only perennial springs in the two hundred and eighty odd miles between Dumeir and Muheiwir, are those of Melossa.

In Palmyrena lies the most easily traversable part of the Syrian Desert, from the point of view of a caravan leader. Direct routes lead eastward to Hit, Abu Kemal and Deir ez-Zor; subsidiary routes formerly branched from these main ones to Salahiya (the ancient Dura), to Mayadin (the former Meshed Rahba) and to Halebiya, north of Deir (once the city of Zenobia). The most famous of these, if not the most useful in modern days, is that connecting Palmyra with Hit, which is some 295 miles in length. It was built by the Romans, who sank wells along it, with stone copings, spaced forty-five kilometres apart; and built pentagonal forts for its safeguarding, four of which are still standing: namely, the fort at Muheiwir, Kasr Amej, Kasr Kebbaz and Kasr Arnab. The Arabs have always called this the *Darb el-Kufri*, or Road of the Unbelievers, because of its Roman origin. The most important route in the Middle Ages, until the coming of the Ottoman Turks, was that between Palmyra and Meshed Rahba. In the Mamluk period this track, which was used by government postal couriers, was known as the *Darb es-Sultan*. From Upper Mesopotamia there is a famous road which runs south from the Euphrates (crossing at Rakka), through Resafa, Taiyiba and Sukhna to Palmyra; and thence to Damascus, or more directly to Bosra eski-Shem. This was once a section of the Roman *Strata Diocletiana* which connected Trebizond with Petra and Akaba, and followed the western edge of the Syrian Desert throughout its entire length. To get to Homs, Hama or any city between Aleppo and Damascus, caravans went through Palmyra, and thence to Homs, along a broad highway which is still well marked by Roman milestones.

Lastly, to reach Aleppo, caravans had a choice of two routes. They could follow the river north-west to Meskineh (the ancient Thapsacus), and then strike almost due west through a country which is more or less arable. Or else, as was usually done, they could strike diagonally across the desert triangle, from opposite el-Ghaim or Abu Kemal, and pass either through or just to the east of the ancient oasis town of Taiyiba.[1]

There is one other, even more northerly route, which was pre-

---

[1] This diagonal route was used almost exclusively from the sixteenth to the nineteenth centuries. It was known as the Little Desert Route. Sometimes, however, caravans chose to cross the desert further north, from Meshed Rahba (Mayadin) to Taiyiba, and join the diagonal route there. In fact, this variation was almost always used during the Middle Ages.

ferred in the pre-Roman period: it traversed the upper part of Mesopotamia, crossed the Euphrates at Zeugma or at Tell Ahmar, and passed to the north-west of Aleppo, directly to Antioch, via Membij (Hierapolis). But this, strictly speaking, lies too far north to be included amongst the Syrian Desert routes. The modern motor route between Damascus and Baghdad, by way of Dumeir, and then south of *Jebel Tenf* to Rutba Wells and Ramadi, was never used before the twentieth century, because of the scarcity of water. From the point of view of the courier, the saving of distance—which is not very great—would have been nullified by the exhaustion of his dromedary. The quickest courier route from Baghdad to Damascus was that from Dumeir, north of *Jebel Tenf*, to Bir Melossa and Kubaisa. This track was sometimes used by caravans also, when rain-water pools were likely to be met with between Dumeir and Bir Melossa.

The points at which the Euphrates was habitually crossed varied in different eras. The Assyrians used the left or eastern bank of the river more than they did the right bank. Their principal crossing was at Tell Ahmar. The Seleucids, who used the routes on both sides of the river indifferently, preferred to cross it at either Zeugma-Apamea or Thapsacus. In the Roman period, both the left and the right banks of the river were used; and the two principal crossings were at Rakka (then called Nicephorium) and at Circesium, where the Khabur flows into the Euphrates.[1] The

---

[1] Tell Ahmar, called Til-Barsib in Assyrian times, was below both Birejik and Carchemish.

Zeugma, which has been called both Zeugma-Apamea and Zeugma-Seleucia, was eight or nine miles above Birejik, and can probably be identified with the site of Bali. As a matter of fact there were several *zeugmas*: the word means *junction*, and was applied specifically to a riverain junction of roads, where there was a pontoon bridge; it was, for example, by the *zeugma* of Thapsacus that Alexander crossed the Euphrates. At Bali, today, are to be seen the remains of bridge-heads; and—as it is fairly well established that Roman engineers of the early second century A.D. substituted a stone bridge at Zeugma-Apamea (Zeugma-Seleucia) in place of the original pontoon bridge—this is one reason for supposing Zeugma and Bali to be identical.

Thapsacus was close to the present site of Meskineh.

Circesium probably became a principal crossing of the Euphrates in the

Saracens had a preference for Kirkisiya, which was their name for the ancient Circesium. Throughout the Middle Ages, caravans destined for either Mosul or Baghdad customarily crossed the Euphrates at Kirkisiya. After the sixteenth century, caravans *en route* for Baghdad crossed further south: at Anna (where once there was a bridge connecting the island with both shores of the river); at Jubba (where there was a camel ford); or else at Hit (where there was the usual pontoon bridge). And later still, in the nineteenth century, Felluja came to be used in preference to all of the more northerly crossings, except when the Euphrates happened to be in flood.

The paths most trodden by caravans were those along which wells or springs were known to exist—such as could be counted upon not to evaporate during the summer months. Of course, there are many wadis in this part of the desert, where water is near enough to the surface to be reached by digging, even in the dry season; but it would take a long time to dig up enough water to supply a caravan of two or three thousand camels! There were two other, not always minor considerations, which gave pause to caravan leaders. One was the payment of tolls; and was best dealt with by passing just outside the custom-barriers of any and every town. The other, a less calculable difficulty, was the semi-chronic menace of the Beduin. This danger will be examined at greater length hereinafter; it is enough to say here that, although nomad raiders were often a just cause of grave concern, they were never so much to be feared by caravans as the settled Arabs who lived along the banks of the Euphrates. Incidentally, river banks were shunned by caravan leaders for another reason. All lowland portions of the desert—particularly between November and June— were apt to be soft and muddy (either from rain or on account of

middle of the third century A.D. After Diocletian fixed the frontier of the Roman Empire along the Khabur River, and fortified Circesium at its mouth, Dura-Europos was abandoned, and the crossing at Dura was no longer used.

Cf. Franz Cumont, *Études syriennes* (1917), pp. 120-125 and 250. *Syria*, vol. iii (1922), p. 207, article by Franz Cumont; vol. x (1929), pp. 186-188, article by F. Thureau-Dangin; vol. xi (1930), pp. 42, 105, 130-132, editorials by René Dussaud.

the annual flooding of the Euphrates), and this made very difficult going underfoot for laden camels. The beasts of burden had always to be considered on this score, because the single-humped camels used in Syria and Irak are anything but sure-footed when travelling over slippery ground; and even a slight skid is likely to displace their carefully balanced loads. For this same reason, level ground, when dry, was always chosen in preference to even slightly hilly country. Alois Musil, in his note on Resafa, gives this reason for its importance in the Assyrian and Byzantine periods; in his opinion it was necessary to divert the merchant caravans along a route which passes by the site of the sixth-century town, because the desert surface in its vicinity offers the surest footing for heavily laden camels.

There are two more desert roads, age-old, which must be considered before turning to the story of desert-borne trade. These two, although not trans-desert highways, have greatly affected the commercial activities on all routes which transect both the northern and the southern areas. One on the west, the other on the east, they skirt the fringes of the Syrian Desert from its northernmost limits to the southern desert zone which loses itself in central Arabia.

The westerly, North-South Route has been the great Arabo-Syrian highway for longer than documents have existed to prove the fact. Even before the Nabataeans made Petraea the centre of their caravan empire, caravan traffic was heavy along the one artery of trade which connected Yemen and all of central and southern Arabia with Palestine and Syria. In ancient days it was the sole western outlet for the spice trade; and after the death of Mohammed it was along this road that the Moslem armies passed into Syria. Later, under the Omayyad Caliphs, it became the post route between Damascus and Medina; and after the great *Hajj* caravans began their annual journeys to Mecca, this was their one and obvious line of march. So that the *Darb el-Hajj*—as one branch of it came to be known in the Middle Ages—was in constant use until the building of the Hejaz railway in the twentieth century. (See Chapter VII, pp. 223-225.) This North-South Route, when Romanized in the Palmyrene period, was the southern portion of the *Strata Diocletiana*. Beyond Damascus, a desert route still continues north-eastward to Palmyra, Sukhna and Resafa, which crosses the Euphrates to Rakka; while a more north-westerly fork leads directly to Homs, Hama and Aleppo.

On its eastern side, the Syrian Desert is skirted by two highways which join each other near Meshed Ali. The northern one, known in the eighteenth century as the Great Desert Route, starts at Aleppo, cuts diagonally across Palmyrena, or the *Little Desert*, approaches the Euphrates near el-Ghaim, and thereafter follows the river south-east to Basra—roughly paralleling its course at a distance of from fifteen to twenty-five miles. (See footnote, p. 171, and Chapter VI, Part 2, pp. 193-205.)

South-west of Meshed Ali—at a reservoir called Umm el-Kurun —the eastern Pilgrim Route, called the *Darb Zubayda* (or the "Darb es-Sitt Zubayda"), crosses the Great Desert Route on its way from Baghdad to the Hejaz. Thence it strikes diagonally southwards to central Arabia, reaching Mecca eventually by the way of Hayil, and returning from Medina by a more direct road. This, though a famous highway, is not one of the more ancient ones. Its use dates from about A.D. 800, when Sitt Zubayda—the favourite wife of *Harun er-Rashid*—caused a caravan track, linking Baghdad and Najaf with the Holy Cities of the Hejaz, to be provided throughout its length with fortified watering stations and reservoirs. Before her time the route was impracticable for large caravans; but it was probably used by individual travellers who were hard pressed for time. It is not possible to date the origin of the Great Desert Route, because there is no knowing just how early the two river routes, the Tigris and Euphrates, were duplicated by a parallel land route to the west of the latter. But sections of it were probably used as soon as the merchants of Syria began to trade with those of Mesopotamia. And it was known in its entirety in the early sixteenth century.

It is easy to see how great an influence the North-South routes have always had on the development of those which cross the desert from east to west. When first there began to be extensive trading along the opposite sides of the desert, it was only natural that the two should find some means of exchanging the products

HIT

R.A.F. official photograph : Crown copyright reserved

of their commercial activities. But on the other hand, as the commodities which were brought to Syria from south-western Arabia
were largely similar to those which found their way to Babylon
from the Persian Gulf (since spices and the products of India and
China were transported along both the eastern and the western
coasts of Arabia), the great North-South Route between Syria and
the Hejaz rarely, if ever, flourished at the same time that the trans-
desert routes happened to be prospering, and *vice versa*. When
Syria was supplied with the exotic commodities of the Orient by
way of the Hejaz, there was a less lively interchange of goods
across the desert between Syria and Mesopotamia; and when
Palmyra was flourishing, because of trading with the cities in the
Euphrates valley, the western highway to the Red Sea was generally in a state of decline—although there was always some traffic
along it on account of the African trade. Possibly, the primary
reason for these commercial fluctuations was political, due to the
fact that the city states of Petra and of Palmyra were rarely prosperous at the same time: when one throve, the other suffered a
period of decay; and the prosperity of both cities, and of the routes
which they dominated, was interdependent. This generalization
holds good alike for Ancient, Roman and Christian times. The
alternating periods can be traced until the seventh or eighth
centuries A.D., but after that the balance was readjusted, owing to
the comprehensive domination of the Mohammedans. During the
Saracen period, both the North-South and the East-West routes
were in constant use, and trade flourished. And after the Ottoman
Turks had annexed all former Saracen lands to their empire, then
both sets of routes were in use, but neither one of them flourished.

2

THE HISTORICAL BACKGROUND OF CARAVAN TRAVEL BETWEEN
SYRIA AND MESOPOTAMIA

In a brief survey of Syrian Desert trade there is no space to include an account of the origins and expansion of commerce in the

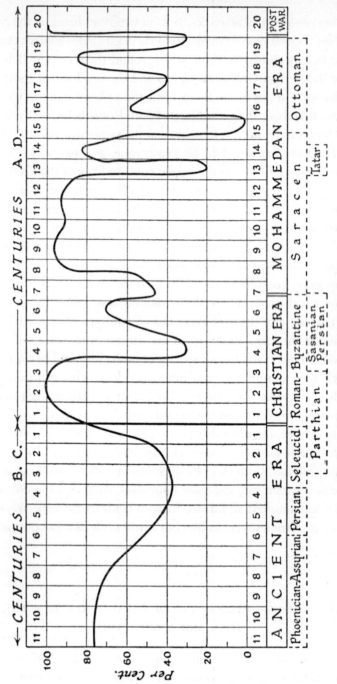

CARAVAN TRAVEL BETWEEN SYRIA AND MESOPOTAMIA
Graph to illustrate the use made of the North Syrian Desert

ancient world, still less an exhaustive analysis of the vicissitudes of trade throughout the centuries. But a sketch of the peaks of commercial prosperity, and their corresponding deeps of decline, is essential in order to enable one to reconstruct a mental picture of when and how these desert routes were used. The accompanying diagram, for example, will serve to focus the commercial periods in their relation to each other, and the periods of maximum and minimum usage of the Syrian Desert as a whole. Then a few words describing the broad outlines of the story of commercial conditions as a whole, and the differing characteristics of the various periods, may give a background for the following chapters which describe in considerable detail several phases of the lives of caravan travellers. When certain of the desert routes were used by the great merchant caravans, and what sort of goods they transported; how the various routes became popular for the use of travellers between the Occident and the Orient, and what their journeys were like; in what way the desert was used by dispatch and mail couriers, to bridge the gap between Mesopotamia and Syria, and to link India with the West; also, and lastly, to give some idea of the modern use of these same routes and the changed conditions of desert travel in the twentieth century.

It is far from easy to outline, briefly, a period of more than three thousand years, which extends, roughly, from 1000 B.C. to A.D. 2000. Perhaps the easiest way is to make artificial divisions corresponding to the successive civilizations which have dominated the Near and Middle East; and then to indicate for each division of time, their comparative conditions of commercial prosperity, with respect, chiefly, to the status of internal and trans-desert trade. As we have but fragmentary statistics (none at all, in the modern meaning of the word), before the twentieth century, for the varying volumes of desert trade, this diagram can only represent relative fluctuations in the use of the northern Syrian Desert routes. The highest and lowest curves of the graph correspond, respectively, to the periods of maximum and minimum usage of the trans-desert routes. Their usage, that is, as compared with those of all other overland trade routes which have connected the Occident with the Orient.

Turning to the diagram, then, one finds that the first and one of the moderately high curves of the graph begins in 1100 B.C. This was the period of Phoenician and Assyrian ascendancy, and lasted until the Iranian Empire—founded by Cyrus—brought the Babylonians and the cities of Phoenicia under Iranian rule, in 538 B.C. But during the Iranian period, and later—after the conquests of Alexander—under the Seleucids, the Syrian Desert routes were little used. Not until after the second century B.C. did these northern desert highways come back into use; because —so long as Petra was supreme in the south, and so long as the northern roads through Anatolia were practicable—they had no chance to develop. With Petra's decline, however, and when Anatolia became a battlefield for the Romans and the Parthians, the Palmyrene routes grew more and more prosperous. Between the end of the first and the end of the third centuries A.D., they enjoyed almost their greatest period of prosperity. But after the destruction of Palmyra, in 271, the routes which this great caravan city had protected declined, and did not have another prosperous era until Justinian took an interest in them in the sixth century.[1] In the early seventh century, Byzantine wars against Iran as well as against the newly Mohammedanized Arabs rendered the desert routes temporarily unsafe for purposes of trade. The eighth century ushered in with it a period of considerable commercial prosperity, and for five centuries thereafter —throughout the Saracen epoch—all of the Syrian Desert routes were in constant use. A partial exception must be made during the troublous times of the eleventh century, and after, when Seljuk Turks and Christian Crusaders imperilled the security of Saracen commerce. In the thirteenth century one of the low-water

---

[1] It was under this same Byzantine Emperor that silkworms were smuggled into Syria, in a hollow stick or cane. It is believed that monks, possibly Iranian Nestorians, brought silkworms into the Byzantine Empire either from southeastern China—Cambodia or Champa—or else from Khotan, in Turkestan; and that they did so at the instigation of Justinian himself. G. F. Hudson (1931), pp. 120-121. Sir Percy Sykes (1934), p. 23.

marks of internal trade was reached: when the Tatars sacked Baghdad in 1258. For a century thereafter, what was left of Saracen trade found its outlet through Egypt; and the newly achieved *rapprochement* between the four Tatar Khanates and the Christian West fostered the use of the Anatolian and Black Sea trade routes. Early in the fourteenth century there was the dawning of a new prosperity in the Saracen lands of Mesopotamia, and especially of Syria—due to the pacificating influence of the Tatars, once they were organized and had, so to speak, become commercially minded. This of course entailed the using of the desert routes anew: so soon as internal connecting links were again needed. Under the rule of the Mamluk Sultans of Cairo, after the Cypriote-Egyptian peace of 1370, there was a brilliant though short-lived revival of Syrian prosperity, and of its newly blossomed trans-desert trade with Mesopotamia. But once again, after the conquest of Constantinople by the Ottoman Turks under Mohammed II in 1453, a period of decline set in. This decline was intensified by the fact that western Christendom abandoned the overland routes and set about finding a way to the Far East by sea. The revival of the sixteenth century was due to the Ottoman Sultans, who found that they could not prosper without trading with the West. The Turks were not anxious to lure back Europeans to the use of the land routes, but they were willing to become the middle-man between Orient and Occident, and to turn the western fringes of their empire into a clearing-house for those products of the East which were destined for the West. It must be remembered that, throughout the Ottoman period, the Turks themselves naturally developed the Anatolian routes at the expense of all the others that crossed their dominions. Europeans, on their side, had not found the long sea route as practicable as they had hoped it might prove; and England had failed to find a convenient north-west passage to Cathay. So Christian and Turk compromised, and came to mutually advantageous terms. The fall-off in the use of desert highways (as indicated on the chart) in the later seventeenth century was caused by internal disorders coupled with an economic decline of

4

the Ottoman Empire. The last year of the seventeenth century in which the desert routes were used by Europeans is 1673; and 1745 is the first year of the eighteenth century in which Europeans resumed their use of them. During the second half of the eighteenth and the early part of the nineteenth centuries, the desert routes were much used, alike by natives and by foreigners; at first, and almost exclusively, by English servants of the East India Company. Even trans-desert commerce experienced a considerable revival until the Suez Canal was opened for navigation in 1869. The "modern" period, so far as desert trade is concerned, dates from 1921. Until the Great War, camel transport was the only medium for carrying on desert commerce. But after aeroplanes and motor cars were used—for the first time commercially in 1923—methods of transportation were revolutionized, and trans-desert trade received an undreamed-of stimulus. One is accordingly tempted to be exceedingly optimistic about the future of the trans-desert routes.

But this too brief outline needs considerable expansion, in order to be intelligible.

Everyone knows that Mesopotamia on the one hand, and Egypt on the other, were the cradles of our modern civilization; and that intercourse between them arose in that dim period called the dawn of history, and became close and constant after 1500 B.C. But perhaps it is less well known that the methods of caravan trading were standardized, and complex conventions for commercial exchanges were regularized, by 3000 B.C.; that there were at that time written contracts and business agreements, in the Sumerian language; and that the substitution of a metal unit of exchange for barter (the predecessor of the coined currency which made its first appearance in the seventh century B.C.) occurred sometime before that dawn of history was illumined by the sunrise of consecutively recorded epochs. And in this early dawn, the main tides of trade flowed between East and West in lines which curved north and south around, and not across, the desert sections of Syria and north Arabia. As has been well said, this desert sea at first divided the Mediterranean from Mesopotamia, before it united them by making of itself a highway for the ships of the desert—otherwise called camels.

About 1900 B.C. the Code of Hammurabi (more elaborate than a similar code of the third millennium) gave merchants the specific sanction of laws to enforce their customs. And for about a thousand years before the conquests of Alexander the Great, Palestine, Syria and Mesopotamia were successively united within the boundaries of various empires: the Egyptian, under the ever-famous Pharaohs of the Eighteenth Dynasty; the Assyrian; the Neo-Babylonian, which was a revival of the earlier Sumero-Babylonian Empire; and, lastly, the Iranian Empire. The first consciousness of unity and a potential solidarity of all the then civilized world arose in the Egyptian period, but was too short-lived to establish that solidarity. The Assyrians, about a thousand years B.C., and their successors the Babylonians, made active efforts to maintain co-operation between East and West. And, con-temporaneously with the height of Assyrian prosperity, the Phoenicians began—under King Hiram of Tyre—their extra-ordinary commercial development on the Mediterranean coast, and beyond. Then it was that there developed direct, if some-what spasmodic, contact between Mesopotamia and the cities of Syria and Palestine: across the desert, from Tadmor eastward to the middle Euphrates—very likely to Circesium —and down either one or both sides of the river to Lower Babylonia.

This first direct route is inferred from the fact that the name of Tadmor (the Palmyra of later days) appears for the first time in Assyrian inscriptions of the time of Tiglath Pileser I, 1115–1100 B.C. It would be difficult to imagine Tadmor as worthy of mention unless the trans-desert caravan trade, on which this caravan city must always have depended, were already established. And this in turn, must have been negligible until camels were imported into northern Syria for use in the desert regions. Now the early Assyrians, who did not use camels, always moved around the Euphrates, and did not venture into the desert at all; and asses, which were always used in the Cappadocian trade of the second

millennium B.C., could only be used on desert tracks during exceptionally rainy winters—and then only upon a few of them. So from these facts, and the negative indication of inscriptions, it is inferred that camels were not known in Syria and the desert before approximately 1000 B.C. Then it was the Bactrian, two-humped camel which was first used on the desert. But the single-humped Arabian camels, which have been used throughout the historical periods of trans-desert trade, were not imported into Syria before the ninth century, or possibly not before the beginning of the eighth century B.C.

During the Phoenician period there was also, possibly, even more direct contact across the desert, between Damascus and the Euphrates: provided that the views of such as Professor Huntington are correct about the change of climate which may have occurred in the desert sections of Syria. If this theory is true, and the periodically arable fringes of the northern desert—the fertile crescent as it was called—was formerly far south of where it is now, then water would have been more plentiful along the more southern routes; and this southernmost track which skirts the *Hamad* would, accordingly, have been practicable for the use of merchant caravans. But it never has proved practicable for such slow-moving traffic within the recorded memory of men. Actually, Alois Musil and several other informed students of Syria's climatic fluctuations seem to have demolished this theory. It has been established that periodically, every four, five or seven years, there is an unusually ample, evenly distributed rainfall over the Syrian Desert. And that during those years, especially throughout the winter months, it is entirely feasible for small caravans to cross sections of the desert which cannot be crossed in normal years; or for nomads and their flocks to make use of oases in which there is, ordinarily, very little water to be found. Also, wherever aqueducts have been constructed—such as those to be found near Palmyra, or between Taiyiba, Ain el-Kom and *Kasr el-Hair*—an appearance of long-established or habitual fertility may be given to the surrounding desert country. But these phenomena do not constitute any actual "change" of climate. Given normal years,

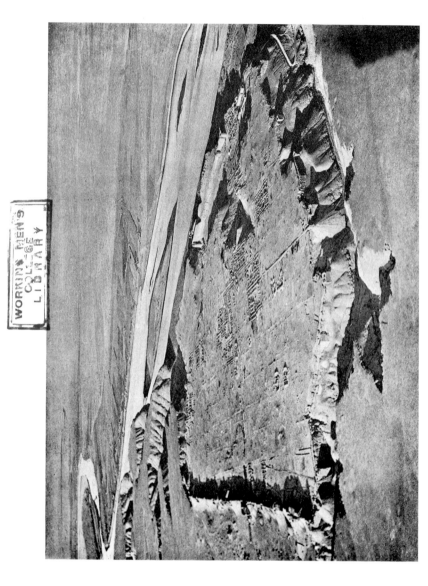

THE ANCIENT FORTIFICATIONS AT DURA-EUROPOS

On the river bank is the citadel and opposite, on the left, the main gate

Photograph by Antoine Poidebard

without any artificial conditions, the desert soon reclaims its own.[1]

The development of a new outlet, between the middle Euphrates and Syria, coincided very fittingly with the effort made by Assyrian kings of the ninth century to dominate the southern routes of Arabia's trade, through the pivotal cities of Tayma in north-western Arabia, and Gerrha on the Arabian side of the Persian Gulf.

The first traceable system of roads was built during the Iranian period; but that the Assyrians before them had built a good many must be deduced from the fact that itineraries were drawn up for their merchants as well as for their soldiers: and an itinerary of routes presupposes the existence of roads. These roads, obviously, were not built in desert country and accordingly have no direct bearing upon desert trade. Nevertheless the perpetual interchange of commodities between various parts of these empires was fostered—both by increasingly favourable trade conditions, and by rulers who were interested in the economic development of

[1] The principal arguments advanced to prove a genuine change of climate in the Syrian Desert are as follows: (a) Numerous authorities have agreed on the former, relatively greater fertility of Palmyrena. (b) Mr H. St. J. B. Philby and Major A. L. Holt agree that there must have been more rainfall in the Great Desert, at least in the Roman period, than there is, on the average, today. For one thing, the line of cultivation in Trans-Jordan extended further east than it now does. For another, the numerous hunting-boxes of the Omayyad Caliphs prove that game was abundant in the seventh and eighth centuries A.D., where now no animals are to be found. Lastly, at el-Jidd, in the near neighbourhood of Jebel Aneza (i.e. in the central Hamad), are the remains of habitations, building-stones, weighing more than two tons, have obviously been carried for some distances, and two water-holes have been cut through 160 feet of limestone. (c) Mr Philby, writing of Arabia, states that there is a "certainty beyond challenge that when the ice-cap of the last Glacial period covered a large part of the northern hemisphere, at least three great rivers flowed from west to east across the whole width of the peninsula" (H. St. J. B. Philby, Arabia (1930), p. xv).

The discovery by Mr Bertram Thomas of the evidences of a dried-up lake in Arabia tends to substantiate this statement. And these theories and proofs of climatic change in Arabia have convinced various students of the Syrian Desert that analogous changes have also taken place there.

their empires. During the period of Iran's supremacy a veritable network of roads and highways came into being; and bridges were built in Mesopotamia and Anatolia, as well as in Iran, which have lasted to this day. Commodities began to flow regularly between East and West; fresh demands were stimulated by the presence of supplies; and trade increased with the proverbial accumulation of a snow-ball set rolling. An added impetus was given to commercial exchanges by the circulation of a stable Iranian currency. The Syrian cities responded to the life-giving movements of trade by growing in size and in importance: particularly Aleppo, Hama, Homs and Damascus; the Phoenician coastal cities of Aradus, Byblus, Sidon and Tyre developed with amazing rapidity; and Petra began to attract a considerable amount of attention, even of misgiving, because of the fearless independence of its Nabataean kings.

But as yet, all this revivalism had only an indirect bearing upon the desert routes: it paved the way for their inevitable resurrection.

The meteoric conquests of Alexander of Macedon left the Near East a temporarily Hellenized unit. And when he died, in 323 B.C., what—for a short time—had been the empire of Alexander the Great, was divided up into two immense territories. The Ptolemies who ruled Egypt also, at first, had suzerainty over southern Palestine and Trans-Jordan; the Seleucids ruled Syria, Anatolia and—also for about a century and a half—the Middle East: east into Asia, as far as the borders of India. This rapid Hellenization of the Near and Middle East served to tighten the bonds of trade, and led to an improvement in such commerical facilities as were at the disposal of the new rulers. They were able to utilize roads already made, and institutions already elaborated. The rivalry which eventually resulted between the Seleucids and the Ptolemies injected fresh economic life into the lands of each, and spurred them to even greater efforts in behalf of commerce. Many new ports and trading centres were founded, particularly in Syria and in Mesopotamia. Articles of Syrian manufacture found their way as far east as Bactria, north of the Indus; and the influence of Syrian commerce can be traced in Chinese art of the Han period.

All this while, Syrian trade found its most convenient channel eastward by the roads from Antioch to northern Mesopotamia, which crossed the Euphrates at Zeugma-Apamea and Tell Ahmar. It may be remembered that the Royal Iranian Highway extended from Ephesus and Sardis to Nineveh, and thence down the eastern side of the Tigris to the Iranian capital of Susa. And the Seleucids continued to favour the northern routes because they were that much further away from any possible interference by the Ptolemies. As for Lower Mesopotamia, its prestige was merely enhanced by the multiplication of trade-centres there. Two natural, and therefore perennial centres for trading exist in the land between the rivers: in their lowest reaches, where they empty into the Persian Gulf; and in the narrow strip of land where the two rivers approach each other most closely. In the first instance, Charax once stood where Mohammera does today; and the ancient mart of Forat was near the medieval and modern sites of Basra. Similarly, further north, a variety of sites—all of them close together—have been successively prominent in the history of commerce: Vologesia and Babylon by the Euphrates; Seleucia, Ctesiphon and Baghdad, on the Tigris.

All of these Mesopotamian cities could be reached by way of Nineveh (Mosul). But of course, as soon as Palmyrene merchants began to trade across the desert, they used one of two routes. If their caravans were bound for Vologesia and Babylon, or else for Forat, they journeyed south-east, through the *Great Desert*, without crossing the Euphrates at any point. Whereas, if they were *en route* for Seleucia, Ctesiphon or Charax, they probably crossed the river at Dura-Europos or else at Circesium, and then cut diagonally across the Mesopotamian plain to the Tigris. From these cities there was direct access to the Gulf. Incidentally, it is likely that the Syrian or Palmyrene merchants transferred their goods at one of the northern towns, and left the merchants of either Forat or Charax to do their own transporting to the Persian Gulf.

As has been said previously, there is no inscriptional evidence to show that Jauf was linked to Mesopotamia by any ancient trade routes. This means that there was not any direct connection between ancient Babylonia and Egypt. It seems almost certain that the highways from, for example, Assyria to the west, passed through northern Syria; and that even the early Assyrian traces found in Jauf (then called Adumu) were derived through Damascus and the Wadi Sirhan. It is possible, but not probable, that under the Seleucids, for the first time, the direct route may have been used between Lower Mesopotamia and the independent caravan state of Petra. But this is not likely.[1] It is to be inferred that the direct route, via Maan and Jafar to Jauf, went no further east than this oasis city, that Jauf (and its surrounding oases) was the terminus of the Petraean caravans, and that Palmyra (then called Tadmor) was the middle-man for the trade between Petra and the cities of the Tigris and the Euphrates. But this brings us to the growth of the Caravan Cities, which were so significant in the development of desert trade.

Undoubtedly the key to the development of trans-desert trade was held by the Caravan Cities, and it is to their rise and growth that we must look to find an explanation of the expansion of commerce by direct desert routes. These cities, with their magnificent public buildings and paved streets, derived vitality and nourishment entirely from caravan trade; so they naturally fostered, in their turn, the trade upon which their existence depended. Two of them, Petra and Palmyra, became in turn caravan empires: because they were the middle-men for all commercial exchanges between Mesopotamia and the Mediterranean, and were able to control all the important caravan routes north of Nejd. It seems almost superfluous to attempt any kind of description of these cities, now that Professor Rostovtzeff has made his researches available to all. Nevertheless, a few words must be said in order to indicate their full significance in this particular connection.

Petra, which was of consequence first in the Iranian period,

[1] See Chapter II, § 1, pp. 37-38 and footnote.

grew into a powerful state when the rival Seleucid and Ptolemaic empires were beginning to be weakened by civil wars and mutual jealousies. She succeeded in keeping her independence, although both rival powers sought to bring the caravan city within their respective orbits. By the middle or end of the second century B.C., Petra had attained her greatest development, and was reaping in full the commercial reward of being middle-man between southern Arabia and the Persian Gulf, on the one hand, and Egypt and Phoenicia on the other. Southern Arabia tapped the resources of Africa, as the Persian Gulf did those of India; and the varied products of all those remote lands had to pass through Petra's territories. Sometimes Gaza, the Ptolemaic city, succeeded in diverting and side-tracking the caravans to and from Egypt; and Ptolemy II, in the third century B.C., had attempted to divert all the Arabian trade directly to Egypt, and thus to cut off both Petra and Damascus; but for the most part Petra controlled all the trade between Phoenicia and the south and east. And as her power waxed stronger, Petra also absorbed the routes leading into Syria, as far north as Damascus. When Pompey added northern Syria to the Roman provinces (in 66 B.C.), Petra had access to all the markets of the Roman world; and even before this, her kings had been taking an interest in the Palmyrene desert routes across to the middle Euphrates. The disintegration of the Seleucid Empire, which had entailed anarchy and commercial instability in Anatolia; the growing power of Parthia in the East, and of Rome in the West: all these unsettled conditions had threatened the safety of the northern Mesopotamian highways; so that the great caravans which travelled to and fro between Mesopotamia and the Mediterranean sought safer and more southerly routes. For this reason, very likely, Tadmor began its growth anew, as a caravan city; and Tadmor, which came to be known as Palmyra, grew into a powerful centre of trade under the protection of the Nabataean kings of Petra. Between the second century B.C. and the rule of the Emperor Trajan, Petra was unquestionably the dominant economic power on the Mediterranean side of the Syrian Desert. Her kings had acquired the ports of Akaba and Leuce Come on the

Red Sea; and they levied such taxes upon caravans in transit through their territories as they saw fit.[1] Her merchants travelled far and wide: in the Near East, and west as far as Puteoli in Italy. But in A.D. 105 Petra yielded her territories to Rome, and Arabia Petraea—from the Dead Sea to the Red Sea—became the centre of the new Roman province of Arabia.

Early in the Christian era, Bosra eski-Shem gradually super-seded Petra and became her commercial successor. And a decade after the latter had finally become the vassal of the great western power, Roman emperors undertook to develop northern Syria and the routes therefrom, at the expense of Petraea. It was natural that Trans-Jordan, half-way between the northern and southern trade routes, should become the commercial centre of gravity when Syrian highways began to displace those further south. The cities which had come into being, originally, because of Petra's northward-reaching policy, automatically grew stronger as the virility of their great neighbour to the south was gradually sapped. The cities of Amman, Jerash and Bosra were the most important of a number of those which flourished on the central and western

[1] Aelana, later called Akaba, was always the great port of the Nabataeans of Petra, from the fourth century B.C. Leuce Come, on the other hand, dates (most probably) from the first century B.C., and was built either on or very near the site of a third-century Ptolemaic city called Ampelone. Leuce Come, at the mouth of the Wadi Hamdh, midway between the Gulf of Akaba and Yenbo, was in a strategic position near the intersection of the two great Arabian trade routes: the trans-Arabian (east-west) route from Gerrha on the Persian Gulf to the Red Sea, and the Arabo-Syrian highway from Yemen to Damascus. Wadi Hamdh, which leads northward from Medina (the ancient Iathrib), eventually curves westward to the Red Sea coast, so that any town built at its mouth would be in direct communication with Medina. Before 100 B.C. the Ptolemies, who were becoming weak politically, had given up any idea of either conquering or isolating the Petraean kingdom of the Nabataeans, and they had turned their attention to Somaliland and were making an effort to secure a more direct trade for Egypt with India. The Nabataeans accordingly advanced their territories southward into Arabia. After occupying Tayma, they pushed south and west to the Red Sea coast; and then it was that they either built a new city at the mouth of the Wadi Hamdh, or else captured Ampelone and re-christened it Leuce Come. Cf. *The Journal of Egyptian Archaeology*, vol. xv, pp. 9-25, article by W. W. Tarn, with notes by Sidney Smith (on Ptolemy II in Arabia).

edge of the Syrian Desert. Bosra, which became the capital of the Roman province of Arabia, was in a key position: in the centre of intersecting roads which led from Syria to Trans-Jordan, and from their joint desert frontiers westward to the coast of Palestine. Once the over-lordship of Rome was firmly established in these lands, all the Trans-Jordanian routes became safe for travel, and caravans traversing them could rely upon efficient protection. But Bosra's leadership soon yielded to that of Palmyra, which was the more logical centre for the northern trade. So that, by the middle of the second century A.D., Palmyra in her turn had become the greatest of the caravan cities, and eclipsed all her southern rivals.

The day of Palmyra's supremacy dawned when Rome and Parthia came to a mutually advantageous understanding, on the eve of the first century A.D. (an understanding which was only interrupted for the very brief period of Trajan's wars against Parthia). Their agreement, which may even have been a written one, stipulated that the routes of northern Mesopotamia, which had become increasingly difficult to safeguard, were to be suffered to die a natural death; and that Palmyra, whose neutrality was guaranteed, and later reaffirmed under Hadrian, was to have encouragement from both these powers. So that it was not long before the city state monopolized all the caravan trade between the Roman and the Parthian sides of the Syrian Desert; and the route which existed between this city and the Parthian fortress town of Dura (on the Euphrates) was made safe and easy for desert traffic. Eventually, as the wealth and power of Palmyra was augmented to almost incredible proportions, she became less and less dependent upon the protection of Rome. A growing feeling of independence, born of a consciousness of her importance in the imperial economy of the Roman Empire, rendered this expanding state increasingly intolerant of either supervision or interference in domestic matters. And as such affairs were inextricably bound up with all her trans-desert trade, and depended upon the organization and regulation of her caravan traffic, Palmyra gradually achieved independence in all but name. Her decline and fall did not come until she attempted to take advantage of Rome's weakness in the

third century A.D., and to establish her autonomy in name as well
as in fact. She thrust her defiance upon the attention of a Roman
emperor: which emperor, unfortunately for her, happened to be
Aurelian. The Palmyrene queen, Zenobia, like a certain cardinal
in Tudor England, refused to fling away ambition until it was too
late to save herself. She was defeated in battle and eventually
captured. Her caravan empire, having invited destruction at the
hands of Rome, was dismembered; and the walls and aqueducts of
Palmyra were levelled to the ground by Roman legionaries. A
later, resurrected Palmyra never succeeded in reviving more than
a pale reflection of her former grandeur. But, not to cover too fast
the ground between the Roman and Byzantine periods, one should
pause for a moment to discover the nature of this grandeur when
the caravan state was young and vigorous.

To write of Palmyra with appropriate brevity taxes one's
powers of self-restraint. There is something so intrinsically fas-
cinating about this oasis city of palms, which spreads her antique
splendour at the gateway of desert hills, that it seems unapprecia-
tive of the true essence of romance to neglect any details, however
trifling. But one must avoid, when possible, trespassing on the
special province of the archaeologist. The modern town, separate
from its nearest important neighbour by more than a hundred
miles of desert, has an interest all its own: it is one of the headquarters of the French Camel Corps and an outpost of the French
Army Air Force. One is also reminded of the medieval importance
of Palmyra by the citadel, which looks down upon the ancient
city from the top of one of the hills behind it. But one is struck
most of all by the lavish display of its ancient ruins. What a city
this must have been in the early days of its glory! It is possible,
from what still remains, to reconstruct in imagination the
Palmyra of the first and second centuries A.D., and to conjure up
a mental picture of this most typical of caravan cities; of the
cultured life which obtained where widely travelled merchants,
the financiers of caravans, set the standard of living; and where
the political life was dominated by four powerful clans. The great
caravan road which crossed the city from east to west can still

PALMYRA AND THE PASS TOWARDS DAMASCUS

Photograph by Antoine Poidebard

be followed: 150 of the original 375 columns stand to this day, their bases buried by the drifting sands; and so do many temples, and the *tetrapylon* which marks the spot in the main street where the ancient caravanserai stood. Their workmanship and the sculptures are less fine than those of Jerash, but they are more extensive. Tombs and votive inscriptions, the foundations of palatial residences and frescoed walls, the statues and altars of Palmyra's gods, all testify to a composite civilization which was a complex *mélange* of the civilizations and pagan religions of Syria, Anatolia, Iran or Parthia, and Babylonia: overlaid by a Graeco-Roman veneer. And as in a first view of Palmyra one's eyes are drawn to dwell on the colonnaded caravan road, just so is the peculiar function of the city predominantly discernible in its statues and inscriptions. Its *synodiarchs*, or caravan leaders, and other officials responsible for carrying on Palmyrene trade—either at home or in the cities and seaports of Rome and Parthia—were honoured by statues and columnar tablets erected in recognition of their services. Altars were presided over by the two Arabian and Syrian deities, *Arsu* and *Azizu*, the patron gods of caravaners. And the fiscal laws of Palmyra were inscribed upon a tablet which bears the date of A.D. 137.

It is to this tablet that one must turn for light on the nature of Palmyrene taxes and customs laws, and for an analysis of the regulations governing trade, which give some idea of the scope of Palmyra's commercial activities. The taxes were apportioned in three ways: certain commodities were taxable, also a few professions and a number of public utilities. In the first category, the highest (variable) taxes were levied, almost equally, upon slaves and perfumes. Perfumes, which came either from India, or else from southern Arabia by way of Petra, were taxed again if re-exported for sale in the Roman Empire, about half as much as for their importation; and the import tax was much reduced if perfumes were brought in in goat-skin bags instead of in alabaster jars. Next on the list, from the point of view of revenue, came olive oil. Then all aliments and dried articles, including dried fruits, nuts, pistachio and pine nuts, beans, straw, and salt fish—

on which last there was a specially heavy duty. Fresh produce, such as cheese and wine, was also taxed, but not so highly as the "dry" products. Woollen materials, dyed purple, which were imported from Phoenicia for re-export to Iran, were dutiable; as were bronze statues and busts, and of course, wood. Apparently duties were imposed by the load, because the different charges made upon imports and exports, according to whether they were carried by camels or donkeys, were roughly in proportion to the differing carrying capacities of the two kinds of animals. There was a transit tax on all varieties of livestock, and on beasts of burden (particularly camels) whether they were laden or not; and this tax was quadrupled for all kinds of vehicles. Sheep were not taxed if brought in only for food; but there was a general pasturage tax for livestock using any part of the desert "commons". Coming to the professions, as defined by the Palmyrenes, per-fumers, prostitutes and shopkeepers were taxed, and all clothing merchants. Lastly, there was a special tariff fixed for the use of the two springs: a water tax which was high, but which varied in different years; and there was a tax on the sale of salt (Palmyra possessed then, as now, outlying salt marshes), as well as on the sale of every sheep-skin or goat-skin sold or imported into the city.

Specific provisions were made to enforce these fiscal laws, and the Palmyrene tax-farmers and collectors were armed with the right to impose various penalties upon recalcitrant citizens. They might demand goods in security against eventual payment; in certain cases of non-payment they were allowed to exact double the amount due; and on rare occasions they might confiscate a man's belongings and sell them at public auction. Whenever there was disagreement with a tax-collector, or a protest lodged against his decisions, a formal appeal was made and the case referred to the Roman magistrate who was resident in Palmyra.

Mention of Rome brings one back to the power behind this and the other caravan cities. They benefited to an unusual degree by the maintenance of the *Pax Romana*. There is nothing more stimulating to trade than security, and this is particularly true of trading carried on through the medium of the desert. The safer the hinterland, the less likely were raiding nomads to make trouble for merchant caravans; and effective protection of the desert frontiers discouraged sporadic attacks on the part of raiders who could be unpleasantly sure of eventual reprisals. The wonderful road system of the Romans, which has been hinted at previously, extended from Anatolia to Arabia. Their roads were protected by garrisons; forts were built to house legionaries; and there was a mobile camel corps for patrolling purposes. Every twenty-eight miles, without exception, wells were dug, fortified and reinforced with stone copings—no matter how far down the diggers had to go to reach water—unless a perennial spring or water-hole could be found ready to hand. For centres of importance, like Palmyra, magnificent aqueducts were constructed and kept in good repair. With such organization behind them, the caravan cities had little to fear. For, so stable was the collective peace, as long as Rome remained strong, that they had no need of specific individual protection. It is thought that Palmyra, again for instance, was what was known as an "open city", during her most prosperous period. It is believed that the walls which were destroyed when Zenobia was captured probably dated from the third century, when Rome's control had temporarily weakened; and when Palmyra was beginning to assert her own self-sufficiency and independence. They may have been built for defence against the Parthians, or against the nomads, or even against the Romans themselves. No one knows exactly when they were built, nor for which of these purposes; but they definitely do not belong to the early period.

. Throughout Palestine, Trans-Jordan and Syria the Romans developed existing roads and built new ones—broad, level highways, well marked by milestones; and the arterial or trunk roads were paved wherever it was advantageous for them to be so. There were two main parallel routes, running from north to south: a coastal road, and the great inland or desert highway which lay to the east of the Anti-Lebanon Mountains and the Jordan Valley. Several transverse roads connected these two, of which two principal Syrian ones began at Palmyra: one ran east to Homs, and through a pass in the Lebanon Mountains to Terablus (the modern town of Tripoli) on the coast; the other connected Palmyra with Hama, Kalat el-Mudik and Tartus (on the coast, between Tripoli and Latakia). The inland desert road, called the *Strata Diocletiana* after it was repaired, improved and paved in part by the Emperor Diocletian, was originally a highway of Trajan's which connected the Black Sea with the Red Sea. It passed through Palmyra and Damascus, skirting the south-eastern or desert foothills of the range *er-Rawak*, between these two cities. There were eight Roman stations on this stretch of road alone, and a fortified post at Dumeir. It was useful for the Romans to have fortified routes along the edge of the desert, both for military and commercial reasons. The nomads were more easily kept in order in this way, and merchants who desired to trade with them, or else who wanted the most flat and smooth-surfaced routes for their laden camels, welcomed the right to use a patrolled and protected highway, along which they could count upon finding water at all seasons.

The trans-desert roads were all equally well protected, and they all joined the Euphrates at garrison towns, where permanent forces were stationed. Dura-Europos, for example, the Dura of the Assyrians, and the Europos of the Seleucids, was one of a chain of river garrison towns, probably all under joint Parthian and Palmyrene authority. And the Euphrates was thus fortified south as far as Hit.[1] The most important desert routes were those between Palmyra and Circesium (on the Khabur), which included a branch to the Palmyrene town of Zenobia; and the road which led directly to Hit, from which branched the track to Dura. The

---

[1] The fortress city of Dura-Europos, which flourished from the third century B.C. until the middle of the third century A.D., was founded by Alexander's Macedonians, probably on the site of an ancient town. Eventually, Dura became a Parthian frontier fort; it grew into a principal centre of Parthian trade on the Euphrates, and was a point of departure for the Mesopotamian caravans. In the later Palmyrene period it was garrisoned by Roman troops. The prosperity of this caravan city coincided with, and was directly dependent upon, that of Palmyra. Shortly after its conquest by the Iranians, Dura-Europos was abandoned.

Palmyra–Hit road, which was fortified throughout, came to be the chief caravan highway for the trade between Mesopotamia and Syria. It is also thought, by Père Poidebard, that there was a Roman track from Damascus to Hit, by way of Dumeir and Bir Melossa, which joined the Palmyra–Hit route before the latter reached Muheiwir.

This glimpse of the caravan cities and their trade may, it is hoped, give an idea of their all-important role in trans-desert trade. Once caravan centres were established, and their special type of commercial activity standardized, they could renew their youth periodically—as often and as lavishly as the general conditions of trade might warrant.

Returning to the survey of commercial life in the Near East, one finds that conditions favourable to trade continued throughout the Roman period—except for short intervals of depression. And after the Eastern Roman Empire had become metamorphosed into the Byzantine, trade flourished in Anatolia and northern Syria from the fifth to the seventh centuries—during such times as the emperors at Constantinople were strong enough to safeguard the trade routes and keep the Iranians at bay. Then, during the early militant period of Islam—directly after the death of Mohammed, in 632—trade suffered a temporary decline. Automatically, and because Arabian irruptions into the northern Syrian Desert, complicated by the guerilla type of Arab warfare, made trade connections unreliable. But the inauguration of the Omayyad Caliphate, thirty years later, fostered a revival of commercial life in Syria; and Damascus became the wealthy centre of Saracen civilization. The Caliph's court was renowned for its luxury, and was only outshone by the even more splendid court of the Abbasid Caliphs, which was established at Baghdad just a century later. So that, from the eighth to the eleventh centuries, the commercial interchanges between Syria and Mesopotamia were resumed on a pre-Mohammedan basis. And concomitantly, as Saracen trade increased, so also did the trans-desert trade, which connected two of the most important land-divisions of the Caliphate. Moreover, in the latter part of the Saracen period, the

Venetians and the Genoese prospered proportionately: especially Venice, after the Fourth Crusade in 1204, when she became the most important Christian power in the eastern Mediterranean.

A special feature of this period, particularly before the era of the Crusades, was the activity of Jewish merchants. Great numbers of these adaptable people traded between the extremes of the Occident and the Orient. Religiously speaking, they were safely outside of the opposing camps of both Christians and Mohammedans; and they profited generally by that fact, as by their ubiquity. Chains of Jewish communities stretched all the way from Spain to China, and their members traded and travelled between the east and the west. Like the Arabs, they had an inherited predilection for wandering; only they preferred to wander over the face of the inhabited world. The name *Radanites*, by which they were known, is presumably indicative of the way they spent their lives in wandering from country to country. They became in consequence the natural middlemen of long-distance trade between the various civilizations. Most of them voyaged to China by the Egyptian–Red Sea route, or else by the Anatolian and Caspian routes. But Ibn Khordadbeh, writing in the ninth century, noted that quite a number of them travelled through northern Syria, crossed the Euphrates at Birejik, and journeyed thence to the Persian Gulf by way of Baghdad. They bartered the slaves, silk (presumably Byzantine), swords and furs of the West, for the musk, aloes, camphor and spices of the East. Incidentally, the Saracen travellers of this same epoch also crossed to the Euphrates by the more direct desert routes, eastward from Palmyra. But Saracen and Jew alike experienced much difficulty in reaching the heart of Iran when they approached it from the Syrian side; and travellers *en route* for Iran were customarily detained if they had passed through or near to Hit.

The eleventh century, with its invasions of Seljuk Turks on the one hand, and of the western Crusaders on the other, marked the beginning of a change for the worse in Syrian commercial history. The Seljuk Turks were the first of a series of Mongol or Tatar invaders who swept westwards to Syria from the central highlands of Asia; successive waves of tribal emigration which had their culmination in the devastating Mongol "horde" of the thirteenth century. These warlike nomads had, at first, neither the taste for trading, nor any comprehension of its potential benefits. So after they sacked Baghdad in 1258, they blocked all the channels of internal trade—with the same wanton disregard of the consequences with which they destroyed the irrigation works of Mesopotamia and all other such evidences of civilization.[1] The Crusaders, on the other hand—like all other Franks who found their way to the Near East—were fully alive to the advantages deriving from commerce and industry. And their appreciation of the commodities and luxuries of Saracen civilization was both instantaneous and comprehensive. The Latin Empire which they founded in Palestine, as well as the more northerly crusader states, would have been as great a stimulus to the development of Syrian and Anatolian commerce, as the Tatars—entrenched in Mesopotamia—were a hindrance; except for the fact that the Crusaders could not refrain from fighting each other.

Meanwhile, the Saracens were finding it difficult to keep the peace amongst themselves. The Fatimid Caliphs of Cairo made repeated attempts to annex Syria in order to possess a convenient base from which to attack their rivals, the Abbasid Caliphs of Baghdad. And the local Arab princes (instead of uniting to make common cause against the intruders) kept alternating their allegiances in order to satisfy their own private blood-feuds. Nevertheless, in spite of foreign invasions and anarchistic tendencies, the twelfth century saw no serious decline in Syrian and trans-desert trade.

In the middle of the thirteenth century, however, there was a definite break in the connections between the eastern and the western sides of the Syrian Desert; paralleled by a diversion of

---

[1] The Moslems had inherited from the Sasanian Iranians a system of irrigation for Mesopotamia which made their province of Irak one of the richest in the known world. The Arabs maintained and improved this system, and so were able to irrigate Mesopotamia by draining the surplus waters of the Euphrates, through transverse canals, to the Tigris.

trade to the north. Soon after the sack of Baghdad, above referred to, the Tatars began to take a more active interest in commerce. Christian missionaries, hoping to find this new type of "heathen" more amenable to conversion than were the Saracens, paved the way for eventual commercial interchanges. The Tatars, on their side, responded to the advances of western Christendom, partly in the hope of acquiring useful allies against Egypt, and partly because their commercial eyes had been opened. From the middle of the thirteenth to the middle of the fourteenth centuries, European merchants had direct access to the Far East, by way of the northern routes, through Tatar territories—so long, in fact, as the four great Tatar Khanates ruled over all central and eastern Asia, the Middle East and most of Russia. And for about half that time, the Tatars and the Christians actually looked upon each other as possible, prospective allies against their mutual enemies, the Saracens. Even after the Tatars were converted to Islam, shortly after the beginning of the fourteenth century, they took to their new religion less fanatically than the Saracens; and so their commercial relations with the West—which had become established on a firm basis, and had never been embittered by religious wars—suffered not at all. The Tatar Khanates were most approachable, at first, through Anatolia; so Europeans, and in particular the Genoese, traded with them through the Kingdom of Little Armenia and the diminutive Empire of Trebizond. This was made easy by the character of these two Anatolian states. The kings of Little Armenia were, at one and the same time, friendly with the Christian west, and vassals of the Tatar Khans; and the rulers of Trebizond, also vassals of the Khans, had been Greek-Christian princes for more than fifty years. At the same time, the Crimea grew into an important centre for the Black Sea routes which connected, by even more northerly and direct highways, with the great silk route of central Asia. It was during this period that the Polo brothers, and young Marco Polo, made their famous journeys to the Orient. But on no one of their expeditions to and from Eastern Asia, did they cross the Syrian Desert.

By the end of the thirteenth century, then, Western Europe

had temporarily ceased to trade across Syrian territory altogether. With the capture of St. Jean d'Acre (Akka) by the Saracens and the Mamluks of Egypt, in 1291, the Latin (or Frankish) power in Palestine finally collapsed. An eloquent gesture of renunciation was made when a Papal Bull of that year was issued, forbidding all commercial dealings between Roman Catholic Christians and the Saracens. Within ten years after the fall of Akka, the *factories* and colonies of the Venetians, the Genoese, the Pisans, and the Catalans of Barcelona had all been transferred from the mainland to Cyprus. And Famagusta flourished exceedingly, because the favourable situation of the Cypriote city made it the clearing-house for caravan produce from the mainland, and for its distribution throughout Europe. For more than a century, then, dating from the sack of Baghdad in 1258, Syrian external trade and commerce was at a low ebb; while her neighbours, Armenia and Trebizond on the north, Cyprus on the west, and Egypt on the south, enjoyed a period of relatively great prosperity. Alexandria, incidentally, had continued to flourish—despite the papal interdict—because the various consuls of French and Italian cities, as well as the merchants whom they represented, persevered in imperilling their Christian souls by frequenting this centre of Saracen trade.

The early fourteenth century saw a gradual revival of Syria's internal commerce. Haltingly, and with occasional set-backs, first Syria and then Mesopotamia regained their prosperity. This was due in part to the pacific policy of the Tatar Khans, and in part to the rule of the Mamluk Sultans of Egypt, whose frontiers reached to the Mesopotamian borders of the Iranian Khanate. For the Ilkhans of Iran, with their recently acquired Mohammedanism, and their quick appreciation of the benefits of commerce, fostered intercourse with the Saracen peoples whom they realized they could not subdue. So it is interesting, but not surprising, to learn from a famous Mohammedan traveller—Ibn Battuta of Tangier—that northern Syria and the Euphrates Valley were far from unprosperous in the first half of the fourteenth century, in spite of a dearth of European merchants. In

1348 Ibn Battuta went from Baghdad to Damascus, journeying by way of Anbar, Hit, Haditha, Anna, Meshed Rahba, Sukhna and Palmyra. He described the district between Hit and Anna as "one of the richest and most fertile" in all the world; and Rahba he spoke of as "the finest town" in Irak. It may be remembered that, before making these observations, he had travelled widely. Sukhna he found, strangely enough, to be inhabited mainly by Christians. Of Damascus he had previously remarked that, in all the East, Shiraz was the only city whose bazaars and orchards could even be compared with those of the "surpassingly" beautiful Syrian city.

Towards the end of the fourteenth century the inevitable revival of Syria's external trade took place. Because, as soon as the Tatars ceased to rule in Asia, Western Europe had been forced to trade indirectly with the Orient, through the Saracens. In 1370 Egypt and Cyprus declared a peace which lasted for more than thirty years; and this fostered a general revival of commerce along the shores of the eastern Mediterranean. Shortly thereafter the Kingdom of Little Armenia was finally overthrown by a Mamluk Sultan of Egypt; and the northern routes, whose principal stations were destroyed by Timur the Mongol, in his wars against the Ottoman Turks, again fell into disuse. So that trade between Syria and Mesopotamia resumed its normal course, from the point of view of the Christian West; and the desert highways connecting them were once more brought into prominent use. Commercial affairs on both sides of the desert were infused with new life, and Syria, in particular, seemed on the point of regaining her pristine pre-eminence. The Persian Gulf, with Ormuz at its mouth (which had been much developed during the century of Tatar rule in Asia), gained a new importance; Syrian merchants began to frequent the terminus of the *Shatt el-Arab*, and even travelled as far as Ormuz and—it is claimed—sometimes as far as Calicut, on the western coast of India. Indian merchants penetrated as far north and west as Basra; and a resurrected Baghdad reassumed the role of middleman for the distribution of Indian, Chinese and Iranian goods to the Syrian West. As for

Syria, the revival which had commenced at the very beginning of the fourteenth century, received a fresh impetus. Many of her cities had been stricken with the plague in 1348, but not, apparently, badly enough to interfere with their commercial development. And the Venetians (doubly impelled by the fact that the Genoese took Famagusta shortly after 1370) lost but little time in re-establishing themselves on the mainland. When the peace between Saracen and Christian was proclaimed, they were on the spot and prepared to exploit their position. Beyrout developed into the principal harbour for the outlet of the caravan trade, with Tripoli not very far behind; Damascus became the dominant city of the hinterland, with Aleppo growing into a closer second; and Venice had her consuls and her *factories* in all four cities, with a few Venetians even in Hama. A regular boat service was established between Venice and Beyrout: a convoy of from three to five galleys making the trip two or three times a year. The Pisans and the Catalans of Barcelona gradually followed the lead of the Venetians, re-establishing themselves in these age-old centres of trade; and eventually even the Genoese (who, at first, had been too busy with their occupation of Famagusta to take an interest in the mainland) also set up their *factories*, or "fondachi", in the cities of Syria.

Only Palestine did not share in this general revival of western trade in the Syrian East. Gaza, which was on the caravan route to Egypt; and Jaffa, Ramleh and Jerusalem—which were visited once or twice a year by European Christian pilgrims—remained fairly prosperous. But the northern coastal cities, especially Sidon, Tyre and Akka, were, commercially speaking, dead; and no Frankish merchants did business even in any of the other Palestinian cities.

Then, close upon the heels of the re-born prosperity, came the Ottoman Turks. During the fifteenth century these Asiatic invaders of Anatolia (the last of the Mongol nomads to penetrate to the Near East) were busily building up an empire. After their capture of Constantinople in 1453, they were busy consolidating this empire. The opening of the sixteenth century saw them spreading southwards. Trade languished in the wake of their

armies; and the habitual interchanges of commerce were summarily—though but briefly—suspended. Our information is necessarily scanty for this period, but we know that trade was never more than temporarily interrupted in what today is called Syria and Irak; even though the old land routes became for long a completely negligible factor in European commercial activities; and even though Western Europe tentatively turned its attention elsewhere.

Meanwhile, at the same time that the Ottoman Turks were absorbing into their dominions the territorial remnants of all former near eastern civilizations, Europe was becoming conscious of new needs. The expanding states of the west became increasingly desirous of additional contacts and more direct communication with the Orient. At the end of the fifteenth century Portuguese explorers inaugurated the long sea route to India, around the Cape of Good Hope. Thereafter the Spaniards explored westwards, and the English searched for a North-west passage to Cathay and India. It was long proverbial that the conquests of the Ottoman Turks, on the one hand, and the Portuguese discovery of the Cape Route on the other, gave a joint death-blow to the Levant trade. It is certainly true that the overland routes were not in commercial use—as links between the Orient and the Occident—for about a century; that Syrian trade fell off very badly—waned, apparently in proportion as Portugal's colonies in the Far East grew in prosperity; and that Western Europe took more interest in sea routes than in those overland. But, in reality, the Levant trade never died at all. It was crippled for a while, but—during the sixteenth century, and particularly under the rule of Suleiman the Magnificent —it definitely began to regain its health. For one thing, Portugal was not long able to corner all the Indian trade, nor to force all commerce with the east to keep to the sea route which she monopolized for her own ships. For another thing, although the Barbary corsairs were a source of great danger to all "infidel" shipping, and the Spaniards were likewise to be feared in the Mediterranean, nevertheless, neither England nor France could be long frightened away from the chance of developing their commercial opportunities in both the Near East and the Orient. Moreover, the sultans of the Ottoman Empire, once their conquests were consolidated and military operations did not necessarily take up all their time, were willing to negotiate with the western states of Christendom; provided, of course, that they could foresee future profits. So that, during the sixteenth century, there was a growing commercial *rapprochement* between Western Europe and the Ottoman Turks, who had thrust their empire in between Europe and Asia. The rival Italian city-states, Venice and Genoa, had been the first to make advantageous bargains with the new rulers of Constantinople, almost immediately after their capture of the city in 1453; although this did not prevent Venice from waging unsuccessful war in behalf of her Mediterranean possessions from time to time thereafter. Over eighty years later Francis I, in behalf of France, followed suit: by negotiating with Suleiman the Magnificent the mother of all modern capitulation treaties. This agreement also gave France freedom of trade throughout the Ottoman Empire, which stretched—by then—from the Black Sea to the Red, and included the hinterlands of Anatolia, Mesopotamia, Syria and Egypt.

England, in her own way, also profited by very friendly, if not altogether official representations at the Porte. In sixteenth-century England the development of merchant companies for the purpose of furthering trade in eastern lands was as significant as it was typical of the spirit of the age. They had, of course, an important bearing upon her future imperial history; but that is outside the special province of this narrative. The Muscovy Company confined its attempts to communicate with the Orient to Russia, and sought an eastern outlet through Muscovite territories and the northernmost routes of overland trade. But the later Levant Company concentrated upon the Mediterranean, seeking to trade with the Ottoman Empire. Its close rival, the East India Company, had at first attempted direct communication with India overland, through Ottoman territories. But owing to the difficulties of land travel, and the complicated character of negotiations with the Turks—as well as the previously mentioned danger to shipping in the Mediterranean, both from the pirates of Algiers and Tunis, and from the Spanish—The East India Company, after its incorporation in 1600, decided to make use of the long sea route to India, by the Cape of Good Hope. Thus, theoretically, the Levant Company had almost a free hand in the Near East; but actually it was much hampered, at first, by the hostility of Venetian merchants, and the costly vexations caused by them to English merchants. Also, the East India Company made difficulties of another kind—in England—for the rival merchant company.

In 1605 the first "perpetual" or permanent charter of the Levant Company was granted; and one hundred and nineteen merchants supplied funds, and an executive committee which consisted of a governor and eighteen assistants. The Company became a legal person, empowered to use a common seal, and to appoint consuls to represent its merchants in foreign lands. This was necessitated in Turkey by the system of the capitulations, which gave judicial immunity, from Ottoman courts of law, to all Christian merchants resident in the Ottoman Empire. "The Governor and Company of Merchants of England trading into the Levant Seas" had also (with respect to other English companies) a trading monopoly in the Levant, and the right of levying both export and import duties on all Levant merchandise. The first consulage dues, as these were called, were levied at Smyrna in 1611; and they amounted to a duty of 2% on the imports and the exports of English merchants resident in that city—otherwise called the English "nation" of Smyrna. Consuls were appointed to Scio, Patras, Tripoli, Aleppo, Alexandria, Algiers, Smyrna and, inevitably, to Constantinople. Sir Thomas Lowe, also governor of "The Company of Merchant Adventurers", was the first governor of the Levant Company under its charter of 1605.

Quite logically, therefore, the old land routes were resurrected in the sixteenth century; and the famous Indo–Syrian highway became once more practicable for merchants of the West. The first European traveller crossed the Syrian Desert before the middle of the century. And in 1598 Van Linschoten wrote of the great merchant caravans from Aleppo that were expected in Basra twice a year, every April and September. Before that time also, caravans had again become accustomed to trading between Aleppo and Baghdad. Furthermore, the European travellers who, as will be outlined in a following chapter, crossed the desert between Syria and Irak in the sixteenth century, and who were numerous between 1571 and 1638, almost all accompanied merchant caravans; and this is a further proof of the commercial exchanges between the various cities of Syria and Mesopotamia. If further contemporary evidence is necessary to prove the resurrection of transdesert trade in this era, one has only to read what various travellers had to say about Damascus, Aleppo, Basra and Baghdad. Leonhart Rauwolff and Pedro Teixeira, to cite only two of them, both described the wonders of their bazaars—more than half filled with foreign goods—and noticed merchants in their streets who came from all the great countries of both East and West.

Actually, the first Ottoman sultans were not averse to fostering commercial relations with the west, in spite of its militant Christianity. And a commercial revival, once allowed to start, was not to be destroyed by spasmodic misrule, nor even by occasional outbreaks of war. After 1600 a general economic decline set in throughout the Ottoman Empire; and the sultans, having failed to divert the whole of the Iranian silk trade through Constantinople, made repeated attempts to extort tribute, in the form of duties on trade, from the *factories* of the various *nations* in their dominions. To make matters worse, civil institutions began to decay; and there was widespread corruption in the governments of the various Pashaliks, as well as at Constantinople. This, involving corrupt practices and a large-scale system of briberies, made it increasingly difficult for foreigners to trade in Ottoman territory. Nevertheless, as a later English visitor to Aleppo expressed it, the distant dependencies of Constantinople flourished like the independent roots of the banyan tree: which, separated from the parent stock, take root from the branches, and have healthy lives of their own. The great cities of Syria and Mesopotamia throve independently, and derived what nourishment they needed from their native industries, inter-urban trade and their extensive commerce with central Asia. Damascus, Aleppo, Baghdad and Basra were not caravan cities—in the strictest interpretation of the title—because their existence was not entirely dependent upon caravan trade. And the same could be said of the smaller cities, such as Homs and Hama. But even so, their native industries could never have supplied all the wants of Frankish merchants. It was their role as middlemen, between the merchants of the West and those of the East, that was the mainspring of their wealth; and they were middlemen only by virtue of their trans-desert trade.

Between 1663 and 1745 there was a marked decline in desert-borne trade; and a variety of happenings conspired to prevent Frankish merchants from using the desert routes. The Ottoman Empire could not keep its own house in order; so it was not surprising that the Sultans found it impossible to maintain order in Irak and Syria, or anywhere else south of Anatolia. They were not able to keep the allegiance of their various pashas in Damascus, Tripoli, Aleppo, Baghdad or Basra, and were forced to besiege these cities from time to time in order to quell their revolts. To complicate the situation, the desert Arabs were the natural and hereditary enemies of the Turks; and there were constant nomadic irruptions and invasions of the northern part of the Syrian Desert, notably by the Shammar Arabs from Nejd. Externally, the Sultans were on bad terms with the Shahs of Iran; and the fringes of their two empires were disturbed by the hostilities indulged in by the Portuguese, the Dutch and the English: in their struggles over the Far Eastern trade. And, lastly, there was a severe recrudescence of piracy in the Persian Gulf. So that, for these eighty years, the Aleppo routes to Baghdad and Basra were studiously avoided by European travellers. Portuguese emissaries continued to use the highway longer than other Europeans (with two recorded exceptions), but even they ceased doing so after 1663.

After 1740, the complex factors in this situation gradually resolved themselves and subsided; and—except for a fresh incursion of nomads from Arabia, the Wahhabis—the Syrian Desert became relatively peaceable. Throughout the second half of the eighteenth century, the Great Desert Route and the Little Desert routes, which are hereinafter described in detail (see also Major Rennell's map, p. 106), enjoyed a period of prosperity and importance. Then it was that travellers, especially those servants of the East India Company who were desirous of travelling as rapidly as possible to and fro between India and England, crossed quite freely and frequently between Aleppo, Baghdad and Basra. Many of them wrote descriptions of the journey; some few made lists of material requirements, and compiled itineraries and advice for those who were destined to follow in their footsteps. Of these, perhaps the most noteworthy were Bartholomew Plaisted, John Carmichael, Colonel James Capper and Major John Taylor, all four of whom were of the East India Company. It is in this relatively prosperous period that we have the most satisfactory picture of Syrian caravans and their organization. Lastly, it is also during this era that one first hears of the revival of a desert postal system, inherited from the Saracens. One of the results of all this activity in the eighteenth century was the establishment of an English dromedary post which served to connect England and India for a hundred years—until 1886.

Such, then, is the background for the following account of caravan travel and travellers. By the nineteenth century, this most ancient and direct highway to the East appeared to have finally emerged from a variety of dark ages into the light of European popularity. Some people believe that its popularity in the nineteenth century would never have waned had it not been for the cutting of the Suez Canal. Certain it is that the opening of an unbroken water-way to the East, in 1869, minimized the usefulness of a long land route, for as long as travel across it was dependent upon medieval methods of transportation. Also, as the Ottoman Empire gradually disintegrated, the conditions of travel through the nomad's-land of the desert grew proportionately more difficult and more hazardous.

In the nineteenth century various railway projects were, in turn, deliberated upon and discarded. The great Euphrates navigation scheme (whereby, in 1837, Colonel Chesney had dreamed of linking the Mediterranean with the Persian Gulf) came to nothing. And in the end, the popularity of the Indo-Syrian route did wane, until once more—after 1886—Europeans had ceased altogether to consider it as a useful short-cut to the Orient. Even Syrian and Ottoman merchant caravans, growing fewer in number because they could no longer compete with modern methods of transport along rival routes, ceased to make much use of it. Thus this shortest of land highways came to be thought of as inordinately long and dilatory.

Once more its eclipse was believed to be total and final; at least so far as the Occident was concerned. And the eclipse of the overland route, dependent upon outworn methods of transportation, necessarily lasted until the methods themselves were revolutionized. But our latest age, following upon the political liberation of the desert regions after the Great War—liberation, that is, from the Turks—is now witnessing what may well prove to be a permanent revival of Syrian trans-desert trade. As will be described in a later chapter of this book, commercial air lines now cross the Syrian Desert—following a trail first blazed by the Royal Air Force; several transport companies have converted caravan routes into motor highways, for the transportation of the mails, travellers and freight; and the survey for a projected railway between Trans-Jordan and Irak has been completed. In so far as can be foreseen, the present use made of the Syrian Desert routes is likely to continue, and the trans-desert trade to increase in volume; always supposing that no political system, or lack of system, is allowed (as in other eras) to menace the relative security of the desert routes.

CHAPTER III

TRAVELLERS AND EXPLORERS OF THE
SYRIAN DESERT

I

EARLY TRAVELLERS

THE desert highways were not monopolized entirely by commercial caravans, nor were merchants the only travellers to make use of them. It is true that the commercial motive was primary and impelling; but trans-desert traffic was consistently increased by numbers of civil servants, diplomats and dispatch-bearers of various nationalities; as well as by a great number of miscellaneous wayfarers whose chief impulse to travel arose from curiosity. The place of these last is relatively important in the history of desert travel. It is true that without the merchant caravans, there would have been neither commerce nor the "highways" exacted by that commerce, between Syria and Mesopotamia. But on the other hand, it is the individual travellers who have given us pictures of this desert crossing, and it is through their eyes that we see the great caravans and their complex organization. An outline, therefore, of the most outstanding of these voyagers should serve as a collective prologue to the stories of their own personal experiences, as well as to their description of desert ways.

The first travellers to leave us diaries or narratives of their journeyings belong to the Saracen period—between the ninth and the fifteenth centuries. They are almost all Mohammedans. Before that time, what little light we have on the conditions of life and the manner of travel in the Syrian Desert is shed by such frontier cities as reflect caravan life in the annals of their foreign trade. Early Christian travellers in the Near East were exclusively interested in

79

visiting Christian shrines and Biblical cities. Roman writers who itemized routes or compiled *itineraria*, specialized chiefly in computing the distances and tracing the roads between places or towns of importance; and with their well-known verbal economy, they conscientiously suppressed pure narrative or description. And in pre-Roman days, the only surviving travel diaries are those describing the marches of armies—Cyrus the Younger, or Alexander for instance, both of whom went north of, rather than across, the Syrian Desert.

Educated Moslems had several inducements to travel in the Middle Ages. The Mohammedan world was of so great an extent —stretching as it did from China to Gibraltar—that its inhabitants were prompted both by curiosity, and by a highly developed commercial instinct, to become acquainted with as many of its regions as possible. Furthermore, it was easy to travel in this vast empire because its provinces were so efficiently organized, intercommunication between them was encouraged and rapid transit was fostered. The Caliph at Baghdad—and later the Sultan at Cairo—took a personal interest in these things. They desired to keep a watchful or a jealous eye (as the case might be) upon the various parts of their realm; so they organized and maintained an imperial postal system. Travellers benefited by the networks of post roads with their caravanserais, and they were often guided on their way by postal couriers. Also, they could equally well make use of the various handbooks that were compiled especially for this service, which contained lists of the principal routes, their postal stations and the distances between each. The most useful of these were written by two government officials of Baghdad, Ibn Khordadbeh and Kudama. In addition, numerous Arab geographers travelled widely themselves in order to obtain their data at first hand; and their geographical works stimulated interest in the lands which they described. One of them, el-Mas'udi, called his book *Meadows of Gold and Mines of Gems* in order, as he said, to rouse an even greater interest in the subject.

There was another, a unique stimulus to travel in the world of Islam. Every year the "faithful" journeyed to the Holy Cities of

Arabia, on a pilgrimage to their shrines—in particular to the *Ka'aba* at Mecca and the Tomb of Mohammed at Medina. All Mohammedans considered it a sacred duty to go thither at least once before they died. The great *Hajj*, or pilgrim caravans (of which there were four annually) drew their pilgrims from every quarter of Asia, the Middle East, Africa and the Mediterranean lands. These immense expeditions, undertaken in a common cause, promoted a sense of Moslem brotherhood. They gave an annual incentive to travel; and the pilgrims, who were accustomed to give and to receive introductions to friends in foreign cities and at the various *Hajj* stations *en route*, made the journey easy for each other.

Of the thousands of Moslems who became acquainted with the Syrian Desert in the Middle Ages, seven are writers of consider-able reputation. One of the first, as well as one of the most interesting, was Mohammed ibn Ahmed el-Mukaddasi, traveller and geographer, who was born at Jerusalem in the tenth century. When quite a young man, he made the Pilgrimage to Mecca. Thereafter he spent twenty years in travelling through the length and the breadth of the Mohammedan world. He journeyed every-where on foot, in order to measure distances and to collect material for a geographical treatise; and he visited all the territories of Islam with the exception of Spain. His *Description of the Moslem Empire* is based on the information he gleaned in various and sundry localities: details concerning their products and state of trade, peculiarities of coinage, weights and measures, the climate, and characteristics of the inhabitants. To get this information el-Mukaddasi mixed socially with every class. He is known to have hawked in the bazaars, officiated as a Muezzin, bound books and made paper, instructed in Koranic law, and even practised medicine as a physician, or *hakim*. His family connections and an excellent education had also fitted him to associate with Saracen princes and officers of high rank. In 985 el-Mukaddasi completed his Geo-graphy, while residing in Baghdad. His book is one of the most scientific and accurate existing descriptions of Moslem lands in the Middle Ages; and the sections on Palestine, Syria and Irak (to the limits of their desert frontiers) are especially valuable.

Ibn Jubair, the Spanish Arab traveller, visited Syria and Palestine and the Hejaz in the second half of the twelfth century; and four famous geographers were presumably well acquainted, personally, with the Near and Middle East. Ibn Haukal in the tenth century; Yakut, Idrisi and Abulfeda in the twelfth and thirteenth centuries, all devoted much space in their geographical treatises to a description of these lands. One of them, Abulfeda, was actually born in Damascus.

Lastly, Shaykh Abu Abdallah of Tangier, so well known as Ibn Battuta, was probably the greatest of all Mohammedan travellers. During the first half of the fourteenth century he visited every one of the Mohammedan, as well as many of the "infidel" countries; and he made the Pilgrimage to Mecca six times. It is estimated that he travelled about 75,000 miles. As far as the Syrian Desert was concerned, Ibn Battuta crossed Palmyrena, from east to west; became familiar with all of the desert frontiers; and made use of both the western and eastern *Hajj* routes into northern Arabia.

It has been said that Moslems were almost the only travellers between Syria and Mesopotamia during the Saracen period. This was inevitable, because, even although the Crusades brought about an active interchange between peoples of the West and of the Near East, the hostility between Christian and Saracen discouraged any individual enterprise on the part of westerners; Christians did not penetrate into Syria's hinterland until after the establishment of the Ottoman Empire. Nevertheless, there is another element to be considered in medieval society. The Jews were more or less free to travel in the Near East, and they knew their way about this territory, in more ways than one. Rabbi Benjamin of Tudela is probably the most famous of them all, because he made a study of the Jewish communities in various Moslem cities. In the latter part of the twelfth century he travelled extensively both in Syria and Mesopotamia.

During the fifteenth and the sixteenth centuries, the Jews were the great land travellers. They were noted linguists, as they had always been, and were reputed to converse in Iranian, Greek, Arabic, "Frankish", Spanish and Russian. Christian travellers found some at least of them very difficult to travel with. Rauwolff, for instance, complained (in the sixteenth century) that they were consistent trouble-makers. They also created a special kind of difficulty: whenever a large group of Jews crossed the desert with one of the merchant caravans, they insisted upon resting during their Sabbath. If they could not bribe a caravan leader to camp for most of that day, they would pay for the services of a guide, or even of an escorting guard, in order that they might ride on ahead of the main body of the caravan the day before, or else rest first and then catch up with it again the day after their Sabbath. Until the sixteenth century, however, even the Jewish merchants used the roads of Anatolia in preference to the desert highways; or else, as in the twelfth century, they took the northern route, from Antioch to Birejik, and thence across northern Mesopotamia.

When the Great and Little Desert Routes were resurrected, in the sixteenth century, they began to be used by Europeans of various nationalities. At first and most particularly by the Portuguese, who soon found a use for this most convenient short-cut to their possessions in India and in the Persian Gulf. It is true that they had a monopoly of the sea-borne trade to the east, and consequently desired to confine all trading with the east to their own ships; and so it was necessarily their policy to obstruct the use of all land routes for purposes of trade. But that very fact made it all the more important for them to have the use of a relatively rapid overland route. So Portuguese officials, merchant travellers and especially dispatch-bearers took to travelling over the Indo-Syrian highway whenever speedy communication was required. Antonio Tenreiro, a Portuguese Jew, crossed the Syrian Desert from Aleppo to Basra, in 1523. He was the first European to do so, as he was the first to make the return journey. It is possible (but most unlikely) that Covilhao, travelling from Ormuz to Cairo in 1487, may have used the Basra–Aleppo route, in part or in whole. In 1528 Tenreiro recrossed the Syrian Desert as the bearer of urgent dispatches from the Governor of Ormuz to the King of Portugal.

The next Europeans to use the desert routes were the Venetians, who had commercial "factories" in both Aleppo and Baghdad. But Caesar Frederick—who travelled eastwards by the river route in 1563, and returned overland sixteen years later—is the only one of their number to leave an account of these early journeys, and that one a brief account. In 1579 Caesar Frederick went from Basra to Baghdad by boat, in fifty days. From Baghdad he travelled to Aleppo, in company with four other Venetians and one Portuguese. His caravan was outfitted with enough food and "beans" for their horses to last for forty days; and the caravan included thirty-two laden camels. The six Europeans also took twenty live sheep with them, of which they ate thirteen. Frederick mentions no specific route, but describes the journey as follows (the translation was made by Purchas—see MacLehose Edition, vol. v, p. 446):

> From Babylon to Alepo is forty dayes journey, of the which they make thirty-six dayes over the Wildernes, in which thirty-six dayes they neither see house, trees, nor people that inhabite but onely a plaine, and no signe of any way in the world. The Pilots go before, and the Carovan followeth after. . . . I say in thirty-six dayes we passe over the wildernesse. For when we depart from Babylon two dayes wee passe by villages inhabited until we have passed the river Euphrates. And then within two dayes of Alepo we have villages inhabited.

The desert short-cut was used freely by the Venetians, and when reported by other travellers, they were said to have travelled with commercial caravans, in groups of from five to nine.

For about thirty years, until 1603, the river route was much in use. All those who went by the Euphrates embarked at Birejik, and most of them disembarked at Felluja, unless they desired to proceed directly to Basra and leave Baghdad out of their itinerary. Dr. Leonhart Rauwolff (in 1573), Gasparo Balbi (in 1579) and Sir Anthony Shirley (in 1599) all went by that way; and so did the pioneers of the East India Company.

In 1580 John Newbery gave the lead to future English merchants, and three years later he pointed out the way (in person)

ANNA IN 1836

From F. R. Chesney : *Narrative of the Euphrates Expedition, 1835-7*

to Ralph Fitch and John Eldred. To the consternation of the Portuguese, these merchants reached Basra, after completing the river trip; and some of them proceeded on their way to India, and entered into negotiations there for the establishing of the East India Company. These are the men who journeyed to the Orient, bearing letters from Queen Elizabeth to the "Grand Mogul" and the Emperor of China.

After the beginning of the seventeenth century, preference was given to the land routes between Syria and Mesopotamia. These, though more wearying, were both quicker and safer than the river. In 1605 Pedro Teixeira crossed overland from Basra to Aleppo, and left the first interesting and detailed account of the desert journey. A year later, Gaspar de Bernardino went from Meshed Ali to Aleppo. Thereafter, the numbers of European travellers who crossed the desert on their way to and from the Orient increased rapidly. In the seventeenth century they were mostly Portuguese, Venetians, Spaniards and Frenchmen. The three outstanding names are those of Teixeira (just mentioned), Pietro della Valle and Jean Baptiste Tavernier.

Pedro Teixeira, like Tenreiro, was a Portuguese Jew. But some-time during the course of his travels, he became a Christian—or possibly he only found it more convenient to profess Christianity. Teixeira was probably a physician, and possibly also a speculator in gems. Lastly, he was a historian, although he was a far better diarist of his own journeys (when he could use the results of his personal observations) than he was a compiler of second-hand information. This versatile man travelled widely in the Orient, lived for long in India, and once even ventured to the Philippines. But the voyage which here concerns us the most is his trip from Basra to Aleppo in December and January, 1604 and 1605. He went by way of Baghdad, with a "little caravan" of 150 camels, 95 asses, 12 horses and an escort of 60 armed men. At Baghdad he delayed some time in order to make sure that Aleppo and the intervening desert was in a relatively safe and peaceful state. When he finally set out for Aleppo, it was with a slightly smaller caravan; and he travelled by a route not in common use, because his caravan *bashi* (or convoy leader) believed a shorter and less frequented track to be safer. At Anna, where they crossed the Euphrates, his caravan was detained for three weeks: hindered by officers of the Emir who, he was told, had been prompted by the "Anali" merchants to keep them in the town as long as possible. His stay there was one long misery: the caravan supplies dwindled to almost nothing; every one of the company suffered with the cold, and was oppressed by "fears" and extortions on the part of the townspeople; they were also tormented by street hawkers in addition to countless beggars. It took the caravan exactly two months to complete the journey between Baghdad and Aleppo.

Teixeira's account of this journey is intrinsically interesting, over and above the fact that it happens to be the first detailed record of a desert crossing. He was an observant, well-informed traveller, and one who took the trouble to be as accurate as possible in every way. He found no feature of his trip uninteresting or unworthy of comment; and he allowed neither fear nor discomfort to interfere with the conscientious, daily recording of all that he observed.

Pietro della Valle was an Italian who took to travelling because he liked an adventurous life. In Egypt, he was the first traveller to enter the second Pyramid; and from that country he sent two mummies back to Europe. Like Pedro Teixeira, he also travelled in Iran and India, but less extensively. He crossed the desert twice, going from Aleppo to Baghdad in 1616, and returning from Basra, by the Great Desert Route, some ten years later. On this latter trip, he shepherded across the desert a coffin, containing the dead body of his Armenian wife, Maani Giserida. He journeyed with a very small party, in the wake of one of the great merchant caravans—spending thirty-eight days on the road. Unlike Teixeira, della Valle did not detour to Baghdad when *en route* for Aleppo; and he kept to the west of Anna in a vain effort to evade the payment of tolls. But where their routes did touch, across the *Little Desert*, and at Taiyiba, the narratives of their two journeys confirm each other very closely, as do the observations which they made concerning the landmarks of the desert and its peoples.

Jean Baptiste Tavernier, otherwise known as Tavernier Bernier, was a Parisian of Dutch extraction. Travelling as a jewel merchant, he made six voyages to the Ottoman Empire, Iran and India; and once he went as far as Java. Tavernier crossed the Syrian Desert twice: once from Baghdad to Aleppo, in 1632; and six years later, from Aleppo by "The Great Desert Road" to Basra. But except in descriptions of incidental happenings on the journey, and anecdotes about the Arabs, the narratives of these trips are not illuminating; and notice was taken of very few geographical, and scarcely any archaeological details. On the second trip, it took his caravan of 600 camels sixty-five days to reach Basra; and in all this time, the palace of Ukhaidir is the only place that Tavernier seems to think worthy of even a brief description.

A few years after Tavernier's second trip across the Syrian Desert, Fray Sebastien Manrique voyaged by an unspecified route from Baghdad to Damascus, with a caravan of 300 camels. His sufferings—which are subsequently discussed in the chapter describing modes of desert travel—were great; so that, taken in conjunction with other information of a similar nature, one is not surprised to learn that the desert became, at this time, very un-popular with Europeans. Certainly the account which he had to give of his journey would not have encouraged others to entrust themselves to this short-cut. The year of his crossing—1643—marks the beginning of a hundred-year period of political unrest and economic deterioration in this part of the Ottoman Empire, which has been previously described (cf. pp. 75-76). It was a time of invasion and turmoil in the Syrian Desert; of anarchy in the Pashaliks which bordered the desert; and of imperialistic rivalries, these latter in the vicinity of the Persian Gulf, between the Portuguese, the English and the Dutch. But despite these un-favourable conditions the desert routes continued to be used for another twenty years, by Portuguese political agents, travelling between Goa (in India) and Lisbon. They had no choice, and travelled when and where they were bid. The Jesuit Father,

Manuel Godinho, who was sent to Portugal on a secret mission, was probably the last of these. He travelled as fast as the anarchistic state of the country permitted, with small caravans: going from Basra to Baghdad, and thence, via Anna, Meshed Rahba and Taiyiba, to Aleppo. Godinho was accompanied by a fellow-countryman, and—if Murray is to be believed—the trip was one prolonged nightmare for the two unfortunate men. Godinho commented upon the extraordinary depopulation of Anna (this was in 1663), and is said to have stated: "They were assured, that no traveller had been lately known to have gone, either by land or by the rivers, without being robbed and murdered; that no inhabitant of Anna durst stir beyond its gates. . . ."[1]

Only two other travellers are known to have crossed the desert before the end of the seventeenth century. John Campbell, a Scotsman, on his way home from India and Iran in 1669, went from Baghdad to Aleppo, via Anna and Taiyiba. Apparently he wrote no account of his own desert journey; but Richard Bell (who was in Aleppo when Campbell arrived there) says that this adventurer made the trip in company with a French priest and a single guide; and that he carried with him a quantity of precious stones, among which was a famous diamond engraved with the royal arms of England. By some miracle Campbell reached Syria, with all his jewels, unmolested by the Beduin.

The other voyager was a Frenchman by the name of Carré, who was on his way back to France from a mission in the Orient. Colbert, with an eye to French commercial expansion, had sent

[1] Murray's *Asia* (1820), vol. i, p. 405. Murray is not entirely to be trusted. Compare, for example, the extremely inaccurate résumé of Colonel Capper's voyage along the Great Desert Route: vol. i, p. 409. Also, Godinho's supposed statement that he saw six tigers (*i.e.* Godinho must have seen lions, not tigers, if he saw any such kind of animal at all, cf. p. 15) near Anna, all at once, sounds rather unlikely. But the inaccuracy in this case may lie with Godinho himself. Unfortunately, Murray's résumé is, apparently, the only English version of Godinho's own narrative. There are two Portuguese editions of this (published in 1665 and 1842 respectively), which the present writer has been unable to consult. However, Godinho's statement regarding Anna, and travelling conditions in general, is near enough to the truth, as we know it, to be believed.

him as an emissary to Madagascar, to report on the potentialities of that island. Monsieur Carré, desirous of seeing as much of the East as possible, returned by way of India and the overland route. It is difficult to say just when he crossed the desert, since the account of his journey was not published until 1699, and he seems to have had (in common with many other European travellers of the sixteenth and seventeenth centuries) a strong disinclination to mention years or dates. He appears, however, to have made this part of his journey between the years 1671 and 1673; and he used the Little Desert Route, going from Baghdad to Aleppo via Anna, Meshed Rahba, a *kasr* on the Euphrates near Rahba, named "Achera", and passing within sight of Taiyiba. Carré complains less of the risks he ran and of the dangers of the road than he does of the extreme heat—he was travelling on the desert in June. Nevertheless, he and his solitary guide were alarmed more than once by various parties of Beduin, and they took care to avoid entering Taiyiba for fear of the robber bands that reputedly made their headquarters there. Furthermore, they "dared" to travel along the banks of the Euphrates only because they had been told that practically all the riverain Arabs (about "ten thousand men") had gone off in a body to plunder the *Hajj* caravan. Carré may have crossed the desert more than once, for in describing the commercial glory that had once been Taiyiba's, and the beauty of its tree-filled oasis, he mentions having seen the town three different times. It is interesting to note that this traveller, and presumably therefore other Europeans who travelled during the seventeenth century, carried some sort of letter of credit. He obtained a "*lettre de change*", as he called it, indirectly (with the help of the Capuchin Fathers) from a merchant of Baghdad, because he was unwilling to carry any more money on his person than was absolutely necessary.

Incidentally, in 1665 two well-known travellers—one of them famous—made a point of travelling around, rather than across, the desert. De Thevenot, who journeyed in Syria with two passports, one Arabic and one Turkish, went from west to east, travelling from Damascus to Aleppo, and thence by the northern route

—via Birejik, Urfa, Nisibin and Mosul. At Mosul he continued to Baghdad down the Tigris, by *kelek*, or river raft. Carsten Niebuhr reversed this journey. After having circumnavigated Arabia, he went north through Mesopotamia, and (by a still more northerly route) via Mosul, Mardin, Diarbekr, Urfa, and Birejik to Aleppo. Niebuhr, with his usual desire to acquire information, cross-questioned a Basra merchant and a Bedu (who had made the desert journey many times) as to trans-desert routes. But though he carefully recorded the desert itineraries, he made no personal use of the information.

No further light is shed upon the rest of the dark age, between 1673 and 1745; although it is possible that one other Frenchman may have crossed the *Little Desert* some thirteen or fourteen years after Monsieur Carré—a certain Soares Sieur du Val, who went to Iran by way of Baghdad, in the last years of the seventeenth century. Neither emissaries nor missionaries appear to have travelled over the Syrian Desert during this hiatus in its use by Europeans. Even the Carmelites, whose puissant settlement at Basra survived from 1623 to 1733, have left in their records no accounts of desert travellings.

2

FOUR GREAT CITIES OF SYRIA AND MESOPOTAMIA: DAMASCUS, ALEPPO, BAGHDAD AND BASRA

Before enquiring as to the travellers of the eighteenth century, it would be well to say a word or two concerning the cities they frequented. Of these, the four great trade-centres were Damascus and Aleppo on the Syrian side; Baghdad and Basra on the Mesopotamian side. And of these four the two most important, during the period of European commercial activity in the Ottoman Empire, were Aleppo and Basra.

Damascus, to begin with the oldest city and the most revered among travellers, was a flourishing town in Phoenician days, and before. The greatness of Damascus as a centre of caravan trade was known to the Occident at the beginning of the Christian era, when it became the chief intermediary between Palmyra and the coast. During the period of the Omayyad Caliphs, from A.D. 660 to 750, Damascus was not only the metropolitan centre of the Mohammedan world, but was the foremost of all Saracen cities as well. The greatness of the city long outlasted the Omayyads, but under the rule of the Abbasid Caliphs of Baghdad there rose commercial rivals to its urban omnipotence, and even to its prestige. Notwithstanding, Ibn Haukal spoke of Damascus, in the tenth century, as "the right hand of the cities of Syria"; and he and his contemporary, el-Mukaddasi, agreed as to the delights and the beauties of this wide-spreading oasis. Idrisi, in the twelfth century, has only praise for the wonders of the city: its Great Mosque, which had first been a Byzantine church of, apparently, unparalleled magnificence; its famous hot baths; the "eight" canals, and the many fountains; its rivers, gardens and fruit orchards. With one accord, Mohammedan writers dwell upon the loveliness of the city and the splendour of its buildings. Damascus, said Ibn Battuta in 1326, "surpasses all other cities in beauty, and no description, however full, can do justice to its charms. Nothing, however, can better the words of Ibn Jubayr in describing it. . . ." [1] Today, the traveller is more impressed by the oasis as a whole, seen in its desert setting, than by the city itself—interesting though its crowded streets still are. But that is another story.

From the eleventh to the fourteenth centuries, Damascus was subjected to a variety of invasions, at the hands of Seljuks, Christian Crusaders and Mongols. But in the early sixteenth century this city regained some of the commercial importance which it had been gradually losing. When the Ottoman Turks ruled the Mohammedan world, which had converted them to its tenets, Damascus became the meeting-place of Turkish and Syrian pilgrims. Each year, from the middle of the seventh century, the

[1] The quotations concerning Damascus are from Ibn Haukal (ed. of 1800), p. 41; el-Mukaddasi (ed. of 1892), pp. 16, 17, 23 and 24; Idrisi (ed. of 1836), i, p. 349; Ibn Battuta (ed. of 1929), p. 65.

Hajj, or pilgrim convoy, had set out from there to perform its pilgrimage to Mecca. Accordingly, Suleiman the Magnificent built at Damascus a lovely mosque and guest-house—to this day one of the most enchanting of all Turkish mosques—where pilgrims from Anatolia might rest after their long journey, and refresh themselves before taking their places in the Syrian *Hajj*. In the intervals, before the assembling and after the return of the *Hajj*, Turk and Syrian transacted business to their mutual advantage.

Damascus remained the centre of the Syrian *Hajj*; but it declined again, nevertheless, commercially speaking. During the seventeenth and eighteenth centuries this decline was increasingly noticeable, in proportion as trans-desert commerce became more and more diverted to the Aleppo route. In the nineteenth century *The Journal of a Deputation to the East* (dated 1849) comments upon the waning prosperity of Damascus, which was so soon to become a thing of the past. Twenty years later, the opening of the Suez Canal gave Damascene commerce its proverbial death-blow. But the prosperity of Damascus has been miraculously revived in the years since 1918; since, once again, this most ancient caravan city has become an important terminus for a great desert route.

Aleppo is probably as ancient a city as Damascus, although it developed much more slowly. Not until the later sixteenth century did it become what Ralph Fitch termed "The chief mart of all the east". Known as *Halpa* to the Hittites, as *Halman* to the later Assyrians, and as Beroea to the Seleucids, this city was finally christened Haleb by the Saracens. That is, today, the name by which it is known to the Arabs and its native citizens. The word Haleb, however, was given an Italian form in the European period. Rauwolff, who described it, in 1573, as the meeting-place of all nationalities—Greeks, Armenians, Arabs, Georgians, Iranians and Indians, "which come and go daily with their caravans"— called it "Halepo"; and here we see the transition of the Arabic name, before it had become completely Italianized.

Aleppo was first heard of (in the second millennium B.C.) as the most northerly Semite outpost against the Hittites. Like

ALEPPO, THE SARACEN CITADEL

Photograph by the author

Damascus, it was mentioned in Babylonian, Assyrian and Egyptian texts; but unlike Damascus, it was still only a small town in the day of the Emperor Julian. Its prosperity dates from the Arab conquest of the seventh century, when Aleppo became the centre, in northern Syria, for the caravan trade of northern Mesopotamia and Iran; and this prosperity was never more than momentarily dimmed by the various conflicts and invasions to which the city was thereafter, from time to time, subjected.

In the seventeenth century Aleppo was considered to be the third city of the Ottoman Empire—next in size and importance to Constantinople and Cairo. Diplomatically speaking, it was even more important than Cairo, because its geographical situation made it the distributing centre for all the correspondence of the Near and Middle East. Travellers commented in amazement upon the variety of languages and of races to be met with there, and the diversity of its bazaar products. They described the public baths, the arched stone bazaars, the imposing Saracen citadel, the great *khans* which housed its merchants, and the ten city gates. One and all, from Teixeira in 1605, to Taylor and Olivier in 1789, Europeans were impressed with the paved streets and stone-built houses, which were said to be the finest in any Turkish city. A *khan* or caravanserai was so built that the lower floor could be used for a caravan depot (or warehouse), and the upper story—as a dwelling-place—could accommodate large numbers of the *Frangi*. Frankish consuls, chaplains and all the more important merchants, however, lived in luxuriously furnished houses of their own. There was a cultured social life, as befitted a city of such diplomatic and political prestige. French, English and especially Italian were spoken at the frequent formal functions; and many of the resident Franks spoke Turkish, Arabic and Greek as well as their own languages.

The European colony, each *nation* of which had its own resident consul and its own interpreter, numbered about two hundred individuals. Of these, about a quarter were English. Such commercial colonies, called *factories*, have already been alluded to; and the members thereof, which were known collectively as the *nation* of whatever country they represented. In the seventeenth century, the three principal *factories* established at Aleppo were—in the order of their relative importance—the Venetian, the French and the English. There were also two Flemish "houses", with a yearly trade amounting to about 150,000 ducats (about £75,000); but they had to conduct their business under the protection of the French. Teixeira, who described them all in detail, tells us that the Venetians had fourteen houses, each of which was a highly organized mercantile community under the control of two heads. The consul of these fourteen houses spent from 70,000 to 80,000 ducats (about £35,000 to £40,000) during his three-year term of office. The French had only five houses, but more than twenty of their ships were annually employed in the Aleppo trade, as against the four to five Venetian ships that were so employed. The French trade brought in about 800,000 ducats (about £400,000) a year. A comment of Teixeira's on the French *factory* is, if unprejudiced, illuminating: "The number of the French who come and go is much greater than that of the Venetians . . . but in other matters they are far from equalling the order, rule and policy of the Venetians". For reasons emphatically not connected with their organization at Aleppo, the French succeeded in monopolizing most of the European trade there, before the end of the eighteenth century. The number of their houses had increased from five to nine; whereas the number of Venetian houses had been reduced from fourteen to two.

Teixeira's remarks upon the three English houses which he found at Aleppo, and their trade (which he estimated as worth about 300,000 ducats, or about £150,000), is not of much significance for the remainder of the seventeenth century, because of a certain coincidence. He was in Aleppo in 1605, the very same year in which the Levant Company—which had been founded in 1586—was reorganized and received its perpetual charter. It was natural that some time must elapse before the impetus, born of the new policy, could result in the great increase of English trade—so noticeable at the end of the century. Visitors, who were entertained some seventy years later by the members of the Company's *factory*, described at length the social and sporting life of the English community. Their chief recreations included handball, cricket, coursing with greyhounds, fishing and duck-shooting in the neighbourhood of Sebkha Jebbul, and the giving of sumptuous banquets. In 1681 the Levant Company was so active that it even sought an entire monopoly of the Red Sea trade, and presented a petition to the House of Commons (which was tabled) asking for the exclusive privilege of importing "raw or wrought silks" into England.

When Dr. Russell wrote his well-known account of Aleppo in the eighteenth century, the total of its population was on the decline. But when the Frankish factories were at the height of their power and influence, Aleppo was at the peak of its commercial prosperity, and the population of the city was computed at between 285,000 and 290,000 people. Monsieur le Chevalier d'Arvieux, French consular deputy in 1680, estimated that the Christians then numbered between 30,000 and 35,000 souls; and that there were in addition some 2000 Jews. The balance was presumably made up of Turks, many of whom were janissaries, and other soldiery under the command of the Pasha. The latter, an appointee of the Sultan, was seldom prevented from exploiting the city for his own enrichment. Even in the most prosperous periods, merchants complained of extortionate duties and injustice in the courts.

In the nineteenth century Aleppo declined, and faded into commercial obscurity—just as did Damascus. But after 1880 Aleppo anticipated the revival that came to Damascus with such suddenness in 1918; and since the beginning of the twentieth century, this city, once so great, has slowly regained a measure of commercial importance.

Baghdad, in comparison with both Damascus and Aleppo, may fairly be called modern. Its setting is venerable enough, since it is near the sites of two very ancient cities, Ctesiphon and Seleucia, and it is not far from the ruins of Babylon. But the contemporary city of Baghdad is medieval, and the original town—the unique "round city" of which no traces are now visible—was founded by the Caliph Mansur in A.D. 762. When the Abbasids succeeded the Omayyads of Damascus, a new capital city was a strategic necessity. Politically, the new Saracen dynasty, which relied upon Iran for support, needed to have its capital closer to Iran, nearer the centre of a Moslem world that was already facing eastward; and as far distant as possible from the Empire of the Byzantine Christians, as well as from the Omayyads of Damascus. Economically, the fertile plains of the Tigris were eminently desirable; and no spot was more so than an Iranian hamlet, already named Baghdad, that was situated on the Tigris just above the mouth of a great Euphrates canal, the then famous *Nahr Isa*. This was near, but not too near to the Syrian Desert "frontier"; and there was adequate river communication with the Persian Gulf. The name Baghdad means, in Iranian, "founded by God". Throughout the Middle Ages Baghdad was officially known to the Arabs as *Medinat es-Salam*, the "City of Peace"; but its older name survived in popular speech; and by that name alone was it known to the Christian West.

There are two divisions in the history of Baghdad: the period before the sack of the city by the Tatars, and the period after this event—from 1258 to the present day. Until the middle of the thirteenth century, Baghdad was not merely an important city, the obvious capital of *Irak Arabi* (as lower Mesopotamia was called by Arab geographers); she was also the brilliant centre of the Saracen world, and the seat of government of the Caliphate. But when Hulagu and his Tatars occupied Baghdad, the political and religious centre of Islam shifted to Egypt, and Syria reasserted its economic importance in the Moslem world. Guy Le Strange, the erudite historian of Baghdad, has said that this great Saracen city maintained its prestige: in spite of wars, sieges, the temporary removal by the Caliphs of the seat of government to Samarra (for fifty-five years in the ninth century), the forty-day sack of the city by the conquering Tatars, and the final removal of the Caliphate to Cairo. But prestige, and the legendary glamour of its greater days, could not restore the splendours and the wealth of the earlier medieval city. After 1258 Baghdad only attained a fluctuating importance, as the economic centre and principal town of Mesopotamia, and it shared with Basra the role of middle-man between Mesopotamia and the Orient on one hand, and Syria and the Occident on the other. The city was ruled first by Ilkhans of the Tatar Khanate of Iran, and later by successive Mongolian dynasties, until—in the sixteenth century—Baghdad and its provinces were added to the Empire of the Ottoman Turks by Suleiman the Magnificent.

Throughout the eighteenth century, Baghdad was as unprosperous as during the preceding century; but less than a hundred years ago, when her western rivals, Damascus and Aleppo, were stagnating, Baghdad had a renewed lease of life. The importance of water-ways to the Persian Gulf was once more recognized, and a new period of prosperity for this city upon the Tigris was the logical result of the revival of the river routes. Under the governorship of Midhat Pasha, between 1869 and 1872, some western reforms were introduced, including the establishment of a telegraph system and the inauguration of a steamboat service between Baghdad and Basra. The concession for this boat service was sold to the then famous Lynch Steam Navigation Company. Later on, the building of the "Berlin to Baghdad" Railway emphasized once again the strategic importance of this perennial capital of Mesopotamia.

Basra, which first saw the light as a Saracen military camp, was founded (by order of the Caliph Omar) a century and a quarter before Baghdad. Mohammedan leaders of the first period of the Arab conquest had considered it necessary to establish themselves at a point where the highways between Mesopotamia, the Persian Gulf and Arabia all intersected. They built their city west of the Tigris–Euphrates, since they also needed a depot of supplies that would be easily accessible to the Arab army. They connected Basra with the river by a great horseshoe-shaped canal, the southern curve of which was famed as the *Nahr el-Obolla*. From this branched a great number of smaller, but navigable channels.

Until the middle of the eighth century Basra and Kufa (sister cities which had been founded within a year of each other) were

7

almost equally important military bases on the desert frontier. After Baghdad was founded, however, Kufa ceded its place to the new Abbasid capital.[1]

From 762 the fortunes of Basra followed fairly closely those of Baghdad; but the former was far enough south to have an independent history of its own. Basra was never a mere satellite town; and in some ways it was more vulnerable than Baghdad, because of its position on the desert frontier. The southern city was often raided by the Beduin, who coveted its extensive groves of date-palms; and it was not immune from either the Mongols or the Iranians. Incidentally, medieval Basra stood more than twelve miles west of the river; but the third and modern city of that name has been built upon the site of its ancient suburb, el-Obolla.

Basra has had three periods of prosperity. Under the Abbasids it was famous as the city of the "Thousand-and-One Nights", and celebrated for its bazaars and the fabulous number of its canals. But the last of the Abbasids saw the end of this first brilliant period. In 1258 Basra and its canal system was, like Baghdad, destroyed by the Tatars. There follows a gap in the history of the city, during which time Basra was rebuilt. In the seventeenth and eighteenth centuries the city had a very busy, if less brilliant period. It was frequented first by Portuguese, then by Dutch and eventually by English merchants, and visited by French and other European travellers. The Carmelites had an influential convent there, and their vicar-general, acting as a French consul, habitually interceded with the governors of Basra in behalf of all foreigners who did business in the city. The very decline of Baghdad in the seventeenth century served to accentuate the strategic position of the Gulf city, and gave the older city a chance to develop.

Some noted travellers visited Basra; among them Teixeira, Pietro della Valle, Tavernier and de Thevenot. They called it

[1] Kufa was founded, also at the command of Omar, a few miles north of the ancient Lakhmid capital called Hira. Gradually Hira became more and more depopulated, until it ceased altogether to exist. Kufa was a populous and important city until Hilla was founded (in 1102); thereafter its suburb, Najaf, displaced it entirely. Najaf is rather better known by the name of Meshed Ali because it contains the tomb of Ali, son-in-law to the prophet Mohammed.

Balsara, or Bassora, and contrasted the miserable appearance of the city with its obvious wealth. They all commented upon the numbers of horses, both local and Arabian bred, that were exported to Ormuz each year—in return for the Indian "merchandizes", spices and drugs that were shipped from the Indian end of the Gulf. Joseph Salbancke, a contemporary of Teixeira's, wrote that ships of "fortie or fiftie tunnes" came monthly to the port of Balsara. Tavernier gives us a picture of the city's brisk transit trade with the West in these words: "Merchants of all countrys, from Constantinople, Smyrna, Aleppo, Damascus, Cairo, and other parts of Turkie, buy such merchandizes as come from the Indies, with which they lade the young camels which they buy in that place; for thither the Arabians bring them to put them to sale".[1]

Basra had a significant peculiarity. During four months of the year, from June to September inclusive, its foreign trade was brisk. The rest of the year trade stagnated. But for these four months sailing-boats had favouring winds to enable them to beat up the Persian Gulf; and there was (in addition to goods from India) a plentiful supply of pearls from the pearl fisheries of the Gulf, particularly from the vicinity of the Bahrein Islands. Every year, in spite of the intensity of the summer heat, an influx of merchants coincided with this perennial commercial revival, so that the number of resident foreigners was more than doubled. House-rents also had a tendency to double in value, and the price of horses and of provisions as well. The ruler of the city, whether an Arab "prince" or a Turkish pasha, made special regulations for his own enrichment; and he decreed that during the monsoon season no individual should either buy or sell anything without his express permission, and through his agency. All the rest of the year the pasha had to content himself with the "gifts" which he extracted from merchants and pilgrims (on their way to and from Mecca), with a four or five per cent customs revenue, and with the taxes which he autocratically imposed upon date-palms, horses and camels. By his command also, mats were frequently

[1] Tavernier, ed. of 1684, p. 89.

spread upon the square in front of his house, and on these were heaped the tithes he exacted from harvests of wheat, rice and fruit. Lastly, Jews and Indians were commercially active, under his personal supervision, both as money-changers and as traders in jewels. The Venetian sequin was the principal medium of exchange.

Early in the eighteenth century, the East India Company established a permanent *factory* at Basra, and this survived for as long as official dispatches and the Indian trade passed westward over the Great Desert Route. Two Englishmen who went through Basra on their way to India, in the latter part of that century, found an English *factory* there, composed of four officials, guarded by thirty sepoys under a coloured lieutenant.

Now, today, Basra shares with Baghdad the return of a prosperity which springs from the renewal of its trade in the Gulf and the two rivers of Mesopotamia.

There is no need to dwell upon the importance of the Persian Gulf in eastern history. Until after the middle of the nineteenth century it played the part in European trade and international politics that has, since then, been taken by the Suez Canal and the Red Sea. The Gulf, with the fortified island of Ormuz at its mouth, was the key to India. During the Saracen period, the Arabs monopolized its commerce; during the century of Tatar rule in Asia, the Tatars did the same; and for a century after the coming of the Ottoman Turks the Gulf still remained inaccessible to the West. But in the sixteenth century Europeans won a foothold on the eastern borders of the Ottoman Empire; and after 1507 the Persian Gulf was open to them. Dominated at first by the Portuguese, it came gradually under the control of the English. But the Arab pirates who infested its waters, and who eventually received active support from the Wahhabis of Nejd, menaced all "infidel" shipping until well into the nineteenth century.

On the west, each one of the coastal towns of Syria had its significant place in the histories of Aleppo and Damascus. Until the end of the sixteenth century Tripoli had been favoured by Frankish merchants; but early in the seventeenth century these came to prefer Alexandretta, then known as Scandaroon or Iskanderun, because, as Aleppo became more frequented by Europeans and the volume of its trade increased, the port which was nearest to Aleppo was found to be more convenient. Late in the succeeding century, however, Alexandretta lost its popularity. The consuls of England, France and Venice went to reside at Latakia, which is nearly midway between Tripoli and Alexandretta; and the English left only a factor or agent to represent the Levant Company at the latter port. There were several reasons for this. Kurdish robbers had made the northern roads unsafe for merchants, especially in the vicinity of the famous Beilan Pass. Then the climate of Alexandretta was found to be very unhealthy for westerners. Lastly, but perhaps most important of all, Latakia was extremely well situated for the trade with Cyprus. Before the end of the eighteenth century, Latakia was visited by six or seven English brigs a year, and by an even greater number of French and Venetian vessels.

South of Alexandretta, and of the long unused port of Antioch at Suedia; south of Latakia, and of the once famous port of Tartus; south even of Tripoli, is Beyrout—which has a better natural harbour than them all. Long before the seventeenth century Beyrout supplanted Sa'ida, or Sidon, as the port of Damascus; but it is too far south on the Syrian coast ever to have been a practicable port for Aleppo.

Much more might be written about the great cities of Syria and Mesopotamia, and about their commercial activities; but it is time to return to the travellers who went to and fro between these cities.

3

TRAVELLERS OF THE EIGHTEENTH CENTURY, AND EXPLORERS OF THE NINETEENTH AND TWENTIETH CENTURIES

It has been shown how, toward the end of the seventeenth century, the trans-desert highways became increasingly unpopular. After the beginning of the eighteenth century, Europeans avoided them altogether. Until 1745 no westerners at all are known to have gone to India by these overland routes. The desert was not even travelled in, with a single recorded exception—namely, the re-discovery of Palmyra by some English merchants (of the Aleppo establishment) in 1691. They were so impressed with Palmyra's imposing ruins that a Mr Henry Maundrell, chaplain to the English *factory* at Aleppo, went to see them for himself eight years later. According to these gentlemen of the Levant Company, Palmyra was "almost inaccessible", because it was "beyond the protection" of the Sultan of Turkey.

When the desert bridge finally came back into use, it was almost completely monopolized by Englishmen, servants of the East India Company; and they used the Great Desert Route which connected Aleppo with Basra. This was the track that was followed annually by the great merchant caravans, which numbered from one to two thousand camels; it will be fully described in a later chapter, so there is no need to outline it here.

William Beawes was the first westerner to cross the desert after this hiatus in its use. He made the trip in 1745; and after him, in close succession, came four other Englishmen: Bartholomew Plaisted, Gaylard Roberts and his son, and John Carmichael. Mr Douglas Carruthers has published their diaries, with very full and scholarly notes, in his book entitled *The Desert Route to India* (1929, No. LXIII of the Publications of the Hakluyt Society). From these accounts, and from those left by four other Englishmen who crossed a little later in the century, anyone interested may obtain an excellent idea of the conditions of desert travel, and of what the Great Desert Route was really like. In 1754 Edward Ives and a group of several other servants of the East India Company carried dispatches from India to England. These Englishmen, who were the last for many years to choose the northern route, went from Basra to Aleppo, via Diarbekr and Birejik. They found the road both difficult and dangerous. Thirty years later Dr. Thomas Howel and two of the Company's servants also chose the northern route, but that was because they wanted to go directly to Constantinople by the fastest road possible; and so they omitted Aleppo altogether from their itinerary. In 1806 Claudius J. Rich, Resident of the East India Company at Baghdad from 1808 to 1821, travelled from Aleppo to Bombay by way of Diarbekr, Mardin and Mosul. At Mosul he went down the Tigris to Baghdad.

Between 1771 and 1790 the second group of four Englishmen crossed by the Great Desert Route. General Sir Eyre Coote, an Anglo-Indian of distinction (on his way home from India), was the first of these. Colonel James Capper, travelling in the reverse direction, was the second. Dr. Julius Griffiths and Major John Taylor followed after Colonel Capper, from Aleppo to Basra, within a few years of each other. They all journeyed in relatively small, private caravans—which was an innovation in desert travel. General Coote's account of his journey is very complete; he describes places like Kasr el-Hair and Taiyiba in great detail, and is equally explicit about the nature of the soil in various sections of the route. General Coote's caravan had one encounter, more rewarding than most in the desert. They met two Arab couriers who were *en route* for Basra. These unfortunate men had been robbed of their camels by the Beduin, but they were still in possession of their mail-bags. The General tells with much gusto how he and his party camped, forthwith, in order to read the European *Gazettes*. It is quaint to visualize such a happening in mid-desert, several hundred weary miles away from any centre of civilization that was even remotely in touch with the western world.

Colonel Capper and Major Taylor had a special and double purpose in mind when they wrote their diaries of the desert crossing. They made a comparative study of the two speediest routes to India (that over the Syrian Desert, and the longer one by way of Suez), with a view to determining which route saved, on the whole, the most time. Their findings are examined in the chapter on the overland dromedary postal services. For this reason they kept close account of their own schedules, and they noted every delay they met with, avoidable and otherwise. Their secondary purpose was to compile a sort of handbook, in order to make the desert trip as easy as possible for such of the East India Company's servants as would be required to travel to India by the overland route. Therefore they made up lists of necessities for the journey, the prices of various supplies, and the cost of outfitting a caravan. They perceived that the Syrian Desert provided a useful short-cut to India, and therefore they were convinced that it should be used, without regard for its monotony or its bodily discomforts. Major Taylor's two-volume work is much more pretentious than Colonel Capper's book, and his copious "statistics" more superficially impressive. But it seems to the writer that there is as much useful information in Colonel Capper's compact outline as there is in the later traveller's two volumes; and that, moreover, there are no discrepancies between the text of Colonel Capper's book and his map, nor any obvious inaccuracies in the former. He wrote up his diary every night while he was crossing the desert, and made very careful notes. From these memoranda he drew the material for his book. The same cannot be said for Major Taylor. His material is not altogether reliable, and his map is remarkably, amazingly inaccurate—as compared with Colonel Capper's relatively excellent map. Also, his judgment in the matter of desert conditions does not appear to have been entirely sound.

There were of course many other travellers during this half-century when the Great Desert Route was so popular. Eyles Irwin, for example, who was chiefly known for his description of the Suez Route, went to Baghdad and Basra in 1781; but though he also kept a diary, he is not one of the more reliable travellers. Various servants of the East India Company are mentioned by name as having gone from Aleppo to Basra, or *vice versa*. Many more are referred to in the diaries of their compatriots, without specific mention of their names. Furthermore, among the anonymous travellers who crossed the desert was one German; and among those whose names are known were three Frenchmen. The first of these, Borel de Bourg, was the only eighteenth-century traveller to have a serious skirmish with the Beduin. They forced him to surrender, after de Bourg had killed several of their number, and, but for the kind-heartedness of their shaykh, he might have been put to death. He was forced to buy his freedom by promising his captors a reward of 200 sequins (about £75) after

his safe arrival at either Basra or Graine. Monsieur de Bourg was
an unlucky man; after escaping thus from the Arabs, he was captured by the English (the year being 1778). André Michaux, who
went from Aleppo to Baghdad in 1782, was the first of a series of
scientifically minded Frenchmen to journey on the desert. He
combined an interest in natural history with the natural curiosity
of the traveller; and spent three weeks in crossing the *Little Desert*,
by way of Taiyiba, collecting as many geological and botanical
specimens as possible *en route*. At the very end of the century
Olivier, a Frenchman of much the same type as Michaux, went
eastwards by the northern route from Birejik to Mardin, and
returned to Aleppo from Baghdad by the way of Anna, Meshed
Rahba and Taiyiba. But he travelled with one of the large commercial caravans from Baghdad to Aleppo, and so was delayed for
ten days at Anna, where his caravan crossed the Euphrates.

The nineteenth century opens with the names of several Frenchmen who are famous in the annals of French colonial history.
Jean-Baptiste-Louis-Jacques (sometimes called Joseph) Rousseau
was for long a well-known figure in the Near and Middle East.
He was born into the diplomatic and consular life, and was educated in its finer points by a distinguished father who had been
consul and agent for the French East India Company at Baghdad,
Aleppo and Basra successively. J. B. L. J. Rousseau himself was
consul-general of France at Baghdad until 1816. Naturally enough
he crossed the *Little Desert* more than once in the ordinary course
of his duties. In 1808 he and his wife and their two children crossed
the Euphrates at Hit, and followed the north-western part of the
Great Desert Route to Aleppo. Having a special interest in
archaeology, Rousseau left the caravan near Kasr el-Hair and went
to visit the twin ruins. During the last twelve years of his consular
service, Rousseau was at work upon a topographical map of the
pashaliks of Baghdad, of Urfa and of Aleppo. He was assisted in
part by a Colonel Boutin, who was murdered by the Arabs in
1815. Lastly, Honoré Vidal, of the French consulate at Aleppo,
travelled widely on the Syrian side of the desert, and he crossed the
Little Desert five different times. Once he accompanied Rousseau;

twice he went from Baghdad to Damascus by way of Palmyra; and twice he went by the "ordinary" route between Baghdad and Aleppo.

The only other well-known traveller in this early part of the nineteenth century is the famous Indian cartographer, Major James Rennell. In his map of Western Asia he charts the Euphrates, and lays down the course of the Great Desert Route (map opposite). For the northern part of the latter he was forced to depend entirely upon the diaries of the various travellers who had preceded him—especially upon the diary of Carmichael, who had taken bearings with a pocket compass from day to day during his journey. Shortly after Rennell, the lower Euphrates was described from Basra to Baghdad by Lieutenant William Heude of the East India Company. The latter journeyed to Baghdad partly by boat and partly on horseback; but he did not cross the desert to Aleppo.

At the end of a long list of English civil servants appears the name of a single outstanding personality. Colonel, later General Francis Rawdon Chesney, who became the commander of the Euphrates Expedition; it was his dream to see river communication established between the Mediterranean and the Persian Gulf. Most of his story belongs to the age of steam; but Colonel Chesney made preliminary investigations of the desert on camel-back, so he also has his place among the travellers of the early nineteenth century. His first desert journey, in 1830, was from Damascus to Anna. From Anna, Chesney decided to finish the journey to Basra on the Euphrates itself, his intention being to make a surreptitious survey of the river. A rough survey of the Euphrates, above Hit, had been made by C. J. Rich at the beginning of the nineteenth century; so Chesney was principally interested in the river between Hit and Basra. He did not attempt a scientific survey, because the Shammar Arabs in the vicinity were supposed to be suspicious of any strange or unusual proceedings, and not a little hostile to strangers. For his purpose, approximate soundings and a knowledge of "the general capabilities of the river" (to use his own words) would be sufficient prerequisite to a future survey by steamboat. Accordingly, Chesney descended the Euphrates as far

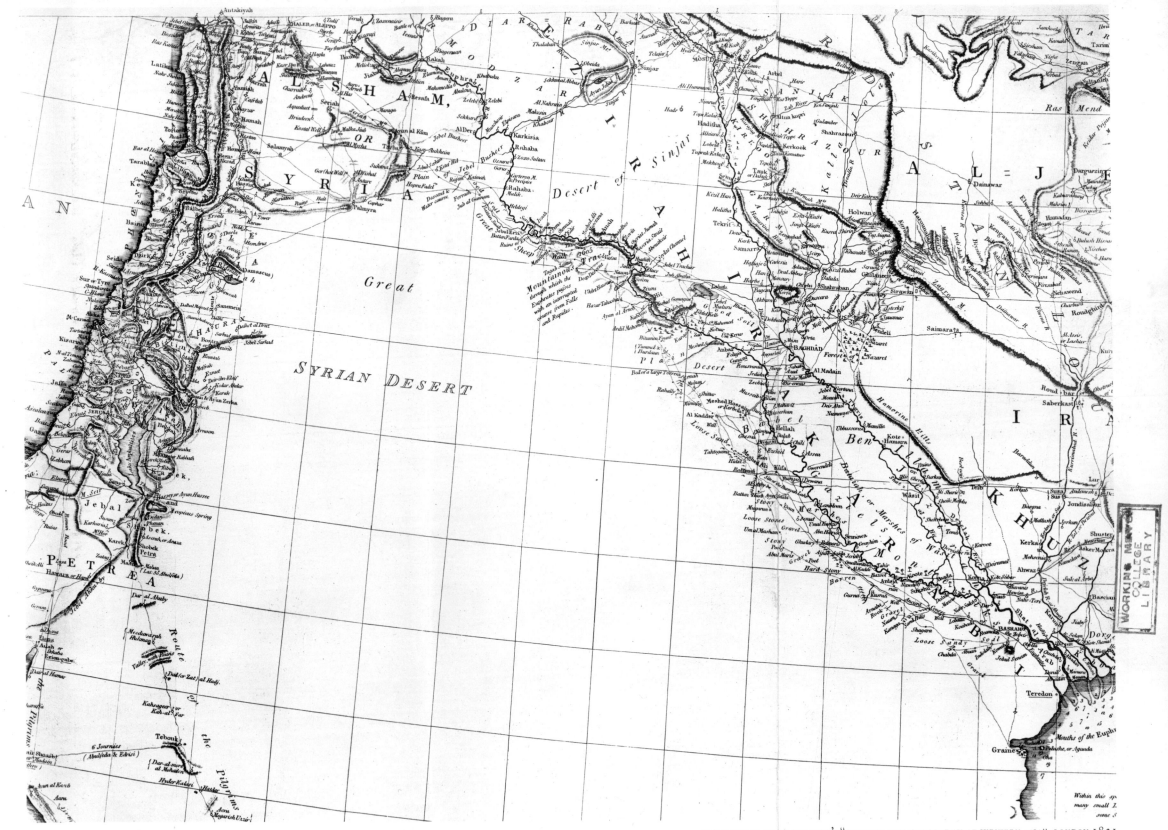

FROM MAJOR JAMES RENNELL'S "COMPARATIVE GEOGRAPHY OF WESTERN ASIA": LONDON 1831

as Hit on an ordinary raft, and then at Hit took a native boat for
the rest of the way. He made a rough sketch of the windings of
the river; took bearings of the principal points with a pocket compass; and took soundings with a ten-foot pole. The raft was fired
upon once or twice; but he succeeded in finishing this preliminary
survey between Anna and Basra. Six years later Colonel Chesney,
when in India, volunteered to carry some important dispatches
back to England. As their delivery was urgent, he had to cross
from Basra to the Mediterranean by the Great Desert Route. He
directed his course by compass, and after reaching the *Little Desert*
he turned westward to Palmyra and Damascus, hoping to reach
Beyrout in time to catch the first homeward-bound mail packet.
He is one of the few Englishmen to have carried dispatches across
the desert at courier speed; and he is, probably, the last western
traveller to make use of the Great Desert Route. Chesney made
the trip, which he estimated at 958 miles, in twenty-two days; he
and the two Arabs who escorted him rode between fifty and sixty
miles a day, and were often in the saddle for nineteen hours.

The Euphrates Expedition, which was organized (under royal
patronage) for the survey of the two rivers of Mesopotamia,
brought several scientists in its train who explored various
sections of the *Little Desert*. Dr. John William Helfer and his
wife, who made a study of ornithology, entomology and botany
for the Expedition; and Mr William F. Ainsworth, surgeon and
geologist of the Expedition. The narratives describing their work,
the twelve maps and the three volumes which Colonel Chesney
eventually published on his historical, political and geographical
researches (though their value is mainly topographical), are the
first genuinely scientific studies that were made of this part of
the world.

While Colonel Chesney was engaged upon this work, a certain
Lieutenant H. A. Ormsby crossed the *Little Desert* by the courier
route from Hit to Dumeir and Damascus. For long it was supposed
that this trip was made by the Arabian traveller Lieutenant James
Wellsted; but Mr Douglas Carruthers has established the fact that
the journey made under Wellsted's name was actually performed

by Lieutenant Ormsby.[1] Apart from this straightening out of mixed identities, little interest attaches to the trip itself; Wellsted remarks only that it took seventeen days of hard riding to go from Hit to Damascus (an incredibly long time); and that truffles were found to "grow abundantly" on the desert.

In 1840, at the end of this decade, a French army officer, Monsieur le Capitaine Callier, made an expedition with one of the large annual caravans of Baghdad. His object was to enquire into the life and organization of commercial caravans. The name of Captain Callier terminates a long period of political interest in the Syrian Desert, and marks the end (until after 1918) of travelling thereon for business purposes. Simultaneously, there opens what may be called the epoch of exploration.

Hitherto, the explorers of the Syrian Desert have, as a group, been neglected. Instead of being given a place to themselves in general histories, a select few of them have been included under sections dealing with Arabia. A book as recent as Sir Percy Sykes' *History of Exploration*, for instance, devotes three chapters to Arabia; and it only mentions a few of the more famous explorers of the Syrian Desert amongst those who confined their wanderings entirely to the "Island of the Arabs"—which is the Arabs' own name for their peninsula. Arabia has naturally overshadowed the lesser desert into which it extends, and is relatively far more important in the study of ethnology and comparative religions. This is one reason why the explorers of the Syrian Desert have not been isolated into a special group. Another reason is the fact that the more celebrated of them have chosen to round off their travels in the Syrian Desert with one or more journeys into Arabia. Furthermore, all but three of the earlier explorers

[1] Mr Carruthers' findings, in his own words, are as follows: that "Ormsby's travels form the greater part of the subject matter of Wellsted's volumes *Travels to the City of the Caliphs*. Although written in the first person throughout, and no other than Wellsted's name appears on the title-page, yet the journeys described are those of Lieutenant Ormsby; Wellsted himself being posted at that date to the *Palinurus* for survey work in the Red Sea." (From Mr Carruthers' private notes, with his kind permission; also pp. 151-152 of Mr Carruthers' latest book, *Arabian Adventure*.)

of Arabia (not counting those who confined themselves to the southern fringes of the Peninsula) either entered Arabia through the Wadi Sirhan, or else came directly from Arabia Petraea.[1] Many of these men prefaced their travels in Arabia with extensive journeying in the south-western portions of the Syrian Desert. For example, J. L. Burckhardt travelled (in 1814) all along the desert frontier of el-Kerak (*i.e.* of the Turkish province which included both Trans-Jordan and Arabia Petraea); he mapped its Roman roads, and he compiled a list of Beduin tribes. After him, G. A. Wallin, the Swedish student of Wahhabism and of the Nejd, went in 1845 from Arabia Petraea to Jauf (where he spent three months), when on his way to Hayil. On a second trip, three years later, Wallin travelled from Tebuk to Tayma on his way to Hayil, and eventually he returned to the Mediterranean by way of Meshed Ali and Baghdad, whence he crossed the *Little Desert* to Damascus, in company with a lone courier of the English dromedary post. W. G. Palgrave also traversed Arabia Petraea on his way to Hayil (in 1862); and C. Guarmani went by another route to Tayma (two years later), visiting Hayil and Jauf on his way back.

Charles M. Doughty, who has been called the greatest of Arabian explorers, first entered Arabia (in 1875, on his way to Hayil) by the Pilgrim Road to Mecca, travelling from Damascus with one of the great *Hajj* caravans. So much did Doughty see of the south-western part of the Syrian Desert, and so much did

[1] The three exceptions are: (*a*) Captain G. F. Sadlier, who was sent by the Government of India to co-operate with the Egyptian Expedition in 1819, and was the first European to cross Arabia from east to west. He landed at el-Katif on the Persian Gulf, and went—by way of Medina—to the Red Sea. Ibn Battuta is supposed to have crossed Arabia from the Red Sea to the Persian Gulf (in both directions, by different routes) in the fourteenth century; Captain Sadlier is therefore the first European, though not the first Arabian explorer, to have accomplished this feat. Cf. Sir Percy Sykes (1934), p. 88. (*b*) Sir Richard F. Burton, who went to Medina and Mecca in 1854. He was able to go without fear into the fanatical Hejaz because he turned Mohammedan, and went as a pilgrim with the *Hajj* from Cairo. It was not until more than twenty years later that he travelled in north-west Arabia and Arabia Petraea. (*c*) Colonel L. Pelly, who went from the Persian Gulf, at Kuwait, to Riyadh, in 1865.

he learn of its inhabitants and their way of living, that he may be considered as belonging as much to the Syrian as to the Arabian group of desert explorers.

Charles Huber, who (with J. Euting) sent the bilingually inscribed stone of Tayma to Europe and was shortly thereafter murdered in the Hejaz (in 1884), had previously visited Palmyra, and had gone from Hit to Damascus—along the courier route, via Bir Melossa. He had also traversed the Wadi Sirhan to Jauf, and mapped with great accuracy the Jauf and Sakaka oases.

Lady Anne Blunt and her husband, Mr Wilfrid Scawen Blunt, belong equally to the Syrian and the Arabian groups of explorers. They are perhaps best known for their *Pilgrimage to Nejd*, but before going to Arabia they travelled extensively in the *Little Desert*, visiting Palmyra and Deir ez-Zor; and they journeyed with a section of the Aneza Beduin through various parts of the *Great Desert*. This was made easy for them because Mr Blunt became blood "brother" to an Aneza tribesman, and was accordingly adopted by that tribesman's clan. Eventually, in 1879, they took the Wadi Sirhan route to Jauf, on their way into the Jebel Shammar region. Lady Anne wrote several volumes which treat, discursively and interestingly, of these journeys. One critic has said that she had but little knowledge, and lacked balance; but even so, the keenness of her powers of observation do much to compensate for these failings; and the tribal lists which she and her husband compiled, and the information they gleaned about the various Beduin, their tribes and their horses, is invaluable to the student of desert life.

A few years before these more famous travellers, Baron Max von Thielmann crossed the *Little Desert* from Kerbela to Damascus (in 1872). And within the next ten years Dr. Theodor Bischoff travelled through Palmyrena; and Černik crossed from the Mediterranean at Tripoli to Deir ez-Zor, by the old Roman route from Homs to Palmyra and Sukhna. Černik went on to Baghdad, descending the Euphrates from Deir. Mention must also be made of an anonymous Englishman who, between 1858 and 1862, made what he terms *Rambles in the Deserts of Syria and among the Turko-*

mans and Bedaweens. He, like Wilfrid Blunt, became a "brother" to an Aneza tribesman; and he travelled in the company of the Aneza and other, anti-Shammar Beduin, even taking part in some tribal skirmishes—that being a period of desert warfare. This anonymous Englishman also describes the Damascus revolt of 1860, and the massacres of the Christians; and tells of his vain efforts to find (and rescue) some of the Christian women who had been sold to the Amarat Aneza by Kurds and Arab Moslems of Damascus.

As the map of Carl Ritter, dated 1852, inaugurates the second of the three conventional periods of exploration in Arabia, similarly Dr. Richard Kiepert's map of 1893 is a landmark in the history of the exploration of the Syrian Desert. He drew largely, of course, on the twelve maps compiled by Colonel Chesney, in which were also incorporated the earlier surveys of C. J. Rich, and he used the sketch maps of other travellers—to such good effect that his became the standard for the Syrian Desert, and was consulted by all desert travellers until after the Great War. His map is not faultless, obviously. For instance, Jebel Aneza is not indicated; and Kasr el-Hair is mentioned under its two alternative names, and located in two different places. Nevertheless, as Jebel Aneza was not correctly mapped until after the War, and as Kasr el-Hair and Kusur el-Ikhwan were not proved identical until 1927 (by René Dussaud), one should not be too critical. Kiepert's map, all things considered, is excellent. A few earlier maps, notably those of Major James Rennell (dated 1809), A. Arrowsmith (1816) and John Walker (1867), had all incorporated the Great Desert Route; but Dr. Kiepert was able to make some important additions to the information contained in their maps. He traced the *Darb es-Sa'i* (or "post-route" as he called it), from Damascus via Bir Melossa to Hit, with relative accuracy; and he also traced the routes followed by Chesney, Thielmann and Huber. Lastly, he included the route of Baron Max von Oppenheim, from Jebel Druze to Palmyra and Deir ez-Zor—a journey which was made in the very year (1893) in which his map was published. Two years later the Danish traveller, J. Oestrup, who had visited

Palmyra, Kasr el-Hair, Taiyiba and Resafa in 1893, published a map of Palmyrena and the Homs region. And before the end of the century Eduard Sachau, who had journeyed through the *Little Desert* twice—approaching it from both the east and the west—published five maps of the district, in addition to his maps of the Tigris and the Euphrates. He had gone out there on an archaeological and cartographical mission. In 1903 Robert Garrett published a corrected version of Kiepert's *Syria* to accompany Miss Bell's book, *The Desert and the Sown*. The next, and the most authoritative maps to be made were begun on the eve of the Great War. In 1914, as very little precise or detailed information was available (particularly as to the southern part of the Syrian Desert), the War Office took the matter in hand, and Mr Douglas Carruthers produced the so-called "one over a million" sheets. His *Carte Internationale du Monde au 1,000,000* covered the whole of the Near East, including the Syrian Desert—*i.e.* the sheets entitled "Esh Sham", "Baghdad", "El Jauf" and "Basra". After the War, Major A. L. Holt made his surveys across the *Great Desert*; Mr H. St. J. B. Philby made a survey of the Wadi Sirhan to Jauf and back to Baghdad; and the French Government in Syria mapped the *Little Desert*.

The twentieth century has, thus far, sponsored two periods of intensive exploration. The first, which began in 1908, lasted until the beginning of the War, and included the first scientific archaeological efforts that were made to identify ancient sites of historical interest. This searching was especially directed to northern Palmyrena, and to ancient riverain towns of the Euphrates. Also, a renewed interest was taken in the *Great Desert*, and some curiosity was evinced in Jauf and in its probable history. In January 1908 Captain Butler and Captain Aylmer, two Anglo-Indians on leave, crossed the *Great Desert* from Baghdad to Damascus, going by way of Jauf, where they spent five days. They wore Beduin clothes, and were the first to go by this route from east to west. Exactly a year later, after a year and a half in Syria and the Syrian Desert (1905–6), Douglas Carruthers began his Arabian travels. He lived and rode with the Beni Sakhr, journeyed through the

Sherarat Wilderness as far north as Tayma, and on his return journey explored the sands of the Great Nefud. Other travellers, notably W. H. I. Shakespear and Gertrude Bell, surveyed the borderlands of the Nefud; but Carruthers was the first to explore the western limits of this unique territory which forms a bulwark for the southern regions of the Syrian Desert. His researches have taken form, chiefly, in cartographical and zoological studies of the north Arabian and the southern Syrian deserts. The value of Carruthers' work is enhanced by the fact that he has also travelled extensively in the deserts of Russian and Chinese Turkestan and Mongolia, and he therefore has an exceptional background for comparative study.

Between 1908 and 1915 three travellers of very different types added greatly to the existing store of knowledge on the subject of the Syrian Desert: Alois Musil, Gertrude Bell and Colonel G. E. Leachman. Musil, to mention them in the foregoing sequence, is justly famed for the wide extent of his travels. As Czech Professor of Oriental Studies in Prague, he had his university to back him; and the Military Geographical Institute at Vienna supplied the necessary scientific instruments for some of his expeditions. Methodically and patiently, for more than seven years, he journeyed up and down and around the Syrian Desert and northern Arabia. This period of exploration was prefaced by two years of travel in Arabia Petraea. There was no region with which he did not become acquainted, from the northernmost tip of Palmyrena to northern Nejd. For the most part he went unaccompanied except by Beduin; and of these the Rualla—in particular his friend, Nuri Shaalan, the great Emir of the Rualla—were his usual companions. On one occasion, however, he was accompanied by Prince Sixtus of Parma. That was in the summer of 1912, and they travelled together in the *Little Desert* and in part of Mesopotamia. Their programme, as outlined in advance of the expedition, included a survey of the route covered; the collection of material for a topographical description of the whole region; the investigation of all remains of ancient civilization; the making of plans; the taking of photographs; the making of copies and

8

squeezes of inscriptions; and the collecting of plants. The titles of his books indicate the extent of Musil's expeditions: *Arabia Petraea, the Northern Heǧâz* (*i.e.* Hejaz), *Arabia Deserta* (*i.e.* "the Great Desert"), *The Middle Euphrates, Palmyrena,* and *Northern Neǧd* (Nejd). Necessarily, however, there were large areas in all of these regions which he never inspected in person. Unfortunately some of the original value of his work was lost on account of the long delay before his books appeared: with one exception these "topographical itineraries", as he called them, were not published until 1926 and after.[1] One serious criticism must be made of these studies. Musil failed to use the works of all who had preceded him, and he did not incorporate into his own maps the surveys of other competent travellers. For example, he did not consider sufficiently either the *Peutinger Table* or the *Notitia dignitatum* in his topography of Palmyrena; he omitted entirely some important authorities for the history of Tayma; and he did not consult either W. H. I. Shakespear or Gertrude Bell for the borderlands of the Nefud. It is a pity that one who covered so much ground should have avoidable lacunae in his written records. Nevertheless, in spite of these and other omissions, he did utilize a great number of ancient and, especially, of medieval (Arabic) sources; and he did some excellent original work at and in the neighbourhood of Resafa. The copious appendices are the most valuable sections of Musil's "itineraries". The narratives themselves are both cold and colourless in comparison with the books of other travellers— such, for instance, as Doughty's *Arabia Deserta.* Musil's best writing and most interesting material is to be found in the most recent of his books, *The Manners and Customs of the Rwala Bedouins*; he considers that the Rualla are the only "pure" Beduin now in existence! In using his maps one must remember that he made all surveys by camel, and that therefore many computations of mileage are bound to be inexact; and that bearings, taken in

---

[1] The first, a three-volume work called *Arabia Petraea,* was published in 1907; but it has not yet been translated from the German. The travels on which this study was based took place in 1896 and 1897. All of Musil's later travels, in the Syrian Desert, took place between 1908 and 1915.

succession through previously unmapped localities, are also (and for the same reason) often inaccurate. One other criticism has been made of the detailed maps which he drew for the whole area of the Syrian Desert. A reviewer, himself an Arabian traveller, wrote of them in the following words: they "allow no blank spaces; every spare inch is filled up with carefully contoured surfaces, every physical feature . . . labelled with its name. This is misleading, for there are no means by which one can distinguish fact from fancy, the 'surveyed' from 'native report'." [1] And this same critic has said that it is often extremely difficult to identify the sites and oases which are shown on his maps. It is only because Musil is so great a traveller that one feels obliged to mention his shortcomings as a geographer. If he had accomplished less, if the task he set himself and the scope of his published work were not, theoretically, all-embracing, there would be no need to call attention to certain of its defects and omissions. Because no other traveller of the Syrian Desert has attempted quite so comprehensive a survey, one is bound to point out the limitations of an otherwise authoritative and excellent piece of work. Philby (on p. ix of the introduction to his popular history of *Arabia*, published in 1930) has said of Musil's six volumes that they "constitute the greatest single contribution to our knowledge of Arabia that has ever been published".

Gertrude Bell is the only woman who has travelled widely in the Syrian Desert without the escort of a man of her own race. Her chief interest was, apparently, archaeology, and she made special and intensive studies of certain places of archaeological interest such as the Palace of Ukhaidir. But she was also a painstaking geographer, receiving the "Founder's Medal" of the Royal Geographical Society eight years before her death. Many of her journeys were through what she called "the Sown", in Asia Minor and Syria; but the Desert had a special lure for her, and she

---

[1] Douglas Carruthers, in the *Geographical Journal*, vol. lxxii (1928), p. 280. Plus conversation with Mr Carruthers. The criticism of Musil's Palmyrene topography was made by René Dussaud in *Syria*, vol. x (1929), pp. 53, 55. Ditto *re* his omissions concerning Tayma.

delighted in the Arabs and their oblique courtesies. In 1911 Miss Bell crossed the *Little Desert*. She, her faithful servant Fattuh and four cameleers, joined the caravan of the Shaykh of Kubaisa at Dumeir, and they proceeded to Hit in company with seven merchants who were on their way to the Euphrates to buy sheep. It was midwinter, and they spent fourteen days on the road, going south of the courier route to Muheiwir, and by the forts of Amej and Kebbaz. This was not her first sight of Roman outposts, because, previously, she had descended by the left bank of the Euphrates from Tell Ahmar to Anna, following the route taken by the Roman Emperor Julian. At the end of 1913 Miss Bell started on her most famous desert expedition. She had long wanted to visit central Arabia; so she set off for Nejd with the intention of seeing some ancient sites *en route*. Her caravan skirted the eastern fringes of Jebel Druze and the lava country, going through Burka, Azrak and then west to Amman on the way to Arabia Petraea. On the way she found Roman, Byzantine and Omayyad remains. When south of the thirtieth parallel (more or less on a line with Jauf) Miss Bell delayed for a while in the *dira* of the Howeitat Beduin; warned against visiting Jauf, she eventually went on to Hayil with a Shammar guide—passing near to Tayma, but without actually visiting this important oasis. On the return journey she went from Hayil to Meshed Ali and Baghdad, and then completed the round trip by crossing from Baghdad to Damascus. This second time she went by way of Palmyra, along (or very near to) what was subsequently identified as the old Roman road from Hit, spending nineteen days on the *Little Desert*. It has been computed that on this journey, from Damascus to Hayil and back, she rode about fifteen hundred miles. During the War an intimate knowledge of tribal personalities and relationships fitted her for the appointment of "Political Officer" in Baghdad, under Sir Percy Cox; and after the War she became "Arab Secretary" to the High Commissioner, and liaison officer between him and King Feisal. She was given the order of C.B.E. for political services to the British Government; but before her death she had recommended archaeological work, founding and

organizing the Baghdad Museum which contains the famous collection of golden objects found at Ur of the Chaldees. Actually,
it was over-work as Director of this Museum that precipitated
her death. It has been said of Gertrude Bell that "she was never
satisfied with mere travel or adventure unless she felt she had
advanced archaeological science".[1]

Colonel Leachman did most of his travelling for political reasons,
and when on active service in Irak. As early as 1910 he studied
colloquial Arabic in Damascus, in order to prepare himself to
journey into central Arabia; and he went thither for the first time
in the company of a Shammar shaykh. At the end of 1912 he went
again to Nejd, to the court of Ibn Sa'ud at Riyadh, where he
paved the way for Shakespear's later mission. On this second
journey he followed the courier route from Dumeir to Bir
Melossa, and then went south along the eastern edge of the *Hamad*.
His escort consisted of a small force of twenty Agails, and (as the
Rualla and various Shammar tribes were warring against each
other after the capture of Jauf by Nuri Shaalan of the Rualla) he
saw the *Great Desert* at its worst, under *ghrazzu* conditions. This
knowledge, and the respect with which the Beduin learned to
treat him, served him in good stead during the Great War, when
he was put in charge of Britain's relations with the tribes of western
Irak. It has been stated, by those in a position to know, that his
influence among these Arabs was so great that he kept them quiet
throughout the War, and entirely unresponsive to anti-British
propaganda and to the overtures of the German "Missmont"
organization. Brother officers of Colonel Leachman have said
that he was the only Englishman who could successfully pass himself off as an Arab—so that even the Beduin did not suspect him
of being a *Frangi* in disguise. Eventually Leachman was transferred
to Mosul as chief Political Officer in charge of northern Mesopotamia. In August 1920, rumours that the riverain tribes of Lower
Mesopotamia were preparing to rise in an organized revolt
brought him to Baghdad; and a heated discussion with a shaykh of

[1] The *Geographical Journal*, vol. lxviii, p. 366. Obituary notice, 11th July
1926.

the Dulaim caused his murder by a member of that tribe. The manner of his death is described elsewhere (see p. 28). Some persons have been tempted to compare the work of Colonel G. E. Leachman with that done, at the same time (on the western side of the Syrian Desert), by Colonel T. E. Lawrence; but their work can no more be compared than their personalities. Their methods of dealing with the Arabs were as radically different as the ends for which they strove. The two men were not faced with the same problems; and even the people with whom they came in contact were possessed of different moral qualities and mental capabilities. The Arabs of the west, who were led by Lawrence, were true desert-bred Beduin; the Arabs of the east were settled for the most part—village dwellers. The marked difference between the desert and the riverain types has already been noted. Leachman worked in closer touch with the Government (in this case the Army) than Lawrence did; and in spite of his intimate knowledge of the Arabs he was often high-handed with them, overbearing and dictatorial. Whereas Lawrence worked and fought with them as well as for them. Colonel Leachman and Colonel Lawrence were both men of courage, endurance and sincerity; but there the comparison ends.

Before the War, Lawrence was engaged upon archaeological work in and near Carchemish, on the Euphrates. During the War, his military and political work was confined, for the most part, to Arabia and Trans-Jordan. Lawrence did his recruiting and fought the earlier battles against the Turks in the northern Hejaz; his campaigns centred in Arabia Petraea and terminated victoriously at Damascus. His was a meteoric figure of the War period. So Lawrence of Arabia cannot be reckoned among the trans-desert travellers. Nevertheless he belongs to the Syrian Desert as truly as Doughty, a man for whom he had great admiration and a vast respect. By virtue of their insight, of their sympathetic knowledge of the Beduin, they have both made their entry into the deserts of Arabia and Syria; they fitted themselves to partake equally of the freemasonry of the nomad tribes. For an understanding of desert peoples, their customs and the lands which they roam, one must turn to both Doughty and Lawrence; and turn again to Lawrence for an interpretation of Doughty and *Arabia Deserta*.

On the eve of the Great War one other traveller crossed the *Little Desert*. Captain T. C. Fowle, of the Fortieth Pathans, took two "language leaves" from India with the intention of learning Arabic and Iranian. On the first of these he crossed the Syrian Desert from Kerbela to Homs via Palmyra. As this was the last desert crossing to be made before the inauguration of motor transport, the circumstances of his trip are of peculiar interest. Captain Fowle started from Kerbela in the company of another Englishman, and because the Great Desert Route was considered too dangerous (on account of the Beduin), their caravan followed the "usual" riverain route to Ramadi, Hit and Abu Kemal, stopping on its way at a succession of "unclean khans". At Abu Kemal Fowle decided against continuing with the caravan to Deir ez-Zor. Instead, he procured a Beduin guide (*daleel*) from a Christian merchant of Abu Kemal, and cut straight across the desert to Palmyra, where he planned to rejoin the caravan before proceeding to Homs and Baalbek. The two men rode horses; they took native pack-saddles, and filled their saddle-bags with enough dates and bread to last them for five days. Fowle slung two small leather water-skins (*kirbas*) on the saddle-pommel, and the *daleel* took a large one (a *matarea*). Blankets and a waterpoof sheet (for the use of the Englishman) were folded underneath the two saddles. Fowle used English stirrups; but he wore Arab dress—not, as he explains, for the purpose of disguising himself, but as proof against long-distance detection and to help pass off casual meetings. He remarked that a caravan track from Abu Kemal to Palmyra was marked on his map, but that he saw not the faintest trace of such a track; and that the country through which they rode was desert "pure and simple", and water was very scarce. His guide agreed to take him to Palmyra for a certain sum of money. This sum was deposited with the merchant of Abu Kemal (who had procured the services of the *daleel*), and it was arranged that the *daleel* should obtain his specified pay from the merchant after returning from

Palmyra with a letter from Fowle as proof of the latter's safe arrival. It may be seen from these details how complicated it had become for the *Frangi* to use the northern desert routes.

After the War, archaeological investigation in Palmyrena became suddenly of absorbing interest. Military manœuvres had led to many fresh discoveries, and missions were sent out both by governments and by universities to exploit their finds, and to organize new researches. The French Government was especially active in this respect; and the English and American universities. As almost all of the *Little Desert* falls within the French mandated territory, it was natural that a special "Service des Antiquités" should be organized by the *Haut-Commissariat de la République Française en Syrie et au Liban*. The field work of this department was done under the protection and with the active help of French officers and soldiers; detachments (often of the Foreign Legion) were detailed for archaeological work, including excavation, first by General Gouraud and subsequently by General Weygand, at the request of the French Academy of Inscriptions. Also, the French Army Air Force was allowed to collaborate with Jesuit Fathers of the University of St. Joseph at Beyrout, notably the Reverend Fathers Antoine Poidebard and René Mouterde, in order to make aerial surveys of the Roman *limes*.

The most notable find made by the British in this territory was at Salahiya. When they occupied the ancient fort there, Roman frescoes were discovered on a near-by temple and reported to Colonel Leachman. Almost his last act before he died was to forward a request—through Gertrude Bell—to Sir Arnold Wilson that these be investigated. James Breasted, the famous Egyptologist, happened to be in Irak just then, so he made the first examination of this strategically placed riverain town, under British military protection. Salahiya has since become identified as Dura-Europos; when first the French Academy of Inscriptions, and later the Americans (Yale University and the Rockefeller Foundation), subsidized extensive excavations there. The scientific and historical side of the work was done by the Belgian archaeologist Franz Cumont, and by the Russian, Michael Ivanovich Rostovtzeff.

Several other names should be mentioned, among the many distinguished archaeologists who have conducted "diggings" in the French Mandate, because they are to be especially remembered for their desert work. Messieurs A. Gabriel and H. Seyrig, both of whom have studied the twin ruins of Kasr el-Hair, and excavated at Palmyra. Also René Dussaud, whose *Topographie Historique de la Syrie Antique et Médiévale* made such a stir when it first appeared in 1927. A part of it has since been supplemented by the more detailed work of R. P. Antoine Poidebard: *La Trace de Rome dans le Désert de Syrie; Le Limes de Trajan à la Conquête Arabe. Recherches Aériennes* (1925–1932). One other writer, an army officer, ought to be included among these French students of Palmyrena. Ct. Victor Müller, commander-in-chief of the *Méharistes* (the French Camel Corps), recently published a book: *En Syrie avec les Bédouins. Les Tribus du désert*. Dussaud said, in a review of this book, that Victor Müller, after six years spent in continuous contact with the moving world of nomads and of semi-nomads, is more qualified to describe them than even the most well-known of the great explorers. This is, presumably, the kind of book that Colonel Leachman might have written, had he been given the opportunity or had the inclination. Their researches would have supplemented each other amazingly well, for Leachman's experiences were primarily in the southern deserts and Müller's were in the northern.

Contemporaneous with the activities of the *Service des Antiquités et des Beaux-Arts* of the *Haut-Commissariat*, the Department of Antiquities of Trans-Jordania began an organized investigation of the desert frontier. But there was so rich and unworked a field in the semi-desert lands of Trans-Jordan, that archaeological work in the desert itself has only recently been begun.

Meanwhile, exploration of the *Great Desert* was undertaken for other reasons, even before motor transport was experimented with further north. In 1920 and 1921 the first reconnaissances were made across the *Great Desert* for a railway survey, between Ramadi and Amman. Major A. L. Holt conducted a number of expeditions to the foothills of Jebel Aneza, and on one occasion he was accompanied by Colonel Leachman. Major Holt also combined with this preliminary railway survey, the laying out of the Royal Air Force Air-Mail Route from Cairo to Baghdad; supervising the marking out of landing-grounds and the ploughing of furrows which should serve as landmarks from the air. He travelled 14,000 miles through the *Hamad*, in Ford cars, and crossed three times from Baghdad to Amman. The "motor route" he thus mapped has been used in times of emergency to supplement the regular Damascus–Rutba motor track. But an account of these surveys, projected railways, and the desert tracks which have been used for motor cars, must be saved for a last chapter on the latest phase of desert travel.

Once the Royal Air Force mail service was in operation, various aerial surveys were made of the region between Amman, Rutba and Ramadi, during the course of regular patrol duty. Notably, Group-Captain Rees discovered a great number of ancient remains, stone sheds and watch-towers in the lava country east of Kasr Azrak. These buildings are thought to be Roman, or possibly even pre-Roman; and they are covered with Safaitic inscriptions. Group-Captain Rees found two hundred of these texts.

A joint expedition was made to Jauf in 1922 by Major Holt and Mr H. St. J. B. Philby, who is so well known for his travels in Arabia. After an inauspicious start in Ford cars, they decided to use camels for their journey. Philby's reason for visiting Jauf was political, and Major Holt took advantage of the opportunity to accompany him in order to reconnoitre the Wadi Sirhan and the country east of Jauf, with a view to the making of a railway survey from Amman to Kerbela via the Jauf–Sakaka oases. The two Englishmen went all the way to Kerbela, a trip of just over 600 miles, although they had not at first planned to do so. The Beduin (who were skirmishing, and in great fear of the Wahhabi raids) caused them innumerable delays and difficulties, so that it seemed wiser to cross to the Euphrates than to return by the Wadi Sirhan.

Nearly eight years later, at the end of 1929, Eldon Rutter, who had previously lived in Mecca and visited Medina, journeyed the length of the Syrian Desert into Nejd. He went from Damascus to the *Hamad*, and thence diagonally south-eastwards to Hayil—along the far side of the Wadi Sirhan and east even of Jauf. Rutter took only two camels with him and a single guide; but for part of the trip he joined a section of the Rualla. According to him, they travelled with extreme slowness, grazing the herds of camels along a front of twenty miles or more.

The last name to be here recorded is that of a German traveller, Carl Reinhard Raswan, who began his journeyings with the Beduin almost a quarter of a century ago. As in the case of Musil, the Rualla were his first hosts; and in their company he became thoroughly acquainted with the *Great Desert* and its adjacent deserts. Raswan's adoption as a "blood brother" by the youthful grandson and eventual successor of Emir Nuri Shaalan gave him an intimate welcome into their tribal life. Like the Blunts, the original and primary motive for his desert sojourns was a consuming interest in Arab horses. Like them, also, he developed a secondary interest in the Beduin tribes. In Raswan's own words, he was not attracted by the "white patches" on the map, but rather by the nomads who wander ceaselessly across this *badia*. Three years before the Great War, and then again, after 1926, he lived (intermittently), fought, raided and migrated with the Rualla. He rode their "war mares" and racing camels, and he drove in "battle cars" with their shaykhs. Once he left the hospitality of the Rualla tents that he might cross Palmyrena and visit the Tai' and Shammar tribesmen of northern Irak. Of the Beduin, of their customs and traditions, and especially of their horses and camels, Carl Raswan has written in *The Black Tents of Arabia*, as also in more than a dozen magazine articles. The photographs which he took during his wanderings are unique, and his many "adventures" are colourfully described.

The first quarter of the twentieth century terminated an era; and this new age of mechanical transport has ushered in with it new types and multitudes of wayfarers. The writer would only add an apology that the preceding chronological list resembles, perforce, Masefield's catalogue of the ships. But all these intrepid people are entitled to be mentioned in their own places, down this thousand-year long line of march; even at the risk of making their personal histories appear dull or repetitious. One must remember that each individual who has ridden through the desert may have felt all the exaltation of a veritable pioneer.

CHAPTER IV

THE MERCHANT CARAVANS

Now at length, after this much explanation and introduction, it is possible to consider the merchants and their caravans. Commercial caravans were, after all, the backbone of desert travel. It was the merchants who fostered intercourse between Syria and Mesopotamia; they kept open the connecting highways; and they themselves were the ambassadorial links between the various cities on both sides of the desert. The travellers who followed in their wake, though interesting in themselves, have been comparatively incidental and evanescent figures; but from their unrecorded beginnings to the present day, the organizing of these immense trading companies, their lading and departure, have formed a pivotal point in the life of all caravan or quasi-caravan cities. As the centuries passed, the early spontaneous and rather haphazard commercial ventures gradually became regularized; and a system involving complex financial arrangements perpetuated itself, despite invasions, revolutions and changing dynasties in the lands adjacent to the desert.

Mecca gives us our first picture of caravan life: Mecca as it was before the lifetime of Mohammed. But so universal are the needs which condition caravan trade, that the caravans of Mecca can be considered as closely analogous (in all essential features) to their earlier Palmyrene prototypes; as well as to the great caravans of Damascus, Aleppo, Baghdad and Basra, from the sixteenth to the nineteenth centuries. These collective emissaries of the caravan cities conformed, from century to century, to a standardized pattern. Their customs became hereditary, because such important matters as the manner of electing a caravan leader and his officers, prerequisite financial arrangements, and sundry details of organiza-

tion were tested and found serviceable. So that what was gradually evolved for the sake of convenience and efficiency, was
handed down from one generation of merchant travellers to
another, as an unalterable part of the institution.[1]

I

THE GREAT CARAVANS OF MECCA IN THE SEVENTH CENTURY

Starting with Mecca, then, at the beginning of the seventh
century A.D., one learns that the whole life of the city centred in
its caravan trade. Everyone in Mecca, rich and poor alike, including women landholders (of whom there were a number),

[1] One of the earliest extant accounts of caravan trading has been discovered
by Professor W. L. Westermann, among the business papers of a certain
Egyptian (of the third century B.C.) called Zenon. When Zenon was working
for Apollonios, treasurer of state under Ptolemy II, Apollonios was en-
deavouring to compete with the Nabataeans in a field which they had
formerly monopolized: namely, the camel caravan traffic. The centre from
which Apollonios' caravans operated (between Sidon, Galilee and Egypt)
was Gaza, the key city on the main road between Egypt and Asia. The Gaza
caravan, described on the papyrus belonging to Zenon, consisted of only four
camels. Incidentally, this is the identical size of a (four-camel) caravan that is
depicted in a graffito which has been found on a house wall at Dura-Europos
on the Euphrates (see Rostovtzeff, *Caravan Cities*, p. 212). The four camels
transported the grain of Galilee, the reed mats and pickled meats of Egypt
and dates that were probably imported into Gaza from Arabia. According to
this papyrus, the Gaza caravan did no trading at its various route stations: it
merely transported a few commodities—cargoes of relatively high value and
small bulk—and received pay only for freightage.

From this account of a caravan in miniature, one can glimpse the caravan
trade of ancient Palestine and Syria; but the caravan described is so tiny a one
that it furnishes no genuine analogy for the great commercial caravans of later
years. The degree of organization required for the outfitting of a four-camel
caravan, and the rules for its management while on the road, would present
none of the problems or difficulties involved in the organizing and governance
of caravans numbering from a thousand to three thousand camels.

This four-camel caravan of Gaza is described in a papyrus of date 259 B.C. It
is No. 2 of the *Zenon Papyri* (vol. i), and is entitled "Account of Earnings of
a Camel Caravan". See *Zenon Papyri* (Columbia University Papyri), i (1934),
pp. 3-10. Edited with notes by William Linn Westermann and Elizabeth Sayre
Hasenoehrl.

was anxious to have a stake in this lucrative business. The powerful families grew richer and more influential with each annual expedition; and the poorer families (from the small-tenant, shop-keeping class) saved every available dinar in order to share in these commercial ventures. All the merchants of Mecca formed themselves into a syndicate, pooled their capital to equip the caravans, and then shared proportionately in the returns from their joint enterprise. There was also an extensive credit system whereby money was collected for the outfitting of the caravans; and exorbitant rates of interest were charged. Hence Mohammed's subsequent denunciation of usury. Generally speaking, a single family would constitute themselves bankers for the occasion, receive deposits from everyone interested in a particular expedition, and then administer the funds as economically as possible in the interests of the syndicate. For an instance, a certain small caravan, of about 1000 camels, once set out for Gaza. The Omayyad family handled its finances; 50,000 dinars were pledged (i.e. about £25,000), of which 10,000 dinars (about £5000) were collected in hard cash; and every citizen of Mecca, even such as were possessed of only half a dinar, had a stake in the enterprise. The initial expenditures were admittedly great, but the calculable profits were even greater. A fifty per cent return on money pledged was guaranteed in advance to all who had contributed toward the organizing of the expedition. Such a guarantee was possible only because the return on the collective investment was always over fifty per cent, and frequently as high as one hundred per cent.

Two large caravans were officially equipped and launched each year. One went to Abyssinia, in the summer; and one to Syria, in the winter-time—water could be depended upon then, and the pasturage was at its best. Other smaller caravans traded locally, and along branch routes of the main highways. These biennial caravans were large, partly in order to increase their security; partly to minimize (as far as was possible) the individual expenses of each merchant. On an average, the camels numbered about 2500 (neither horses nor mules were used) and there was an escorting guard of from 100 to 300 men. In the matter of protection, a great deal of both energy and money were expended. For example, there were certain well-known spots along the route where caravans would normally expect to be ambushed—where it was only too easy for brigands to lie in wait for them. The convoy leader had to take extra precautions to ensure the safety of his caravan. If such a place were near a town, he would arrange to be met in advance by a special escort of soldiers; but if the expected ambush were in the open desert, some friendly nomad tribe would be called upon to provide a temporary guard while the convoy passed through the danger zone.

The question of expenditure was all-embracing. The necessary annual expenses seemed innumerable, as were the risks incurred by each yearly expedition. Hence, of course, the exorbitant rates of interest charged for the outfitting of the caravans. There were general charges, for maintenance and protection *en route*: the upkeep of the caravan, until its return to Mecca, its revictualling on the road, and the fees payable to guides and other necessary officials. A large proportion of the annual costs was incurred by the necessity for subsidizing the nomads through whose territories the caravan had to pass. Transit tolls were exacted, indemnities for the use of wells and pasture lands, and subsidies in exchange for a guarantee of immunity for the annual convoys: a guarantee which had to cover every kind of molestation and attack.

One additional and inevitable expense resulted from an ingenious kind of insurance system. Since Meccan camel cargoes (spices, perfumes, aromatics, ivory, gold, silver, etc.) were not perishable, nor their eventual market prices adversely affected by abnormal delays, it was possible to evolve a simple method of protecting merchandise against damage or loss. A single leader was put in sole charge of the caravan, who could be held accountable for its safety and welfare. A man of some distinction was always chosen, and one who was both respected and feared by the nomads. On his shoulders rested the sole responsibility for the safe-conduct of all caravan goods. If any property in his care was damaged or stolen, the caravan leader and his kinsfolk were obliged to recompense its owner. He and his kin were responsible to the syndicate of merchants for each and every bale of goods in the convoy. Therefore, in order to enable him to make good any loss or damage and to ensure the employing of as reliable and efficient a man as possible, a very high remuneration was paid to the caravan leader. He had additional duties, such as the maintaining of discipline within the convoy and the conducting of all negotiations with the nomads, and it was up to him to see that they kept their agreements. Occasionally, an elected caravan leader would have to appoint a substitute, whose powers on the march would be identical with his own. But he himself was still accountable to the syndicate of merchants for the safe-conduct of their property—that was a responsibility that could not be transferred to the shoulders of any other man. Actually, the best guarantee for the security of a caravan was the personal prestige of its chosen leader, and the awe inspired by the fact that he was a representative of some distinguished family or clan; so that he almost always conducted the convoy in person.

Incidentally, in this connection, it is interesting to know that Palmyra had been accustomed to raise statues in honour of her outstanding caravan leaders, and that Beduin shaykhs were often entrusted with the Palmyrene convoys. A column of the second century A.D., which was found recently on the Palmyra-Hit caravan route, bears a significant inscription in honour of a certain Soados Boliadou. Because of his "repeated good offices", and the fact that "in many and important circumstances" he had "aided with princely generosity merchants, caravans, and such of his fellow citizens as were established at Vologesia", Soados had been honoured by two Roman emperors. Furthermore, the Senate and the people of Palmyra, as well as "various caravans", had erected four statues of Soados—at the expense of the treasury; and three other statues had been erected in his honour at Spasinou Charax, at Vologesia, and at the caravanserai of Genneas.[1]

Next to the caravan leader, the most important personage in the caravan was its official guide, or *daleel*. This word is still used today,

[1] The text of this inscription is printed in *Syria*, vol. xii (1931), pp. 105-107.

in the north Syrian Desert, to designate the "pilot" of a caravan. But in the Meccan convoys the *daleel* also regulated the length of the day's march, the daily halts, and all other details of the itinerary. Some guides, during periods of political unrest or of warfare, acted as spies and political agents; and some were well-informed interpreters. But this was definitely outside the range of their regular duties. First and foremost, the *daleels* were guides. Incidentally, the nature of their duties was such as to make their profession an hereditary one; and a father would take a young son with him on caravan journeys, as an apprentice, to teach him the fine points of his calling, as well as all the landmarks on the road.

The couriers were also important members of the convoy unit. These were called *basheers* when they carried good news, and *nadeers* when their news was bad. Caravans in danger or distress were accustomed to dispatch a *nadeer* for aid; and such a messenger was recognizable from afar by his reversed saddle and his rent garments. Citizens of Mecca, upon sighting a *basheer*, would assemble in the market square to welcome their caravan. The arrival of a convoy was a public event, often greeted by the beating of drums; and holiday crowds were wont to witness the counting of its cargoes and a display of the goods therein contained.

The humblest members of the caravans were the camel-drivers. There is little to say about these underfed cameleers who plodded so many hundreds of miles by the side of their charges. Either they were paupers, employed by camel-owners for a pittance; or else they themselves were the owners, reduced to driving their own camels because they happened to be in debt to one or more of the syndicate of merchants, or were otherwise indebted to some member of the family which was acting as banker for the expedition.

There was a minor and subsidiary outlet for the commercial activities of the citizens of Mecca. The nomads through whose lands the annual caravans journeyed were anxious to have some small share in the long-distance trade of the great caravans. Such

Beduin as were friendly, and at the same time commercially minded, reaped an annual harvest of subsidies in return for their co-operation, active and passive. Naturally enough, they desired to spend a portion of their annual income upon a few necessary commodities. Their most common needs were for iron and copper ware (particularly in the shape of cooking utensils), cloth vestments, and weapons. And they were eager for occasional luxuries such as coffee. The result was that every caravan that went out from Mecca laded some of its camels with goods to be sold *en route*, and—wherever it encamped—displayed its wares, like a peripatetic fair, to do business with the nomads.

2

THE ANNUAL CARAVANS WHICH TRADED BETWEEN SYRIA AND MESO-
POTAMIA FROM THE SIXTEENTH TO THE TWENTIETH CENTURIES

It is not until the end of the sixteenth century that we have any detailed information about caravan life on the Syrian Desert, and then it is chiefly to European travellers that we are indebted for our facts. Van Linschoten, writing in 1598 of his visit to Basra, was the first to comment at any length upon the trade caravans which journeyed annually between Syria and Lower Mesopotamia. Piecing together his remarks with the statements of several other travellers, contemporary and otherwise, one gathers that a large merchant caravan from Aleppo made an annual round trip to Basra and back; and that a Basra convoy made a similar round trip to Aleppo and back, also once a year. There was in addition a caravan of unladen, desert-bred camels which went out from Basra yearly, to be marketed in Aleppo. And there were an uncertain number of small merchant caravans which made annual journeys to and fro between Aleppo and Baghdad, as well as between Basra and Baghdad. To be as specific as possible, there were four merchant caravans which made the journey annually between Basra and Baghdad; and usually three which made the journey between Baghdad and Syria. Generally speaking, a

Baghdad caravan went to Damascus once a year and Baghdad caravans went to Aleppo twice a year.[1]

It was during this period that Europeans fell into the habit of calling caravans *caffylen*, or, more usually, *cafilas* (*i.e. kafilas*). This is a phonetic equivalent for the Arabic word which is used to designate "companies of people and camels". Pedro Teixeira, and later Portuguese writers, often used the word *kafila* loosely, to mean a convoy of ships or boats on the Tigris or the Euphrates. But most other Europeans used it more correctly, as a synonym for caravan.

Van Linschoten does not describe these caravans or *kafilas* in much detail. He gives one a vague picture of a vast throng of people and pack-animals, who "ryde all in order like a battell that marcheth in the fielde", escorted by a guard of several hundred Turkish janissaries. "Victualers" followed behind the main body, supplied with luxuries such as honey, dates, sheep, goats, hens and even eggs to sell to the merchants *en route*. Now to say that the great caravans were guarded by janissaries is to say that they were actively protected by the Ottoman Turks; which in turn means that the Sultan and his pashas were making a definite effort to foster trade between Syria and Mesopotamia. This inference is confirmed by the further statement (made by the same traveller) that a large guard was scarcely necessary for the safety of a *kafila*, because even before the beginning of the sixteenth century, Arabs had left off their plundering along the desert routes.

Van Linschoten also remarked upon the fact that merchants of all nations whatever were allowed to travel with the *kafilas*, excepting only Spanish and Portuguese travellers, who were looked upon with grave suspicion! Which is an interesting evidence of the unpopularity of the subjects of these two nations, then so

---

[1] Until the end of the eighteenth century these figures remained the same for the annual numbers of caravans trading from Baghdad to Aleppo and Damascus.

It is interesting to compare this traffic with that which went to Anatolia by the northern route. In 1800 there were, customarily, two or three monthly caravans of from 30 to 40 donkeys, that went from Baghdad to Mosul; and two annual caravans, of from 150 to 200 mules, that went from Baghdad to Constantinople.

powerful. The Spaniards were feared, because of their efforts to ally themselves with the Iranians; and the Portuguese were disliked because of their commercial ascendancy in the Persian Gulf. Some few of them, however, managed to travel with the *kafilas* disguised as Frenchmen, Englishmen or Venetians—which nations were tolerated because of their commercial establishments in Aleppo. In any case, Portuguese couriers would rarely have had the time to loiter along with a large caravan: they were generally the bearers of urgent dispatches. With this exception, then, for the next 150 years (after 1598) Europeans who crossed the desert did so in company with the merchant caravans. An occasional traveller, such as Pietro della Valle, found it too uncomfortable to travel with such an immense crowd, and decided that the attendant delays were intolerably irksome. He compromised by allowing the *kafila*—with all the other Aleppo-bound Europeans—to precede him; and then set out in its wake, three days after its departure, with a tiny caravan of his own, hoping thus to avoid the inconveniences, as also to benefit indirectly by the proximity and protection of the great caravan.

The Aleppo–Basra caravans followed, for the most part, the Great Desert Route (see map of Major Rennell); with the exception that at Taiyiba—or rather Kasr el-Hair—they preferred to take the direct road to Meshed Rahba and thence to follow the Euphrates down to Kubaisa, before going out into the desert again. Some of them, however, especially such *kafilas* as were organized entirely by Arabs and unaccompanied by any Turks, followed the ancient Roman route between Palmyra and Hit, north of Bir Melossa. But the Great Desert Route was used in its entirety before the middle of the seventeenth century. Incidentally, Basra-bound merchandise was generally destined for Ormuz, but it was sent down the Persian Gulf by boat, from Basra to this island clearing-house at the mouth of the Gulf.

It is interesting to note that until about the middle of the seventeenth century a novel kind of courier system was employed. Every caravan kept in touch with either its base or its destination by means of homing pigeons. While on the road, Basra or Aleppo pigeons would frequently be released by the caravan *bashi* to announce the whereabouts of the *kafila*, or else to report upon the safety of the way (for the benefit of smaller, unofficial caravans); sometimes even to ask for help or reinforcements, should the caravan fear attack. This use of homing pigeons by caravan leaders was only an incidental part of a widespread organization within the Ottoman Empire. The extent to which this system was developed is explained more fully in the chapter which deals with the desert postal services.

Between the sixteenth and the nineteenth centuries the institution of the caravan gradually assumed its modern form. There grew up an elaborate ritual of preliminary preparation, which resulted (after the lapse of two or three months) in the assembling of this mobile unit, of complex composition, which was known as the *kafila*. When the time came to begin preparing for an annual expedition, the first step was to choose a caravan leader. This important official was elected in a general assembly of all the merchants and camel-owners concerned. Their choice had then to receive the sanction of the Pasha. Thereafter the caravan leader, who was known by the Turkish title of *bashi* (though he was always an Arab shaykh), attended in person to all of the joint business of the caravan. He it was who fixed the schedule and picked out the route to be followed; he supervised the collecting of provisions and equipment for the trip; and almost his first duty (in collaboration with the merchants) was to standardize the quality and the size of each individual camel-load of goods, and to decide upon its value. By the end of the eighteenth century the rate for transport charges varied (it is said) between 80 and 110 Turkish piastres (about £20 to £27) a load. It would not be safe to make a generalization as to prices before then, although individual price quotations can sometimes be found for specific expeditions.

When, after two or three months of preparation, the *kafila* was ready to take the road, the caravan *bashi* became its commanding officer; and he remained in charge of its general administration. First of all, he divided up the cameleers into troops of from twelve to fifteen camel-men each. Every one of these small companies, called *barkaness*, was under the immediate supervision of its own chief cameleer or shaykh, and all the shaykhs were answerable to the principal shaykh, who was the caravan *bashi*. He gave them their marching orders, designated their respective places in the line of march, and assigned to each company its share of the escorting guard. This share was determined upon a proportional basis. A single guard was allotted to each camel-load of cloths or silk; but only one was considered necessary for every two loads of heavy or alimentary merchandise, such as sugar, coffee, pepper, etc.

As in the Meccan caravans, *daleels* were used, but as much in the role of scout as of guide. Other officials of the *kafila* included a *muezzin*, whose duties were purely religious and judicial; a *kahweji*, the official maker and distributor of coffee amongst the various shaykhs, merchants, camel-drivers and soldiers; and the *bayrakdar*, or standard-bearer, who rode just in advance of the convoy. Most important of all was the *bashi's* principal assistant, the *shaous*, who might be likened to an aide-de camp. His primary duty was to police the *kafila* and help the *bashi* to maintain order and discipline in so large a company; he also gave the signal for daily departures, when so instructed; and (on the side) he doctored both man and beast when there was need! The shaykhs of the *kafila* were jointly responsible for paying the *muezzin*, the *kahweji* and the *shaous*.

Once on the march, the various groups, each one closely attended by its armed escort, straggled along the desert way; the escorting guard marched on foot, as close about the laden camels as was feasible. The *bayrakdar*, at the head of the caravan, kept his banner furled except at a time of crisis or danger. The *bashi*, in company with all the lesser shaykhs, preceded the rest of the caravan by about three miles' distance. Mounted on horses or dromedaries, they constituted an advance-guard. Whenever they felt like waiting for the caravan, they would have an hour in which to rest, drink coffee and smoke, while the main body caught up with them.

Night halts and encampments were only made after a careful reconnaissance, and all camping arrangements were well ordered and carried out with dispatch. The *bashi* was accustomed to have his tent pitched in the centre of the spot which he selected for a camp site. Round about his centre tent the shaykhs pitched theirs. All the camels were unloaded and turned loose to graze for the space of two or three hours: a camping-ground was always picked with an eye not only to available water, but also to a pasture-ground of *shik* or camel-thorn for the camels to feed upon. Some guards, called *segmenes*, or *segmans*, were detailed to tend the grazing camels, and to bring them back to camp at nightfall. But before entrenching themselves for the night, the *muezzin* called the whole company to evening prayer. And then a community supper was served. Small circles were formed, separate groups of shaykhs, merchants, cameleers and soldiers, while they ate their one cooked meal of the day. After supper, a general council was held for the morrow: a shaykh-council or assembly, presided over by the *bashi*. First they would arrange the next day's itinerary; thereafter they deliberated upon matters of justice. This council had full judicial rights over every person in the *kafila*, laid down laws for the common good of all, and imposed penalties upon transgressors. The *bashi* and the *muezzin* both presided over judicial matters, and they two, giving a joint pronouncement, were comparable to the *kadi*, or civil judge. Since the safety of the whole caravan was dependent upon obedience to the *bashi* and his ability to maintain effective discipline, decisions were arrived at with less argument than is customary among Arabs, and the orders of the council were enforced without difficulty. Camps were arranged either in a square or else in circular formation; and the bales of merchandise were stacked to make a low wall around the tents. The camels were couched, each with a leg tied under him, outside the rampart made by their packs; though occasionally, if a night attack were feared, they were made to lie down inside— between the tents and the surrounding wall of bales. And throughout the night, whether or not an attack were apprehended, the *segmans* (divided into watches) stood sentinel for the sleeping caravan.

The only variation of the daily routine was in event of imminent danger, if a *ghrazzu*, or raid, were expected. In such an eventuality, the various companies making up the caravan would march in close order, practically joined each to the other, and every one flanked by its foot soldiers. Or else, if an unfriendly tribe of Beduin was actually encountered, a pitched battle resulted. If a robber band managed to take the *kafila* entirely by surprise, the resulting fight was a disordered skirmish in which the *segmans* defended their charges as best they might. But if a desert raiding party was unable to conceal its proximity, the caravan *bashi* would have warning of the impending attack. Then a defence could be properly organized, and the assembled *kafila* was made to resemble (in part) a night encampment. The camels were couched behind a rampart of their own packs, arranged in square or circular formation; which rampart formed a wall from four to five feet high. As each camel's load consisted of twin bales of merchandise weighing roughly from 250 to 300 pounds apiece, the outer bulwark was a fairly stout one. All the members of the caravan, including the *segmans*, fought from behind the camels: they were an improvised, entrenched army.

Arrangements for the safe-guarding of caravans were the one element in caravan organization that underwent a change between the sixteenth and the nineteenth centuries. In the early part of the Ottoman period caravans were protected (more or less efficiently) by Turkish janissaries, under the command of a Turkish captain. But these professional and alien soldiers became overbearing toward their Arab associates, and were consequently unpopular with them; and they were always intensely disliked by the Beduin, so that they eventually ceased to be considered as reliable escorts for the merchant caravans. Gradually another kind of protection was substituted for that of Turkish mercenaries. A certain tribe of Nejd Arabs, called Agails, interested themselves in the carrying trade, and made a practice of providing escorts as well as camels for the commercial caravans. In the eighteenth century a Pasha of Baghdad had invited the Agails to leave their homelands in central Arabia, in order to assist him in putting down a rebellion. These

Agails, after helping the Pasha most efficiently, decided to remain in the north instead of returning to Nejd. Many of them settled on the west bank of the Tigris at Baghdad; more of them in the village of Zebeir, near Basra; and some few of them also in Damascus and Aleppo. Being a tribe with both military and commercial inclinations, the Agail Arabs became relatively popular with the Turks (even helping them to keep the janissaries in order from time to time), and they soon made themselves indispensable to the Pasha of Baghdad. The result of all this was that they won many privileges for themselves, not the least of which was a monopoly of the caravan trade between Mesopotamia and Syria. By the end of the eighteenth century, they alone had the right to form caravans and to protect and lead them across the Syrian Desert. Generally speaking, therefore, every caravan *bashi* was an Agail, and his picked escort of soldier-guards were also Agails. But sometimes the Agails leased or farmed-out this privilege to a friendly tribe, or subdivision of a tribe; and these made the only exceptions. This was not all. Most of the soldiers were also camel-owners who hired out their camels to the merchants. So that, in the event of fighting *en route*, the guards would be defending their own live property as well as the merchandise which they were paid to protect. Such a double interest in resisting an attack would account for their proverbial zeal and bravery. And yet, over and above any motive of self-interest, the Agails appear to have been exceptionally courageous fighters. However, there were fewer pitched battles on the desert after the Agail soldiery displaced the Turkish, because these Nejd Arabs were on excellent terms with most of the Beduin. They were particularly friendly with the Aneza, that other Nejd tribe which (after 1700) became the most important as well as the largest single tribe in the Syrian Desert.

The relations of the Agails with all other Beduin form part of a still more comprehensive and difficult question, involving the attitude of the Beduin to all caravans that crossed the nomad's-land. This subject cannot be fully covered until the private caravans of European travellers are discussed (see pp. 172, 184-185, 212-216). But on the whole it may be said that, although the majority of Beduin tribes were more friendly toward the merchants' caravans than toward the private ones, they were often irresistibly attracted by the former. A caravan of merchandise had a far stronger appeal to their plundering instincts, so lavish was the reward of a successful raid. By an intricate system of subsidy or tribute, the senior shaykhs of the principal Beduin tribes exacted money payments (*khifara*) from every *kafila* that crossed the desert, in return for which they guaranteed immunity from attack by their own tribesmen. The amounts paid for this guarantee varied directly in proportion to the size and the wealth of each *kafila* that took the road. At first each caravan *bashi* made a special arrangement with the Beduin, in person, every time a caravan set out; and the greater his personal prestige among the desert shaykhs, the more favourable were the terms he was able to make in behalf of his caravan. After the Agails undertook all these arrangements, a regular understanding grew up between them and the Beduin, which made it possible for caravan *bashis* to dispense with individual negotiations each time that a merchant caravan set out to cross the desert. As Major Taylor put it, in western phraseology, an Arab agent was stationed in all the big cities bordering upon the desert, who was delegated to act as a collective representative for all the tribes amongst whom prospective caravans would need to journey. This agent "readily" furnished a "pass", upon demand, to any Agail caravan *bashi*. A sum of money was paid for this pass, which was in proportion to the number of camels in the proposed caravan. The agent divided amongst the various Beduin shaykhs concerned the money he thus obtained (after deducting a commission for his own services as intermediary), and they in return honoured the "passport" of their agent by according the caravan in question a safe-conduct through their respective portions of the desert.

Still another factor entered into the situation, and that was the general condition of rest or unrest which the desert might be enjoying when a caravan set out. Van Linschoten, in 1598, had remarked upon the comparative safety of the Great Desert Route. Less than seven years after he wrote, the conditions of desert travel had begun to change for the worse. Pedro Teixeira described both alarms and attacks. Near Meshed Ali his *kafila* got wind of a raiding party of fifty Arab thieves: so, in his own words, they all "marched on the look-out, and in the best order we could keep. The best-armed took the vanguard, and went prancing and shouting war-songs, to encourage themselves in their own defence, and that of the company" (see the 1902 edition of Teixeira's work, p. 43). And later, on that same expedition, Teixeira's caravan was attacked one day, before the break-up of camp, by 300 mounted Arabs armed with spears. The raiders drove off 200 camels with their loads of dates and some merchandise, and even stripped the clothing off a number of merchants. The sequel to this story shows very clearly just where and how the Beduin drew the line in their looting: they subsequently returned all the 200 camels (which happened to belong to the Emir of Anna) when they learned from the cameleer (whom they had captured with the camels) that the animals were in his charge, and that he himself was a brother-in-law of one of their own shaykhs. It was not recorded that the loads were returned with the camels, and it is unlikely that they were, since the merchants only rented the camels in question.

Twenty years afterwards, Pietro della Valle had a lot to say about the dangers and difficulties of desert travel. There were, of course, special complications in 1625, when he made the desert journey. It happened to be one of the interludes when Baghdad was being governed by a Khan, who represented the Shah of Iran. At that time the Shah was bringing influence to bear, not only upon the Khan of Baghdad, but also upon a powerful Beduin ally of his, the Emir Nasir, to intercept and rob the annual *kafila* from Basra. In this particular instance the Emir played into the Shah's hands; he succeeded in holding up and robbing the caravan, and even impressed many of its members into his service to help him carry on a personal feud. The *bashi* was killed, and his son was forced to take over the leadership of the caravan in his stead. But, fortunately for Syrian Desert trade, it was not often that the independent Beduin found it to their interests to join forces with

the Iranians. They derived too much profit from the annual subsidies which were paid them by the caravan *bashis* in exchange for
their guarantee of safety.

Finally, Jean Baptiste Tavernier had tales to tell of still another
kind. Once his caravan was held up and detained by "one of the
most potent Emirs of Arabia". The caravan *bashi* tried to buy
off the Emir with costly gifts; but the gifts were refused, and a
payment of 400 crowns (about £100) was insisted upon. And
yet, while robbing them on the one hand, the Emir sent over
baskets of provisions to feed all the members of the caravan for
the three days during which he detained them. On another
occasion a raiding party led by two young shaykhs held up
Tavernier's caravan, and insisted upon exchanging presents of
food for merchandise. They ransacked all the personal baggage,
and found, among other things, some engraved pictures which
belonged to Tavernier. Twenty of these they insisted upon
"buying", for twelve ducats, in spite of the latter's protests. It
must be added that Tavernier's caravan was an exceptionally
small one, numbering only 600 camels, and that he was one of
the last Europeans to travel between Aleppo and Basra for almost
a hundred years. Conditions on the desert grew steadily worse
thereafter, until the eighty-year period of anarchy, which, as has
already been explained (p. 76), did not terminate until practically
the middle of the eighteenth century.

William Beawes, the first European to use the Great Desert
Route in the eighteenth century, wrote that the Aleppo–Basra
"road" (in 1745) was "commonly more secure than any other,
tho' not so safe, however, as to make unnecessary their going
well provided with arms and ammunition, it being impossible
to adjust with all the wanderers of the desart; nor do they think
it worth while. But altho' the lesser tribes are generally awed by
the greater, yet opposition sometimes happens, and whole caravans
are plundered, as was the last year's [caravan] from Damascus to
Bagdat." [1] For more than a century after Beawes' voyage, the
Great Desert Route (as described in Chapter VI) was that in most

[1] Beawes, quoted in Hakluyt (1929), *op. cit.* p. 34.

general use. It was referred to by Edward Ives, in 1773, as "the common route of the caravan from Aleppo to Bassora".

Less than seventy years later, in 1807 to be exact, Olivier was able to say that a well-ordered caravan, with an adequate guard, had nothing to fear from petty Arab raiders; and could trust themselves to the safe-conduct of the greater shaykhs because of the tolls, or gifts, which they paid to them.

The Basra caravans, as they had evolved by the mid-eighteenth century, had interesting and rather special features of their own. The merchants of Basra had no fixed time of departure each year. When their opportunity came, they had to request permission from the Pasha of Baghdad, whose territories intervened between them and Syria, and receive a special licence from him. Sometimes, in order to obtain the desired permission, they had to pay the Pasha a sum of money as great as he could hope to collect from them in tolls or duties, were they to traverse his entire *pashalik*, and go to Aleppo by way of Baghdad and Mosul. But carriage was so much cheaper by the desert route, and the road tolls so much less, that it was actually worth their while to drive so costly a bargain with the ruler of Baghdad. All things being equal, the merchants usually awaited the arrival of the ships from India, particularly those from Bengal, which generally arrived in June. In this event, the *kafila* would leave Basra about mid-July.

With this exception, the Basra caravans were organized much as were those of Baghdad, Aleppo and Damascus. The merchants elected their own *bashi*. Each merchant contributed his proportionate share towards the general, collective, expenses. And whenever there happened to be extraordinary expenses (which had not been budgeted for), due to unforeseen dangers or the like, all the merchants of the *kafila* were "assessed" equally. But the Basra merchants were relatively sociable amongst each other, throughout their long journey of 770-odd miles; and their solidarity was sufficient to inspire them to make common cause in the matter of common grievances, such as, for example, the occasional insolence of their cameleers. Also, the merchants travelled in comparative comfort, each one of them providing himself with a tent and other similar conveniences; and they made a practice of halting at noon to drink coffee or take some form of refreshment.

But the merchant caravans were, if anything, less important than the caravans of unfreighted camels which left Basra each year for Aleppo. So great was the demand in the Ottoman Empire for light camels, that dealers could always count upon selling from 3000 to 4000 of them a year for ready money. Accordingly the annual departure of this caravan was always fixed to coincide with the height of the market in Syria; and that necessitated its leaving Basra some time between the middle or end of April and the middle of June. Beduin owners would drive all their marketable camels to Aleppo, sell as many of them as possible, and then return, after loading the unsold animals, if any, with Syrian merchandise. Whenever it was feasible, they would join forces with the merchant caravan which was also due to return to Basra some time in November or December, after the rains had begun to fall. Plaisted, who travelled with a camel caravan in 1750, was able to expand the bare facts given us by Beawes and Carmichael, both of whom travelled with merchant caravans. He informs us that the animals for this caravan were all desert-bred, and that a large proportion of them were supplied by the Shaykh of el-Hasa, which is a district east of Nejd, on the Persian Gulf opposite to the Islands of Bahrein. His camels furnished the nucleus of the caravan, and this nucleus was usually doubled or trebled within five or six days of starting out, as they travelled through other camel-breeding districts. The Shaykh of el-Hasa furnished the guard, which numbered about 150 men mounted upon dromedaries. And the bulk of the caravan's personnel were genuine Beduin. As for the camels, they were not tied together—in lots of seven or eight—as was the custom in Iran; they were instead allowed to go loose and without order, browsing as they went. The carrying of merchandise was officially debarred from this type of caravan, but a few people, nevertheless, usually contrived to carry some. On the whole, the camel caravans were not pleasant to travel with, from a European's

point of view. They were possessed of fewer conveniences than
were the merchant caravans; they did not habitually stop for noon
refreshment; and no one of their members carried or set up tents,
not even the caravan *bashi*.

It is difficult to generalize concerning the average size of the
annual caravans. The numbers of the merchants and their hired
pack-animals depended upon so many things. Primarily, as was
inevitable, upon general trade conditions, and the fluctuations in
the demand for any given commodity. This in turn was dependent
upon the ultimate, rather than the immediate destination of the
merchants' cargoes. The risks of each separate commercial venture
were, at best, considerable enough without adding to them the
hazard of an uncertain market. Of course, in a sense, commercial
dealings were necessarily less flexible in the eighteenth century
than they have been since the nineteenth century. In the earlier
days there was little speculating upon untried commodities, for
which there was no established demand. Merchants were apt, as
far as was possible, to confine their exchanges to articles of proven
popularity. At least this was true of the trade that was carried on
across these desert routes.

One finds that various travellers give widely different estimates
of the numbers of camels in their caravans. The recorded numbers
of a very few of the great, or annual caravans, were 600 or 800
camels; many of them were declared to number 1200, 1500 and
2000; and from time to time even larger estimates occur, such as
2500 and 3000; once, as many as 4000 camels were specified—in
John Eldred's caravan, when it journeyed from Baghdad to
Aleppo. Possibly the average round figure for good years, was
1500. Then again, whenever there were any great numbers of
European travellers accompanying a *kafila*, the numbers of camels,
as often of other kinds of riding animals, increased. Three provision camels were usually considered necessary for the use of any
European attached to a *kafila*. Carmichael, who crossed from
Aleppo to Basra in 1751, mentions that there were 7 Jews in the
caravan; about 20 Turks; 33 Christians, merchants and passengers;
and an escort of 240 soldiers. And there were "about 1200 camels",

THE GREAT KHAN OR CARAVANSERAI AT DAMASCUS

Starting-point and terminus of innumerable caravans

Drawn by W. H. Bartlett, 1835 : British Museum

50 horses and 30 mules. Olivier, who travelled with the merchant caravan of 1797 from Baghdad to Aleppo, gives us another sample list. There were in his *kafila* 20 merchants and travellers, 150 Arabs, 50 *segmans* and 2000 camels. On the other hand, the camel caravans were always larger than the merchant caravans, as was natural—considering the nature of their commerce. That with which Plaisted travelled, for instance, numbered 5000 camels—after a second drove had joined the Basra herd near Kubaisa. And these caravans scarcely ever numbered less than 3000 camels.

A special feature of caravan travel, which might easily be over-looked by those unfamiliar with desert conditions, was the necessity of taking a sufficient number of provision camels to keep the whole *kafila* in food and water during the long journey. Such supply or store camels would greatly add to the numbers of a caravan, without bringing in any commercial returns at all; and the numbers of these would account for some of the acute variations in the figures reported by travellers as to the sizes of caravans, from year to year. Teixeira refers to a prevalent custom which provided that, when a merchant hired camels to carry his merchandise, he was allowed, for every ten laden, one extra camel for his personal baggage. Tavernier, for once, is even more explicit on the subject. According to him, a merchant was "generally" allowed an extra camel to carry his provisions, for every six camels which he had laden; and, proportionately, he was entitled to half a camel's load for three laden camels; but if he had upwards of twelve laden camels, he might have as many extra baggage or provision camels as he wanted. Then, there was always a reserve supply of unfreighted camels to replace casualties, whether temporary or otherwise. To return again to figures, out of the 600 laden camels in Tavernier's caravan, only a scant 50 carried merchandise for sale at the journey's end; but this small-sized caravan had to provide for 400 men. And again, out of 2000 camels, Beawes reports that "about" 400 were loaded with merchandise, and another 400 with passengers and baggage. In Carmichael's caravan, as many as half of the 1200 camels were so laden. A few of the annual *kafilas* included from 75 to 100 asses

10

and mules. The figures given above, illustrating the ratio of loaded camels in a caravan, seem much too small in proportion to the size of the *kafila*. But one must remember the three-day distances between some of the watering-places, which might upon occasion be lengthened to a four- or five-days hiatus. And one must also bear in mind the fact that food was as difficult to count upon finding *en route* as was water; and that tents and equipment were accounted as provisions, as well as food and water. Again, one should not forget that reported numbers (whether of companies of men, camels, their cargoes, or the prices of things quoted in desert regions) are necessarily open to question. It is easy for anyone to be mistaken as to the exact numerical size of any large group or company. Furthermore, whenever travellers had to rely upon the Arabs for their figures, such figures are always suspect, because the Arabs are notorious for the generous stretches of their imaginations and of their memories when reckoning such matters.

Those who are interested in distances and mileages, or rates of travel in general, will find another peculiarity in discussing the subject of caravan travel. Until the modern period, desert distances have always been reckoned by the number of caravan hours it would take to go from one place to another. But how compute the "speed" of a caravan with any accuracy? It depends upon so many extraneous things. Riding camels or dromedaries can cover the ground at approximately five miles per hour for ten or eleven hours a day, for a stretch of about twelve days at a time—under normal conditions. Sixty miles is not an excessive or unusual distance for a dromedary to travel in one day, and an eighty- to ninety-mile stage is altogether feasible.[1] Camels laden with merchandise, on the other hand, take about twice as long to do a day's march as a dromedary; and unladen pack-camels travel faster than those loaded, but do not approach the speed of a

[1] The writer is indebted to Mr Douglas Carruthers for the following dromedary records, which, on his authority, are quoted in order to substantiate the preceding statements: 60 miles a day for nine days in succession; 250 miles in three and a half days; $62\frac{1}{2}$ miles between 10 P.M. and 5 A.M. Also T. E. Lawrence once rode 90 miles in 22 hours; and Guarmani claimed to have ridden 182 miles in two stages.

dromedary. There is also a kind of light pack-camel which carries a small load and has an intermediate speed. But there our comparisons must end. Such approximations do not give reliable figures when long distances are involved; and they cannot be used as an exact basis for computation when given unusual conditions of travel. If the ground surface is exceptionally slippery, or unduly rocky, or strewn with flints, then a camel's average rate of speed will naturally decrease. There will be a similar decrease if weather conditions are adverse or unfavourable: if there are strong head winds, heavy rain, hail, frost, snow or the "poison-wind" called *simoom*. Extremes of cold or heat or drought lead to casualties, sometimes even to deaths, among the camels of a caravan; and such a calamity in turn results in the overloading of the uninjured camels of a caravan, and its consequent slowing up for the remainder of the journey. Most caravans met with at least some of these unfavourable conditions during the course of an annual voyage between Aleppo and Basra, or Baghdad and the Syrian cities. So the reader will not be surprised to learn that the annual Basra–Aleppo caravans took anywhere from 30 to 70 days to perform the appointed journey; and that those which travelled between Aleppo and Baghdad took from 25 to 36 days. Smaller caravans, of course, made either journey in much less time than the great commercial *kafilas*. And naturally, the longer the distance to be covered, the wider the variation in the time required by various caravans to cover the allotted distance.

Nevertheless, several caravan travellers made careful studies in order to ascertain the average rate of travel of a camel. Their conclusions give us an average maximum figure but no minimum figure for this rate. Major Rennell in *A Treatise on the Comparative Geography of Western Asia*, which he wrote as an introduction to the various painstaking maps which he made of the Near and Middle East, took a vast amount of trouble to determine the average rate of laden camels under ordinary conditions. In his own words, "The caravans between Aleppo, Bagdad and Basrah, of which we know the most, certainly go at the rate of two and a half (2·5) miles only per hour. . . ." This statement he qualified else-

where by adding that the caravan rate was even less if its camels were more than 2000 in number. Major Rennell's findings and those of all other noted travellers across the Syrian Desert—most of whom he cited—are in substantial agreement. Although a few, such as Dr. Thomas Howel, believed that the average caravan could proceed at the rate of three miles per hour over average good tracks.[1]

Some travellers made their estimates by walking alongside of a camel and timing his various paces, their lengths at different hours of the day and over different types of country, and then taking the average of these computations over a space of ten or twenty days. Others made mathematical calculations of a different sort. Major Taylor, for example, who reckoned that a camel which is "not overloaded" usually makes forty steps a minute, and that each of those steps is, on the average, five feet and six inches in length, arrived at the more general conclusion that the usual rate of such a pack-animal was 2·5 miles per hour. Many travellers, even although their estimates as to the average rate of travel of a camel were in agreement, differed, nevertheless, when it came to computing the distance of a caravan journey. Whenever a journey exceeded twenty days, their computations of its actual mileage were at variance.

There is little more to say concerning the general character-istics of the great merchant caravans. The countless anecdotes and descriptive material that is available would, in essence, be merely repetitious. So the story must now turn to the purely commercial interests of these trading convoys.

3

DESERT COMMERCE AND CARAVAN TRADE

From the days of King Hiram of Tyre until the era of the Mohammedan conquest, the articles in greatest demand were

---

[1] The miles in question are "British", or English statute miles, i.e. 69·16 E.S. miles are equal to one degree of latitude. For the verbatim quotation see Major James Rennell (1831), vol. i, p. li.

gold and frankincense and myrrh. These may be considered to typify the precious metals, drugs, aromatics and perfumes (especially essences) that found their way north to Syria from southern Arabia; and with them were included spices, which also came, more remotely, from the Orient as well as from Yemen. The articles most often specified were: cinnamon, spikenard, resin, myrrh, balm and incense. In the period of Mecca's commercial importance, gold, silver and iron were all mined in the Hejaz; and the principal export of Mecca, even before gold-dust and leather, was silver. Some Syrian-bound convoys were laden exclusively with silver in the form of bars, and even wrought into various shapes such as vases. These caravans also carried Chinese silk, received via Aden; slaves and ivory, from Africa; and dried raisins from Taif (the hill station of Mecca). They brought back to Mecca from Syria: grain, olive oil, wine, silken materials and various other textile fabrics that were a mixture of both silk and linen; also arms, which they smuggled into the Hejaz in spite of policing and the Byzantine customs officials.

In the Saracen period, especially during the Crusades, Syria began to import an increasingly varied assortment of goods from India via southern Mesopotamia; and articles from Iran, Central Asia and eastern China were imported through northern Mesopotamia, or indirectly via Baghdad. At the end of the fourteenth century, caravans brought gum and raw silk to Syrian markets from Iran; rhubarb from China, fine rugs and delicately woven fabrics (silk and otherwise) from both Iran and China. In the later sixteenth and the early seventeenth centuries, Rauwolff, and after him Teixeira, found the following articles for sale in the *souks* or bazaars of Aleppo: in addition to the usual spices, an assortment from India which included long pepper, turbith, cardamoms, cloves, nutmegs and mace; precious stones from Iran; pearls from Bahrein, in the Persian Gulf; various roots and "delicate cups and dishes" from China; indigo, rhubarb and "the best sincerest musk". There were also many jewels from India, such as garnets, rubies, sapphires and diamonds, which were smuggled into Aleppo by the caravans which came across the desert from Basra and from Baghdad.[1] Similar articles found their way to Damascus, also for distribution to the Occident as well as for Syrian consumption.

By the end of the eighteenth century, the large annual caravans were bringing to Aleppo and Damascus (in addition to their usual Oriental wares) Mocha coffee from the Persian Gulf; Iranian-grown tobacco, cherry-wood pipes and silks from Iran; muslins and shawls from India; and rose-water which had been distilled at Basra.

In the matter of exports, Syria continued to trade with the same staples that were exported from Damascus to Mecca in the Byzantine period. In addition, el-Mukaddasi (writing in the tenth century) noted sundry oddments of native manufacture that were also articles of commerce: such as brass-ware, mirrors, lamp-jars, needles, paper, carpet-stuffs, ropes, glass beads and glass-ware (reminiscent of Phoenician days), dried figs and raisins. The travellers Sigoli and Poggibonsi, who visited Damascus in the fourteenth century, and Ghistele, who visited Aleppo in the latter part of the fifteenth century, reported having seen these same articles in the city bazaars, as well as the famous steel-bladed swords and daggers of Damascus workmanship. Timur the Mongol transferred the steel industry of Damascus to Iran in the early fifteenth century; but Damascened weapons, of inferior quality, continued to be manufactured and exported from Syria.

In the seventeenth century there were a few Syrian articles for which there was a genuinely great foreign demand. Damascene taffetas and brocades (what country did not know of the "damascs" of Damascus?) were transported as far east as Java and the Moluccas, or Spice Islands. There was a Mesopotamian and an Iranian market for the silks and cotton cloths of Aleppo, as well as for the pistachio nuts and the various kinds of "hard" soap for which Aleppo was noted. And both Damascus and Aleppo made,

---

[1] Rauwolff states that the merchants of Aleppo smuggled in jewels from India, because they were afraid to pay customs duties on them, and thus advertise their possession of the jewels. They were in constant fear of robbery. See "Dr. Leonhart Rauwolff's Itinerary" (1573–74), published in vol. i of *Ray's Travels* (1693), pp. 85 and 86.

for use in Syria as well as for export, brass-ware, copper utensils and silver ornaments; especially the ornamental brass and copper-ware, so famous today, which is inlaid with silver. This industry, like that of the weaving of silk and combinations of silk and cotton, has never died out in either of these cities. Today their bazaars are hung with every colour and variety of silk materials, covers and silken garments; the silversmiths still fashion silver jewellery, inset with semi-precious Iranian stones; and every article of use or beauty, which could conceivably be made out of brass and copper, is exposed for sale.

After the inauguration of the Ottoman régime, caravan trading became even more complex. To the number and variety of the exchanges made between the Near East and the Orient there was added the commerce which Europeans conducted on both sides of the Syrian Desert. Sir Thomas Roe of the East India Company, writing to his colleague Sir Thomas Smythe in 1616, tells of receiving a mysterious packet of Italian letters and bills. By means of this anonymous windfall, the East India Company learned that there was an overland trade between Aleppo on the one hand, and Iran and India on the other; that this trade was carried on by Italians and "some English"; and that "the sums and goods mentioned in the particulars" were "very great".[1]

The commodity most perpetually in demand in the seventeenth century was raw silk; but the silk trade had two close rivals. Indigo was in great demand, and so were "galls", or gall-nuts. To give instances of the freight carried by two typical caravans, one "very large" and the other small, reference may be made to the Venetian archives. Late in April of the year 1618, a Baghdad caravan arrived in Aleppo bringing 1000 packs of silk, 2000 casks of indigo, 5000 cordovans, and some loads of rhubarb and linen goods. By contrast, a caravan set out from Baghdad in early April 1628 with only 500 loads of goods for Aleppo; these included 160 loads of Iranian silk. In the matter of the gall-nut trade, Teixeira (to cite only one contemporary European) claimed that more than

[1] *Letters to the East India Company*, 27th November 1616, vol. iv, pp. 248 and 249.

12,000 camel-loads of galls were exported annually from Diar-bekr to Aleppo, Tripoli and Damascus; as well as to Baghdad and Basra, for India or China.

The most popular European imports into the Near and Middle East were cloths and coarse woollen materials, English and other-wise. Silver bullion was imported from France; gold coin and Venetian cochineal; English tin and lead. From 5000 to 6000 pieces of woollen cloth were annually imported from Venice; and from 12,000 to 15,000 cloths from England.[1] English merchants, after experimenting with the packing of this sort of goods for camel transport, found that only "three pieces" of English cloth should be packed into a single bale, lest the camel be overloaded. It did not take them long to find out that a bale or chest should weigh only 250 pounds, and that two such "parcels" constituted a full camel-load. The English traded first with Syria and Iran; but in the eighteenth century, English broad-cloths and thin woollens were also being sold in Irak, notably in Basra. And, speaking of Basra, there was a special luxury trade instituted by the English *factory* there. Burgundy wine was brought to the city, for the consumption of the English merchants in residence, by the great Aleppo caravans—all the way from the Mediterranean by camel!

There was one other type of trading in which the merchants of Aleppo, Hama, Homs and Damascus, as well as of all the towns of the Euphrates, engaged, though with little profit to themselves. Amongst the Beduin of the Syrian Desert there has always been a ready market for a few staple commodities. Coarse cloths, such as black and blue "calicuts", for their skirted garments; weapons, or knives of various sorts, and (eventually) fire-arms, when they could afford them; iron and copper-ware, particularly in the form of cooking utensils. These things are necessities to all but the most impecunious Beduin. So also are the woollen cloak, the *aba*, and the cloth turban, or *keffiya*, which they wear—although the desti-tute nomad makes for himself a goat-skin or camel-hair burnous;

---

[1] Cf. *The Venetian Calendar of State Papers* for 5th October 1635, pp. 460, 461. Also Pedro Teixeira (1902), p. 120.

and the comparatively rich as well as the very poor make their tents and their rugs out of this same kind of wool. In more modern times, coffee has become practically a necessity to them, and tobacco a highly prized luxury. To finish the list, they have a continuous need for a small amount of flour and of grain. Ordinarily, their payments for these things could not be made in specie. They have been forced to pay in kind; and in their case, that meant chiefly in camels. In fact, without the breeding of these pack-animals it is doubtful if they could have lived in the "empty" spaces of the desert at all. Such nomads as raised horses sold them as well as camels; and such of them as lived in relatively fertile districts also traded with sheep or goats and their produce; or with dates, if they happened to own palm-groves near the Euphrates.

4

TOLLS, CUSTOM DUES AND THE EXACTIONS OF THE BEDUIN

The greatest thorn in the flesh of all merchants who transported their goods by caravan was the matter of tolls. Tolls, custom dues and so-called gifts were a source of endless worry and perennial expense. This was one reason for the general popularity of Syrian Desert routes. The half-dozen tolls, more or less, which were payable along the desert highways were a mere bagatelle to the innumerable exactions to be met with along the roads of northern Mesopotamia. When a caravan's destination forced its *bashi* to choose the northern way, tolls had to be paid not only to cross rivers such as the Euphrates, but at every streamlet where it was necessary to use a ford; each city—Sharmley, Urfa, Diarbekr, Mardin, Nisibin, Mosul—and most villages exacted a transit tax and required the examination of all bales of goods. Tavernier tells us that, in the seventeenth century, a city toll amounted to two and a half piastres (or about 12s. 6d.) per horse- or mule-load. Every frontier crossed (in Turkish times, the borders of each *sanjak* and *pashalik* as well) required a transit toll. Often, also, the soldiers of a Pasha would ride many miles in order to force a caravan to go out of its way to pass across another customs barrier. Likewise, every rest-house (*khan* or caravanserai) had a fixed rate of charge; a head-tax on both man and beast. And it almost goes without saying that, in towns or districts where *khans* had been erected, it was necessary for the safety of a caravan that it should lodge there overnight: within, under no circumstances without, its gates.

Tolls and dues were, for the most part, levied by the load. But in cities such as Aleppo or Basra, there was a ten per cent *ad valorem* duty to pay on all goods, whether imported or exported. At Birejik, the charge for ferrying merchandise across the Euphrates was two piastres (or about 10s.) on every load of goods. At Anna there were special complications. The transit dues on goods and merchandise were paid to the Emir of Anna; but a "small royalty" was payable to the Turks in addition. Furthermore, goods were divided into two classes: "fine" merchandise, such as silks, cloths, indigo, spices, etc., which was charged five ducats (about 50s.) on each load; and "heavy" commodities, like galls or dates, which were only subject to a toll of one ducat (or about 10s.) per load. This, according to Teixeira, was the theoretical charge; but he assures us that in fact these tolls were literally doubled to ten and two ducats a load, respectively, by the extortionate demands of the customs officers.

The Great Desert Route naturally evaded most of the above-mentioned exactions. There were, nevertheless, certain inescapable tolls on the passage across. Pietro della Valle enumerated them for us in the seventeenth century. There was a customs due upon leaving Basra. At Kuwebda, near by, the shaykh charged five piastres (about 25s.) for every camel-load of fine merchandise, valued "at the rate of Indian cloth"; and a "much lower rate" for every other kind of load, valued "at the rate of tobacco". For passing through the territory of the Emir of Anna there was a toll of six piastres (about 30s.) on every load (even though a caravan might take care not to approach the city itself), plus an added "gratuity" of two piastres (about 10s.) on the six to satisfy the soldiers who collected the toll. At Taiyiba there was a variable charge for every person, of from four to twenty piastres (from about £1 to £5) a head—and a charge of less than a *larin* (*i.e.* less than 10d.) on each camel, loaded or light. This unusual arrangement was for the purpose of obtaining an adequate yearly revenue from the Basra caravans of unfreighted camels, destined for sale in Syria. As at Anna, "gifts" were also demanded by the collectors. Finally, at Aleppo, the usual ten per cent duty on all imports had to be met.

The unique type of desert toll was that exacted by the Beduin shaykhs. Della Valle stated that there were three principal shaykhs who claimed the perennial right to charge from three-quarters of a piastre to one and a half piastres (approximately 3s. 6d. to 7s. 6d.) for every kind of load, regardless of its nature. But unfortunately for the merchant, there were usually a number of shaykhs, encountered more or less accidentally, who considered themselves entitled to exact transit fees from any and every caravan. Tavernier has a good deal to say on this subject, and some of his details are picturesque. It was apparently customary for these desert shaykhs to "come to the caravans, to take their tolls, and to change their Crowns, Reals, or Ducats of Gold, for Larins. If . . . the merchants will not change their money, then will they refuse to take their toll"; they will "go a-hunting", and leave the merchants to think it over! But "if the caravan goes on without paying their tolls, these Arabian Princes will either cut them in pieces, or take away their camels, or rob them of all they have, as they have several times done".[1] Apparently gifts were always exchanged with Beduin thus encountered; when money was demanded, it was an additional expense to the merchants. The caravan *bashi* often anticipated money demands, in the hope of forestalling them altogether, by making an instantaneous offer of costly gifts. The moment a Beduin tribe was reported by a *daleel* to be either on the march or encamped in the neighbourhood of a caravan, the *bashi* would send its shaykh a choice selection of pieces of scarlet cloth, satin, gold or silver brocade, saddles ornamented with silver, or armour

---

[1] J. B. Tavernier (1684), vol. ii, p. 1. For the value of a *larin* see table of moneys and exchange (p. 316). The *larin* was the one silver token-coin in use on the desert, principally in the neighbourhood of Basra and the Persian Gulf.

—according to the rank and power of the shaykh; often copper cauldrons as well, if his tribe were desert-dwelling. In exchange for gifts or money accepted, the shaykh would send the merchant caravan a gift of food, usually dates, honey, etc., or else camels.

In the eighteenth century sometimes tribute only was exacted, such as a charge of one sequin (about 7s. 6d.) for every camel carrying merchandise. And sometimes a lower tribute might be exacted, together with certain stipulated gifts. In one case the presents itemized were: a hawk, two pieces of broadcloth and twenty pairs of Turkish boots.

5

STATUS OF MERCHANT CARAVANS IN THE TWENTIETH CENTURY

Such, for four centuries, were the conditions of caravan commerce and the methods of desert trading, a system which prevailed, almost intact, until the eve of the Great War: except for the fact that trans-desert commerce declined rapidly after the opening of the Suez Canal; and the Great Desert Route was scarcely even used after the middle of the nineteenth century.

Today there is no caravan trade from Damascus to and fro across the desert. The modern motor and lorry services to Baghdad have displaced it entirely. What remains is a local traffic, or short-haul trading which serves the length and breadth of Syria along its desert frontiers. Thus Damascus is still a focal point for the remnants of its former caravan trade: the exchanges between Damascus and Aleppo, via Homs, Hama and their neighbouring desert villages, are still effected—in part at least—by means of caravans; and so is most of the necessary trading between Jebel Druze and Damascus. Camel-owners use their camels chiefly to carry certain kinds of produce, such as ripe grain, at the particular season for selling or trading therein.

Aleppo, on the other hand, is differently situated. The villages in the semi-fertile districts of the northernmost part of the desert are not yet readily accessible—except those on the modern road which goes from Aleppo to Meskineh, where it joins the modern riverain motor track. Trading between these villages is still done in the ancient way; and caravans still cross the northern end of the desert between Aleppo and Deir ez-Zor. Small *kafilas*, of from five to eight camels, carry on a modern trade, chiefly in butter, sheep, wool and grain. Their organization has been described to the writer by a certain *Hajji* of Damascus, by the name of Selim Sawwaf, a merchant who used to supply the *Hajj* caravans with 2000 camels a year, and who has made some thirty-odd trips to Mecca.

Except for the informality of their arrangements (a result of their very small size), the modern caravans are organized on traditional lines. The merchants, who come together spontaneously, elect one of their number to lead the joint venture, and they all share equally in the risks and profits of the expedition. Apparently, being so few in number, the merchants are comparatively more independent and self-assertive than formerly— but that is the only noteworthy difference.

The safety of the modern *kafila* is provided for by the mediation of the *Akhwan*, or brotherhood. This institution has been loosely described as a "sort of freemasonry of the Beduin". What it means, actually, is something both more specific and more effective. A certain member of one tribe becomes the adopted "brother" of a certain member of another tribe, and so is bound to receive the same hospitality, consideration and safe-conduct through the desert at the hands of this other tribe as the man whose "brother" he has become. The resulting brotherhood is a serious affair, binding unto death; and there is no desert-dweller who would not recognize and respect this relationship. The ritual ceremony of adoption seems to vary amongst different tribes. In some cases an actual commingling of the blood of the two men is considered necessary; but sometimes there is only an exchange of gifts and an oath sworn, in the presence of one or more tribal witnesses. Occasionally, even, a money payment suffices (according to the *Encyclopaedia of Islam*). The "brothers" thereafter are received interchangeably by the tribes to which they respectively belong; and the friends and relatives of one man automatically become the friends and relatives of the other one. Two tribes, as collective units, can also become "brothers", each to each—and so, quite literally, brothers-in-arms.

The bearing of this unique system of "brotherhood" upon the safety of a commercial caravan is as follows. Some one of the merchants of the *kafila* would have a "brother" in every town or village on the route by which the caravan was intended to pass. That "brother" would pave the way—with money or its equivalent—for the arrival of the caravan; and he would come out from his village to meet the caravan, and conduct it in person to the next village, where he would give over its safe-keeping into the hands of some other "brother". Of course these "brothers" were well paid for their services by all the merchants of the caravan, because they benefited equally with the merchant "brother". Other escort than that of a "brother" is dispensed with. An armed escort for so tiny a company as the modern *kafila* of only six or seven camels would be too costly a proposition with respect to the calculable profits.[1]

This explanatory definition of the *Akhwan* is a fitting conclusion to a chapter on desert commerce. Fitting, because in its latest commercial phase the brotherhood system still plays a not insignificant part; just as do the Agail Arabs who were described in another part of this same chapter. The Agails, as guides and "brothers", have greatly aided in the development of the Damascus–Baghdad motor services.

[1] Incidentally, this general institution of the *Akhwan* must not be confused with any specific organization of *brethren*, of which there have been several in Arabia. The most modern example are the Wahhabi *Ikhwan* (i.e. *Akhwan*) of Ibn Sa'ud: the "militant-salvationist agricultural colonies" (to use the words of Philby) which the great Arabian leader planted in Nejd in 1912. Cf. H. St. J. B. Philby, *Arabia* (1930), p. 226.

CHAPTER V

EIGHTEENTH-CENTURY TRAVEL ACROSS THE DESERT

I

THE FOUR PRINCIPAL ROUTES AT THE DISPOSAL OF THE
TRAVELLER

THUS far only merchants have been considered, and their manner
of travel across the *Badiet esh-Shem*. But one must not assume that
all those who voyaged between Syria and Mesopotamia were
bound to follow the orthodox routes of commerce. Nor was all
desert travel bound to conform to the elaborate and conventional
pattern of the great caravans. Many European travellers, as has
been previously noted, chose to travel independently. Some of
them preferred a voyage down one of the great rivers, or a
round-about journey to Baghdad (across northern Mesopotamia),
to the direct desert crossing. Others had no particular objection
to travelling with a small merchant caravan. The smaller *kafilas*,
although their procedure and organization was closely modelled
upon that of the great caravans, were free to vary their routes;
and they were correspondingly more flexible in the matter of the
daily routine. Such flexibility was even more pronounced in the
case of the small, privately hired caravans which were independent
of the exigencies of commerce. In any case, a prospective trans-
desert traveller was able to select his own variation of the route,
and could decide upon his own mode of travel: neither the one
nor the other was preordained.

Between the sixteenth and the eighteenth centuries, the Syrian
Desert was thought of as a useful though hazardous highway
between the Orient and the Occident. The "land route to India"
(as the highways connecting Aleppo with Baghdad and Basra

came collectively to be called) was one of the three principal East-West routes; and it was the only one of the northern land roads which had not been either blocked or monopolized by the Ottoman Turks.

After the middle of the eighteenth century, the popularity of the Syrian Desert was definitely in the ascendant. Travellers, and particularly servants of the East India Company, who had to choose a way for going from England to the Orient (or *vice versa*) became increasingly persuaded of the greater relative advantages of the "land route" to India. Then it was that the Syrian Desert came to be thought of as a bridge between East and West, and was recognized as a most convenient short-cut between Mesopotamia and the Mediterranean.

The three practicable ways of travelling between England and India were as follows: by boat around the Cape of Good Hope— a very long and tedious trip in the days of small sailing-ships; by boat to Egypt, overland to Suez, and (again by boat) down the Red Sea and around the Arabian Peninsula; thirdly, to Mesopotamia: either overland to Constantinople (via Ostend and Vienna) and thence to Baghdad; or else by sea to Cyprus or one of the Syrian ports, and across the desert to either Baghdad or Basra.[1] From the delta of the *Shatt el-Arab* (the Tigris–Euphrates rivers), travellers had to go by boat through the Persian Gulf to Bombay. After 1745 no one who was free to choose, travelled long-sea; even though some of the record-making sailing-vessels carried passengers to Madras or Bombay in from three and a half to four months. The sea voyage was too cramped and monotonous, and the weather apt to be extremely bad in the vicinity of the Cape. Also, to journey overland across the width of Europe, Anatolia and the length of Mesopotamia, was too tiring a trip for the average voyager, in spite of the fact that this was admittedly

---

[1] In the eighteenth century European boats habitually called, at least once a week, either at Cyprus or at one of the Syrian ports: Beyrout, Tripoli, Latakia or Alexandretta. The most frequent Continental sailing-boat services were those from Marseilles, Leghorn and Venice. It was always easy—when the weather was good—for a traveller to find a passage on a Cypriot or Syrian vessel, if he desired to cross from Cyprus to Syria, or *vice versa*.

CARAVAN AT WATER HOLE BETWEEN SUKHNA AND RESAFA
Photograph by the author

THE CARAVAN LEADER
Photograph by Douglas Carruthers

the speediest and least expensive of all the routes—for a person who travelled with the minimum luggage. So that in reality the choice lay between a series of inconvenient (and often dangerous) boat trips, via Egypt, and the more balanced journey, via Syria, in the course of which sea and land travel were pleasantly combined. Furthermore, as soon as the routine of desert travel became more or less standardized, and a series of journeys had been made by Englishmen on their way to and from India, would-be travellers over the desert way were less prone to be intimidated by its supposed dangers and difficulties. Demonstrably—after William Beawes' desert crossing in 1745—it was both safe and practicable for a European to travel to India via the Syrian Desert.

Once a traveller had made up his mind to cross from Aleppo to Basra (or *vice versa*), he could then choose between four different variations of the crossing. His choice would depend, primarily, upon the season of his arrival at Aleppo or at Basra; and, secondarily, upon whether the opportunity of travelling with some particular caravan—ready and prepared for departure—presented itself. But, all things being equal, the Great Desert Route, on its own merits, would be more likely to attract prospective travellers than that through northern Mesopotamia, the Little Desert routes, or a river journey.

For purposes of comparison, these four alternative itineraries may be briefly summarized.

The Northern (or Mesopotamian) Route went from Aleppo to Birejik on the Euphrates, and across the river to Urfa (which was the Edessa of crusading days); thence to Mardin, Mosul (called the "great junction" of caravan routes), and down the Tigris—either literally, by *kelek* (raft), or else along a riverine road—to Baghdad. By this way the traveller really evaded the issue: going around, rather than across the desert.[1] There were a few definite advantages to this route, but—in general—the disadvantages appear to have

---

[1] It is interesting to note that in Tavernier's day the country between Aleppo and Birejik was fertile and efficiently irrigated; and that a century later (at least by 1750) the land had become a desert.

outweighed them. In summer the trip was more comfortably cool, and the water supplies were more plentiful, than along the more southerly highways; but, on the other hand, it was painfully cold and wet during the six winter months. The Northern Route itself, being round-about, was disproportionately long. Its length was emphasized by the fact that caravans invariably delayed to trade *en route*, and went out of their ordinary way to avoid Kurdish marauders, with whom the mountains were swarming. The only safe way to travel through this robber-infested region was with one of the large merchant caravans, composed of from 500 to 700 animals, consisting of horses, mules and donkeys. Europeans so travelling had to resign themselves to all manner of delays and impositions; often they were even forced to pay—unlawfully of course—local capitation taxes to which the native Christians were subjected. Sometimes the Pasha of the district made restitution upon complaint; sometimes not; it depended upon the Pasha; and often he was unapproachable. By way of compensation the traveller passed through many towns, ancient and interesting from an historical point of view, and some beautifully varied mountain scenery. And these same towns, in which were comparatively comfortable rest-houses or caravanserais, afforded relaxation, refreshment, change of diet, and doctors if need arose. At Mosul there were inevitable delays and inconveniences due to the necessity of making fresh transport arrangements. Either one had to transfer to another caravan and hire fresh riding and baggage animals therefor, or else, if southward-bound, arrange to be poled down the Tigris on a raft. This method of river travel was supposed in the eighteenth century to be dangerous, owing to the peculiar construction of the *kelek*: poles were lashed in rectangular formation—like a grid—to a layer of inflated goatskins, which made excellent floats; but these skins had been known to burst. Actually there would be little reason for alarm even if a goatskin were to burst (which was likely to happen whenever one was scraped too often over a stone or sand-bar), because the Arab boatmen are skilful in patching and sewing up a skin. Moreover, the bursting of one or more goatskins could only cause a raft to capsize if it were to happen while the *kelek* was negotiating rapids. When Sir Hubert Young descended the Tigris by this same primitive sort of raft in 1913, in the month of October (when the river was about dead low), he thought there was "no more idyllic way of travelling". The contrast of the peace, coolness, lack of dust and freedom from the perpetual bargaining for supplies, as compared with land travel, fascinated him. Imagine sitting on such a raft, trailing one's feet in the cool water, while the raft turned slowly round and round, as it spun downstream with the current! At low water it took about ten days to reach Baghdad.[1] Altogether, under favourable conditions the traveller would have to allow between fifty-two and sixty-five days to accomplish a trip by this northern route, from Aleppo to Basra; and rather more if travelling in the reverse direction—on account of going upstream. But, as a matter of fact, boatmen never attempted to pole these rafts upstream from Baghdad to Mosul. Usually, after a downstream voyage had been completed, the raft would be broken up; its poles would be sold, and the goatskins deflated so that they could be carried up-river to make a new raft for another down-river voyage. But between Basra and Baghdad, one could travel up the Tigris in small boats which, unless there was wind enough to fill a sail, had to be towed upstream by ropes in the hands of their Arab boatmen, who "tracked" along the river-bank.

The river journey, *par excellence*, was that down the Euphrates. This was recognized by those earliest pioneers of the East India Company, Ralph Fitch, John Newbery and the other merchants who, in the early summer of 1583, followed the still earlier lead of Caesar Frederick. These enterprising Englishmen, after disembarking at Tripoli from the *Tygre* (the ship which was later immortalized by Shakespeare's reference to the expedition),

[1] On Tavernier's fourth journey to the East (1651–52) he descended the Tigris, from Mosul to Baghdad, in eleven days. He explained that a *kelek* was made by "binding long poles together, five or six, one on top of the other, like a floating raft of wood. . . . They are made square, and underneath are placed about a hundred goatskins (inflated)." Tavernier also remarked that most of the rafts used on the Tigris were even larger than the one he described. R. C. Thompson (1910), pp. 147–148.

crossed the mountains to Aleppo in seven days—by what had originally been one of Rome's principal high-roads to the coast. Then they made a further caravan journey to Birejik, which they reached in the record time of two and a half days, and there they finally hired a native boat in which to voyage to Felluja. This they accomplished in sixteen days: another record trip. Then, after selling their boat for less than a sixth of what they had paid for it at Birejik, they went on to Basra by way of Baghdad. Eldred, who also went by the river route that same year, took almost twice as long to get from Birejik to Felluja as did Fitch and his comrades, but he probably voyaged more slowly because of travelling when the river was low. On the other hand, when contemplating a trip down one of these great rivers, one had to bear in mind that when the snows melted in the mountains of Anatolia, the Tigris and Euphrates would be in flood, often dangerously so. Thus rapids which could easily be navigated at low water were occasionally impassable at high water, when the river's current was strong; and the Euphrates—in particular—bred dangerous whirlpools.

Birejik was the usual point of departure for anyone embarking for Baghdad or Basra, and it was also the place where travellers had to cross the Euphrates on their way to and from Mosul. Situated in a kind of natural amphitheatre, with mountains to the north and west, this town had always been an important caravan station. It is at this point that the Euphrates finally leaves the narrow rock-cut walls of its upper, mountainous reaches, and enters the Syrian-Mesopotamian plain; in other words, the river here becomes navigable for the first time, and the country on either hand most easily accessible. The original (Aramaic) name of the town was "Birtha", meaning fortress, on account of its famous citadel, built on a cone of rock. "Birtha" was changed to "Bira" by the Arabs, became "Bir" to medieval travellers, and finally came to be known by the Turkish form of the name, Birejik. In the Seleucid period a boat-bridge may have spanned the Euphrates at Birejik, and one or more boat-bridges were in use there in the Middle Ages; but a "ferry" service was eventually substituted for them.[1] In the late seventeenth century, Maundrell saw "a great many ferry boats" at "Bir"; and in 1836 Colonel Chesney found sixteen of them there. They were great ungainly boats, with an exaggeratedly gondola-like bow, and an absolutely square stern, the end of which was open, so that all manner of beasts of burden might easily be driven in and out of the commodious interior, where they were herded for the crossing. Except for these ferries, the boats to be had at Birejik, for a voyage downstream, were ordinary *feluccas* such as one sees on the river today: rather unwieldy sailing craft which are also capable of being rowed. In 1745 a boat could be hired for sixty Levant dollars (about £15) to take passengers as far as Hilla; there they would tranship to a larger boat in which to finish the voyage to Basra, or, if desirous of proceeding via Baghdad, they would disembark above Hilla, at Felluja, and ride the forty-odd miles between the two rivers. Rafts similar to those used on the Tigris could also be hired; but as their speed depends entirely upon the strength of the current, they are excessively slow, because the oars with which they are equipped are used only to steer the raft, or else to fend it off from hitting the banks or islands in the river, when carried too close in-shore by the current. At Hit, and wherever else there are bitumen deposits near the river, one finds a curious kind of craft: a framework of light wood and branches is made, plaited through with a kind of basket-work of reeds and straw; this in turn is coated, inside and out, with melted pitch into which sand and earth have been admixed. The hull is thus rendered water-tight, with its double layer of asphalt or bituminous

---

[1] It is believed that Birejik was called Macedonopolis in the Seleucid period. Until recently it was thought that Zeugma-Apamea was situated opposite Birejik, on the Mesopotamian bank of the Euphrates, and that a bridge connected the two. But since Bali has been identified as the probable site of Zeugma, it is possible that there was no bridge at all at Birtha, or Birejik, until after the river-crossings at Tell Ahmar and at Zeugma (which were below and above Birejik, respectively) had lost their popularity. See, in this connection, Chapter II (footnote, p. 41).

For the history of Birejik compare *The Encyclopaedia of Islam*, article on Birejik; Franz Cumont (1917) (*op. cit.*), pp. 120, 130-132 and 250.

cement. Noah built the "ark" in this fashion, according to Genesis (vi. 14), and the modern visitor to Baghdad will recall a variation of the type: the round, black *guffas* which (even to this day) their boatmen load to the rims with sacks of grain, merchandise and animals.

On the whole, a voyage down the Euphrates is interesting, especially from an archaeological point of view, and attractive at most seasons of the year, and would be likely to appeal to the tourist of any age or century. The chief drawback has always been the river Arab. Riverain shaykhs are noted for their lawlessness and greed; each man for himself is the traditional attitude. They impose countless tolls on hapless river-farers, and see that they are exacted; and they take no pains to prevent their peoples from plundering such as travel by the river route. Only a disproportionately large and costly escort would preserve a traveller and his belongings from the nightly—and in some cases daily— menace of banditry. The boatmen were and still are as much afraid of river thieves as those who hire them, if not more, and generally insist upon sleeping on shore every night of the journey, the more easily to protect themselves. Occasionally boatmen have been persuaded to anchor in mid-stream for the night; but not often, and always under protest. So that if a traveller were pressed for time, the river route would prove to be impracticably slow—in addition to the fact that during three-quarters of the year the normal sluggishness of the current makes the journey very long-drawn-out.

The inconvenience of the river trip was also against any general use of the Euphrates. Rauwolff, for instance, was much impressed with its inconvenience from several points of view. When he voyaged down the Euphrates (in 1573), he found that the boatmen were very unskilful in sailing their miniature fleet of boats in unison. Some they ran on sand-bars; others were allowed to ram each other; a good deal of merchandise was inadvertently capsized; a part of the cargoes thus capsized sank, and the balance had to be dried in the sun for several days together. It was, apparently, unusual when he could report that on a certain day the "navigation proceeded very well". Rauwolff also had a good deal to say about the annoyance of river tolls and the examinations to which travellers and merchants were alike subjected, by both Arabs and Turkish customs officials.

It is only fair to native boatmen to say that, even below Birejik, it is not easy to take a boat—still less a number of boats—down the Euphrates. Colonel Chesney, in the nineteenth century, visualized the establishment of a steamboat service to connect Anatolia and northern Syria with the Persian Gulf; and so convinced was he of its imperial importance, both to trading interests and travellers, that he dedicated many years of his life to its inauguration. But, as will be described in another chapter, he found that the Euphrates (with its rapids, its winding course, its shallow rock-filled waters, shifting shoals and changing river-bed) did not lend itself to such a service.

While on the subject of river routes, it might be as well to mention the two that were most frequently used by travellers: those along the lower reaches of the Tigris and the Euphrates. Since Baghdad is situated on the Tigris, the easiest way for those desirous of reaching Basra would appear to be by that river. But so tortuous is the Tigris, so many and fantastic are its loops and bends, that the actual distance between the two cities is more than doubled by this water-way. Only those who were indifferent to time would consider descending, to say nothing of ascending thereby. However, with a strong favouring current, the voyage downstream could be made in between fifteen and eighteen days; whereas, travelling upstream against the same strong current, travellers have been known to spend anywhere from forty to eighty days in "tracking" from Basra to Baghdad. Tavernier even claims that tracking upstream occasionally took three months, especially if there were an adverse wind.

The one popular and frequented river route was that between Hilla and Basra. The Euphrates is most easily navigable along this stretch; Baghdad is a scant two days from Hilla (on horseback) and the voyage thence to Basra could be made in ten days. Travelling in the reverse direction, provided that the opposing current were not too strong, the voyage upstream averaged only sixteen days. Dr. Thomas Howel made this journey *en route* to Constantinople in 1797; and judging from his account thereof, he derived not a little amusement from the trip, which he made in company with two other Englishmen. He mentions in passing that all their belongings were stowed away most carefully at the bottom of the boat: completely inaccessible because they were buried under a cargo of dates! So they all three went portmanteauless until the dates were sold, at a village called "Devanoe", where they fetched a profit of about thirty per cent.

Most diaries of river travel portray the guide-interpreters and the boatmen as excessively timorous. Sometimes this timidity was only feigned, in order to extract the maximum pay and baksheesh from their passengers; but more often it was a genuine fear of roving Arabs. They perpetually conjured up stories of ambush, murder and robbery with, and even without, the slightest provocation. That all this was not pure imagination has been proved both before and since Dr. Howel's journey. Even as recently as 1934 (on 7th March, to be exact) this was most tragically proven: two young men who rashly undertook to paddle themselves down the Euphrates, without any sort of escort, were both murdered by the Arabs. There is, however, another side to the story. Dr. Howel and Lieutenant Heude (the latter made the river trip twenty years after Dr. Howel) both seemed to think that there was more to fear from the rashness, imprudence and quarrelsome dispositions of Turkish river guides than from the Arabs. The guides of their day apparently made a point of inviting trouble; and there is no doubt that Turks of any description were unpopular with the Arabs. But this is only a partial explanation, because not all river guides were Turks, and most of the boatmen were Arabs.

Generally speaking, travellers were anxious to cross the desert as speedily as possible. Very few people travelled to the Orient in the eighteenth century except on urgent business; and a trip between Western Europe and the Far East was long enough at best. This being the case, the more direct and calculable desert routes were usually preferred. Of these there were two: that across the

Little Desert, and the Great Desert Route. The *Little Desert*, it may be remembered, is that northernmost part of the Syrian Desert which has already been described as triangular in shape; it is synonymous with the district of Palmyrena. Both of these routes crossed Palmyrena diagonally, keeping well north of the *Hamad*— the stony, waterless desert. The Great Desert Route was merely a continuation of the shorter route and, instead of crossing the Euphrates at any point, skirted the eastern edge of *as-Samawa* (or the *Great Desert*) to reach Basra.

If a voyager had business in Baghdad *en route* to Basra, or conversely to Aleppo, he would naturally choose to cross the Euphrates either at Anna, or by the camel-ford of Jubba, or at Hit. Before the seventeenth century, the favourite crossing was at Kirkisiya, via the Saracen post road; and later on (sometime after 1850) Felluja came to be generally used. But at the time of which we are speaking (in the seventeenth, eighteenth and early nineteenth centuries) the example of the great annual trade caravans was usually followed, in crossing the river at Anna.[1]

After crossing the Euphrates, caravans continued the journey to Baghdad by cutting diagonally across the Mesopotamian Plain; and since small convoys could travel much faster than the large commercial caravans, they took, on an average, only twenty days to cover the distance between Aleppo and Baghdad. Of course this average could be shortened, as well as uncertainly and disconcertingly lengthened—especially if delays were caused by winter snow and rain.

[1] Teixeira, when on his way through Anna in 1605, stated that "through this territory pass most of the *cafilas* or caravans between Aleppo, Tripoli, Damascus and Baghdad " (Teixeira, *op. cit.* p. 86).

For a late eighteenth-century example, the merchant caravan with which Olivier was travelling (in 1797) went from Baghdad to Anna, crossed the river there—taking ten days to accomplish this—and then followed the Euphrates north to Meshed Rahba, before branching westward to Taiyiba for Aleppo.

At Anna, bridges had once connected the island in mid-stream with both the right and left banks of the river, but by the seventeenth century the bridges had ceased to exist, and caravans had to be ferried across.

There was a little-used variation of this Little Desert Route, one which is usually associated in our minds with the overland dromedary mail: namely, from Baghdad to and from Damascus. Large merchant caravans never used this direct route, because it hugged rather too closely the central belt of waterless desert. They were forced to follow the ancient road connecting Hit with Palmyra, and to travel thence to Damascus along the *Strata Diocletiana*. But the *tatars*, or Turkish dispatch-bearers, and certain small caravans occasionally used the more direct route which went from Damascus to Hit via Dumeir, Bir Melossa and Kubaisa. Theoretically, a caravan could cross by this track in fourteen days. In 1643 Fray Sebastien Manrique (on his way home from India and Iran) travelled, with a caravan of 300 camels, from Baghdad to Damascus by "the most desert route": an unusual one, as he noted at the time. Their exact itinerary is somewhat obscure, but it is plain that they went either by way of Bir Melossa or else—just possibly—via Rutba Wells. The only landmark in Manrique's account of the journey is "a place of seven wells", wells so deep that the water in them was almost invisible. His caravan took thirty-seven days to cover the distance, which was two and a half times as long as the caravan *bashi* had reckoned upon taking. This was partly explained by the fact that, through fear of the desert Arabs, they abandoned the "direct road" in favour of the "solitary deserts". Everyone suffered dreadfully from thirst before the caravan finally reached the cultivated lands, two "easy" days to the east of Damascus.

Manrique's reason for going by way of Damascus is interesting. He had heard that the Turkish custom-house officials made as many difficulties as possible for travellers arriving from India.[1] They professed to believe that every person on his way home from the Orient had pearls and diamonds sewn into his clothes; and accordingly they made a drastic and excessively disagreeable search in the hope of finding jewels on the person or amongst the belongings of every traveller

[1] The mint and the three custom-houses of Aleppo were farmed out to Jews (in the sixteenth and seventeenth centuries).

coming from the East. Such treatment of foreigners by the officials of Aleppo must eventually have been modified, because no similar complaints were made during the eighteenth and nineteenth centuries.

Last, but far from least, we come to the Great Desert Route—that long land road which for almost a century was travelled, written about, mapped and discussed by the servants of the East India Company. This unique travel route was no longer either an accidental nor yet an incidental section of the four-months voyage between England and India. To some travellers it was the most dreaded part of their long trip—more on account of its discomforts than its dangers. To others it was the most attractive section of their trip, full of new experiences and interesting and unusual sights—both humanly and archaeologically speaking. The desert journey, between 765 and 780 miles in length, usually took between twenty-four and thirty-eight days.[1] A traveller spent the whole of that time in the open desert. He had to live the life of a desert Arab, with all that implies of discomfort and monotony; he suffered from heat in the day-time, from cold at night, and from wind at all times; he went thirsty if the water failed; and he was in as much danger of being robbed or murdered by marauding Beduin as were the least of his caravan. All this was incontrovertible. But on the other hand, unless the trip were made in midsummer or midwinter, neither heat nor cold were extreme; and only the seasonal *simoom* (as the hot "poison wind" of the desert is called) was to be feared. Also, in midsummer only was there a possibility of water shortage, because the route was planned to lead a caravan on from one well or spring to another, with a maximum interval of three

[1] The exact mileage of the Great Desert Route (which has not been used in its entirety since the latter part of the nineteenth century) cannot be accurately computed, partly because the total mileage of a desert trip depended (in each case) upon how closely the meanderings of the Euphrates were followed. Similarly, the speed of a caravan was also variable: the smaller the caravan, the more quickly the voyage could be completed; and it may be remembered that the great *kafilas* often spent from forty to seventy days on the road.

days' travel between them. Desert villages as well as those on
the banks of the Euphrates, were, it is true, avoided; but that
was no loss! And the caravan *bashi* approached closely to several
of the smaller ones, where the toll-frontiers were of minor
consequence; and after crossing Palmyrena, the river was frequently in sight.

As regards the safety of the route, the open desert was unquestionably safer than the more settled regions, whether of the
Euphrates or of the northern (Mesopotamian) uplands. The
hierarchical tribal systems of the desert plateau, which have resulted in the quasi-omnipotence of a few powerful shaykhs, made
it possible to bargain for safe-conduct. Before setting out, a
caravan would secure indirectly the goodwill of these shaykhs,
who, in return for whatever gifts of money or valuables they
had accepted, would guarantee the immunity of the caravan
from the unwelcome attentions of their tribesmen. No Beduin,
from the least to the greatest, ever thought of disobeying the
mandates of his shaykh. Accordingly, every caravan *bashi* engaged
the services of *rafeeks*—or "human passports", as they have most
aptly been called—to accompany them across the desert. A *rafeek*
was a member of some one of the tribes or sub-tribes under the
jurisdiction of one of the greater shaykhs; he would carry an
easily recognizable symbol, such as the banner of his tribe, and
his presence would prove to any brother-tribesmen whom they
might encounter that their shaykh had pledged his honour on
behalf of the safety of that particular caravan. Not only would
the *rafeek's* own brother Beduin respect the caravan which had
engaged his services, but the members of any tribe which valued
the friendship of his shaykh would also refrain from molesting it
in any way. The only Beduin to be feared were outsiders: those
who did not belong to any one of the great tribes of the northern
desert, and whose shaykh or shaykhs, therefore, did not supply
rafeeks for the safeguarding of caravans, or make terms with
what were, to them, alien tribes. The Shammar Arabs, when they
first swept northwards from Nejd, furnished an example of the
type of outsider most to be feared; as were also the Wahhabis,

who did likewise at the very end of the eighteenth century. They, of course, were as much of a plague to the indigenous nomad tribes as they were to passing caravans; but even they were more apt to demand tribute, or "free gifts", from the caravan as a unit, than to plunder it wantonly.

So much safer was the way by the open desert, and so relatively free from tolls, that travellers to and from Iran sometimes travelled across the *Little Desert*, between Baghdad and Aleppo, instead of going by one of the two more direct northerly routes which terminated at either Smyrna or Constantinople. Tavernier, who went to Iran several times in the middle of the seventeenth century, recommended this way. He himself made the following journey, travelling fast, with a single guide:

Alexandretta to Aleppo	.	. .	2 days
Aleppo to Taiyiba	.	. .	3 ,,
Taiyiba to Meshed Rahba	.	. .	5 ,,
Meshed Rahba to Anna	.	. .	5 ,,
Anna to Baghdad	.	. .	4 ,,

Total . 19 days

Thence into Iran, via Kenghavar to Ispahan: 13 more days.

By this itinerary, with a good boat connection and a favouring wind in the Mediterranean, Tavernier claimed that a man could travel between Paris and Ispahan in two months.

As early as 1626 a Venetian ambassador, writing from Constantinople to the Doge and Senate, had reported as follows:

The way from Persia to Damascus by Diarbekir is bad, long and dangerous . . . but by the desert it is short, perfect and safe. . . . From thence to Damascus messengers can go in twelve days and a caravan in thirty. The route is quite safe for caravans and persons on horseback. Small companies might be robbed, but not murdered. . . . I have this from many Turks of Aleppo, who have been in those parts.[1]

The relative safety of the open desert was, if anything, even more to be credited after 1740 than before 1640.

2

METHODS AND MANNER OF TRANSPORT ACROSS THE DESERT

Before describing the Great Desert Route at length, it may be well to explain how a prospective traveller would be likely to set about preparing for his journey. To begin with, having once decided upon the long desert road, because of its greater security, its brevity and freedom from unnecessary delays—especially from those caused by the officiousness and "impertinences" of Turkish officials—he had then to determine upon his manner of travelling.

A traveller might make the crossing almost alone, escorted only by one or two Arab guides. Those who made the journey thus, few in number though they were, congratulated themselves upon escaping the delays and vexations attendant upon travelling in company with a great number of men and beasts. It was obviously less safe for two or three men to travel alone, more particularly if one of them were not a native of the desert, than to make the trip with a well-escorted caravan. But it was much more speedy. Two or three men mounted on dromedaries could cover about fifty miles a day, and thus reach their destination in fifteen or sixteen days. If the maximum speed were necessary, a traveller could obtain permission—through the Resident of his country—to travel with a Turkish dispatch-bearer, or *tatar*. This was also the cheapest way to perform the journey, because the *manzel* (or imperial order) which authorized a traveller to accompany a government messenger entitled him to all facilities, and exempted him from all incidental expenses. For instance, William Heude went thus

[1] Quoted from the *Venetian Calendar of State Papers*, No. 690, p. 503. For Tavernier's route to Iran see J. B. Tavernier (1676), vol. i, p. 286.

from Baghdad to Constantinople for only £30. Both these ways of travelling, however, were very fatiguing. Even the ordinary caravan journey meant forced marching for the novice; but forced marching at top speed, on meagre Arab fare, was a veritable endurance test. Furthermore, dromedary-riders were unable to take any baggage with them, because they had to ride as light as possible. This was a drawback, because, unless a man shepherded his own belongings across the desert, he had to finish the rest of the journey before they could catch up with him. When Tenreiro rode post-haste from Basra to Sukhna, on his way to Aleppo in 1528 (with a single guide), the two riders were equipped only with dates, biscuit, "round balls of dough" to feed their dromedaries, and water-buckets.

Ordinarily speaking, the average voyager would expect to join a caravan of merchants, either one of the two great caravans which made the Aleppo–Basra journey annually, or else one of the smaller trading caravans. The smaller the caravan, the faster it would make the crossing; the larger the caravan, the slower its progress and the greater the number of inevitable delays, but the more adequate would be its escorting guard. However, the ordinary traveller would have no choice but to accompany any caravan that was ready to set out; if he missed one opportunity, he might have to wait from two to four months before he could be certain of another—although very small caravans did make the trip with variable frequency.

By far the most comfortable way to make the trip was to hire a private caravan. But, though satisfactory from all other points of view, this was also—and very naturally—the most expensive way to travel. In addition, this way entailed a delay of from ten days to two weeks, in order to get together the full complement of men and equipment for a private caravan. Delay was apt to be especially protracted at Aleppo, where the requisite camels were harder to collect than at Basra. Furthermore, the proposed caravan *bashi*, or leader, had to be chosen with the greatest care imaginable, because on him would rest the whole responsibility for the success of the expedition. It was necessary, therefore, that the *bashi* be efficient as well as trustworthy. Major John Taylor, who went very carefully (but not always accurately) into the subject of comparative expenses (after crossing the desert in 1789), stated in his report to the Directors of the East India Company that an adequate private caravan might be hired for the purpose for between £500 and £600. Such a unit would include an armed escort of from forty to sixty men, and twenty baggage camels for tents, water-skins and one's personal belongings. One could thus perform the journey in about twenty-eight days. Major Taylor himself, who travelled as one of a party of five (including two servants), paid only "£333 : 10s. 8d." for a caravan which included sixteen baggage camels, and a guard of Arabs: forty in number, who were "well-armed, with match-locks and scymeters".

Everyone who dealt with Arabs was insistent upon the necessity of making any agreement with them as formally binding as possible. A written contract was imperatively enjoined upon all prospective voyagers; and honest caravan *bashis* were, apparently, always ready to sign such a written agreement in the presence of witnesses. The more trustworthy ones showed themselves to be scrupulous about faithfully discharging their obligations.

At this point it may be both interesting and illuminating, psychologically speaking, to reproduce one of these contracts verbatim. Colonel James Capper, in company with two other Englishmen and three servants, desired to cross from Aleppo to Basra in the year 1778. As there was no caravan "likely to set out" for Basra, the Consul formed a "light caravan" expressly for them; and at the last minute this was joined by a Jewish merchant who offered to double the escort if he might be allowed to avail himself of the opportunity of thus transporting thirty camel-loads of goods across the desert.

The following contract was made with a certain Shaykh Suleiman of Aleppo:

This writing is to certify, that we the under-written of the tribe of Arabs Nigadi, have of our own free will agreed to accompany and conduct the bearer of this contract, Colonel

Capper, an Englishman, and those of his company: and that we oblige ourselves to take with us seventy guards of the tribes of Arabs Nigadi, and Agalli and Benni Khaled, who are all to be armed with muskets. . . . And we do promise also to carry with us nine refeeks with their muskets, two of whom of the two different tribes called Edgelass, two of the two tribes Il Fedaan, one of the tribe of Welled Aly, one of the tribe of Benni Waheb, one of the tribe of Lacruti, one of the tribe of Baigee, and one of the tribe of Sarhaani . . . and it is agreed, that we the under-written are to bring with us our own provisions, and the provisions for the guards and refeeks above-mentioned, and the same provisions are to be loaded upon our camels, the hire of which camels is to be paid for by us; and we likewise agree to buy ourselves thirteen rotolas of gunpowder, and twenty-six rotolas of balls, the cost of all the aforesaid things are to be paid for by us, and not by Colonel Capper.

And we also oblige ourselves to provide for him and his people nineteen camels, for the use of himself and his company, to carry their tents and baggage, water and provisions for themselves and for their horses, besides those nineteen camels above-mentioned; we also oblige ourselves to provide them two other strong camels to carry the mohafa [or camel-panniers for passengers—see p. 182] in order that they may change every day one camel . . . and a person to lead the camel . . . and a person to take care of his horses.

We . . . do promise Colonel Capper, by our own free will and consent . . . to pay all kafars and giawayez [duties] to all the Arabs, and to the Sheick . . . and all the Sheicks of the tribe of Beni Khaled, and to all other tribes of Arabs whatever; and we make ourselves responsible for all what is above-written, and further when we approach the tribe of Arabs called Il Aslam, and Shammar and any other tribes, we oblige ourselves to take from them a refeek to walk with us till we have passed their confines.

We agree to carry no goods, or even letters from any other person or persons, excepting the goods from Khwaja Rubens,

12

which are thirty-one loads, for the hire of the said goods from Khwaja Rubens we have received in full . . . according to the receipt in the hands of the said Khwaja Rubens: moreover we have agreed with our free will to provide for the said thirty-one loads, for every load two camels, in order to keep up with the above-mentioned Colonel Capper, and never separate from his company till our arrival at Graine; [1] and we also oblige ourselves to pay the dolleels [scouts] the maadeb, the birakdar [standard-bearer], and the chaous [officers of the guards] all the said persons we are to pay ourselves, and not Colonel Capper. We have agreed also with our free will, with the said Colonel Capper, to carry him and his company safe in thirty-six days to Graine, from the day we depart from . . . Nayreb [one of the first caravan-stations to the south-east of Aleppo. It is not named on Rennell's map]; but in case . . . Colonel Capper should be desirous . . . to rest a day or more . . . the . . . delay is not to be reckoned in the . . . thirty-six days. And we the under-written also engage three days before our arrival at Graine, to dispatch a messenger from our parts with Colonel Capper's letter to the agent of the British nation in Graine.

And by this instrument it is stipulated and agreed between . . . Colonel Capper and us the under-written persons, that he pays us for all the services above-mentioned dollars 941¼ [about £235] in Aleppo, which sum we have received in full; besides which . . . Colonel Capper does oblige himself to give us on the road dollars 500 [about £125]; and moreover at our safe arrival at Graine, on our having fulfilled this our agreement with him, he . . . to pay us dollars 800 rumi [about £200], and in case we should fail in performing any part of our agreement with him, we then are to forfeit the last-mentioned 800 dollars, and all we the underwritten are responsible one for the other, for the performance of the promises as above agreed between the contracting parties. In witness whereof, we have signed

[1] Graine is on the Persian Gulf, about seventy miles from Basra (see Rennell's map). Colonel Capper went direct to Basra, but Khawaja Rubens and his merchandise took the track to Graine where the Basra track forked.

with our fingers this the sixteenth day of the moon called Shewal, in the year of the Hegira, 1156 [*i.e.* October 1778].

SULIMAN EBBEN ADEYAH
MOHAMED IL BISSHIR
ALLY EBBEN FADDIL
[and five other names].
The Witnesses to the agreement are:
IL HAGGI OMAR ULLEED
[and six other names].[1]

This is a typical example of the "usual" eighteenth-century contract. And Shaykh Suleiman was as good as his word, in every respect.

From Colonel Capper's day to the twentieth century, those who hired caravans to cross by the desert routes customarily made similar written agreements. Baron Max von Thielmann, for a later example, who crossed the *Little Desert* in the last quarter of the nineteenth century, made a contract with an Agail camel-driver for safe conveyance from Baghdad to Damascus. The agreement which was drawn up provided for six camels and two guides, and for transport by the way of Hilla, Kerbela and Palmyra, within a seventeen-day time limit; the remuneration agreed upon was thirty-two Turkish pounds (which, according to the rate of exchange in 1875, amounted to about £29 sterling) to be paid in advance. A bonus of £3 : 4s. was to be paid in Damascus at the end of the journey, if the caravan arrived on the appointed (seventeenth) day; otherwise not.

This question of remuneration was a thorny one, chiefly because no bargaining with Arabs can be lightly undertaken. Bargaining is a ritual, an interminable process, involving complicated exchanges of meaningless courtesies, over-much coffee-drinking, and frequently the bestowal of gifts. But the essence of its success is an apparent unconcern with the matter in hand! The unfortunate foreigner, who feels himself at so obvious a linguistic disadvantage, must try to make it appear that his proposed journey is of

[1] Extract from Colonel James Capper (1783), pp. 55-58.

much less consequence to him than the driving of a good bargain; and that time spent on bargaining is emphatically not time wasted. This, being contrary to the truth, is difficult to achieve. Such methods and the psychology required to employ them convincingly are, to say the least, alien to the Anglo-Saxon temperament. Also, it was generally impossible to pretend for long that the time factor was unimportant. So that, on the whole, the would-be Anglo-Indian traveller was at a decided disadvantage in all ways. The one saving grace, especially in those early days, was the relatively unsophisticated outlook of even town-bred Arabs, and the comparative simplicity of life in the Near East in all its material aspects.

Bargaining for transport was further complicated by the difficulty of securing a thoroughly reliable caravan leader. It was no economy to drive a hard bargain with an inferior type of caravan *bashi*, when inefficiency on his part, not to say dishonesty, might cost a traveller very dear. There were so many ways in which such a one could make up the difference between what he considered a fair and an unfair bargain—the foreigner was absolutely at his mercy, once the desert voyage had commenced. A merely incompetent leader was almost as bad, since he would, however unintentionally, be continually subjecting the members of his caravan to daily annoyances and constant, avoidable dangers. The hazard of unscrupulous caravan *bashis* can be well illustrated by the case of a "Mr J.", which was noted by Dr. Julius Griffiths in 1786. This unfortunate man arranged, and paid in advance, for conveyance from Basra to Aleppo. The time limit agreed upon was twenty days. But throughout the entire journey detours were made, on the pretext of avoiding tribes of supposedly hostile Arabs; and the *bashi* kept demanding more and more money for travelling by the circuitous way. "Mr J." had, of course, no choice but to pay the exactions, otherwise he would have been abandoned, helpless, in mid-desert. His caravan took seventy-two days to reach Aleppo—fifty-two days overdue—and the English Consul there could obtain no satisfaction whatever for "Mr J." The Consul was able only to prevent these same Arabs from being employed on any future occasion. This, though, is the darkest side of the picture. It is worth noting that Dr. Griffiths speaks of the "ill-usage" "Mr J." experienced as "unusual" and "unaccountable". It is accountable, actually, in the light of the above warning. And the moral of the tale is that "Mr J." could not have chosen his caravan leader with sufficient care. Dr. Griffiths goes on to say:

In justice to the Arabs . . . it must be confessed, circumstances of this kind seldom occur. . . . Strictly faithful in their agreements, it is only requisite that these agreements should be perfectly understood; and, in general, a perfect reliance may be made upon the execution of the treaty.[1]

As to the expenditure necessitated by joining and travelling with a merchant caravan, the range of costs was, not unnaturally, very wide. Anyone who could afford to travel in luxury would expend between 1500 Indian rupees (about £150) and 2000 Indian rupees (about £200) for his riding and baggage animals, equipment, food and sundries, and for the services of an Arabic interpreter. But a poor or very economical traveller could cut down this expenditure to approximately 200 Indian rupees (about £20). So that any figure between these two extremes is entirely credible.[2] The average man who crossed the desert between 1745 and 1790 would not need to spend more than £50 to £60. And this moderate outlay would ensure him a certain amount of comfort. For instance, it cost Bartholomew Plaisted only £48 to travel with a camel caravan from Basra to Aleppo in 1750. A full half of this sum he spent upon a *mohaffa* camel and three baggage camels, with their equipment and six skins of water. The balance he expended upon various sizes of leather water-bottles and skins, food (including bread, rice, sugar, coffee, "clarified" (or boiled)

---

[1] Quoted from J. Griffiths (1805), p. 320. The incident is described on pp. 386–388. The full name of "Mr J." is never given.

[2] In the above quotations the rupees in question were presumably Indian rupees, though this was not specified. See table of moneys and exchange in the eighteenth century, p. 317.

butter, onions, pepper and salt), a servant and a carpet. But his list does not include the indispensable tent and a "travelling kitchen" —both of which were loaned to him by a friend. Major Taylor, in his list of expenses inevitably to be incurred by anyone travelling with a caravan, confirms all these items, including the four camels, the tent and the "kitchen", and he adds bedding and blankets to the list. A box of medicines was also considered highly useful, both for the traveller himself and also for "charitable ministrations" to any Arabs or fellow-travellers who might fall ill during the journey and be in need of simple remedies. In the matter of food, many more articles of diet might be included, but those specified above were the desert staples. In addition, any one or all of the following were acceptable to desert voyagers: fruit drinks (especially the citrous fruit-juices), "essence", vinegar and a kind of sour shrub punch; cold fowls, "potted" meats and tongues, cheese, soup extracts and "dried articles"—such as quinces, spices, sago and biscuits. Also alum was often taken to purify the water that was found *en route*. But potted meats generally turned bad in the summer months; hares, sheep and fowls could be bought on the way, sometimes even goat's milk and eggs, and—from villages such as Kubaisa and Shittat—dates and barley also; and liquor or wine was apt to prove unhealthful, especially in the hot weather. The best drink of all, for those who did not object too strongly to the taste, was—and still is—the native *leben*, a cooling and healthful drink made from sour milk.

The question most difficult to decide was how a person should travel comfortably over the desert. The *mohaffa* was always recommended, but it was far from popular. This was a sort of wooden box to sit in (about five feet high), carried upright like a crude sedan-chair; it was heavily curtained, or hooded, against the sun; sometimes it was padded to ease the jar, or fitted with mattresses, but more often not. A pair of these "panniers" or "cradles", slung from a pole on either side of a camel, would—when occupied— constitute a full load. A *mohaffa* camel was thus enabled to carry two people, or one person and his equivalent in weight on the other side. This was double the capacity of a palanquin-carrier, on which only one person might sit. Some travellers did not mind travelling in these cages, or at least found them preferable to walking or riding in the hot sun. Others preferred to ride the camel Bedu-fashion, or else to ride a horse or an ass, or even to walk—finding the *mohaffa* intolerably stuffy and cramping. William Beawes, in language reminiscent of Pepys, described one as follows:

Our mahoffi terribly fatigues us, and was certainly only intended for such who have only no legs or can bestow them independent of their bodies. It is impossible to maintain a tolerable easy posture for two minutes together, and the motions moreover are so diabolical that I have frequently in a day worse qualms than a breeding woman and am sorer bruised by night than Sancho in his government. However, it keeps the immediate heat of the sun from us, which we should probably find at this season [*i.e.* August] insupportable; tho' here also the benefit is not much greater than being baked instead of roasted, and therefore the mahoffi is but a trumpery machine, and a wheelbarrow in comparison to a princely carriage.[1]

After which indictment it would be hard to persuade the uninitiated of the advantages of this sort of "camel-pannier". The best plan seemed to be to alternate walking—in the cool of the day—with variable periods of "rest" in the *mohaffa*. Or else, as Gaylard Roberts advised, to ride a horse, a mule or a large-sized donkey part of the time, and sit in the "covered cage" during the heat of the day. He particularly recommended large donkeys, which had an easy motion and could be bought quite cheaply, especially in Basra. A horse was an expensive proposition at best, and horses are prone to lameness when driven to work hard in the hot weather on blistering sand-tracks. They are relatively delicate compared to camels and asses; and even when considerately treated and watered regularly, they do not stand up very well under the prolonged strain of a desert crossing. On the whole, horses require

[1] Extract from the diary of William Beawes, 1745, as printed in Hakluyt, lxiii (1929), p. 12.

better food, more water and greater care than the other beasts of burden.

In this period, the cost of a camel varied between £4 and £7; where a reliable "hack" cost at least £8, in Aleppo, and a really good horse could not be had under £37. In Basra one could buy a horse for about 500 Basra rupees (about £37 : 10s.), spend another 100 upon carriage and provisions for the same, and then hope to sell it in Aleppo for about 300 Basra rupees (about £22 : 10s.): if—a big if—it reached there in good condition. In spite of these drawbacks, however, many Englishmen preferred to entrust themselves to an animal with which they were familiar, rather than to travel for so long a time in great discomfort.

Perhaps the worst problem of all was to determine upon one's costume. Was it advisable to wear native dress, or was it not? Should one, or should one not, attempt to disguise oneself? Opinions differed on this important matter. Some averred that to dress in Arab clothes, without being able to speak and act like an Arab, was worse than useless; that such an action would be interpreted as a mark of either servility or cowardice, and the wearer would accordingly be treated with insolent contempt—or worse. This school of thought held that Christians, and especially Englishmen, would be respected so long as they did not lower their dignity by masquerading in the clothes of some other nationality. The opposing school of thought maintained that to travel in native dress was not to attempt an unsuccessful disguise; that the wearing of such a costume would merely evince a spirit of friendliness to the inhabitants, and would be interpreted as a mark of respect and courtesy to one's hosts in an alien land. That to refrain from proclaiming oneself a foreigner would only indicate—on the part of the wearer—a sympathetic tolerance of strange customs and differing religious beliefs. Lastly, it was argued that to be inconspicuous in a throng of people would ensure immunity from unwelcome attention—freedom from incidental discourtesies and random insults. These were the two sides of the question—in theory. In fact, it had apparently been necessary, in the seventeenth century—for safety's sake—to wear native dress; and the custom was handed down to the travellers of the early eighteenth century as almost obligatory. By the nineteenth century, however, it was no longer essential to dress thus in order to travel in the desert. To quote Major Taylor again, it was advisable to compromise: to wear a turban and outer garments of Arabic design; but not necessarily to grow a beard and whiskers! And one should be careful not to wear Mohammed's favourite colour, which was red; nor green, since that was a colour sacred either to those who had made the pilgrimage to Mecca, or else to descendants of the Prophet. Generally speaking, it was believed that to ensure the maximum civil treatment one had to conform a little to the customs of the country.

This question as to the proper and fitting costume to be worn also involved the even more delicate one of weapons. Inexperienced travellers on the desert always insisted upon carrying arms of some sort; but those who knew the ways of Arabs believed, and still believe to this day, that there is no surer way to rouse the ill-feeling of the Beduin, and that an atmosphere of suspicion and ill-feeling generally results in hostilities. A man who is unarmed proclaims, in the most convincing fashion, that he trusts the people he is amongst; and Arabs are peculiarly susceptible to this sort of flattery. Put on their honour to behave chivalrously, they are apt to be chivalrous. But show that you dislike or mistrust them, or ask for trouble by meeting their natural pugnacity more than half-way, and they will show themselves quick to pick a quarrel, eager to find an excuse to plunder a foreigner, and ruthless in their attacks upon him. On the other hand, of course, if a man were travelling under the protection of an armed escort, he might as well be armed as not. One armed man more or less would not incite chance-encountered Beduin to attack a large caravan; so that the *Frangi* (or foreigner) might better be able to reinforce his own guard in case of need. In other words, if one were definitely outnumbered on the desert, one's only salvation would lie in propitiation, in showing extreme trust and friendliness. Otherwise, if the odds were fairly even, then one should carry weapons openly, and show an almost reckless willingness to fight. The Beduin admire personal courage, and therefore, were enforced hostilities to go against a person, they would be more inclined to be generous to a brave—if routed—foe, than not.

The following incident (in the eighteenth century) is indicative of this; and it is not by any means unique, except in its details. A certain young man had joined a merchant caravan bound for Basra. Somewhere beyond Kubaisa, the caravan was waylaid and attacked by several hundred mounted Arabs. The caravan resisted the attack gamely, and the young man, who was armed, did his bit to help repel the robbers. He never knew exactly how the affray turned out, because, in the thick of the fighting, he was knocked on the head. Later that night he came to himself, stripped of all his clothes and tightly bound with cords. By the light of a camp-fire he could make out the faces of some of his captors squatting around it. Having heard stories of their chivalry, he made up his mind to appeal to the shaykh of the tribe. With great good luck he succeeded in picking out the right man, and managed to roll himself (barrel-wise) over to the feet of the shaykh, only to find that this personage knew no language with which he was acquainted. Nothing daunted, he indicated by means of comic grimaces that he was half frozen and hungry. Some of the Arabs were stirred to laughter by his antics—which helped; and the shaykh gathered the impression from his pantomime that the captured Frank was throwing himself on his mercy—which was just what the young man had hoped to achieve. For a painful moment his fate hung in the balance. Then some eloquent—or it might have been some comic—gesture touched the shaykh to magnanimity. The Frank was suddenly released, his own clothes restored to him, and he was served with a hearty meal. The next day the shaykh, all friendliness, sent him on to Basra in the care of a special escort. In such circumstances, a chance remark or action could turn the scale; and, as in this case, the impulsive, child-like Beduin, who react spontaneously to their emotions, can be moved to generosity.

From the preceding explicit details it may be gathered that the journey over the *Great Desert* presented no insuperable obstacles. Quite the contrary. But the traveller who liked things conventionally and tidily arranged, who detested haggling in person or bothering about innumerable details, such a one would find the preparations for this journey irksome. The person who liked to be understood when he talked or issued orders in English, who preferred to ignore alien customs and prejudices, or temperamental differences in his servants and guides, would dread such an expedition as an almost intolerable trial to the spirit; and the daily discomforts of the crossing itself would prove almost equally insupportable to the flesh.

On the other hand, the adventurous traveller, who liked the savour of alien peoples and strange customs, who enjoyed the novelty of the preparations for his trip, who—in short—was intrigued by the playing of a sort of new game, whole-heartedly, would be not at all abashed in the face of a desert crossing. Zest for the game would enable him to cope with all things humorously and in good part. Such, for instance, were Lady Anne Blunt and her husband—though they explored the Syrian Desert and visited the tribes of the Aneza in a leisurely fashion, and were not driven by the compulsion of having to cross in a given direction in the least possible time. Lady Anne saw to the making of their great silken tent, arranging for tent-makers to come to their house in Aleppo to sew it together under her personal supervision. Mr Wilfrid Blunt was vastly interested in trying out—in person— and bargaining for their horses, and in selecting their baggage animals. And on their journeys, every new stretch of desert or oasis to which they came was eagerly explored, and fully appreciated for its beauty or interest. Moreover, the prospect of spending several months completely out of reach of "Christian aid" seems to have inspired them with but few actual qualms.

Certain of the diaries of those who adventured in the *Great Desert*, a century earlier, show traces of this same questing spirit, this interest in the new and the unknown; in spite of the fact that the earlier travellers undertook their journeying from purely business motives.

CHAPTER VI

PRIVATE CARAVANS OF THE GREAT DESERT ROUTE

I

ROUTINE OF TRAVEL AND DAILY INCIDENTS

WE have seen the preparations necessary for a desert crossing, the traveller's choice of routes and manner of travel, his contracting for transportation and requisite equipment. It is now possible to think of the journey itself, and conjure up in imagination the routine of daily travel across the Great Desert Route, and to some extent, the Route itself. And since a separate chapter is devoted to the organization and customs of the merchant caravans, it will simplify the picture to consider only an example of one of the smaller, privately hired caravans.

Suppose an imaginary company of five Englishmen were ready to set out for Basra, with a guard of forty armed Arabs to escort them; then they would need sixteen baggage camels to carry their personal boxes, water and other supplies. In addition, imagine them to desire three riding horses, for which two extra camels would be needed to carry food and water; and a *mohaffa* camel, on which two men might be carried simultaneously, in panniers slung on either side of the animal. Half a dozen spare camels would have to be taken along, in case some of those laden were to sicken or die, as well as an extra *mohaffa* camel—since, on account of the necessity of having a balanced load, the double *mohaffa* could never be divided between two camels.

The first day out from Aleppo, only a few miles would be covered, because, with the best intentions in the world, there would be innumerable delays in getting all the caravan together, and the places of each and all assigned in the line of march, in

accordance with the dictates of the caravan leader. So a word as to
the ruler of this highly organized little community, which was a
self-dependent and very nearly a self-sufficient unit, is necessary.
The caravan *bashi*, or leader, was (as has before been hinted) solely
responsible for the welfare of the caravan under his charge. This
meant that he was an absolute dictator, whether in the making of
important decisions or in the details of organization. He it was
who decided when to load and unload the camels; he apportioned
the siesta hours, chose the camp site, and gave the signal for brief
halts and for the evening meal. The scouts who preceded the
caravan took their orders from him alone, and made their reports
to him. If the *bashi* decided that a detour was expedient, or necessary for safety's sake, the necessity was unquestioned by the rest
of the caravan; if he decided that a forced march was essential,
there was no appeal. Like the master of a ship at sea, his word was
law until the desert crossing had been made, safely or otherwise.

The rising hour of the travellers and the daily loading of the
camels always took place very early in the morning. The decision
of the caravan leader as to which particular hour it should be—
between two in the morning and sunrise—depended upon the
season of the year; the hotter the month, the earlier was it necessary
to start, in order to accomplish the day's allotted stage; but it was
never later than sunrise, and usually just before dawn. A day's
march was spaced according to the distance between supplies of
water, unless a time-limit for the journey had been agreed upon in
the contract, when the daily stage was allotted more arbitrarily and
artificially.

But to return to the daily schedule. As soon as the *bashi* gave
the signal, the cameleers helped to pack up tents and camp
utensils, and then proceeded to load their camels as speedily as
possible. They would already have swallowed hastily a cup of
bitter black coffee; and the travellers would drink theirs while the
men were loading, and perhaps have some Arab bread to go with
it. Once under way, the caravan—as a unit—did not halt until
midday. Then the noon hour was whiled away with some more
black coffee and some light, uncooked refreshment: dates, perhaps,

or any of the dried articles which were itemized in the preceding chapter. For this brief halt, the camels were not lightened
of their loads. After one or more hours, the caravan continued on
its way until an hour before sunset, having covered roughly thirty
miles in the course of the day's march. Whenever possible, it was
considered advisable to halt early enough in the day to pitch camp
comfortably before the sun went down. Occasionally, when the
caravan was not pressed for time, the noon halt was much
lengthened, or even prolonged over the rest of the day—especially·
during the summer months. The merchant caravans often travelled
by moonlight, thus marching later, or breaking camp earlier in
the morning than private caravans. The latter, after all, were
generally able to make some small allowance for individual
comfort.

As soon as the site had been selected for the night's camp, the
camels were unloaded, hobbled, and then turned loose to graze.
Camel-thorn was the best they had to hope for, except in the
season when the spring grasses flourished. Camel-thorn and dried
dung furnished the only available fuel for the camp-fires, which
were laid and lighted directly after the tents were pitched. The
tents of the *Inglesi* were generally set up at a little distance from the
main body of the caravan, to windward, if the lie of the land permitted. The evening repast, the only cooked meal of the day,
was then prepared.

Food was a problem to all but the Arabs. Unless the Englishmen
had brought special food for themselves, the "luxuries" such as
potted meats, biscuits, preserved fruits, special drinks and so forth,
they would have to share the communal rations. Boiled rice, as the
foundation for some variety of pilaff, was the staple dish. Perhaps
a sheep had been bought of wandering Beduin for from three to
seven Turkish piastres (roughly, 15s. to 35s.), or some fowls at
half a piastre (2s. 6d.) apiece. If they had passed near a village—
such as Shittat—the caravan might have obtained dates and barley
as well, or even milk and eggs. If a camel fell sick, and was obviously incurable, it was killed and eaten with relish—by all except
the *Inglesi*. Still, the best suppers of all were eaten when part of

the day's march had been passed in hunting. Hares were plentiful almost everywhere on the desert, and so were a kind of partridge or grouse. The hares were often cooked by baking them in the ground, much as the native bread was made. Tavernier gave a circumstantial account of this bread-making, a process which does not vary from century to century. "The people", as he called the Arab members of his caravan, dug a round hole in the desert, six inches deep, and from two to three feet in diameter. This hole was filled with "bushes", to which they set fire. Then they cleaned the heated hole, and packed into it dough, which had been pre-pared in a round copper utensil. Lastly, they covered over the holes with hot stones, and left the dough to bake overnight. Arab bread, when baked in this way, is about two fingers thick and as "big as an ordinary cake".

Partridge- and hare-hunting was a welcome diversion in itself, quite aside from the fact that its results—if any—helped to vary the evening menu. Occasionally, Arabs would bring falcons with them, to give added interest to the chase, for they were reputed to be very skilful in hunting and killing hares with a "stick", which they flung so dexterously "as seldom to miss their aim". Once in a while the escort would treat the company to another sort of entertainment, a sword dance, in the performance of which they circled about their banners, planted upright in the sand, and kept time to a kind of high-pitched, toneless music which they chanted lustily as they danced. This "compliment" was of course always rewarded by a gift of twenty Turkish piastres or so (about £5), and followed by a special supper—at the expense of the *Inglesi*.

Such in brief was the routine of desert travel. There was little occasion for its variation, and but few opportunities for its enlivenment. Not infrequently a traveller, when mounted on horseback, would leave the caravan for a few hours or more in order to explore some near-by village or ruin of archaeo-logical interest. But with the exception of such brief excur-sions, there was little change from day to day in the orderly life of the caravan.

2

DESERT LANDMARKS, AND ITINERARY OF THE ROUTE

At this point in our narrative, the attention of the reader is called to Major Rennell's map of the Great Desert Route (see p. 106). This is the only authoritative and contemporary map on which this particular desert road was traced. The sketch maps which were made by some travellers are interesting; a few, such as Colonel Capper's, are even quite good; but they are all inaccurate. This map of Major Rennell's, on the other hand, is more nearly accurate than any other map of this region which was made previous to the middle of the nineteenth century; although it must be admitted that most of the mountains indicated in Palmyrena are incorrectly placed. Furthermore, Major Rennell consulted the works of all the travellers who had preceded him, and he used their information in his tracing of the desert road. This, as may be seen, is embellished with descriptive remarks concerning the nature of the country traversed thereby. It is interesting to compare the differences in the spelling of Arabic names as they appear on this map, dated 1809, with the same place-names on modern maps. For example, Al Kadder on Major Rennell's map is the modern Ukhaidir; Ayun al Kûm has become Ain el-Kom; and Kasr Aukheim, which was the older form of the name Kasr el-Akhwan, is now generally known as Kasr el-Hair. For the convenience of the reader, every place mentioned in the following itinerary will be given in its modern form, and followed (in brackets) by Major Rennell's spelling of the same name.

Landmarks, or places of importance along the Great Desert Route, number little more than a dozen. The first place to be noted by the East-bound traveller is the *Sebkha*: "Sebkha Jebbul", the Valley of Salt. This is a vast saline depression which lies southeast of Aleppo. It is turned into a lake by the winter rains, and it evaporates into caked, crystalline deposits of salt in the summer. But, except for its geological interest, and the fact that it long

13

supplied the *Pashalik* of Aleppo with salt for trading purposes, the *Sebkha* is less spectacular than an ordinary mirage. Near the western end of the depression the Route passes through two mud villages, clusters of domed huts which have been likened by some travellers to beehives, and by others to sugar-loaves. The first of these, Sfira, was the customs station for Aleppo, where all caravans travelling thither from Irak were inspected. After leaving the second of these villages, Hikla (Hagla), the caravan descends into a plain, leaving Jebel Shubait on its left and the long ridge of Jebel el-Hass on its right.

Thereafter, until the Bishri ranges (Jebel Busheer) come into view, the flat surfaces of sand and shale yield nothing of interest to the sightseer. Nothing, that is, except an occasional encampment of black tents, the "houses of hair" which mark the temporary resting-place of a Beduin tribe. These mushroom villages look today as they have always done, rows of little sloping-roofed, rectangular tents, set up in straight lines which flank a broad centre path, or "street". Dozens of stray dogs—efficient scavengers— bark the stranger on and off the village premises; and the community life of all its inhabitants centres in the *raison d'être* of the encampment, a spring or well with its crudely fashioned trough, equipped with a goatskin bucket or an earthenware jar.

Taiyiba (often called Tayba, Tibia or Tiaba by the earlier travellers) is set high on a fortified citadel to the west of the Bishri Mountains. The Route passed alternatively through this town, or else four or five miles to the north and east of Taiyiba, through Ain el-Kom (Ayun al Kûm), which was then, and still is, noted for the excellence of its numerous mineral springs. Several other villages grew up on the slopes and along the foothills of the ranges that run diagonally south-west from the Euphrates to Palmyra— wherever, in fact, springs found their way to the arid surface. But Taiyiba has always been the most noteworthy of these villages. The first mention of Taiyiba—originally called Ord—was in the annals of Assurbanipal, about 638 B.C. In the sixteenth and seven- teenth centuries it was a walled and fortified town with possibly as many as 600 inhabitants. Pedro Teixeira, who described it in the first decade of the seventeenth century, noted the remains of Christian buildings and the belfry which had been converted into a mosque; and he counted over 250 houses there. But the glory of Taiyiba was her springs; as at Sukhna, further to the south-west, and at Palmyra, there were hot sulphur springs as well as the sweet waters for drinking. Unquestionably, this town was once prosperous and important. In 1625 Pietro della Valle even mentions that a certain Italian-speaking Arab, by the name of Berekiet, posed as a "Factor or Procurator of the Franks, saying he had the authority so to be from the Consuls of Aleppo". At that time both Taiyiba and Sukhna, or Sukana (as it was then called), were held by the Emir of Anna as a *Sanjak*, in fief to the Sultan. But before William Beawes crossed the desert in 1745, Taiyiba had been deserted and almost entirely ruined.

Sukhna, also a walled town, was only visited by caravans which were on their way to or from Palmyra; and Teixeira states that in his day it was only about half the size of its more northern neighbour. He claims to have been told that, in the days before the Turkish conquest of the region, both these towns were founded to serve as forts in aid of caravans: Sukhna on the Damascus–Palmyra route between Baghdad and Basra, and Taiyiba on the Aleppo branch of the route to these Mesopotamian cities. He adds that guards were accustomed to escort caravans to one or the other town, and then turn them over to the garrisons of Sukhna or Taiyiba—according to their destination—where further guards were provided to escort them on their way.

Today, both Taiyiba and Sukhna are only small mud villages; and the latter—to which the few remaining inhabitants of the older Taiyiba fled in the eighteenth century—is now the larger of the two. The modern Arab village of Taiyiba is built on top of the high citadel which probably formed the acropolis of the ancient town.

Occasionally one sees the tomb, become a shrine, of some Moslem *Hajji*, set high on a hill-top in the neighbourhood of Sukhna and Taiyiba. General Sir Eyre Coote described such a shrine when he visited Taiyiba in the latter part of the eighteenth century. He climbed the hill to the southward of the town, to see what the building on its summit might contain. In the tomb he found the embalmed body of a "saint", stretched upon a canopied bier; oil lamps were set in niches round the walls, and these were kept lighted (presumably by the Arabs); verses from the Koran were inscribed upon the walls, and the roof of the cupola was adorned with ostrich eggs.

Whether caravans passed through Taiyiba or went more directly through Ain el-Kom, they all followed the same mountain pass to the south-east, the southern entrance of which is guarded by the ancient ruined castle called Kasr el-Hair (Kasr Aukheim). Since this is the most interesting of all the isolated ruins in the middle of the Syrian Desert, it is worth describing in some detail. Kasr el-Hair is a double ruin: two splendid square buildings, constructed of reddish brick and yellowish white limestone. The larger one, though less well built than the small *kasr*, is almost twice its size; many towers are built into the walls of them both. It is conceded by most authorities that the two forts were built at different periods. The smaller one, which may have been a fortified summer palace, is almost certainly pre-Islamic; its ornamentation is definitely Byzantine, and indicates that it may have been built at the same time as the Byzantine town of Resafa-Sergiopolis. The larger fortified building was probably a walled town of the Omayyad period, and may have been built about A.D. 728–729. According to one theory, it seems likely that an agricultural colony, whose colonists were mainly from Homs, grew up near the already existing fortress-palace; such a colony would have had the protection of its garrison and the benefit of its irrigation system. When a permanent refuge became necessary, on account of the Beduin, the settlement was walled. A watch-tower stands between the two *kasrs*, which are more than 125 feet apart. There are the traces of walled gardens and orchards, and the remains of two aqueducts which once supplied the twin buildings with water in abundance. The finest of these aqueducts was laid along the fourteen-mile stretch of desert separating Kasr

UKHAIDIR

el-Hair from Ain el-Kom. In the immediate vicinity of the two buildings are also the traces of a huge enclosure: a section of its retaining wall is still standing, a wall that is buttressed and pierced with very low arches at regular intervals. Archaeologists disagree in their explanations of the use to which the arches of these walls were put. One hypothesis is that there was once a great artificial lake, measuring five and a half miles in length by almost a mile in width; and that the low arches of these walls were probably equipped with sluice-gates to regulate the distribution of the water thus enclosed. A reservoir of this sort would have assured a constant supply of water for extensive gardens in the neighbourhood of the *kasr* and its walled village or town. A conflicting hypothesis, which depends for its validity upon the assumption that the annual rainfall of Palmyrena (as recently as the beginning of the Saracen period) was more abundant than it is today, holds that these walls were used to enclose vast gardens, for which these low arches provided the necessary drainage. Modern gardens in the oasis of Palmyra and in some of the villages of Jebel Druze are enclosed with similar (arched and buttressed) walls: these modern enclosures furnish a possible analogy for the walled-garden theory. According to this latter hypothesis, the aqueducts would have brought additional supplies of water to Kasr el-Hair, but there would have been no need for so large a reservoir. If the whole of this desert triangle was formerly much more fertile than at present; if flocks pastured the year round where now the spring grasses grow most thickly, then there is reason enough to believe the legend that gardens once bloomed amongst these hills between Ain el-Kom, Taiyiba and Kasr el-Hair. At least, as recently as 1909, Musil stated that with the aid of irrigation the whole vicinity of Taiyiba and Kasr el-Hair might be cultivated.[1]

After passing the *kasr*, the hills are left behind, and the caravan

[1] Alois Musil, *Palmyrena*, pp. 77 and 81. A controversy on the subject of the enclosure at Kasr el-Hair has been carried on in the pages of the archaeological publication called *Syria*, by A. Gabriel and Henri Seyrig. Monsieur Gabriel originated the reservoir theory, and Monsieur Seyrig subsequently evolved the enclosed-garden hypothesis. Cf. *Syria*, vol. viii (1927), pp. 304-322; vol. xii (1931), pp. 316-318; vol. xiii (1932), pp. 317-320.

crosses a very level tract of desert to the Jubb el-Ghanam (Jub al Gannam). This "Sheep's Well", or rather group of wells, was a much used watering-place at the convergence of several caravan routes. One at least of the wells is rock-cut and extraordinarily deep. The whole group is in the heart of a region that Major Rennell marked on his atlas as a "Great Sheep Walk", when the surrounding land was capable of supporting many more flocks of sheep and goats than it is able to do at present. Teixeira, who was most painstaking and accurate in his descriptions, mentioned passing many encampments of "Turkymanis" with their flocks of cattle, sheep, camels and mules all the way between Sukhna and Anna; and he described all this country as "fertile". Just south of here the Wadi Suab (Battan Suab) must be crossed, the first of a series of wadis on this Route, the greatest of which is the Hauran. And soon thereafter the western foothills of *Jebel Erzi* are rounded.

Near el-Ghaim (Guiam) the Euphrates is sighted for the first time; and by this wide bend of the river, one of the two principal Baghdad routes cuts across to Anna (Anah). Unfortunately for such travellers as liked to see interesting places, Anna (known to the Assyrians as Anat) was rarely if ever approached near enough by the Basra caravans for side trips to be made to that town. In the seventeenth century Anna was built on both sides of the Euphrates. It had two main streets which ran for several miles along each river-bank, and its citadel stood on a walled island in mid-stream. When Teixeira passed through, this ancient town boasted an unusual number of large water-wheels, "great mills", spindle shops for the weaving of wool and cotton, two-storied stone houses, and "thirty great boats" for trading on the river. Today, Anna is still an important market town for the Beduin, and its chief produce is cotton.

Hit, even more ancient than Anna, was equally out of the path of the Basra-bound traveller. Though smaller than Anna, and less well built, it was still more famous because of its wells of liquid pitch.[1]

---

[1] Hit, as early as the ninth century B.C., was known as *Id* (on account of its pitch springs); and the name *Id*, after being called *Is* by Herodotus, eventually took the form of Hit.

Ibn Battuta, who visited these towns almost three centuries earlier than the often-quoted Teixeira, described the country between them as one of the most fertile and therefore beautiful regions he had seen in all his travels. In his eyes, the country of "the River of China" was its only rival—so attractive were the tilled fields along the Euphrates, and the widespread orchards of fruit, olive and date trees. But after the eighteenth century much of this district was laid waste. The Turkish garrisons of Anna and Hit were first reduced and eventually withdrawn; the Emirs troubled very little about keeping their fortifications in repair; and the inhabitants, less and less able to defend themselves against the Beduin, sadly declined in numbers as well as in prosperity. But notwithstanding this decline, a twentieth-century date-palm census of Hit gives an estimate of 50,000 trees.

However, this is digressing too far. The Great Desert Route kept well out in the desert, from fifteen to thirty miles west of the river. Caravans occasionally left the customary track to approach the Euphrates more closely, but such was not their habit. At one of the few places where the river was approached within about five miles, it was for the purpose of crossing the Wadi Hauran at the most convenient spot. An exception in the other direction was made between Felluja (Feluja) and Kerbela (Meshed Hossain). Along this reach, where the Euphrates sweeps eastward toward the Tigris, caravans consistently kept almost fifty miles distant from the river. A desire to travel as fast as possible was partly responsible for their cutting across the desert, beyond the numerous bends of the river. But fear of riverain thieves, and a determination to avoid the payment of all unnecessary tolls, were undoubtedly the chief considerations. For instance, after crossing the Wadi Hauran, caravans usually made a fairly wide detour to avoid Kubaisa (Kubessa). Individual travellers, or some members of the escorting guard, often went in to forage for extra supplies; but the caravan itself generally encamped from one to six miles outside Kubaisa, frequently at Ain el-Arnab (Ayan al Arneb), the Hare's Pool. This spring is more than five miles away from the village, which is set in a large grove of date-palms. Only caravans which purposed crossing the Euphrates at Hit, *en route* for Baghdad, had to leave the Basra track there and go through Kubaisa.

The next landmarks south of Kubaisa, not counting one of the inevitable wadis, are the pitch spring or "bitumen fountain"— *Abu Kir*—and an abandoned mud fort called Thumail (Tammel). These two places are about twenty-five miles west of Lake Habbania, a lake which, in the spring months, often unites with the Euphrates to flood all the land between Ramadi and Felluja —which land remains thus inconveniently inundated for many weeks.

Thereafter the caravan was obliged to skirt two more oases, Rahhaliya (Rahally) and Shittat (Shittar), for the same reasons that Kubaisa was avoided. These towns have very fine date-palms, and with their produce the inhabitants trade with Basra; but in the eighteenth century they both had evil names. Shittat in particular was notorious for its thieves, and for the shelter it afforded marauding nomads.

Possibly the most imposing ruin which travellers had the opportunity of seeing was that of Ukhaidir (Al Kadder): an immense fortress-palace, thought to have been built in the Lakhmid period. It is almost fifty miles due west from Hilla (Hellah).[1] This walled building, or rather group of buildings, constructed of brick and stone, stands alone near the edge of a wadi. Tavernier, in the seventeenth century, described its three large courts, two-storied arches, and a lake with a brick-paved canal leading from it. A century later John Carmichael gave a much more detailed account of Al Kander, as he called Ukhaidir. So "magnificent" were these ruins that he was "almost persuaded" they were a part of ancient Babylon! He noted its many bastions and turrets, the even more numerous arches and arched gateways. The "envelope" or outer walls which surround the castle, stables and "parades" or courtyard, form a square that actually measures over 500 feet each way.

[1] Until the twentieth century, Ukhaidir was not well known; one of the best modern accounts of the place has been given us by Miss Gertrude Bell.

Carmichael found "plenty of water" there, but he makes no mention of any lake.

Another ancient ruin, of nearly as much interest, is to be found where the Eastern Pilgrim Road crosses the Route. This is Umm el-Kurun: a large reservoir, fifty yards square, presided over by an imposing fort.

Twenty miles north of there, the caravan must have passed within sight of the famous golden dome of Meshed Ali, which shines at a distance like a "globe of fire". Unlike the Shi'a shrine at Kerbela, Meshed Ali—or Najaf as it was also called—was near enough to the Basra route to be visited by travellers. But its inhabitants, like those of the other Shi'ite town, were exceptionally fanatical Moslems of the official Iranian sect. It was not safe for an unbeliever to stay in Meshed Ali, and it was as much as his life was worth to try to see the tomb of Ali, the Prophet's son-in-law. William Beawes inspected the town (one of the four most holy cities of Islam) and the outer courtyard of the mosque; but he was not allowed to visit the shrine or to see the tomb, which was supposed to be adorned with matchless jewels. He saw that the mitre-shaped dome and the minarets of the mosque were sheathed with plates of gilded copper; and that the outside of the building was tastefully decorated with azure and gold "fret work"; but the rest of his observations were perforce restricted to the town itself. He, like other and earlier travellers, found the houses to be mean and neglected, "more like heaps of rubbish than dwellings", the only building of any consequence being the *khan*, or caravanserai, which had been built and was maintained by various Shahs of Iran for the housing of Iranian pilgrims. But the intermittent periods of Turkish domination had been long and disastrous; the conquerors, who were orthodox Sunni, had reduced the Shi'ite inhabitants of Najaf to poverty and their town to a shell. They had respected only the shrine itself. Half a hundred years after Beawes' visit to Meshed Ali, Dr. Julius Griffiths stopped on his way to Basra to see the Holy City. Taking advantage of the siesta hour, he was rash enough to look inside the Mosque of Ali. On leaving, he was stoned (almost to death) for his sacrilege. Within the mosque, what chiefly caught his eye were the ornaments of the shrine: balls of ivory, glass, ostrich eggs, "a prodigious number of lamps", two huge silver candlesticks and a great many, very small "rich carpets" on the floor.

Meshed Ali is the last town of interest near the Route; and after crossing the *Darb Zubayda*, the caravan passes only an occasional, shapeless ruin, an infrequent Arab encampment or mud village, and two wadis. This last stretch of more than two hundred miles was, apparently, the very worst part of the whole journey. The desert proved excessively sandy and bare, the weather was always hotter, and the frequent watering-places supplied only the most brackish and unwholesome water.

Two to three hours' distance from Basra is the mud village of Zebeir (Zobeir), the caravan station where tolls were collected. There, if any merchandise was being imported into Basra, caravans were detained for inspection and the payment of their dues. There also were all accounts settled with desert shaykhs who exacted tribute for their safe-conducts. At Zebeir travellers would leave their camels and ride on ahead of the caravan into Basra, generally on fresh mounts. Horses were customarily provided by the Resident, who was in the habit of sending out an escort to meet any incoming caravan of whose approach he had been notified by advance messenger.

So much for what one of our travellers, Bartholomew Plaisted, would call a barren description of a very barren country. And yet, according to the preceding itinerary, it was not so very desolate after all. This same Plaisted, who was so impressed with the barrenness of the country through which he voyaged, made a few general remarks upon the nature of the passage over the "Great Syrian Desert". As he summarizes very neatly what a number of his compatriots also thought about the same journey, it may not be out of place to quote a few sentences from his closing paragraphs.

I have been the more particular in making my observations on the nature of the soil as we passed along, because this desert has generally been represented as a level sandy plain; whereas in reality the greatest part is a hard sandy gravel like some of our heaths in England. In some places it is full of large loose stones, and in others full of small hills, which are more barren than the valleys or plains, for these are generally full of shrubs, and the lower the situation the more green they are. However, these are but few in comparison of the rest, for the greatest part are dry and parched by the heat of the sun, insomuch that they will take fire as readily as shavings; and yet these are all the food the camels have to live upon. [Plaisted, it may be remembered, crossed from Basra to Aleppo in the months of June and July.] All the hills between Busserah [Basra] and Tayba [Taiyiba] seem to be little else but stones.

There is no want of water, as is commonly supposed, when you travel the common track; but then it is generally bad, and therefore it is the quality but not the quantity that is most to be complained of. . . .

But though the water is so bad, the air, except in the rainy season, is always pure and serene. . . .

Before I entered the desert, I apprehended there would be great difficulty in travelling such an extent of ground; but I soon found myself mistaken, for the road is easily found, unless you are obliged to leave the common track. Their rules are always to call at the same watering-places, to which they are guided by the hills and valleys, which are well known to those who have often passed that way. Besides they are assisted by the sun; and in many places the way is beaten like our footpaths in England, where the tracks made by the camels are very visible. Indeed, in some places there is no such thing to be seen; but then it is where the land is marshy or the soil loose and sandy, and then they are directed altogether by the sun and hills. Sometimes, perhaps, they may stray a little out of their direct way, but they soon get into it again. The tracks are very easily known, for there are many of them running parallel to each other for several miles in breadth; insomuch that it is almost impossible to make any mistake. Besides, there are single men who carry

letters every month from Busserah to Aleppo, which could not
be so easily performed if the road were difficult to find. Add to
this, that there are other tracts which run across the desert from
one watering-place to another. In short, there is not the least
danger in mistaking the way to those who are the least used to
the road: but if a caravan is obliged to wander out of their
knowledge, then they may be reduced to the greatest extremities
for want of water.

Apparently the prospective travellers of Plaisted's day were
known to be nervous about getting lost on the desert. He might
have added for their comfort what another English traveller remarked upon, namely, that sometimes all tracks were completely
obliterated by sand, whenever high winds or dust-storms occurred,
but that if ever a caravan *bashi* and his men got lost, they pitched
camp and waited for the night to fall, in order to get their bearings
from the stars. Desert Arabs are excellent navigators at night.

This record of a journey from Basra to Aleppo is very detailed
and full of advice to desert travellers. The author was at much
pains to make a note of everything which he considered useful.
His account was intended to be a sort of compendium of helpful
hints for various friends in Bengal who might, at some later day,
be called upon to travel home by the desert way. Thinking himself to be the first English traveller to cross with a camel caravan
(he had joined one of the great caravans numbering about 5000
camels), Plaisted excused himself for verbosity in the following
words:

I know that letters have been sent from Aleppo by a few who
have past this desert, but without many particulars of their
journey over it, either because they kept no journal or because
they were so immersed in pleasures at Aleppo that all their
former hardships vanished out of their mind. However I am the
first who crossed it with the camel caravan, and probably have
been the greatest sufferer on that account; and perhaps am the
only person who was at the trouble of writing each day's

CAMEL CARAVAN WAITING TO ENTER ZEBEIR, NEAR BASRA

occurrences, after having been cooped up in a cajava [*mohaffa*] for thirteen hours together.[1]

Plaisted does not appear to have been a particularly patient traveller, or a man who was easy to please and knew how to take things as he found them; so his own disposition may account for his slightly jaundiced view of the desert journey as a whole. It is possible that his Indian experiences, and various quarrels with fellow-servants of the East India Company, accentuated a certain irritableness of temper which is traceable in his writing. Also, he crossed the desert in the most uncomfortable of all ways, with a large caravan of unladen camels.

3

DIFFICULTIES AND DANGERS OF THE DESERT CROSSING.
ADVICE TO TRAVELLERS

This seems an opportune place to examine the question of risks. What exactly were the dangers, and how serious were the discomforts of this desert crossing? It may be easier to enumerate the lesser hazards first, in order to relegate them the more quickly to an appropriate limbo of oblivion. As was sagely observed by the first Anglo-Indian to travel by the Great Desert Route: ". . . it is supposed that those who undertake to travel any parts of the East are informed that long stages, a slow pace, course far[e], and a warm sun are to be the common trials of their patience and constitution". Still, the stages were often longer and slower, the daily rations worse, and the sun much "warmer" than the traveller bargained for; and there were other trials, such as insect pests, vipers and poisonous scorpions—particularly rife in the summer months—which often made caravan life very hard to bear. But these also

---

[1] The above quotations are from "A Journey from Calcutta in Bengal, by Sea, to Busserah: From thence across the Great Desert to Aleppo", by Bartholomew Plaisted, as printed in Hakluyt, Second Series, No. lxiii (1929), pp. 90, 91, 100-102. Plaisted crossed the Desert in 1750.

were doubtless expected—with some trepidation. Then there was the wind which was ever-present. In September the north-east wind was grumbled about because it raised "thick clouds of fine sand" (*i.e.* dust-storms). In April and May it was the north-west wind, which blew as from a "glass furnace", and resulted in both sore eyes and painful lungs. Pietro della Valle complained bitterly of the wind in June, that "blows continually in the Desart"; it first shattered and finally destroyed all the "little pavilions" in his caravan, so that for the rest of the journey they bivouacked without tents, and had to improvise shelters made of their clothes. The worst of all the winds blew from the south-east; it was known, in summer, as the "poison wind". So devastating was this simoom (called *shamel*, or *samiel*, by Europeans in the eighteenth century) that even Arabs died from inhaling it, and could only hope to survive if they kept their mouths covered. In summer, too, the heat was often more than just a trial. Teixeira commented on the deaths of over eight camels and several asses, all from the exhaustion caused by heat and thirst. But even so, one rarely reads of human beings dying from this kind of exposure. One of the few such tragedies was that of a Mr Hayes, the travelling companion of Dr. Julius Griffiths. Fear of Arabs drove their caravan out of the track; a well which the caravan *bashi* had counted upon using was found to be dry; and the caravan was forced to travel without any water at all for several days. Mr Hayes was not in good enough health to survive forty-eight days of such travelling, with the thermometer registering between 95° and 116°, so he died before reaching Basra. And yet, his little daughter, Marianne, who was only seven years old, lived through the ordeal. A Captain Currie, when he returned from India to England shortly after 1786, took Marianne Hayes back across the Syrian Desert to Aleppo.

In winter, the hardships caused by bitter cold winds, freezing nights and heavy downpours of rain, were severely trying to the traveller; although conditions resulting from intense cold are more disagreeable than harmful. Still, tents were not infallibly waterproof; and damp bedding, to say nothing of wet clothing, is not exactly healthful. One Englishman, who was painfully surprised by the intensity of the desert cold, remarked that ice even "attached itself to our whiskers"; and more than one traveller noted that not only pools, but also the water in the goatskins, froze so solid that they could not get a drink from the skins until noon or after. In some places the ground would become so slippery in the rain that laden camels could not keep their footing; and if the camels slipped badly enough to fall, a caravan would have no choice but to halt until the rain was over. Or, if a freezing surface caused the camels to slip, a caravan would have to wait until the sun thawed the ground. But extreme conditions such as these occurred only in midwinter. Sometimes in January or February there were even snow-storms; at least a series of snowfalls, each sufficient to delay a caravan for several days at a time, so that a journey normally taking only six weeks might require nine weeks of travel. A special difficulty confronted those who counted upon using water pools rather than wells or springs. If they were shallow and frozen over, they would yield—when broken—only a mixture of mud and ice.

While on the subject of water supply, one might as well stop to consider this perennial problem. As Plaisted said, there was generally plenty of water along the "common track", but it was usually bad. This was certainly true of most of the water obtainable in the summer months. "Foul" was the adjective most often applied to it. Shallow pools were bound to be salty or brackish; the water of many of the springs was extremely unpalatable— either sulphurous or bituminous to the taste—and often it was unhealthful enough to cause intestinal troubles. In midsummer, many wells and water pools went dry, or partially so. Then it was less a question of finding water than of reaching it ahead of some- one else. Suppose a watering to be barely adequate for a small caravan of fifty people plus their animals: consider their position if a nomad tribe found it first. Mercifully, many travellers appear to have been ignorant of the possibility of such an accident, though one or two thought to enquire why their caravan *bashis* so often planned to reach a watering-place at break of day. But a traveller's most trying experience was to see a clean spring or water pool fouled by the animals of his own caravan. This happened whenever the animals got a chance to stampede, which they did frequently in the hot weather. Thirsty camels could smell water long before it was visible to humans. Moreover, in the large merchant caravans, Arabs customarily allowed their animals to drink before they filled their own water-skins, in case there was not enough water to go round. This custom grew out of rivalry between the cameleers, each one of whom was determined that his own charges should be adequately watered. They were so dependent upon their camels that they were forced to consider them and their ability to carry on before even themselves. After the camels and other pack animals had been watered, the Arabs would then draw their own water; when they would occasionally treat it in the following way before refilling the goatskins. They were accustomed to boil such water first (as Miss Bell has stated), and then throw into it a powder which they ground from a white chalky kind of stone; and after this powder had precipitated the mud at the bottom of the boiling pot, they would be able to pour off clean water. But Musil claims that the Beduin drink muddy (even fouled) water without first treating it in any way. Europeans naturally gave much attention to this problem, both to the quality and the quantity of procurable water. They were always advised to make a special arrangement with the caravan *bashi* for the replenishing of their supplies *en route*; and they were assured that one camel could carry enough for three men, since it was reckoned that three days was the maximum distance between watering-places. It was also earnestly recommended that travellers buy their own water-skins, and supervise (in person) their refilling at each and every place, in order to make sure that they were always given their own clean skins to drink out of. Six full water-skins were reckoned to be the maximum load of a single camel. Travellers also had various devices for filtering water. The easiest and most accepted method was to strain it from the large goatskins, through several thicknesses of muslin, into the small leather bottles which they carried on their persons. Some people tried to purify it first with alum; but when they did, they were disappointed to find that one bad taste had merely been substituted for another. The water of certain mineral springs, when jostled about in goatskins for about twenty-four hours, generally became sweet to the taste. This, as one Englishman remarked, "was but small compensation" for having first had to drink it in its original and "nauseous" state.

Turning from the subject of mere physical hardships to more tangible difficulties, there were the Arabs. To read the accounts of some travellers, one might think that the European members of a caravan were imprisoned in a den of thieves; they believed themselves to be tricked and robbed by every Arab in the caravan, from the leader to the cameleers. They were perpetually apprehensive of thieves within, and of stray robbers without, who might prowl about the encampment at night; and they particularly feared *ghrazzus* (more accurately *ghazw*), or raids by Arab bandits. These raiding bandits they visualized as swarming over every section of the desert route, either lying in wait to attack each caravan which crossed, or else actually in league with their caravan *bashi*. He, as the unavowed partner in all contemplated robberies, was pictured as ever ready to betray the company in his charge to Beduin shaykhs, in return for a substantial share of the profits.

To what extent were such dark suspicions justifiable? That is a very difficult question to answer fairly. It is as though one were to ask how dangerous highwaymen used to be, in the days of stage-coaches! There were just enough examples of all the things that were feared to justify such apprehensions. But there was not enough continuity in this kind of incident to support extravagant fears. All had occurred at one time or another; but very rarely to the same caravan. Thieving and robbery, whether on a large scale or a small one, was spasmodic, like the "crime waves" of a more modern era.

Consider the caravan *bashis*, for example. Some of them were dishonest, as in the previously cited case of "Mr J." (see p. 180). Others were dishonest in other ways, insisting upon hiring unnecessary guides for pointless detours, or borrowing money for "unforeseen" expenses and tolls—which money they never paid back. Some *bashis* were out and out villains, like the one who

14

conspired with a traitorous Pasha of Baghdad to lead his caravan into an appointed ambush, and then, when it was set upon by an armed band of horsemen, withdrew to one side with his escort and watched the plundering take its course. This sort of thing, however, rarely happened after 1750. Leaders of the merchant caravans sometimes tyrannized over Franks who joined them. They would exact payments from them on one pretext or another, quarrel with their servants, and encourage Beduin (who stopped the caravan for customary tributes) to ransack the luggage of the *Frangi*, and demand as a "gift" whatever they found to covet. The Beduin did not, of course, hesitate to hold up private caravans as well, in order to ransack travellers' luggage. Pietro della Valle, who crossed from Basra to Aleppo just in advance of a great *kafila*, twice lost many of his belongings in this fashion: some arms, clothes, curios, silk, a fine bit of amber, an Iranian turban of silk and gold and several porcelain dishes. In one case the shaykh of the tribesmen who had done the ransacking returned a few of his things to della Valle, and offered him a meagre payment for those which they kept. But here again, such treatment of foreigners was usual only in the seventeenth century. On the whole, caravan *bashis* showed themselves increasingly prone to desire the steadier profit which a good reputation would bring to them. It didn't pay them, any more than it did the cameleers, to make a practice of dishonesty. Flagrantly dishonest caravan leaders have been denounced and deserted by their own Arab followers, men who preferred the surer—if slower—rewards of honest service in behalf of the *Frangi*. So that, in general, they took a pride in their responsibilities, and earned a name for fair dealing. Naturally, the more important a man's position (a *bashi* was nearly always a shaykh), the less he could afford to have a bad reputation. No testimonial could be more reassuring than that of Colonel Capper. After giving the *bashi* of his caravan an excellent character for the entire trip, he made the following note about the settlement of their account: "So far from finding him mercenary and selfish as these people are generally represented, he behaved to us with a politeness and liberality that would have done honour to the most polished European". Shaykh Suleiman refused to count his money in the presence of his employer, and (according to Colonel Capper) could not have followed him to Basra had there been an error.[1]

As for incidental robberies within a caravan, they occurred—of course; but they generally took the form of petty pilfering. The following anecdote illustrates the sort of thing, and the psychology of the thief as well. John Carmichael, when travelling with one of the merchant caravans, had his blanket stolen a few days out from Aleppo. After suffering in silence without it—the length of one cold night—he bethought him of a "stratagem" to recover it. He mentioned its loss to several Arabs in the caravan, telling them incidentally his belief that it had been taken away by some mistake or other, because Arabs were so celebrated by travellers for their honesty. "This", said he, "had the desired effect; the Arab who had it, fearful for the national honour, returned it, pretending he had found it on a camel. On the recovery of my property, I complimented the thief on his not deviating from the integrity of his countrymen."[2] Other travellers might profitably have taken a lesson from Carmichael in the use of such diplomacy.

Stray, night-prowling robbers caused frequent alarms, but they were rarely able to make off with anything, because every properly organized caravan was in the habit of setting an efficient night watch. Teixeira's caravan was troubled more than most by such alarms, as well as by the day-time attacks of heavily armed bandits. He himself was obliged to take his turn keeping watch, alternately with his fellow-travellers. Once a stray thief attempted to steal a camel. He was prevented, just in time, but succeeded in escaping and took with him the turban of a Moorish merchant instead. Near Meshed Ali there was a scare of thieves, and Teixeira described in detail how bands of Arabs used to ride out on camels to waylay a caravan—two men on each camel. Before attacking they would dismount, hobble their camels (by fastening one knee

[1] James Capper (1783), p. 85.
[2] Printed in Hakluyt (1929), p. 139.

in a bent position) and advance to fight, armed with lances, bows, swords, shields and scimetars. Many of the fighters were also mounted on horses. This was in 1605. And on that same journey Teixeira's caravan encountered another, a very small one (just outside Anna) which had come all the way across the desert from Damascus, unescorted. Less than a dozen unarmed merchants had brought a hundred loaded camels across in safety. They reported the Aleppo road to be safe, and the city itself "open and in good order". Here was a contrast, in these two merchant caravans, of a kind most common on the desert.

As for the Beduin, they were dangerous in fits and starts only. It has been described how all the important tribes of the northern desert kept *rafeeks* at both Aleppo and Basra, who were available for the use of caravans. They were hired by the caravan *bashis*, and paid regular salaries which they divided with the shaykhs of the tribes they represented. Their safe-conduct was valid, as far as it went; and no places in the desert were traversed, nor any wells visited, unless they were under the jurisdiction of a tribe which had representation in the caravan. But it took a long time to perfect the *rafeek* system, and in the seventeenth century there was much more reason to worry about the Beduin, and much more interference with caravans than during the later eighteenth century. Of course (and obviously) the *rafeek* system never gave adequate protection when the Beduin were engaged in fighting among each other, or—still more—when they were on bad terms with the Turkish Pashas of either Aleppo, Damascus or Baghdad. The desert was particularly unsafe if any of the desert Arabs were carrying on guerilla warfare with the established government of either Syria or Mesopotamia. In such circumstances, the escort (if it happened to be Turkish) would furnish a most welcome target for their attentions. A modern instance of the truth of this is the Druze Rebellion of 1925 and 1926. At war with the French Government of Syria, the Druze Arabs attacked and plundered all mail and passenger convoys which crossed by the modern route via Rutba Wells, or by any track within reach of Jebel Druze. Even on that by way of Palmyra, which was temporarily substituted for their regular one, the French were forced to supply special escorts for the convoys as far east as the Irak frontier.

Spasmodically also, as has previously been said, new tribes (such as the Shammar Arabs, the Aneza and the Wahhabis) pushed northwards from central Arabia, tribes which were bound by no traditional alliances or allegiances and which had made no agreements to respect property that they might covet. The only way to ensure good treatment from such as they, was to avoid meeting them altogether. The large *kafilas* could not hope to keep their whereabouts unknown; their only hope was to double their escort, when possible, and make minor changes in the route—which they did whenever their scouts reported a large encampment to be in the vicinity. But the small and privately hired caravans were much more mobile; and, as their departures were rarely long premeditated, they were able to prevent a knowledge of their departures and proposed destinations from being spread abroad. When on the road, small caravans were able to make wide detours, if they found themselves to be in hostile country; and if ever they encountered a few unknown and mounted Arabs, they would—when practicable—detain them forcibly, and make them accompany the caravan for three or four days, lest they report its whereabouts to a hostile tribe.

But the most consistent menace to all caravans did not come from the Beduin at all. The worst offenders against desert neutrality were tribes of vagabond Kurds, or similar mountain dwellers, and bands of deserters from the Turkish forces which were stationed as garrisons in Damascus, Aleppo, Birejik, Urfa and various other smaller towns. Hill peoples (after attacking a caravan) could always retreat to their mountains, and seek a safe refuge in Syria or northern Mesopotamia when reprisals were attempted. And deserters—already outlawed—had nothing to fear except capture, and no loyalties to restrain their plundering propensities. Still, one does not read of many caravans being thus waylaid along the open desert routes; only in the neighbourhood of towns, and on the northern (and therefore more dangerous) route. Scarcely any such incidents occurred on the desert after the middle of the eighteenth century.

Two generalizations may safely be made. First, that the more accustomed Arabs became to dealing with Europeans in general (and Englishmen in particular), the more they chose to let them alone and to consider them as a privileged class. Familiarity, in this case, bred a doctrine of *laissez aller, laissez faire*, in its most literal sense. Secondly, that the Beduin have always been intermittently dangerous to any and all desert travellers. Being nomads, no purely governmental system of pacification has been able to subdue them and cope with them all consistently. This is natural enough when one stops to consider that the Arabs only respond to personal contacts (a system means nothing to them) and that the faith and goodwill of a tribe is embodied in its leader. The honesty and reliability of the various shaykhs naturally differs with each individual.

The following story throws light on the relations between a government and an Arab shaykh. The instance is a modern one, and all the more illuminating because the government in question is the British, which has been on better terms with the Arabs in all respects than the former Turkish Government ever was. A certain shaykh in Trans-Jordan made a treaty with the British, through a Commandant of the Trans-Jordanian Frontier Police Force. The shaykh was an important one, with several tribes under his jurisdiction, and he had the name of being an exceptionally humane and honest man. By the terms of his agreement with the Commandant, he undertook to keep his tribesmen in order; to prevent their robbing foreigners resident in Trans-Jordan, and —specifically—to refrain from waylaying and plundering all motor cars which used the roads from Amman to Jerusalem, and from Amman to Tiberias. He kept his word faithfully, to the letter, for many months: until, in fact, all the native inhabitants of Trans-Jordan began to suffer acutely from the effects of a severe drought (this happened in 1932). Finally, on one day, he and his men held up and robbed thirteen cars on the Jerusalem road, in a pass near Jericho. Four days later he contrived to send a message to his "friend" the Commandant. The Commandant was begged to accept the sincere apologies of the shaykh for the recent robbery; he, the shaykh, had kept his tribesmen from banditry of any kind as long as he possibly could—until they were literally reduced to starvation by the drought; but what could he do then? How otherwise were they to get food? As the father of his people, could he allow them to starve to death? Of course he would guarantee that no more robberies should occur, unless Allah chose to prolong the terrible drought. Allah was a witness to his deep regret that two of the men in the motor cars had been injured—unintentionally—by his people.

A comment on this recent happening would be superfluous. But it tempts one to make a further and final generalization—not on the characters of the Beduin (who, presumably, have remained unchanged during the last four centuries), but on their relations with Europeans. Their attitude toward the *Frangi* has definitely altered in one important respect. Within the last fifty years or so all Arabs have learned what caravan *bashis* were the first to learn: that it does not pay to injure a foreigner, be he English or European. They know that to kill is to invite retribution; that even a single murder will result in eventual chastisement—possibly in the punishment of a whole clan or of an entire village. There is one kind of modern banditry which typifies this attitude, one to which the Trans-Jordanian Arabs are especially prone. They will hold up a car, rob its occupants of everything they possess, including their clothes, and then send them on their way again. Sometimes the robbers will take the car as well, or at least all its spare parts; but generally not. In any case, when their victims eventually reach civilization, they will be uninjured, but stripped of every least article of clothing, wrapped about with newspapers, or—if they are lucky—clad in the seat-covers and the curtains of their car. One of the first similar cases of this kind (on camels instead of in motor cars) was reported by Baron von Thielmann in 1867: two Englishmen reached Jerusalem, one clad in a copy of *The Times*, and the other in *The Times Supplement*. This kind of banditry has frequently occurred since the Great War. But formerly, Arabs were not in the least afraid of hurting a foreigner, and they had no reason to expect an effective reprisal if they did. They held their own lives very cheap; it would be strange if they valued the lives of Westerners any more highly. The only consideration potent enough to counteract their natural indifference to the taking of human life was a commercial one: it paid them better to treat the *Frangi* well. By dealing with them on a fair basis, they stood to gain more than they could hope to reap from indiscriminate robbery and manslaughter. Gradually the Beduin came to realize that frequent raiding of caravans tended to discourage desert traffic, and so to decrease the profits derived from transit tolls. Their tribute payments would dwindle in proportion. Between 1663 and 1745, the *Frangi* showed clearly that they could be frightened away from the desert routes altogether; and the Arabs were the losers in consequence, commercially speaking, until the desert once again became safe for foreigners. In other words, it was a desire to exploit commercial potentialities, rather than a fear of consequences, which influenced the Arabs in their earliest treatment of foreigners. That, and the fact that the most self-respecting Arabs have always been scrupulously honest according to their own lights. Their ideas of honesty and fairness differed often and emphatically from western standards; but that was only to be expected. To extort "gifts" and money payments from a merchant caravan was, in the eyes of a desert shaykh, not an extortion at all, but his right and just due. He considered himself entitled to exact tribute from every caravan that crossed any part of the desert which was included within the orbit of his tribe, or its fixed range of migration (see pp. 22-23). Likewise, he would only guarantee the safety of a caravan in return for a fixed payment; this was collected through the *rafeek*, whose salary was only a part of the total payment required. When Colonel Capper's caravan was stopped by Shaykh Fadil (near Taiyiba), the Shaykh demanded that a tribute of one sequin (about 7s. 6d.) be paid him for every camel carrying merchandise; but he did not delay the caravan unduly, nor did he insist upon any other (extra) payments at all, because a *rafeek* from his tribe was travelling with the caravan. So that a merchant by the name of Rubens was the only loser in this encounter with Shaykh Fadil's tribe.

This seems to exhaust the topic of desert hazards and perils in all its phases. In conclusion, there is a word to be said on the subject of the advice which was indiscriminately proffered to travellers. Some of it was rather naïve. Much of it was superfluous. Most of that covering their contacts with Arabs may be inferred from the preceding account. Nevertheless, since a modicum of advice was thought to be a necessary adjunct to one's equipment for the journey, it must not be omitted altogether. First of all, travellers were warned never to rouse the cupidity or avarice of an Arab by displaying—unnecessarily—"finery", arms or curios. On the other hand, it was considered wise to avoid the appearance of poverty, lest the members of one's caravan should take advantage of a man whom they thought to be friendless and of no consequence, and therefore not worthy of respect. To inspire Arabs with a feeling of respect and (when possible) awe was thought to ensure deferential treatment from them, and to prevent their attempting to extort any sort of unwarranted payments. At the same time, one was advised to wear native dress in order to obtain the maximum civility! In dealing with the Arabs in a caravan, a cool head and an equable temper were urgently recommended; the foreigner was advised to disregard well-meant impertinences or unwelcome curiosity; and always to make an effort to treat even "the lowest Arab of the caravan" as though he were on an equal footing. In the case of a theft or an unpardonable insult, a traveller was warned never to chastise (personally) the offender; but to make a calm statement of the case to the *bashi*, who would see that justice was done. The most emphatic advice of all was given on the subject of the caravan leader. In every matter relating to the desert, and in every emergency throughout the entire journey, complete confidence should be shown in the *bashi*, regardless of the traveller's true feelings. One should appear, "unequivocally", to place entire trust in his judgment and in his good faith, because the *bashi* would be as susceptible as all other Arabs to this sort of flattery. Never for a moment let him suspect that anyone in his charge disbelieved in him. His honour thus appealed to, indirectly, he would respond with all the peculiar chivalry of his people. Lastly, a traveller should never tempt Providence by straying from his own encampment, or by wandering off into the desert alone, away from the main body of the caravan. If there were ruins or a place like Meshed Ali to be visited, an escort should be taken, or—at the very least—a guide who spoke Arabic. It was particularly foolhardy to go through Arab villages or encampments without an adequate guard; several near disasters from this cause were only narrowly escaped.

Teixeira made an observation which is so inclusive in its general application that it must be included with all these other more specific warnings. His remark was prompted by the conduct of a certain Diego de Melo, a headstrong and hot-tempered fellow-traveller. This foolish man had foundered his horse in order to reach Meshed Ali before the rest of the caravan, and at another time he had threatened a cameleer with his sword. Teixeira's comment upon Diego de Melo was that ". . . unpleasant things befell him during this journey, for that he would not consider and distinguish times and places; which, if a man cannot do, he had better stay at home".[1]

This cryptic admonition is an appropriate last word, an inverted *pax vobiscum* to prospective desert travellers.

[1] Teixeira (1609), p. 101.

CHAPTER VII

THE GREAT "HAJJ" CARAVANS

I

THE ISLAMIC PILGRIMAGE

THERE is a well-known type of caravan which is neither a merchant convoy nor a private company of independent travellers. It pertains to both, and conforms to the pattern of neither. Namely, "The Great Hajj", or annual pilgrim caravans. These have a special life and history of their own, which is as unique as the purpose they have fulfilled for more than twelve hundred years.

Between the seventh and the twentieth centuries, Mohammedan pilgrims have made annual journeys to Mecca and Medina, the holy centres of Islam, from every Moslem land between Western Africa and China. Those from Iran, Mesopotamia, Syria and Egypt have been particularly numerous. Mohammed himself founded the Islamic Pilgrimage, *el-Hajj*. He instituted annual ceremonies at the Ka'aba, which was a very holy pre-Islamic shrine at Mecca; and thus incorporated ancient rituals in the new monotheism. Pilgrimage to a sanctuary was an old Semitic custom in Arabia; and the fundamentals of the *Hajj* ceremonies were pre-Mohammedan, just as the core of Mohammedanism was pre-Islamic.

The Mosque at Mecca contains the Ka'aba, or "Black Stone", which has been an object of veneration since the days of Abraham; and pilgrims who "circumambulate" the *Beit Allah* (House of God) in pilgrim dress (*el-Ihram*) touch and kiss this Stone. In the words of the Koran (Rodwell's translation, edition of 1929, p. 395), "the pilgrimage to the temple is a service due to Allah from those who are able to journey thither". At Medina, in a mosque

of four minarets, and under a green dome, the Prophet Mohammed is buried; accordingly all Moslems who perform the pilgrimage to Mecca also visit Medina; but this is a meritorious action
merely, not obligatory as is the *Hajj* (or *Hajjat el-Islam*). The tomb
of the Prophet is not approached in the *Ihram*, but rather in the
best clothes which the pilgrim may possess; and a visit to the
Mosque of the Prophet at Medina is called *Ziyarat*, or "Visitation".
After performing the rite of "circumambulation" (*el-Tawaf*) of
el-Beit Allah at Mecca, a pilgrim becomes a *Hajji*; after visiting
the tomb of Mohammed at Medina, the *Hajji* is also called *Zair*.
In Mohammedan belief the "House of God" at Mecca is the holiest
spot in the whole world, but Medina is considered holier or more
"venerable" than every part of Mecca save only the *Beit Allah*.
This in brief is the nature of the annual *Hajj*.

It has been said that the pilgrimage to Mecca is obligatory. That
is, it is required of every Moslem, at least once in a lifetime. Every
Moslem is understood to mean every adult Mohammedan, man
or woman, who is free and of sound mind. Slaves are exempt; and
exceptions are made for those whose health is chronically too bad
to stand the strain of so arduous a journey, and for those who
literally cannot afford to leave home. If a man is too poor either
to pay or work his way to Mecca, or if he could not adequately
provide for his family during his absence, that man is absolved
from the necessity of performing the pilgrimage. Women who are
in bad health are likewise absolved, as well as those who have
neither husband nor relative to accompany them—since women
are not supposed to travel alone to Mecca. As Islam expanded, the
obligation of the *Hajj* became an even more stringent duty. A
sick man, who remained incurable, and was therefore without any
hope of eventually making the pilgrimage, would endeavour to
send a substitute. Noble princesses who did not perform the
journey in person were accustomed to send camels, laden with
water, for the benefit of the poorer pilgrims. In certain cases the
Hajj could be performed vicariously, after death, if specific testa-
mentary provision was made, and sufficient funds were bequeathed
for the purpose. A poor man could honourably accomplish the

Hajj by hiring out his personal services to a fellow-pilgrim, as a servant or a camel-driver. Any True Believer who made three pilgrimages to Mecca felt assured of Allah's special protection in the next world.

A pilgrim, before setting out, made special preparations for the journey. He would set his house in order; pay his debts, wind up all business matters, arrange family affairs in order to safeguard his wives and children, and give charity or alms to the poor. The prospective *Hajji* arranged everything as though for death; his preparations amounted almost to a spiritual and material rite of purification, in anticipation of an act of supreme devotion. On the other hand, many pilgrims set out for Mecca with the idea of worldly or commercial gain (self-advancement). Profitable commercial ventures could be undertaken at both Mecca and Medina, and merchants in particular could trade *en route*. Each of the great *Hajj* caravans was a veritable travelling city of from five to ten thousand people, so there were countless opportunities for trading among the pilgrims, as well as among both townspeople and Beduin at the various *Hajj* stations. Furthermore, the *Hajj* journey was a broadening experience in the life of every Moslem. A man travelled hundreds, or perhaps thousands of miles in the company of Mohammedans of various nationalities; and the pilgrimage offered some men (the poor and the very busy) their only chance of a voyage in foreign lands. For others, the pilgrimage was sometimes only the beginning of a life of travel and adventure. Ibn Battuta is the most famous example of a medieval traveller who prefaced a lifetime of voyaging with a visit to Mecca. He began his career by performing the pilgrimage, acquired thus a taste for travel, and spent the rest of his life in wandering from one end of the Moslem world to the other. Most typical of all, however, is the story of a certain merchant of Baghdad named Ali Cogia; most typical, that is, of the mixed motives of an average Mohammedan pilgrim, and of his experiences after reaching Mecca. The interested reader will find this story in *The Arabian Nights' Entertainments*, where it is told in picturesque detail.

Several decades after the death of Mohammed, when the Omayyad Caliphs chose Damascus for their capital, an annual pilgrim caravan was organized from that city. The Abbasid Caliphs, from motives of convenience and because of the zeal of Sitt Zubayda (wife of Harun er-Rashid), subsequently organized a *Hajj* centre in Baghdad; to be imitated still later by a Pasha of Basra; but the Western *Hajj* continued without interruption to leave annually from Damascus. Iranian pilgrims, such as were not too vehemently *Shi'a*, joined forces with their *Sunni* brethren; but they generally, though not invariably, chose to travel by their nearest route to Mecca, which was via Baghdad or Basra. (For the distinction between *Shi'a* and *Sunni* Mohammedans, see glossary, p. 309.) West of Damascus, a fourth *Hajj* centre was organized at Cairo, for pilgrims from Africa and the Mediterranean. Thus, for nearly thirteen hundred years, the major divisions of the *Hajj* have started (almost simultaneously) from four different focal points. Pilgrims have congregated at Damascus, Baghdad, Basra and Cairo, to join one of these great convoys. The Aleppo *Hajj*, like the caravans of Turkish pilgrims from Constantinople and the rest of Anatolia, have always joined forces with the greater *Hajj* of Damascus, because that city was on their most direct line of march to Mecca. Since the Mohammedan year is divided into twelve lunar months (or 354 days), the pilgrimage is made at no fixed season; but each year the date for its departure is advanced eleven days. The *Hajj* months always follow directly after Ramadan, the Moslem month of fasting. Ramadan is the ninth month of the Mohammedan calendar, and every thirty-three years it occurs in midsummer.

The Eastern *Hajj*, as the Baghdad and Basra pilgrimages were called, followed two different routes across the south-eastern end of the Syrian Desert. The *Darb es-Sitt Zubayda*, as the most famous of these routes is called, was originally marked out and provided with fortified watering-places as long ago as the ninth century A.D. At each *Hajj* station the Lady (*Sitt*) Zubayda caused a rest-house and one or more reservoirs to be constructed.

General Sir Eyre Coote described one of these stations in the eighteenth century. The rest-house he inspected was a square building of stone, about thirty feet high, which was "casemented on three sides with very good arches; and with four good chambers on each side"; near by was a deep well, the top of which was "styned" with stone and lime, for ten feet below the surface; a large square *birket* (reservoir), and two oblong ones that seemed once to have been arched over, had been built between the well and the rest-house. The *Darb Zubayda* runs from Meshed Ali to Hayil (and, formerly, to Fayd), via Jebel Shammar, and thence to Medina and Mecca. Today, scarcely any of its *birkets* and rest-houses could be used; in the north-east they have been mutilated by a variety of invading powers, and in Nejd a great number of them have been destroyed by the Wahhabis. Colonel Leachman reported that only the *birket* at Jumeima (which lies south of the thirtieth parallel of latitude) remains in good condition.[1]

The *Darb el-Hajj*, or Pilgrim road of the Damascus caravans, followed the ancient Arabo-Syrian highway, along the desert frontier of Trans-Jordan and Petraea to the Hejaz. The route has been changed several times since the seventh century: at first the *Hajj* followed the track which runs east of Jebel Druze to Trans-Jordan; and south of Amman the *Darb el-Hajj* has oscillated between the three tracks which lie east of the Jordan and Dead Sea valleys. But since the sixteenth century the pilgrims have adhered to a single track, because of the fortified watering-places which the Ottoman Government built and kept guarded on their behalf. In the nineteenth century, between 1819 and 1902, four European travellers followed and described this Western *Hajj* route. According to Burckhardt, Fridolin, Doughty and Castiau, the principal stations north of the Hejaz were as follows: Mezerib (considerably to the west of Jebel Druze), Kal'at Mafrak (in 1932 the Iraq Petroleum Company established one of their principal camps

---

[1] The *birkets* were described by General Sir Eyre Coote in the *Journal of the Royal Geographical Society*, vol. xxx (1860), p. 206; Colonel G. E. Leachman in the *Geographical Journal*, vol. xxxvii (1911), p. 267.

at Mafrak), Kal'at ez-Zerka (north of Amman) and Maan.
Between Zerka and Maan are four famous *kal'as*, or forts—those
of el-Belka, el-Katrani, el-Hasa and Aneza. Beyond Maan the
Darb el-Hajj goes straight to Akaba esh-Shem (so called to distinguish it from Akaba el-Masri, on the Gulf of Akaba), where
the caravan is obliged to wind through a deep gorge to the plain
below. Thereafter, in the Hejaz, the *Hajj* route passes through
Mudowwara, Tebuk and Medain Saleh to Medina. Finally, the
pilgrims had a choice of two main highways between Medina
and Mecca. At Mezerib and Maan, as at one or two towns in the
Hejaz, the *Hajj* caravan was in the habit of stopping for a rest of
two or three days. Therefore, important annual market fairs were
held in these towns. The caravan was usually delayed much
longer at Mezerib (from eight to ten days) in order to make all
final arrangements, and to enable all pilgrims from Palestine and
the southern Lebanons to join the *Hajj* convoy. It was there that
William of Tyre, in the twelfth century, attended the great fair
which he described as being held among the pilgrims before
their departure for Mecca. In the early part of the nineteenth
century (according to Burckhardt) the caravan also spent a whole
day at Kal'at ez-Zerka: during which the pilgrims amused themselves by hunting the wild boars which were said to be plentiful
in the Wadi Zerka. Marcel Castiau noted that *kal'as* were spaced,
along the *Darb el-Hajj*, about thirty-four miles apart. He described them as ancient massive constructions, approximately
sixty feet square, which were occupied by at least one Beduin
family, and were often garrisoned by three or four Turkish
soldiers as well. There were always two reservoirs, which had
usually been dug in a near-by wadi; they were joined together by
a canal, and the smaller of the two served as a drinking trough
for the animals. In years of drought, village Arabs and Beduin
carriers were hired to fill at least one of these reservoirs at each
station in advance of the great caravan; and such water-carriers as
had to be employed were paid out of the special *Hajj* fund with
which the Sultan, as official (self-appointed) protector of the
Holy Cities, customarily subsidized the pilgrimage. Supplies of

food, forage and other necessary stores could be replenished at any one of the *kal'as*.

The *Darb el-Hajj* was not a made road in any sense of the word, but a serried multitude of tracks which had been trodden into hard paths by the feet of countless generations of beasts of burden. Those tracks are today clearly visible along the northern part of the route (near Mafrak, for example); but south of Maan there was no trodden *Hajj* road even in Doughty's day—all was empty desert. Through ravines and narrow defiles, a single well-worn track indicates that the huge caravan has always been forced to wind its way in single file. Throughout the length of the route, bleached bones and the skeletons of camels, horses and mules can be found; and at intervals little mounds of rock are to be seen, which serve as tombstones for the pilgrims who have died on their way to or from Mecca.

The Western Pilgrim Route has been described in more detail than the Eastern, chiefly because it passed through larger places, the names of which are better known; and also because there is more specific information regarding it. Ibn Jubair, for instance, who travelled from Mecca to Baghdad in the twelfth century, gave an interesting account of the *Eastern Hajj Route*; but his description would mean little except to those who were already acquainted with the deserts of Nejd and of Irak. For the same reasons, it seems wiser to confine a description of the pilgrim caravan to the Damascus *Hajj*. The analogies are obvious and the differences but slight, between this most familiar convoy and its three sister caravans.

2

THE ORGANIZATION OF THE PILGRIM CARAVANS

For as long as the Imperial Ottoman Government lasted, the Damascus *Hajj* was led by two Turkish officials. One, always of high social standing, was called *Emir el-Hajj*, and was usually a palace nobleman of Stamboul; actually, until within the last hundred years, the *Emir* was generally a younger son or relative of the Sultan. The other, a Pasha, was in actual charge of the organization of the convoy, and solely responsible for its daily business and routine; he was also the officer commanding the military escort, and paymaster of the Arab shaykhs. By his side rode the "pilot", or *daleel*: a native of Damascus who had been trained to intimate knowledge of the Road and its landmarks by a long apprenticeship. For the rest, the caravan was so meticulously organized that even a pilgrim's camel-place in the line of march was appointed and, once decided upon, was unalterable. The Emir and the Pasha alone were privileged to outride the caravan, and smoke and rest until the rest of the convoy should catch them up.

When Maundrell witnessed the setting out of a certain pilgrim caravan, at the end of the seventeenth century, the Pasha of Tripoli was the *Emir el-Hajj* for that year. The "cavalcade" was very heavily guarded by three troops of *segmans*, mounted troops of spahis, janissaries and "mailed soldiers" of Damascus; and in addition, eight companies of *mugubrines* (infantry detailed for desert duty) were taken to replace the garrisons of various *kal'as* on the *Darb el-Hajj*. Maundrell also commented upon forty-six dervishes (or "religious madmen") who led the procession, carrying silk streamers of red and green and of yellow and green.

A perennial feature of the *Hajj* was the *mahmal*. This was a large and beautifully decorated palanquin, a litter of wood which was covered with black, green or red silk, brocaded (or embroidered) with gold and ornamented with tasselled fringes and silver gilt balls. The *mahmal* was a symbol of sovereignty, a great litter which carried only a copy of the Koran and a finely wrought Turkish prayer rug: both gifts of the Sultan, Commander of the Faithful. The new rug was intended as a covering for the tomb of Mohammed; and each year the sacred carpet which had been carried to Medina the preceding year was brought back in the otherwise empty palanquin. The *mahmal* camel, always an especially large animal, was customarily exempted from bearing burdens forever, after the completion of its first pilgrimage.

Monsieur Gaudefroy-Demombynes, a noted student of the *Hajj* and its ceremonial customs, believes that the *mahmal* is a comparatively modern institution: that it was unknown during the Omayyad and the Abbasid Caliphates, and that it was probably introduced into the pilgrimage by the Mamluk Sultans of Egypt, in either the twelfth or the thirteenth century. The idea may have originated in imitation of a Beduin custom. Certain tribes of Arabia and the *Great Desert* kept tribal palanquins for use in war: *el-otfa*, or *el-merkab* (the latter kind was decorated with ostrich feathers), in which a daughter of the senior shaykh of the tribe would be carried into battle with her tribesmen, to encourage them to fight. Until 1918 the Rualla were possessed of a *merkab*, which accompanied their men into war. An analogy might be made between the *Hajj* and an Arab tribe preparing for war against infidels. The term *jehad* means a holy war against intangible evils and demons of the flesh, as well as against unbelievers— though the latter is its more common meaning; so the *jehad* led by the *Hajj* might also carry its symbol or standard of spiritual battle. Once *el-mahmal* became an important element in the *Hajj* ceremonial, it insensibly developed a political as well as a religious significance. Mongol rulers sent a magnificent *mahmal* with the Eastern *Hajj* (between 1321 and 1472); and independent princes of Yemen had their *mahmal* claims and "rights" in the fifteenth and sixteenth centuries. After 1517 the Sultan of the Ottoman Empire sent a royal *mahmal* with the Damascus caravan, as the symbol of his supreme spiritual authority, and to affirm his title of Protector of the Holy Cities; but even during the Ottoman period, the Pasha of Egypt continued to perpetuate the Mamluk custom, and to send an Egyptian *mahmal* with the Cairo *Hajj*.

The *Hajj* fund, to which reference has already been made, has been administered, since the sixteenth century, by a personal representative of the Sultan. During the latter part of the nineteenth century the annual subsidy for the pilgrim caravan amounted to something over 300,000 Turkish pounds. (The Turkish (gold) pound has fluctuated only slightly during the last century. After

the monetary reforms of 1844, it was quoted at 18s. 2d.) A grant
for this sum was made from the Ottoman public treasury, but
almost one-sixth of the total was obtained by a direct tax levied
on the Turkish Province of Syria. The moneys were expended
in the following way. Annual gifts were made to the Shaykhs of
Medina and Mecca, and to the shaykhs of all villages that lie
along the *Darb el-Hajj*; annual subsidies were given to the Beduin
shaykhs, which payments were usually made through the heads
of the various villages; the caravan's armed escort—numbering
between one hundred and one hundred and fifty men—had to
be paid, as well as the caravan officials, local guides, water-
carriers, etc. About 50,000 pounds (Turkish) was reserved for
the upkeep and protection of the road and its water supplies, and
for the permanent guards that were maintained at certain of the
fortified watering-places.

The question of protection for the caravan was a serious one.
The Sultan's relations with the desert nomads who inhabited the
waste lands of his dominions were precarious at best, and often
strained to breaking point. The Beduin instinctively looked upon
the pilgrims as their natural prey. Nevertheless, if they were
adequately bribed (and they considered themselves the sole
judges of the adequacy of their annual subsidies), the Beduin
would refrain from molesting the *Hajj*. Burckhardt, when re-
marking that most sections of the Aneza claimed passage money
from the Syrian *Hajj*, quoted the amounts of several of the subsidies paid them. One tribe alone, for example, took a yearly
surra, or tribute, of fifty "purses" (about £1000). There were,
however, a great number and variety of tribes who ranged the
desert fringes of the *Hajj* road, and they all believed themselves
entitled to a regular annual payment; and if the Porte defaulted,
ever so slightly, they felt at liberty to indulge their inbred taste
for plunder and surprise attacks. So, despite the vigilance of their
scouts and the habitual bravery of the mercenary guard, to say
nothing of the numerical strength of the caravan, pilgrims were
often subjected to robbery and violence.

To consider expenses from another point of view, that of

the pilgrim, a few generalizations may be made. The minimum cost of a trip to Mecca and back was forty Turkish pounds, and this sum was calculated on the assumption that the maximum weight of a pilgrim and his belongings should not exceed three hundred pounds. For the maximum fare, there was of course no limit. Wealthy pilgrims could take their own servants and special food; and even hire a private litter, or "camel coach", at a daily cost of one Turkish pound.

There lives in Damascus today a certain silk merchant, by the name of Selim Sawwaf, who formerly owned 2000 camels and was a contractor for the *Hajj* caravans. Between 1875 and 1910, Selim Sawwaf made thirty trips to Mecca, and on the basis of his long experience he gave (to the author) the following information concerning the supplying of the great caravans. Camel "owners", according to him, had always been in the habit of buying their camels each year, as cheaply as possible, from the desert Arabs who raised them. Then they hired out these animals, at the highest possible price, to prospective *Hajjis* and convoy officials; and sold them at a profit, after their return to Damascus. Possibly the Pasha of medieval Damascus once had a monopoly of this lucrative trade, as did the Pasha of Basra in the seventeenth century; but fortunately for Selim Sawwaf, there was no such government monopoly in his day. In order to take part in contracting for the pilgrims, a single owner or else a collective group of camel-owners, acting as a unit, had to contribute a minimum "share" of two hundred camels. The potential market of the *mukowams*, or camel-masters, depended directly upon the numbers of the pilgrims to be convoyed. These numbers varied year by year; varied so greatly that, within the thirty years' experience of this particular contractor, the demand for camels had fluctuated between four thousand, in some years, to as many as twenty thousand in others.

The great caravan as a whole numbered many more than its camels; baggage mules and even donkeys were also used; the armed escort rode either horses or dromedaries; and many of the ordinary riding camels carried two riders. No satisfactory conclusion has ever been reached, however, as to the average number of pilgrims who have made the annual journey from Damascus to Mecca. The numbers guessed at by medieval travellers are wildly improbable; hearsay carries no conviction; and there is no certain way of telling just what proportion of *Hajj* camels carried pilgrims, and what proportion carried baggage, stores and tents. Possibly a fair estimate for the Damascus *Hajj*, within the last century, would be an average of 5000 pilgrims a year. On the other hand, it is well known that the size of these caravans has been gradually on the decrease, and that the *Hajj* as an institution has actually been declining since the eighteenth century.

Selim Sawwaf gave the writer some further information, of considerable importance, concerning the influence of the *mukowams* on the history of the *Hajj*. Strangely enough, although religious laws regulated most of the life of the caravan and decreed the time and manner of fasting, ablution and prayer, the strictest of all the regulations was believed to be secular in origin. The camel-masters originated a law which was, at least in more recent times, ruthlessly enforced: namely, that the entire trip should never take more than forty days and forty nights to perform. Five days, not counted in the forty, were spent in Medina, but that was the only exception countenanced. No halts of more than one hour were allowed by day, and a great part of the journey was performed by night. Sometimes, if the caravan accomplished a thirty-mile stage with exceptional speed, in less than the allotted time (in, for example, ten or nine hours instead of twelve), a halt of two or three hours was granted at the first watering-place encountered thereafter. Otherwise, on every third day, an hour's rest at some village was arranged. But that was all. Were a person to fall ill, or to die, or a woman to weaken under the strain, even so, no exception could be made to this stringent regulation. Once embarked upon the pilgrimage, it behoved the pilgrim to persevere to the bitter—sometimes very bitter—end. Anyone who failed in this self-imposed duty, and was literally unable to travel, was left behind: even, upon occasion, to the mercy of the marauding Beduin. But when at last they reached their objective and finally arrived at Mecca, the caravan stayed there for more than three weeks. Only a short time was exacted in the Holy City for religious purposes (all the prescribed duties of the *Hajj*, that is to say, could be performed within three, or at the most six days), but a long rest was allowed the pilgrims: partly for the purposes of trade and commerce, and partly so that both men and beasts might have a chance to recuperate from the long and exhausting trip. The return journey was made exactly as the outgoing one had been, in forty days, the only change in the routine being a shortened stay at Medina. According to Selim Sawwaf, the camel-owners and contractors were solely responsible for this forty-day test of endurance; and the reason he gave was that a great and disproportionate expense would be incurred by them for every extra day spent on the road, beyond the time they had contracted for.[1]

The preceding details of routine and organization give the skeleton framework of what must have been one of the greatest of medieval pageants. Unfortunately no future travellers, such as Ludovico di Varthema or Charles Doughty, can see or travel with it, for the *Hajj* no longer journeys between Damascus and Mecca. One can only imagine the great horde of humanity that formed the pilgrim caravan, and picture its progress along the nine hundred miles of the *Darb el-Hajj*. Averaging about two miles an hour (so huge a caravan naturally travelled more slowly than smaller convoys), the procession would drag out its length for some two miles. Generally speaking, not more than three or four camels swayed abreast of each other; camel drovers and

[1] After leaving Maan, and especially after Tebuk, the *Hajj* has always been accustomed to press forward with all possible speed (travelling most of the night, as well as all day long). This was accounted for, to the satisfaction of those interested, by the lines in the Koran which urge pilgrims to "pass on quickly" when they approach the Holy Places (Koran, *op. cit.* p. 359). And these words also furnished the camel-masters with a religious argument and pretext for insisting upon the maximum speed during the entire journey. The passing centuries have witnessed minor changes from time to time, in the number and length of the daylight halts, as well as in the route of the pilgrim caravans; and the relative scarcity of water in the Hejaz has necessitated many a forced march.

servants walked wearily beside their charges. Behind the pilgrims followed a score of smaller caravans: camels in single file, laden with merchandise, tied together and strung out one behind the other, the long line led by a small donkey—such as one may still see in Syria today. Occasional litters furnished bright splashes of colour, with their red and gold and green trappings; especially, at the head of the procession, the litters of the Emir and the Pasha; and the *mahmal*, most resplendent of all, which housed the Sultan's personal gift for the tomb of the Prophet.[1]

But when the serpentine caravan halted for an hour or two, it suddenly became a mushroom city of tents. These tents were crowded compactly together to facilitate their defence, but with a middle street where hawkers might do a hectic trade during the brief halt, and at one end of which traders were at liberty to set up their booths and display their wares for sale. For the pilgrim caravan was invariably accompanied by small caravans of merchants, whose presence and activities were expressly sanctioned by the Koran. Their camels usually numbered somewhat above two hundred; so that the whole convoy resembled a travelling *souk*—a perambulating bazaar. No trading, however, was allowed while the caravan was on the march. The merchants carried goods of every description: food to supplement the meagre fare which the *Hajj* commissariat provided for the pilgrims; clothes and weapons in case any pilgrim should desire to increase

---

[1] Burton stated that, while on the march, the *mahmal* was stripped of its embroidered cover; that its camel carried the "framewood" unadorned. Cf. Sir R. F. Burton (1893), vol. ii, p. 65, note 3.

In discussing rates of caravan travel, Major Rennell makes the following statement: "The rate of the Mecca caravan falls so low as 1·96 (m.p.h.), owing doubtless to the great number of camels (which are said to be sometimes 15,000), and the excessive length of their days' journeys". Also, because both African and Syrian camels, *i.e.* animals of two different sizes, were used in the Damascus *Hajj*, the whole convoy was still further slowed up. Doughty remarked upon the fact that "the great *Hajj* camels" never browsed on the road; they were fed at the halts with clots of "boiled pulse" and with a "long knot-grass forage" called *thurrm*.

See Major James Rennell (1831), vol. i, pp. xlix, l and li; C. M. Doughty, (1933), vol. i, p. 65.

his stock during the journey; and large quantities of cloth and silk, brass and copper-ware to sell to the Beduin encountered *en route*. The clothing merchants generally did not go all the way to Mecca with the caravan, finding it more profitable to wait at Tebuk or some other *Hajj* station and trade there until the *Hajjis* returned northwards. There was no imaginable commodity with which these merchants were not able to tempt buyers, so that— between needy pilgrims, avid nomads and eager villagers—they generally made a profit of about twenty-five per cent on their trading stores.

Ludovico di Varthema went to Mecca, in 1503, as one of the mercenary guards of the Damascus *Hajj*. After him, until the time when Charles Doughty accompanied the Syrian pilgrims as far south as Medain Saleh, the few Europeans who visited Mecca went there and back by way of the Red Sea. Joseph Pitts (in 1680), Ali Bey (in 1807), Giovanni Finati (in 1811), J. L. Burckhardt (in 1814) and Sir Richard Burton (in 1853) all went to the Hejaz via Egypt. Since Doughty's day, Mecca has become slightly more accessible to Europeans. Both H. St. J. B. Philby and Eldon Rutter, for instance, have actually lived in the city; but Mecca is still forbidden to all except Moslems, and since the consolidation of the Wahhabi power under Ibn Sa'ud, "anti-infidel" regulations have been applied with all their old rigour. It may interest the reader to know that a single woman, Lady Evelyn Cobbold, has recently visited Mecca; and that she became a Mohammedan before doing so.

In the first years of the twentieth century, the Sultan began the building of the Hejaz railway to facilitate the transport of pilgrims from Anatolia, through Syria, to Mecca. By 1908 this railway had been completed as far as Medina. Thereafter, until various sections of the road were put out of commission during the Great War, the *Hajj* travelled most of the way by rail. Since the Armistice, Syrian and Turkish pilgrims have gone regularly from Beyrout to Jedda by boat. Between 1904 and 1911, the Eastern *Hajj* was not able to use any of the Nejd routes to the Hejaz, on account of the unsettled state of central Arabia. It went via Damascus, or else more usually by boat from Basra, through the Persian Gulf and around Arabia. After 1908, pilgrims from Irak and Iran began to use the new railway, and today, since 1926, they have used (almost without exception) the Nairn track—crossing by motor car or lorry from Baghdad, to join the *Hajj* ship at Beyrout. Within a few years it is likely that the Irak pilgrims, at least, will once again use the *Darb Zubayda*, which is in process of being opened to motor traffic. Lastly, the Egyptian pilgrims now cross the Red Sea by boat instead of crossing the Sinai Peninsula by caravan (as they did in the Middle Ages); and the richer pilgrims may soon be flown across to the Hejaz, in planes provided by an Anglo-Egyptian aviation company.

It is almost incongruous to think of this essentially medieval expedition being perpetuated by twentieth-century mechanical transport. One wonders how far such mechanization will mar the spirit of the *Hajj*. Some of the stricter Moslems may feel that the Pilgrimage is thus in danger of losing its intrinsically religious character. After all, the arduous nature of the journey was considered a virtue in itself; a process of spiritual purification to be wholeheartedly undertaken by the True Believer. In Moslem theology the word *Hajj* means "aspiration"; and the term has been used to express a conviction that man is only a wayfarer here, on his way to another and a better world. A belief has thus arisen, and persisted through the ages, that the greater the hardships of the pilgrim on his way to Mecca, the greater will be the ultimate reward of the *Hajji* at the hands of Allah.

CHAPTER VIII

ELEVEN CENTURIES OF POSTAL SERVICE

I

THE "BERID" OF THE ABBASID AND MAMLUK PERIODS

CARAVAN trade and desert travel have been variously, and in some aspects lengthily, described. But there is one type of traveller, the desert courier of the dromedary post, who has hitherto been mentioned only incidentally. Four separate and distinctive postal services of the Syrian Desert now remain to be discussed. Since the ninth century A.D., the Abbasids, the Mamluks, the Ottoman Turks and the English have successively made use of a dromedary post, to bridge this desert which intervenes between Syria and Mesopotamia. In a later phase, during the eighteenth and nineteenth centuries, the British dromedary post became a link in an imperial, Anglo-Indian service; and the Near Eastern trans-desert postal system was only the intermediate section of an organization that united the Occident with the Orient. In this period it was best known, at least to Europeans; but the desert postal services were no less interesting or important in their earlier phases.

Before the coming of the Saracens, Iran, Mesopotamia and Syria had all three been serviced by couriers and express messengers, for purposes of state. The early Iranians and the Seleucids, as well as the Romans, had inaugurated government services for the forwarding of official and military dispatches. After them, the Sasanian Iranians and the Byzantines had perfected the imperial postal services, which they had inherited, and added to the number of existing post-roads. But no one of these earlier empires had incorporated a trans-desert service in their otherwise comprehensive postal systems. In the ancient period, as has been previously explained, no trade routes crossed the Syrian Desert. All the principal Near and Middle Eastern highways converged in Anatolia, and all trade and postal routes that connected Syria with Mesopotamia crossed the Euphrates well above the northern limits of the *Little Desert*. Under the Romans and the Byzantines, when the desert stood between them and the rival empires of Parthia and Sasanian Iran, there was no occasion to bridge it with courier services. A neutral Palmyra traded across the *Little Desert*; and more than one military highway traversed Palmyrena. There was constant communication between Palmyra and her commercial colonies on the Euphrates and in Mesopotamia; and the legions of the Roman army kept in touch with their outpost garrisons; but neither merchants nor soldiers could be called postal couriers, in spite of the fact that they carried messages and dispatches in the course of their desert travellings. Both Romans and Byzantines, however, maintained a provincial postal service in the settled sections of Syria; and the Theodosian Code legislated as to its functions. Not until Saracen days, not until a single power ruled Syria, Mesopotamia and the intervening desert, was there an impelling reason to connect the eastern and the western sides of the desert with a regular and official courier service. The *Berid*, or "post service", was established, with an efficient desert section, as soon as the Caliphs set about organizing their Moslem Empire.

Under the Omayyads, the Byzantine postal organization was perpetuated; both the institution and the name were borrowed from their predecessors. The Roman word *veredus* had first been used to designate a post-animal, or horse; it was later applied to the courier who rode the horse, and then to the institution of the post itself. Most Arabic writers agree that *veredus* is the root of the word *berid* (or *barid*, as it is spelled in the *Encyclopaedia of Islam*); and that *veredarii* becomes the Arabic *beridiyin*, meaning postal couriers. On the other hand, the Abbasids inherited and adapted the postal organization of the Sasanian Iranians; and there is an Iranian word that might also have formed the root of *berid*. *Beridedem* was a term applied to mules whose tails had been cut;

and short-tailed mules were invariably used in the Iranian period to carry government dispatches. The Omayyad Caliphs appear to have re-established the Byzantine postal services west of the desert; and the first Abbasid Caliphs apparently perpetuated the Iranian institution east of the desert. After the beginning of the ninth century, the two systems were unified and established on an imperial basis. Arab historians credit Harun er-Rashid, or rather his famous Barmecide councillor, Yahya, with reorganizing and remodelling the *Berid*. The office of postmaster-general was created; and the *Sahib el-Berid* was held responsible by the Caliph for the efficient working of the system, in all the provinces of the caliphate. So widespread an organization required meticulous administrating and book-keeping. Official lists of postal stations and their personnel were compiled; and among these are to be found some of the most valuable works of Arab geography. Interesting accounts of this postal system, as it existed in Syria and Mesopotamia, have been handed down to us by four "road books" of the ninth century; two of them are particularly relevant, those written by Ibn Khordadbeh and Kudama. In the tenth century el-Mukaddasi, who travelled so extensively through his Saracen world, corroborated these earlier accounts.

It goes without saying that the network of post-stations which, with their relays of post-horses, were established in the populated districts, could scarcely have been introduced into the desert sections of the various routes. Instead, hard-riding, desert-trained postmen were provided with the best of dromedaries. These men covered incredibly long distances in the course of a day's "march", obtaining remounts only occasionally—at some of the larger oases. The strict regulations whereby the *Sahib el-Berid* kept a check on the postal officials under his charge, would, however, have applied equally to the desert couriers. A dossier was kept of their names, their appointments, their expenses, and the number of their relays; also, as exact reckonings as possible of the distances they covered. Although, obviously, it was not possible to hold them so strictly to account in the matter of punctuality as their brother couriers who travelled the more settled regions by the ordinary relay routes.

The elaborate system of high-roads which radiated from Bagh-dad included two so-called trunk roads for communication with Syria. One of them followed the right bank of the Euphrates north-west to Rakka, which had become a focal point for the Syrian Desert routes. But the main post road reached Rakka by the roundabout way of Mosul, branching south-west from that city to the Euphrates at Kirkisiya; there it crossed the river and turned north-west, after joining the other trunk road. From Rakka, which is on the Mesopotamian or left bank of the Euphrates —about one hundred and fifty miles north and slightly east of Palmyra—the post of that era had a variety of roads to choose from. From opposite Rakka, along the right bank of the river, there was a route due west to Aleppo; also, three routes south and west, all of which passed through the ancient Byzantine town of Resafa. A courier might travel directly from Resafa to Homs, or to Damascus; or else, by means of the old Roman *Strata Diocletiana* to either Damascus or Bosra eski-Shem, by way of Taiyiba, Sukhna and Palmyra.

Between the eleventh and the thirteenth centuries, the wars and revolutions which took place in various parts of the Abbasid Caliphate led to a gradual decline in the efficiency of the *Berid*. The *Sahib el-Berid* himself had something to do with the deteriora-tion of the postal services. That official had acquired so much power that he was thought of with jealousy by other heads of government departments, and was looked upon with suspicion by the Caliph. The *Sahib el-Berid* had gradually assumed the office of chief supervisor of the provincial officers. This gave him the oppor-tunity of spying upon the provincial governors (in behalf of the Caliph); and it also made it possible for him to connive in revolts against the Caliph. Accordingly, the powers and the purse of the *Sahib el-Berid* were indirectly curtailed, and his department was subjected to innumerable restrictions. An institution such as the *Berid* needed the active backing of the Caliph, and the full co-operation of the provincial officials. After the eleventh century, these officials ceased to co-operate; and the Zengid Caliphs alone gave their consistent support to the postal services. Furthermore, in addition to the weakening of the administration of the *Berid*, the postal routes became increasingly unsafe; and from time to time the imperial service had actually to be suspended. After Baghdad was for the last time besieged by the Mongols, and sacked by them in 1258, the whole postal system was disrupted.

Three years after the last Abbasid Caliph took refuge with the Sultan of Egypt, and the centre of Saracen political power shifted to Cairo, the postal services were reopened. In 1261 the great Mamluk Sultan, ez-Zahir Baybars I, reorganized the *Berid*. One reason for this was the Sultan's desire to reunite the forces of Islam in the east, and to bind all the provinces more closely to Cairo— under his personal supervision. Three officials of the Cairo Chancellery, el-Omari in the fourteenth century, el-Kalkashandi and el-Makrizi in the fifteenth century, have given us very full accounts of the *Berid* and its development under the Mamluk Sultans of Egypt. The service, as they have outlined it, was organized as follows. The postmaster-general, then known as the *Emir el-Berid*, or (more technically) the *Sahib diwan el-insha*, was under the immediate supervision of the "Secretary of the Secret Chancellery" (*el-Katib es-Sirr*). Similarly, deputy postmasters in the six provinces of Damascus, Aleppo, Hama, Tripoli, Safad (Tiberias) and el-Kerak took their orders from the governor, or *Na'ib*, of each of these provinces. The *Na'ibs* were responsible for keeping the Sultan fully informed as to all current events; and for this purpose an imperial courier, or *beridi*, reported twice a week at Cairo, with the latest news from all the six provinces. The moment a *beridi* reached the palace, he was brought without delay into the presence of the Sultan. Three officials conducted him to the audience-chamber; and after the courier had kissed the ground in the royal presence, the dispatch was handed to the Sultan, so that the ruler himself might be the one to break the seal. Then the dispatch was handed to the Secretary of State, the aforementioned *Katib es-Sirr*, whose duty it was to read the contents aloud to his master. Even if some Emir happened at that moment to be in audience, he was expected to stand apart while the document was being read to the Sultan. Before setting out on a tour of the provinces, every *beridi* was given a silver plaque, about the size of the palm of his hand; one side bore the name of the reigning Sultan, and the other a religious inscription. This metal tablet was supposed to be hung around the neck of the courier, inside his cloak; and a yellow silk scarf had to be worn on his back, outside his outer garments. By the yellow scarf he could instantly be recognized as an imperial *beridi*, and by that sign he was able to obtain relays at the post-stations. The silver plaque was returned to the Chancellery at the termination of each round trip.

Four days were allowed by the imperial schedule for a courier to ride between Cairo and Damascus, and five days to ride as far as Aleppo; but occasionally the journey took even less time than that. *Khans* were built at all the post-stations on the Cairo–Aleppo highway; but they were not necessarily equidistant from each other. The distances between *khans*, in the country districts, varied according to the availability of water; and every important town was required to have a *khan*. At these post-stations the courier could count upon obtaining water, food, forage and any necessary equipment, as well as a remount; and a saddled horse was customarily kept in readiness. The principal trans-desert postal route in the Mamluk period was from Damascus to Meshed Rahba, via Karyetain, Beida, Tadmor (Palmyra), Arak, Sukhna and Kubakib. Rahba and the whole of this *Little Desert* route was under the jurisdiction of the *Na'ib* of Damascus, whose province was the most important of the six Syrian provinces. Beyond Rahba, the postal service was extended to Mosul; but that was also beyond the jurisdiction of the *Niyaba* of Damascus. The more direct courier route to Baghdad, via Dumeir and Hit, was also used upon occasion.

It has been said by more than one student of the Saracens, that the *Berid* was one of the most important institutions of Islam. The building of many *khans*, the digging of wells along arid sections of the post-routes, and the greater security of the roads all gave a great impetus to trade and travel. The roads were considered so safe that even a woman could journey by any one of them, on foot or on horseback. Furthermore, the best type of responsible government employee was developed in the *beridi*. Every courier was an Arab chosen from the militia; he was liable for service, day or night, on the Sultan's business; and he was necessarily a man of intelligence, discretion and tact. Occasionally the *beridi* was sent on private and very delicate royal missions; and sometimes he was even charged with collecting the royal taxes.

2

THE "TATARS" OF THE OTTOMAN EMPIRE, AND THE PIGEON POST

After Timur the Mongol invaded Syria in the fifteenth century, the imperial *Berid* was suspended. In fact, after 1426, the postal services ceased to exist in both Syria and Egypt except for purely local purposes. They were not resurrected until the Ottoman régime was firmly established in the lands of the former Caliphate. During the first century of their rule, the Ottoman Turks gave more attention to perfecting their military organization than to developing civil and political institutions. It is not, therefore, until the middle of the sixteenth century that one hears again of a postal system in the Near East.

When Europeans began to travel extensively in the Ottoman Empire, two types of courier service were in use in Syria and Mesopotamia. One, a local messenger corps to link cities and serve the country districts; the other imperial, and part of a central organization to link Constantinople with the provinces. Most of the large cities had each its own courier system, which was maintained for commercial purposes and to facilitate the business of its merchants. Take, for example, Aleppo. A large permanent corps was kept there, all of whose members were under the orders of a single shaykh, known as the *Shaykh es-Sa'a*. He alone was responsible both for the honesty and for the efficiency of every one of his messengers. They were divided into two noninterchangeable groups: the couriers allotted to the settled regions, who invariably travelled on foot; and the desert couriers, speci-

16

ally picked for courage and intelligence, who performed their journeys on the best available dromedaries. Anyone desirous of thus dispatching either letters or valuables (whether in the form of money or not) without waiting for the departure of a caravan, would make a personal and private arrangement with the shaykh of this courier organization. There was no fixed tariff for such services, because the cost of sending a messenger to any given place varied greatly. The charge made depended upon the season of the year, the supposed difficulty or danger of the journey contemplated, and the time-limit agreed upon for delivery of the message. Accordingly a special bargain was driven in each case; after which the shaykh would choose a messenger (for whom he personally accepted entire responsibility) and then, after giving him his charge, he would—in person— set the courier on his way. The couriers assigned to the Aleppo–Baghdad route were, comparatively speaking, few in number. This was partly because there was not much call for their services; but an added reason for their scarcity was the fact that it was difficult to find many men who were sufficiently reliable and resourceful to be entrusted with dispatches of value. Even as in the twentieth century, desert couriers had a great deal to contend with. They rode hard, often out of reach of water; and they had to be ever vigilant, constantly on the look-out for avowed enemies or unknown Beduin raiders. Several times a day a courier might have to leave his dromedary and scout from hillocks in order to reconnoitre the country which he was about to traverse; often he would have to change his route, perhaps at a moment's notice, and make a wide detour around some spring or oasis where he had counted upon finding food, or water, or both. Of course, travelling alone, the courier had several advantages over a cumbrous caravan. He was unhampered by the delays of routine, elaborate encampments and the use of many and slow-moving animals; and he was free to take as many difficult short-cuts as were either practicable or necessary. So that the courier often covered the distance between Aleppo and Baghdad within a week's time.

As for the *tatars*, or dispatch-bearers of the Ottoman Government, they were a corps entirely separate and distinct from ordinary couriers. They were paid out of the Turkish treasury, and were organized to carry political and administrative dispatches, mandates or bullion through the length and breadth of the Ottoman Empire. On trunk routes they were provided with relays of horses at numerous post-stations, and were expected to travel night and day if their business was urgent. Ordinarily speaking, they were required to perform their journeys within certain definite time-limits; they were penalized if this limit was exceeded; but they were often awarded a bonus in addition to their pay when they made extraordinarily fast trips. On the Baghdad–Constantinople route they were "often" supposed to cover the distance (which was between 1400 and 1500 miles) in twelve or thirteen days. And once even a *tatar* was said to have travelled from Baghdad to Constantinople in eleven days. At least these record journeys were reported by Dr. Thomas Howel, a servant of the East India Company, who travelled home from India via Baghdad in 1797.[1]

There was this much interchange between the two courier systems: if any person could show that he had pressing need (for business or other vital reasons) to send an urgent message, the government would grant a special permit for the hiring of a *tatar*. Such permission was the more to be valued because, not only was the greatest speed thus assured, and the use of all government facilities *en route*, but also identical protection was accorded to *tatars* when carrying civil dispatches as when they were engaged upon government business, under imperial orders. From time

[1] Thomas Howel (1797), pp. 43 and 115. There is a note in the French edition of Dr. Howel's *Voyage en Retour de l'Inde*, to the effect that the word *tatar*, in Turkish, means courier or messenger. Many eighteenth-century writers mistakenly spelled the word for courier, *tartar*; and thus arose the prevailing, erroneous idea that Turkish couriers were, in general, Tatars (then invariably spelt Tartar), which was not the case. Cf. Howel, *ibid.* p. 43 note.

This note is given here for what it is worth, although it must be admitted that the most up-to-date Turkish dictionary does not substantiate the statement.

According to the Oriental Department of the British Museum, the most approved modern spelling for both Tatar (the race) and *tatar* (a courier) is without the first "*r*".

to time, however, the *tatars* were complained of because they delayed to escort merchants or to convey merchandise in person. But this, of course, never happened when they were upon government, or Turkish business.

There was another, a totally different kind of postal system, which supplemented the *tatar* and municipal courier services. The pigeon post was a highly developed institution that had its origin in the early Saracen period. The Arabs and the Turks both realized the potential advantages of such a post, and utilized the birds as much as was practicable, in desert as well as in mountainous regions. The Caliph el-Mahdi, third of the Abbasids, was the first to organize a pigeon post (in the latter part of the eighth century). Homing pigeons were bred in Mesopotamia for the use of the government; and the egg of an exceptionally fast bird is said to have been worth as much as twenty dinars (about £10). The Caliph also authorized the importation of the best available homing pigeons, the prices of which varied between 700 and 1000 dinars (approximately £350 to £500). In spite of their popularity in Mesopotamia, it was some time before homing pigeons were imported into Syria or Egypt. The first ones were brought to Syria from Mosul in the twelfth century—in 1160, to be exact. Eventually, the Fatimid Caliphs of Cairo created a special government department just for the purpose of supervising the pigeon post, and of keeping track of the genealogies of the various birds employed. Messages, written in code on very thin paper, were carried by pigeons between Cairo and Basra, and between Basra and Constantinople. These birds were also used on the *Little Desert* courier route, between Damascus, Palmyra and Meshed Rahba.

In the Ottoman period, the first travellers who commented upon the use made of homing pigeons were Rauwolff and Van Linschoten. The former noted that they were used between Baghdad and Basra, and between Aleppo and Alexandretta, for commercial purposes. The latter described how "doves" carried news of great importance from Basra and Baghdad to Aleppo and Constantinople. He also claimed that pigeons of the Turkish post sometimes flew as far as a thousand miles. This they were able to do because there was a highly organized system of relays, which provided towers for the birds on an average of every fifty miles. A certain Master Thomas Dallam, who was in Aleppo in 1600, stated, from his own observation, that homing pigeons (they were usually called "carrier pigeons" in his day) flew from Aleppo to Alexandretta in only four hours. Tavernier later remarked that the English and French vice-consuls, who were stationed at Alexandretta, notified their consuls at Aleppo of the anchoring of one of their country's vessels by sending one or two pigeons across the mountains. The news was thus received within four or five hours after a boat's arrival, instead of two or three days later.

By the nineteenth century the pigeon post had been discontinued; although the Basra and Iskanderun breeds of homing pigeons were famous even in Europe. Captain Callier claims to have been told (in 1837) that the pigeon post of the early eighteenth century had been even more popular than the courier services—at least in Mesopotamia. He also said that no one in Baghdad had been able to give him any satisfactory explanation as to the reason for its abandonment by the Ottoman Government. The Reverend Henry Teonge, writing from Aleppo in the seventeenth century, stated that European merchants had given up using pigeons "by common consent". He gave a reason for this, as follows. A certain carrier bird was killed on its way to Aleppo from the coast. A merchant, on finding the note that was tied to its wing, learned that there had been a sensational rise in the price of gall-nuts in Europe. The merchant, acting on this information, bought up all the available gall-nuts in the neighbourhood of Aleppo, and resold them to his own great profit. This led to so much ill-feeling among the *Frangi* in Syria that they all agreed to guard against any future misadventures of the kind.

3

THE BRITISH DROMEDARY POST

As soon as commercial relations between the Sultan's government and the nations of the West were established on a sufficiently

firm basis, Frankish merchants began to penetrate into the remoter
parts of the Ottoman Empire. The *factories* and commercial companies which did business in Syria extended their activities and
their spheres of influence; and Christian merchants vied with each
other to exploit Mesopotamia and western Asia, which had been
inaccessible to them for so long. Then, directly the Portuguese, the
Venetians, the French and the English entrenched themselves on
the eastern side of the desert, they were faced with the necessity of
maintaining some sort of communication with their older and
more important bases on the Syrian side. Like the contemporary
Turks and their Saracen predecessors, the Christian commercial
communities were forced to find some way of bridging the desert
that divided them.

As the English alone of these four Christian powers developed
a genuine desert postal service, and as they alone persisted in using
the desert routes between the seventeenth and the twentieth centuries, it is permissible to consider the postal courier problem
entirely from their point of view. In the first place, the initiative
was taken by the *factors* of the East India Company who were
stationed at Surat—more than a century before the permanent
establishment of their *factory* at Basra. From letters of servants of
the Company in India, one learns that their first attempt to send
dispatches overland was made in 1615, and that assistance was
earnestly "entreated" from the Consul of the Levant Company,
stationed at Aleppo, to co-operate in forwarding them on to
England. But the real impetus for the establishing of overland
communication via Aleppo came two years later, when the Surat
Factory planned to extend its activities into Iran, and so became
conscious of more need to send packets to England as quickly and
as safely as possible. Edward Connock spared no pains to persuade
the officials in London of the wisdom of such relatively rapid
communication. And then, from Ispahan, he wrote at length to
the Consul in Aleppo, Mr Chapman, to make arrangements for a
regular service via Baghdad. He asked that the Consul send him
"two footmen of the Arabb nation, and such as have wife and
children or parents in that your city of Alleppo" (who might be

regarded as hostages for the good conduct of the "footmen"). "Such men they must be", he wrote, "as are both honest and painful, and that know the way from Bagdatt" (Baghdad) "to you through the desert without a guide." Furthermore, these men should receive "sufficient reward for their service, either yearly or by the journey", because "our occasions will be great and often and requireth speed, nor will shame at petty expenses".[1] When such letters were sent thus to Aleppo, the Consul was asked to forward them to England either by way of Constantinople or else by a Dutch, an English or a "Mercellian" ship (from Alexandretta, Latakia, Tripoli or even Beyrout)—whichever way, in short, might prove to be safest and most expeditious.

It was not long before dispatches were being sent across the Syrian Desert with some regularity. Such packets of letters, incidentally, were always sent in duplicate, by "double conveyance"; and they were dispatched with more or less frequency for the next twenty years. But the Baghdad–Aleppo route, although long in use by the Venetians and the Portuguese, was never popular with the East India Company's servants, because of their belief that English mail packets were intercepted and stolen by the Portuguese agents in Baghdad. So that, after 1636, dispatches were sent to Aleppo by way of Basra whenever possible. Also, until the trans-desert service was properly systematized in the following century, there was considerable complaint about delays and time lost *en route* to England. Packets of letters dispatched from Iran or India took from nine to eleven months, occasionally more, to

---

[1] Quoted from *Letters to the East India Company*, vol. v, pp. 285 and 286. It must be remembered that the English *factory* at Aleppo was an agency of the Levant Company, and, therefore, totally unrelated to the East India Company. Any service performed by members of one, for servants of the other, was a purely gratuitous kindness. As witness, for example, the following extract from the Court Minutes of the East India Company (p. 148), for 27th January 1636: "Mr. Wansford, the Consul at Aleppo, having sent two packets to the Company costing 7*l.* or 8*l.*, this sum is ordered to be paid to him with a gratification of 20*l.* in acknowledgement of his courtesy". Several such reimbursements (for postage and conveyance of letters, together with additional gratuities for "courtesy") were made by the East India Company in subsequent years.

arrive in London. Much of this delay was actually caused by the packet-boats, which had always to await favouring winds, but never waited for overland dispatches.

The chief objection to using the desert routes for mail was the unsettled condition of the country, particularly towards the latter part of the seventeenth century. The Ottoman Empire was believed to be in a state of political and economic decline; and it was a fact that the Sultan found it impossible either to maintain order, or to afford protection to foreigners, in any of the lands which bordered upon the Syrian Desert. To make matters worse, the Sultan was on bad terms with the Shah of Iran, and professed to fear an alliance between Iran and England which might threaten either Turkish trading interests or his remoter territories. Rumours kept persisting to the effect that no Englishman could travel safely in the Ottoman Empire, still less through or across it. Sometimes even, a "footpost", already started on its desert way, would turn back again—particularly when incidents occurred such as the deaths of William Finch and his companions in Baghdad (in 1613) and the subsequent confiscation of his property by "the currish and tyrannical Turks". Add to all this the fact that desert Arabs were irreconcilably hostile to the Turks, and one can picture a nomad's-land in which anything might happen in the way of fatal surprises. Occasionally also fatal mistakes occurred, like one which was recounted by Tavernier. A certain express messenger had been dispatched from Ispahan with a packet of letters for a consul at Aleppo; he set out in company with two Capuchin friars and an Arab guide. Somewhere between the Euphrates and the mid-desert oasis of Taiyiba, they encountered a caravan of Damascus merchants whom they mistakenly thought to be robbers. They rashly attacked the caravan, and one of the friars killed one of the merchants; whereupon the merchants naturally retaliated by killing all four of the travellers. The packet of documents, however, was recovered and eventually reached the hands of the consul for whom they were intended.

On the whole, however, the open desert was considered relatively safe during the early seventeenth century, and far less dangerous than the mountainous country north of the Euphrates. Venetian, Portuguese and French emissaries all used the *Little Desert* routes until the middle of the century; although there appears to have been no thought of maintaining any regular system of communication between the European communities of the Near and Middle East. In the eighteenth century, conditions gradually improved; but between 1673 and 1745 it is not recorded that any European dispatch-bearers crossed the desert. Before the middle of the eighteenth century, however, Englishmen once more turned their attention to the short-cut to India. Servants of the East India Company began to cross between Aleppo and Basra (in 1750), and the Company's dispatches were safely carried to and fro across the desert.

Once the general use and feasibility of the Great Desert Route was thus proved, there was agitation for the organizing of a permanent and regular overland postal service. The proposition was opposed, at first, on the ground that a mail route via Suez would provide a quicker, and therefore better, service. Between 1780 and 1800, all possible routes to the East were variously and statistically debated; and the Directors of the East India Company received copious documents and lengthy reports on the subject from its agents, and from others interested in the development of communication with India. The case, briefly stated, was this. Servants of the East India Company travelled to India by three different routes; but the sea voyage around the Cape was considered too long for the use of the Company's dispatch-bearers. This meant that one of the other two routes would have to be developed for mail purposes. The quickest known route was by Suez, but it could not be relied upon throughout the year, especially for the passage home (travelling from east to west), on account of seasonally adverse winds in the Red Sea. For six years or so the East India Company had made use of the Suez Route for the transmission of Indian dispatches; but after the withdrawal of their agent from Cairo in 1782 (for reasons commercial and political), the Aleppo–Basra Route had become the most popular one of the three. And after 1798, when a permanent resident was appointed to Baghdad, they had the alternative use of the Little Desert Route from Aleppo to Baghdad. The desert part of the overland journey (some 770 miles in length) took, on an average, only twenty-five to forty days—unless a messenger were to allow himself to be delayed by travelling with a large merchant caravan. But the time required to complete the entire journey from India to England was three and a half months; and frequently it took six months or more. For example, Messrs Irwin and Smyth, of the Madras and Bombay Establishments, left England on the 26th of October 1780, and did not arrive in Bombay until the 29th of the following May; and they did not linger *en route*, because they were the bearers of urgent dispatches. Between England and Syria the boat connections were infrequent and erratic; and before beginning the desert portion of the trip, there was always delay due to the time wasted in getting together and bargaining for a sufficient number of guides, camels and the adequate provisions. So that occasionally the time consumed on the overland route very nearly approximated that spent at sea on the Cape Route.[1]

Colonel James Capper, who crossed the *Great Desert* in 1778, suggested that all three routes be employed in rotation:

By the several ways of the Cape of Good Hope, Suez, and Bassora, we shall be able to send dispatches to and from India at all seasons . . . the best season for leaving England, to go by the Cape of Good Hope, commences in November, and ends in April; that by Suez commences early in April, and ends in June; and that by Bassora will be the best route all the rest of the year.

Such a scheme would ensure "a constant succession of intelli-

[1] According to Major Taylor, the record passages made by sailing ships to India, via the Cape of Good Hope, were—up to January 1799—as follows:

To Bengal	.	. 4 months
„ Madras	.	. 3 months 10 days
„ Bombay	.	. 3 months 20 days
	and	4 months 15 days

gence".[1] It was also his idea that, when the desert route was used, the Company should make use of the ordinary post from England to Vienna, and employ couriers from there to Aleppo and Basra who should go by way of Constantinople. This, although too tiring a journey for the ordinary traveller, would be the speediest of all routes for a mail service.

On the other hand, Major John Taylor advised concentrating upon a single route, and that one via Egypt. He also crossed the *Great Desert* (eleven years later than Colonel Capper), and it took him six months to perform the journey; so that he considered the Suez Route as definitely preferable for the establishing of a regular mail service. After returning from India he made a lengthy comparative study of both the Syrian and the Egyptian routes, with elaborate tables of statistics to prove that, at any time of year, and by any imaginable variation of the two voyages, at least thirteen days could always be saved on the Suez Route; and he believed that under the best conditions (that is, with favouring winds in the Red Sea) more than twenty-six days might thus be saved. Major Taylor was convinced that, if connections were speeded up, the Suez–Red Sea Route would ensure mail deliveries between India and England in from fifty-two to sixty-six days; as against eighty to one hundred days on the Aleppo–Basra Route —even allowing for the time which might be saved by a somewhat similar speeding up of the service via Syria. It is to be noted that in his calculations for the overland route, Major Taylor reckoned upon only sixteen days being spent between Aleppo and Basra. This, because he never visualized making use of Europeans on the desert, either as couriers themselves or as escorts for Arab messengers; since the difficulties and hardships attendant upon fast desert travel were too great for such as were not accustomed to dromedary-riding. In his own words:

I condemn Europeans being ever employed to carry dis-

[1] Quoted from *Observations on the Passage to India, through Egypt, and across the Great Desert . . . with remarks . . .* by James Capper, Esq., Colonel in the Service of the Honourable East India Company (London, 1783), p. xi.

patches either out or home, where expedition is required. It is safer and cheaper to dispatch three expresses by different routes, than to trust one European. Letters in cypher falling into any hands can be rarely attended with bad consequences; and it would be hard indeed if one did not escape.

Eventually, the Marquis Wellesley was to prove Major Taylor wrong in his minimum calculations for the Basra Route: this service, as run during the early part of the nineteenth century, normally took between sixty-eight and eighty-five days, from Bombay to London.[1]

In whatsoever way these various suggestions might eventually have been modified, co-ordinated and put into execution by the East India Company, had they been dealt with in times of peace, their solution in fact was determined by war and the exigencies of Anglo-French politics. The plan finally adopted was that recommended to the Company by the Marquis Wellesley, who in 1800 was Governor-General of India. He was very insistent in writing to the Court of Directors of the East India Company, and almost demanded that—in some way or other—communication between India and England should be accelerated. In view of the then existing Anglo-French hostilities, the Governor-General of India felt a pressing need to communicate as often as possible, not only with England but also with the English forces in Egypt. And during the Napoleonic wars it was only natural that he should consider the Basra Route the only safe one. Also, although the Suez Route might have been potentially more rapid, it was a fact that unless elaborate and impracticable improvements were made via Suez, the Syrian Desert Route was the most rapid

[1] *Travels from England to India, in the year 1789, by way of the Tyrol, Venice, Scandaroon, Aleppo, and over the Great Desert to Bussora; with instructions for travellers; and an account of the expense of travelling*, by Major John Taylor (of the Bombay Establishment), 2 vols. (London, 1799), vol. ii, pp. 20-22, 31-40, and 294. Also an earlier work by Major Taylor, published in 1795, embodying *Considerations of the practicability and advantages of a more speedy communication between Great Britain and her Possessions in India:—with an Outline of a Plan for the more Ready Conveyance of Intelligence over-land by the way of Suez.*

in use at that time. In 1800 the Marquis Wellesley wrote to the Court of Directors as follows:

I trust you will establish the monthly packet over land from London, and also monthly vessels of intelligence. . . . The object is of the utmost importance; in the present year I was nearly *seven months* without receiving one line of authentic intelligence from England . . . so that I suffered almost insupportable distress of mind. . . . Speedy, authentic, and regular intelligence from Europe is essential to the conduct of the trade and government of this empire.[1]

Before outlining the details of a plan for the establishment of an official dromedary post, the Marquis Wellesley had obtained as exhaustive reports as possible on the subject of alternative desert routes between the Persian Gulf and the Mediterranean. The contents of the reports which were submitted by the two agents who were stationed in Irak, may be summarized as follows. From Basra, Mr Samuel Manesty wrote that the desert service from Basra to Aleppo had proved its great usefulness; that his messengers were "active and careful", and anxious to please from motives of self-interest; that the Consul John Barker at Aleppo, who employed *tatars* to forward the mail to Constantinople, had most zealously co-operated with him; and that the various desert shaykhs—whose tribes roamed over the Great Desert Route—had promised safe-conduct for his messengers, and given repeated assurances of friendship. He added that he had always been careful to refrain from sending any packets across the desert which had the slightest appearance of containing valuables, lest Arab cupidity be tempted. For fifteen years (from 1784 to 1799) the Basra–Aleppo courier route had been successfully and uninterruptedly used by agents of the East India Company. Successfully, that is to say, with the exception of a brief period in 1799, when their desert messengers had been molested and even robbed by marauding

[1] *Despatches* (1836), vol. ii, p. 394. Letter to Hugh Inglis, Chairman of the Court of Directors, 6th October 1800.

nomads—probably Wahhabis. Mr Manesty finished his report
with a statement of his own conviction that the recent epidemic
of robberies on the desert was, though very regrettable, a purely
temporary phase; because he had got into touch with the shaykhs
of the offending tribesmen and they had given satisfactory guaran-
tees as to the future good behaviour of their people.

On the other hand, the resident newly appointed to Baghdad,
Mr Harford Jones (later Sir Harford Jones Brydges), strongly
recommended the use of the Baghdad–Constantinople high-road,
on the ground that this route would give more speed and greater
security. More speed, because dispatches sent from Basra took six
days to reach Baghdad, and thence (after only a day's delay) could
be carried on to Constantinople in twenty days or less—making a
total of, at most, twenty-seven days. This schedule could be
shortened by several days between January and June. Whereas
from Basra, although dispatches sent via Aleppo might take only
twenty-seven days in summer, there was no certainty as to how
much longer they would inevitably take in winter, when the going
was made harder by rain or snow. If the Baghdad–Constantinople
Route were to be used regularly, Mr Jones thought it would be
necessary to obtain a firman from the Porte, giving the English
Resident at Baghdad the right to employ four *tatars* for the exclusive service of the Anglo-Indian mails. The Company would
have to pay each one of these *tatars* an annual salary of ten Turkish
pounds (which, at that period, would have amounted to less than
£9 sterling), with additional bonuses for unusual record deliveries.
Altogether, Mr Jones believed that it would only cost about £15
(sterling) to send a packet of dispatches from Basra to Constantinople by way of Baghdad. This, he thought, was rather less
than the usual cost of sending them via Aleppo. The greater
security of the Baghdad Route lay in the fact that, if a *tatar* were
ever lost, his dispatches could be traced—as could he—from town
to town by means of special arrangements with the Pashas of
Baghdad, Mosul, Diarbekr and Sivas.

After due consideration of the Marquis Wellesley's proposals,
the East India Company decided to inaugurate a double service

for the consular mail from Basra to Constantinople via both
Baghdad and Aleppo. Arrangements were made to send monthly
posts to and from Basra, an original dispatch and its duplicate. One
was to be forwarded to Constantinople via Aleppo, and one via
Baghdad; the original to go alternately by each of the two routes.
A special note was to be appended if the dispatches were intended
to go by express messengers. Also, careful notes were to be kept
at Basra, Baghdad and Constantinople, of the dates on which such
packets were received and sent off, and of their final arrival at the
latter city, in order to discover which of the two routes was
definitely preferable.[1]

This overland mail service proved as satisfactory as the Marquis
Wellesley had hoped; but after a few years the Basra–Aleppo
Route came to be preferred to the other via Baghdad, and was
used almost exclusively until the Suez–Red Sea Route was reopened in 1833. Soon a fortnightly instead of a monthly service of
packet-boats was established in the Persian Gulf. These packets
were only small sailing-vessels, but they habitually made the
voyage between Bombay and Basra in from ten to fifteen days,
even in the face of the dreaded south-west monsoon. So that mail
deliveries were made between Bombay and London in from sixty-
eight to eighty-five days, and the service maintained its name for
efficiency. After the reopening of the Suez Route, interest waned
temporarily in that through "Turkish Arabia" (*i.e.* the Great
Desert Route); and this service was even suspended after 1833,
until Colonel Chesney urged a revival of the desert post. This
was the Colonel Chesney who was in command of the famous
Euphrates Expedition which was attempting to establish river
communication between Syria and the Persian Gulf; and who
took a vast interest in all supplementary services. However, although the Euphrates Expedition was doomed to failure (in the

[1] See the *India Office, Home Series*, Miscellaneous, 470: the Governor-General
—No. 9 official, 18th February and 12th March 1800, with enclosures from
the Residents at Baghdad and at Bussorah, in answer to enquiries made by the
East India Company as to "the means of forwarding with the utmost possible
security and dispatch, the public (national) Correspondence from India to
Constantinople".

matter of its principal objective), the desert post was resurrected in 1837. But several modifications were made in the service: the "Arabian Route" (as it was then called) was used only for the forwarding of duplicate dispatches, and the route itself was changed. Before the middle of the nineteenth century, the Mediterranean was linked with the Persian Gulf by means of a dromedary post which cut almost straight across the desert from Damascus to either Hit or Ramadi, and proceeded thence via Baghdad. This was the old direct desert road of Roman and Saracen days, which is still known to the Arabs as the *Darb es-Sa'i*, or "Road of the Courier". It is a road practicable only for fast travellers, because water is so scarce *en route*. A single group of springs known collectively as Bir Melossa is the chief watering-place between Dumeir and Muheiwir; and that is the only perennial water supply (in a distance of almost 280 miles) where a courier could count upon finding plenty of water at any season of the year. This very fact gives anyone using the route a certain immunity from interference by the Beduin, and particularly from such of them as migrate annually northwards and southwards, accompanied by their families, in search of water and pasturage for their flocks. The service was further quickened (after 1837) by the use of a steamboat on the Tigris: the East India Company maintained one steamer on the river to ferry the mails between Baghdad, Basra and Mohammera on the Lower Tigris–Euphrates. West of the desert section, the mails for Europe were carried by special horsemen to Beyrout, for a Mediterranean packet-boat connection.

In addition to alterations in the route of the dromedary post, internal changes were also made in the service. "Postage" at fixed rates was levied on articles thus dispatched; and the Government of India subsidized the line to the extent of a monthly grant of 200 Rs. (about £20), in order to supplement its normally meagre receipts.

All this while, however, the principal Imperial Post, containing the originals of all dispatches, was sent every month by way of Suez. This shorter route (which was made the official one in 1837) inevitably became the favourite as soon as it was realized that steamboats—especially when used in the Red Sea—were capable of overcoming the chief drawback of this service. Even before the Canal was opened, the journey between England and India, via Suez, was actually shortened to twenty-eight days. Another practical advantage of this route lay in the fact that it was equally well adapted for both passenger and mail traffic. This was emphatically and obviously not true of the "Arabian" route; still less so of the new desert way which entailed such hard riding. By the end of the nineteenth century, for instance, couriers often took only six days to go from Baghdad to Damascus—though it must be admitted that their average time for the desert crossing was eight or nine days.

Before continuing, two interesting facts must be noted. First, that the Syrian Desert postal service was never actually incorporated with the Indian postal system—notwithstanding the subsidy granted it by the Government of India. Secondly, that between 1844 and 1862 there was no direct communication between India and the Persian Gulf—scarcely even any trading in the Gulf by British merchantmen. The result of this unusual state of affairs was that all the Indian mail from both Basra and Baghdad had to go backwards: across the desert to Damascus, and through the Red Sea to India!

After the year 1862, the Government of India became again actively interested in the development of the Persian Gulf. A mail steamer service was inaugurated which, after a dozen years, became a weekly one; the Euphrates and Tigris Steam Navigation Company was further developed; and the Indian postal system was extended to include the lands bordering upon the Persian Gulf, and even established post-offices at Basra and at Baghdad. But in spite of the greater speed and efficiency thus assured to the desert mail service, the Indian Government lost money on the line: it cost them Rs. 489 (about £49) a month to maintain the service via Baghdad and Damascus. So that the government was reluctantly forced to withdraw its subsidy in 1871. The result may be imagined, particularly in view of the fact that the Ottoman Empire maintained a rival trans-desert post during the eighteen-

17

eighties (in addition to the fortnightly *tatar* post which went from Baghdad to Constantinople via Mosul and Diarbekr), and made a series of persistent endeavours to oust the Indian post-offices from Turkish Irak. The only thing which kept the British dromedary post going at all was its superior trustworthiness—or so one may infer from certain remarks made by Baron Thielmann on the subject. During the year 1886 the British desert service was officially closed after a century's use.

After 1886, the only dromedary post was that of the Ottoman Government. In 1889 the Sultan re-established the direct service between Baghdad and Damascus, which had been suspended two years previously; and a weekly desert post was thereafter maintained until the outbreak of the Great War. Seventeen years later, Aleppo became the foremost Syrian station instead of Damascus; because the route thither was safer, and because it was a more convenient headquarters for the forwarding of mails to Constantinople than was the more southerly city. Nevertheless, *tatar* couriers continued to use the shorter route alternatively, from time to time. Sometimes, when the service happened (temporarily) to be doubled, the Damascus and the Aleppo track were both in use. But so robber-infested had the Damascus–Hit route become that it was known as "the road of death". Twice in the year 1909, Arabs (who were said to have been of the Dulaim) robbed the mail and killed the courier of the post. The Baghdad mails left twice a week for the Turkish capital. On Mondays they went by the northern *tatar* post, via Mosul; and on Thursdays via the *Little Desert*, for either Damascus or Aleppo. The desert couriers were, as they had always been, mounted on the best available dromedaries; and they rarely if ever conveyed money or valuables in their mail-bags. They always made a point of carrying some tobacco, and the latest news: two most acceptable gifts for any of the Beduin whom they could not avoid encountering. Generally speaking, couriers travelled alone; but occasionally they were commandeered to act as guides. This happened once, for instance, in 1911, when the joint caravan of Miss Gertrude Bell and the Shaykh of Kubaisa had need of such aid. The Shaykh hired the

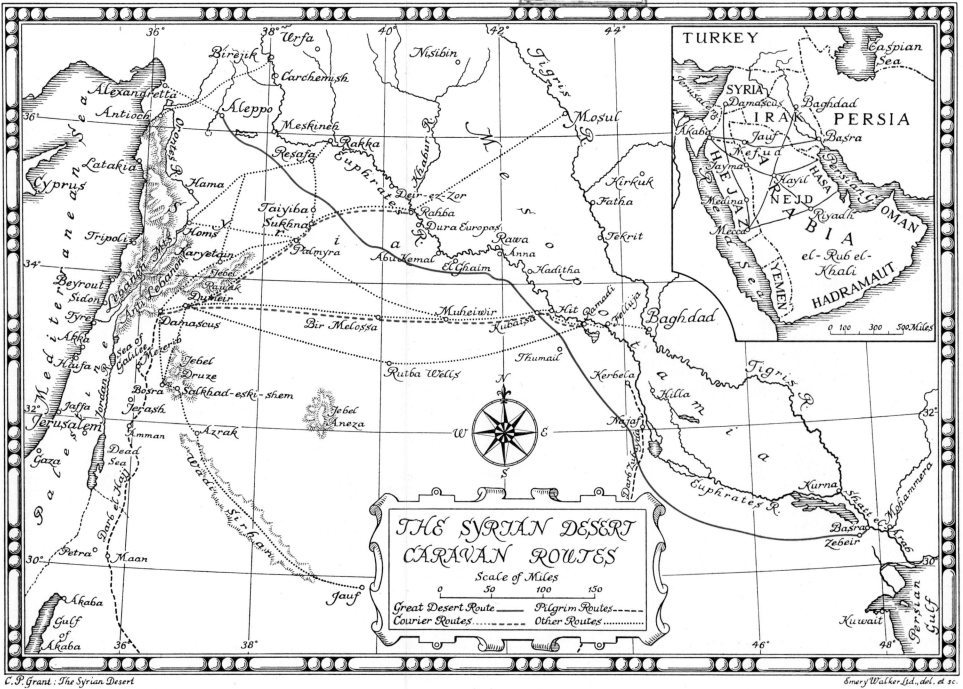

THE SYRIAN DESERT
CARAVAN ROUTES

Scale of Miles

0   50   100   150

Great Desert Route ——— Pilgrim Routes ------
Courier Routes ········· Other Routes ········

TURKEY

Caspian
Sea

SYRIA
Damascus   Baghdad
Jerusalem
Akaba   IRAK   PERSIA
Jauf   Basra
HEJAZ   Kefud
Tayma   Hayil   HASA   OMAN
Medina   NEJD
Mecca   Riyadh
ARABIA
YEMEN   el-Rub el-
Khali
HADRAMAUT

0   100   300   500 Miles

C. P. Grant : The Syrian Desert

Emery Walker Ltd., del. et sc.

desert postman (possibly bribed is the more accurate word), who was about to set out for Baghdad, to guide their caravan from Dumeir to the Euphrates. This did not take the courier out of his ordinary route, but it necessarily delayed him.

Very soon after the Ottoman Government entered the Great War, all trans-desert services were inevitably suspended; and here ends the story of the dromedary post, obviously and most appropriately. The later history of the Overland Desert Mail belongs solely to the mechanical era; and the influence of these revolutionary changes on the methods of desert transportation will be described in the following chapter. The inauguration of motor transport, the opening of new desert highways for motor traffic, the development of modern trans-desert postal organizations, both the air and the motor services—all these dramatic developments came after the final disappearance of the dromedary post. Solitary couriers, capable of carrying only small dispatch-bags, have given place to mechanical couriers of unlimited carrying capacity; and the prolonged and arduous days of desert journeyings have been superseded by rapid and only briefly wearying trips. Undeniably, the foresight of such as the Marquis Wellesley has been justified. A mail route which was of vital importance, even under the disadvantages of medieval methods of travel, has now doubly proved its importance under modern conditions of transport. This desert link, once the most brittle of an imperial chain, is now of unquestioned strength.

CHAPTER IX

THE ERA OF MECHANICAL TRANSPORT

No one of the preceding chapters has been brought up to date. In each the story has ended at the dawn of a mechanical era, before the Syrian Desert had once more come to be thought of as an important link between East and West. This, the last chapter of a survey of desert travel, should contain an outline of the various modern plans which have contemplated the use and improvement of the desert short-cut to India.

I

THE EUPHRATES EXPEDITION

In the first of these plans, the Euphrates river—rather than the actual desert—was visualized as the connecting link. "The Steam Committee of the House of Commons" recommended, and Parliament subsequently voted, a grant of £20,000 for an experiment to be made for steamboat communication with India by Syria and the Euphrates. A supplementary £10,000 was later subscribed: half by Parliament, and half by the East India Company. Preliminary investigations by Colonel Chesney in Asiatic Turkey, Syria, Arabia and Iran paved the way for such parliamentary action; the fact that the Euphrates Route was estimated to be 1230 miles shorter than the Suez Route was a telling argument in its favour; and the personal interest which King William IV took in the proceedings did much to put the scheme into active execution. Colonel Chesney conducted the expedition, and various departments of government contributed to its outfitting. After an explicit agreement with the Sultan of Turkey, and in spite of the unspoken opposition of Mohammed Ali, temporary docks and slips were constructed on the Euphrates some two and a half miles below Birejik. At this new river station, named Port William by the Englishmen, two steamboats were launched in the spring of 1836. These iron paddle-wheel steamers, named the *Euphrates* and the *Tigris*, had been transported from the mouth of the Orontes to the Euphrates, across the Lebanon Mountains. They were moved in sections along a corduroy road, except where they were rafted along such stretches of water as the Lake of Antioch—an amazing feat that took almost a year to accomplish. Sometimes a boiler, even though mounted on a wagon and dragged by forty pairs of oxen, could only travel at the rate of half a mile a day. For an adequate description of this undertaking, and a wealth of picturesque details, the reader is perforce referred to Colonel Chesney's own *Narrative* of the Expedition.

Before the survey of the Euphrates was actually begun, coaling stations were established at Deir ez-Zor and Anna; and the Arabs were prepared for the coming of the steamers by a special and friendly mission. Sections of the Aneza made a "treaty of amity and permanent peace", entailing commercial facilities, with His Majesty's Government; but the Montefik Arabs of the Lower Euphrates proved suspicious and unfriendly. The river was actually descended and surveyed all the way to the Persian Gulf, in spite of the loss of the *Tigris* and twenty of her men in a violent hurricane near el-Ghaim. Eventually, parts of the Tigris and the Karun rivers were also surveyed, as well as the lands adjacent to these water-ways.

The Expedition did not result in the opening of a steamboat service on the Euphrates, though a concern called the "Euphrates and Tigris Steam Navigation Company" subsequently established a steamboat service on the Tigris between Baghdad and Basra, to connect with the Gulf service of the "Peninsular and Oriental" and "British India" steamers between India and Basra. A re-examination of the Euphrates convinced even enthusiasts that this river was unfitted for swift and continuous steam navigation, on

CHESNEY'S RAFT DESCENDING THE EUPHRATES

Nearing Haditha

From F. R. Chesney : *Narrative of the Euphrates Expedition, 1835–7*

account of the periods of torrential flood which alternate with periods when the river is shallow and pool-like. The net result of the Euphrates Expedition appears to have been to turn the spotlight of European politics upon the Mesopotamian Valley; to convince European governments of the desirability of opening some sort of practicable commercial short-cut between the Continent and India. England was the first of the Great Powers to take any active steps to bring this about.

2

RAILWAY PLANS AND PROJECTS

Naturally enough, a railroad was the next medium of communication to be considered; and successive railway projects were formulated and received governmental consideration. Even after the opening of the Suez Canal in 1869, it was argued that the opening of an alternative route through "Turkish Arabia" would have immense commercial and political advantages. The "Euphrates Valley Railway" was the first of these schemes; and it was originally broached in or about 1840. The river itself proving intractable, a riverain railway appeared to offer the second-best solution for turning its valley to account. Twenty years after the disbanding of the Euphrates Expedition, a company was organized to promote the construction of a railway which should connect the Mediterranean with the Persian Gulf. Colonel, by then Major-General Chesney, and W. P. Andrew, chairman of the Scinde Railway Company and of the European and Indian Junction Telegraph Companies, were the moving spirits of the plan. Under their leadership the project took definite shape; the East India Company became genuinely interested in it; and the British Government instructed Viscount Stratford de Redcliffe (their Ambassador at Constantinople) to support General Chesney's efforts to procure a favourable concession from the Porte. The Sultan was asked to grant a ninety-nine-year free lease of the land on the right bank of the Euphrates for the construction of

the railway, plus a 6 per cent dividend per annum on a capital of
£8,000,000. In return for this concession, the railway was to
become Turkish property at the end of the ninety-nine years,
though a perpetual (English) right-of-way was to be guaranteed.
It was intended that the railway should connect Seleucia, the
ancient port of the Orontes, with Antioch, Aleppo and the
Euphrates; and that at first, until the track was completed as far
as Basra, there was to be a steamboat service on the river: from
"Jaber Castle" (about half-way between Meskineh and Rakka)
to the Persian Gulf. A concession was actually obtained from the
Porte, but the project had to be abandoned in England, because
the "Euphrates Valley Railway Company" failed to obtain a
financial guarantee for the enterprise from the British Government of the day. W. P. Andrew revived this project in 1871,
even though the concession for the railway had lapsed. A
Parliamentary Committee reported very favourably on the plan;
but once again the "Euphrates Valley Railway Company" failed
to secure a financial guarantee for its proposed railway, so the
scheme was necessarily and for the last time defeated.

Between 1840 and 1856 most of the arguments were used, in
favour of a Euphrates Valley Railway, which have grown so
familiar since that time; and which applied thereafter to all the
British schemes in turn which advocated making use of the Syrian
Desert as a short-cut to the East. It was considered "essential to
the vital interests of England in the East" to "cut in half" the distance to India. By this means England could keep in closer touch
with India; the advance of Russia, "the barbarian Colossus",
might be checked in the East; and English trade with Iran would
increase, as well as Anglo-Indian traffic and commerce. The Ottoman Empire was also brought into the question. The opening and
development of the Euphratean territories was held to be "essential to the well-being of Turkey". Aleppo and Baghdad, both
populous cities and centres of caravan commerce, would be greatly
benefited.

After 1872, when the Euphrates Valley Railway project was
finally scrapped, other trans-desert railways were projected and

debated in official and unofficial circles. There were two schools of thought on the subject, both of which desired a railway to bridge the Ottoman Empire; but one group believed that northern Mesopotamia offered the best route; and the other was convinced of the greater advantages of a desert route. Some people thought that a railroad laid through desert country could never be made to pay, and that therefore the only practicable route was across northern Mesopotamia, where fertile plains and urban centres— alike well-peopled—would help to increase the returns from the railway. On the other hand, many people realized the political complications that might arise from such a move; England, France, Germany and Italy, to say nothing of Russia, all claimed to have "vital interests" in the Ottoman Empire. Moreover, the Sultan could not be trusted to refrain from interfering in any public service which might be organized in his own dominions, within reach of Constantinople.

The political implications of any Anatolian or northern Meso- potamian railway project were not over-estimated. Eventually, after prolonged international bickering and the most delicate political negotiations, Germany obtained a concession from the Porte, and commenced the much-discussed Berlin-to-Baghdad railway. The Great War interfered with its completion; but the western branch of the post-War railroad of Irak (a Basra–Baghdad section was opened as early as 1920) will soon connect with this Anatolian line. The story of the building of the Berlin-to-Baghdad railway is a whole book in itself—a book that has already been written in interesting detail. All that may be said about it here is to mention that its eastern section bridges the Euphrates at Jera- blus (south of Birejik), and crosses the Mesopotamian plain south of the Urfa–Mardin caravan route; and that it has been completed as far as Nisibin. The post-War Mesopotamian boundary of Syria follows this railway line between Jerablus and Nisibin; and the Syrian railroad joins the Anatolian line at Muslimiya, a little north of Aleppo.

Advocates of a desert route have proposed several alternatives. The Turks (in 1873) and the French (in 1930) discussed the possibility of a *Little Desert* railway which should cross from Homs to Palmyra, and then follow the medieval courier route to Deir ez-Zor. The first of these proposals was never followed up seriously because engineers reported to the Ottoman Government that, since water was not available, it would be impracticable to run a railway over so long a stretch of desert. An alternative plan, similar to the one that was eventually adopted for the Berlin-to-Baghdad railway, was suggested to the Sultan instead. The French Government in Syria, however, have revived the scheme. Water has proved to be available, since the Iraq Petroleum Company, while laying the Tripoli branch of their oil pipe-line, found that they were able to sink artesian wells in the desert. The London *Times* of 17th September 1930 reported that a Homs–Palmyra–Deir ez-Zor railroad was "now fully planned", with a probable branch line from Gabaji to Abu Kemal; that its desert length would approximate 400 kilometres, and its estimated cost was 200,000,000 francs.

British statesmen and engineers, on the other hand, have concentrated their attention upon a *Great Desert* route. This was inevitable, since recent British interests in Egypt, Palestine and Irak have required the emphasis being laid on a more southerly route; especially as such a one would give more direct access to India, and be farther removed from interference by Turkey or any one of the other Great Powers. It was on these grounds that the Euphrates Valley scheme was finally abandoned—plus the fact that a railway which actually followed the right bank of the river would have been unnecessarily roundabout, and would have had to serve country that is as much desert as any part of the *Great Desert*, from the point of view of local freights and traffic.

Three principal (alternative) *Great Desert* routes have been suggested. As early as 1878 it was proposed that a railway should cross Palestine and Trans-Jordan from Haifa, or from Akka, to Salkhad, which should be carried thence down the length of the Wadi Sirhan to Jauf; and that from Jauf the main line should continue to Kuwait, with a branch line to Basra. Should the desert section of this route prove to be impracticable, it was thought possible that a railway might be built more directly across the desert, from Salkhad "due east" to Basra. It was this second plan that was followed, at least in part, in the railway survey which was made after the War. But before any survey was actually made, a third plan was formulated. It was suggested, by C. E. Drummond Black, in 1908 that a railroad might be constructed from Port Said, via Akaba and Jauf, to Basra (with a branch to Kuwait), which should follow, more or less closely, the thirtieth parallel of latitude. After crossing the *Shatt el-Arab*, the railway was to go on to Quetta, by way of Shiraz and Nushki. It was stated that there would be as few engineering difficulties in the building of an Akaba–Jauf–Basra line as had been encountered in the construction of the Damascus–Medina sections of the Hejaz railway.

There were two perennial drawbacks to any *Great Desert* railway project. In the first place, the Beduin could be counted upon to make trouble—if only spasmodically. Secondly, the extreme poverty of the country that would be served by such a railway gave cause for other apprehensions. Even the heartiest advocates of a desert railroad were apt to take their stand mainly on its political (or military) desirability; they questioned whether, in the long run, it would pay its own way, and so justify (economically) the expense of its construction. Nevertheless there seems today (since the Great War) good reason to think that it might be profitable to open, by this way, the Irak and Iranian markets to Europe. The surplus products of Irak, in particular, have increased both in quantity and in variety; and they will continue so to increase, on account of the extensive irrigation projects which are in process of development. The Hindiya barrage (near Hilla) and the great Habbania escape (designed to store up the wasted flood-waters of the Euphrates) are only the beginning. If a short-cut freight line to the Mediterranean could guarantee the barley-wheat crops of Irak and Iran an immediate outlet, these would reach the European markets a whole month earlier than the crops of all the other barley- and wheat-raising countries. In other words, these particular products would supply a perennial international demand, so their marketing value would not depend upon any world-wide system of competitive selling. Furthermore, Irak may once again become a cotton-growing country. Experiments have shown that cotton of fine quality can be grown there; so that, if the locust problem can be satisfactorily solved, an increasingly large surplus may be grown for export. It is scarcely necessary to add that the dates of Irak are as famous for their flavour as the date-palms of the country are for their profusion. Lastly, important oil-fields have been discovered in Irak and Iran; but the export of oil is a special problem which is being solved independently in a unique way. In the case of Iran, the question is not so much one of handling an increase of exportable products as it is of finding another outlet for her existing trade. Originally Iran traded overland, making use of the Anatolian and Syrian caravan routes. Eventually, in the later nineteenth century, much of Iran's trade was diverted northward, and reached Europe mainly through Russia. But since the War, and after the collapse of the Russian railways, Iran has once more begun to seek an outlet to Europe through the Mediterranean. There is always the Persian Gulf route, coupled with that around Arabia to the Red Sea; but, as in the case of Irak, a speedier and more direct overland outlet (such as would be provided by a trans-desert railway) would be an inestimable boon to Iranian merchants. There are some who think that multiple lorry services, across the modern motor tracks of the Syrian Desert, would solve the problem, at least for the present. According to their calculations, relays of lorries could handle most of what Irak and Iran would be capable of exporting for many years to come; and what could not be transported to Mediterranean ports in this way should either be shipped from Gulf ports by boat or carried by rail from Nisibin through Turkey. Certainly this would be an inexpensive solution of the problem, without involving any large initial expenditures, and without taking any risk of future losses and failures. On the other hand, a government that refused to take this chance might conceivably lose (by default) a valuable trading monopoly.

One other possible railway route was proposed before the War, along a line that is intermediate between the *Great* and the *Little* Deserts. It was suggested that a road-bed might be laid almost "straight across the desert", from Damascus to Anna. Strategically, and from an engineering point of view, this would be the most practicable of all the proposed routes; but politically, before the War, such a railway would have fallen between two stools; and since the War, neither England nor France have desired that a railway should traverse a section of desert which lies partly in Syria and partly in Irak. A motor track was eventually opened across this intermediate desert, and it passes through the desert zones of both Syria and Irak; but that is another problem altogether. Motor routes are more flexible than railway lines; and motor car or autobus companies can be run on either a competitive or a monopolistic basis, without loss to their efficiency.

It was after the motor services were organized that the French revived the railway project, referred to previously, for an all-French line between Homs and Deir ez-Zor via Palmyra. Its Mesopotamian extension would consist of two lines, one to Mosul and one to Baghdad. Meanwhile, the British have shown an even keener interest in the projected construction of an "all red" railway route between Palestine and Irak. In 1922 Major A. L. Holt made a preliminary survey across the *Great Desert*, north of Jebel Aneza; and ten years later a final survey was made along the line which he had marked out. Major Holt had also examined an alternative alignment via Jauf; but his considered recommendation was in favour of the more direct, northerly route. Everything else aside, it would of course be preferable to have a British-run railroad go north of, rather than across, any of the territory of Ibn Sa'ud. At all events, the Haifa–Baghdad Railway, as projected in the completed survey of 1932, would, in the words of Major Holt, be entirely feasible and present but slight engineering difficulties. Such a line would cross the *Hamad*, north of the peak of Jebel Aneza, and connect Mafrak with Rutba Wells and Rutba with Hit. A promising estimate of the probable passenger traffic of this proposed railway was predicted, in the event of its being constructed. The estimate was based upon an analysis of the figures recorded for travellers (excluding pilgrims) who crossed the Syrian Desert between the years 1926 and 1931 (inclusive). But since this estimate, as incorporated in the report on the survey for the Haifa–Baghdad Railway, has not as yet been made public, no details or figures thereof may be given here. However, the undertaking of such a project depends upon a number of things, of which the estimated traffic and financial returns are but a part; so the construction of a *Great Desert* railroad has been postponed, perhaps indefinitely.

3

THE ESTABLISHMENT OF MOTOR TRANSPORT

After detailing so many projects which have not as yet materialized, it is a pleasure to be able to turn to certain transport schemes that have actually proved themselves a success. Shortly after the Great War, plans were made to bridge the *Great Desert* by air; and almost simultaneously motor transport was talked of across the *Little Desert*, and feasible motor routes were experimented with. The development of land transport should be first described because, in journalistic language, it represents a more literal "conquest" of the desert than aerial transport. In addition to which, the motor companies which have established themselves on the desert are genuine desert services, whereas the trans-desert air lines are through services to the Far East, and their Syrian Desert sections are but short and incidental parts of far-flung imperial routes. The following outline, necessarily compressed, can only indicate how much there is in the story to capture the imagination.

Early in 1923 several people collaborated to make an experimental trip between Damascus and Baghdad. Mr C. E. S. Palmer, H.B.M.'s Consul at Damascus; Hajji Mohammed el-Bassam (called Ibn Bassam by most of the Europeans in Syria), a wealthy Baghdad merchant; and Major D. McCallum, British liaison officer with the Haut-Commissariat at Beyrout, planned a joint expedition. They obtained the co-operation of Mr Norman Nairn, of the Nairn Transport Company of Palestine and Syria, who loaned them cars and the services of the Company's chief engineer-mechanic, Mr Edward Lovell. El-Bassam, who was a personal friend of most of the Aneza shaykhs, was well acquainted with the desert and its tracks. He, in partnership with a Syrian merchant, had run a contraband trade in gold to Irak, until the French intervened to prevent their smuggling gold out of Syria. Originally they had conveyed the contraband across the desert by camel via Deir ez-Zor, and thence down the Euphrates to Felluja. But as soon as el-Bassam conceived the idea of using motor cars to transport the gold, he began to look for a more direct (as well as a less frequented) way of reaching the Euphrates. It was only after several successful trips had been made by motor car for this purpose that el-Bassam offered to assist Mr Palmer in looking for the shortest route between Dumeir and Ramadi.

On 2nd April 1923 the reconnaissance party set out in three cars: a Buick, an Oldsmobile and a Lancia. They took enough food and water to last the party for ten days; and sufficient petrol and oil to carry the cars well over 1000 miles—in case they might be forced to turn back when almost within reach of Baghdad. On the second day out their convoy came upon the "air-furrow" —the Royal Air Force route-marking between Amman and Ramadi. Within three days they reached the Euphrates, at Ramadi; and on the evening of the third day the citizens of Baghdad gave an enthusiastic welcome to the twelve members of the Palmer–McCallum expedition. Incidentally, four of these twelve were Englishwomen. Their desert crossing had been uneventful, except for an accident to the Lancia that "Ted" Lovell was able to repair *en route*; and British officials were thereby convinced of the feasibility of establishing a motor route along the tracks made by these three cars. In particular, Major Douglas Gumbley, then Postmaster-General of the Irak Government, became keenly interested in the development of a new land route. Actually, it was at his request that the Nairn Transport Company subsequently organized their desert service. In spite of the enforced brevity of this outline, a word must be said about the Nairns and their company.

Norman Nairn and his younger brother, Gerald, are New Zealanders. During the War they served with the British forces in the Near East, and throughout the Palestine campaign they were both with the Mechanical Transport division of the R.A.S.C. After being demobilized in Palestine, they went into the motor-car business, and, in partnership with an Assyrian of Haifa by the name of Nasser, they instituted a Haifa–Beyrout service. In time they obtained mail contracts from the governments of Palestine, Egypt and Syria. In time, also, the Nasser–Nairn concern was liquidated, and a new all-British company was formed. The Nairn Transport Company, recruited entirely from among ex-Service men, instituted a daily passenger and mail service between Palestine and Syria. After 1922 this organization made a name for itself by carrying the Egyptian mails from Haifa to Beyrout in just over four hours.

When the Nairns were approached by sponsors of this projected desert route, Norman Nairn was not slow to grasp the potentialities of the situation, and he lost no time in beginning a personal survey of the desert between the Anti-Lebanon Mountains and the river Euphrates. During the spring and summer five more trial trips were undertaken, in Nairn cars; and each one of these expeditions reconnoitred large areas of desert to the north of, as well as to the south of, the first route that had been followed when el-Bassam led the way. It was thus established that the first route had in fact passed over the most easily traversable section of desert, and this was the track that was finally chosen for the Nairn convoys.

The Overland Desert Route, as it came to be called in the English press, follows the Damascus–Aleppo high-road northwards for about fifteen miles before branching east to Dumeir. From Dumeir, Nairn drivers steer south of east until they reach Rutba Wells in the Wadi Hauran, which their speedometers show to be 261 miles distant from Damascus. On their way to Rutba, Nairn cars pass to the south of Jebel Tenf, which is the

THE FIRST MOTOR CROSSING, 1919

Behind Arabs watering their flocks are the Ford cars en route from the Euphrates to Palmyra and Damascus

Photograph by Lt.-Col. Kenneth Mason

only mountain landmark on the route. From Rutba, where the
only wells now to be found on the route are situated (the only
water of any kind, for that matter, until the river is reached), the
"Nairn Track" turns to the north of east, and follows the "air-
furrow" into Ramadi. At Ramadi the track joins the ordinary
riverain road along the right bank of the Euphrates, and continues as far as Felluja. Until the spring of 1932 cars had to cross
to Mesopotamia by a pontoon bridge, or—if this had been cut
to save its being swept away in time of flood—cars were rafted
over by a ferry. Today a steel and concrete bridge spans the river
at Felluja, so that one of the few hazards of the trip has been
eliminated. A straight and dusty road covers the thirty-five miles
between Felluja and the outskirts of west Baghdad. The total
distance from Damascus to Baghdad is 534 miles; and from the
sea-coast at Beyrout to Baghdad the mileage is 606. As may well
be imagined, the only metalled road on the entire route is that
between Beyrout and Damascus; and over this part of the route
the desert buses never travel. This is also the only mountainous
district that has to be crossed; and the two ranges which intervene
between the desert and the sea, the Anti-Lebanon and the Lebanon
Mountains, are crossed at an altitude of 4000 and 5000 feet respectively. They form a beautiful, almost a breath-taking contrast to the 445 miles of desert which lie to the east of Damascus.
As for the desert section of the route, drivers on the "Nairn
Track" are confronted with but few physical difficulties. The
Wadi Hauran is the only deeply cut wadi that has to be crossed,
and at Rutba its ravine is more easily traversable than it is at any
other point nearer to the Euphrates. In dry weather the desert
surface is smooth and hard-packed, covered in places with gravel
and shale, and occasionally spattered with flints; its whole wide
extent is a potential road-bed. Hundreds of heavy motor vehicles
have gradually worn deep grooves in passing over this smooth
surface; and these grooves constitute what is known generally
as the "Nairn Track". In wet weather rain-water collects in the
occasional depressions, and in these cars are sometimes mired.
Also, about seventy miles east of Rutba Wells are a series of mud-

18

flats which the rains render extremely treacherous. Lastly, whenever the Euphrates is in flood, convoys are unable to use the
riverain road from Ramadi to Felluja; they are forced to make an
eighty-mile detour around Lake Habbania. The Habbania track,
which is strewn with pumice sand, has the name of being one of
the worst of desert tracks.

It has already been mentioned that the Nairn desert service
was organized at the request of the Irak Post Office. Early in
October 1923, after the most efficient preparations had been made,
the Nairn Transport Company opened a weekly service (between
Damascus and Baghdad) that was scheduled to connect with the
weekly Anglo-Indian (P. & O.) mails to and from London. An
irregular, extra trip a week was also provided for passengers
"when necessary". Postal notices were duly published, informing
the public that articles destined to be carried over the new route
should be superscribed "Overland Mail Baghdad–Haifa". At
first there was a surcharge of threepence, no parcel post was
accepted, and there was no insurance system—only ordinary
registration. But eventually, of course, the surcharge was abol-
ished; and parcel post and insurance were undertaken, as by any
normal postal service. The mail contract with the Irak Government was for a period of five years; and by its terms the Nairn
Transport Company was bound to deliver the mails between
Baghdad and Port Said within a sixty-hour time limit. From
Haifa to Egypt the mails were to be transported by rail. Provision
was made for the payment of a fine—for every additional hour
over the sixty—if ever the mails should be delayed; but such a
fine was never imposed.

Of primary importance in the organizing of this desert service
were the precautions that were taken for the safety of the
convoys. The Nairns made a contract with Hajji el-Bassam to
arrange for a safe-conduct for their cars across the Badia. He was
to subsidize the Beduin tribes on behalf of the Company, and his
men—detailed to escort the convoys—were to be *rafeeks* as well
as guides. It was agreed that el-Bassam and the tribes should together receive a certain fixed percentage (one-third, to be exact)

of the mail-contract returns. This subsidy amounted to approximately £2000 a year. Once this arrangement was made with el-Bassam, and through him with the Beduin tribes, Nairn drivers and convoy leaders ceased to carry any fire-arms whatever. The guides who were supplied by el-Bassam were Agails, and all of them were, inevitably, of the *Akhwan*. The significance of this designation has been explained elsewhere (see pp. 157-158), as well as the importance of the *rafeek* system in desert travel (pp. 172 and 212); and the psychological reason for travelling among the Beduin without weapons of defence (so easily mistaken for weapons of offence, see pp. 185-186); so there is no need to repeat these definitions and explanations in this specific connection. Only it is interesting to call attention to the fact that medieval customs and ideas still obtain on the desert, even in this twentieth century. The Nairn Transport Company continued to use Beduin guides for about eighteen months after the opening of its service; and the contract with el-Bassam remained in force for three years. When his valuable services were finally dispensed with, in 1926, el-Bassam received a block of the Company's shares.

Other general precautions were also taken, to ensure both the safety and the comfort of trans-desert passengers, by order of the Irak Government; and these were supplemented by special regulations of the Nairn Transport Company. No car was allowed to cross the desert alone, or unprovided with government-inspected passes; nor could any car leave or arrive at either Baghdad or Damascus without due notification by wireless. Sometimes as many as twelve or fourteen cars would travel together, each of which was kept to its own appointed place in the convoy. Cadillac and Buick touring cars were used by the Nairns for the first three and a half years, and each one of them had special water and petrol tanks fitted to its running-boards, and was required to carry spare parts, tyres, shovels and ropes, and a week's rations of food and drinking water. Night encampments, which were the inevitable accompaniment of the touring-car (single-driver) era of the Nairn Transport Company, were made caravan fashion: the cars were formed into a square, within which beds were set up; and the men passengers took their turns standing watch with the guides and drivers.

The Irak Government was not alone in backing the Nairn Transport Company. Special franchises, such as the duty-free importation of petrol, tyres and cars, were granted by the Syrian Government; and there was even talk of a small subsidy for the Company, though nothing concrete came of the suggestion. But in fact nothing could have helped the Nairns more than the official and benevolent policy of non-interference in their affairs; because it saved them from being hampered at every turn by bureaucratic red-tape.

A month after the opening of the Overland Desert Mail, Messageries Maritimes advertised a "combined service with the Nairn Transport Company" via Marseille; a "ten-day journey", with a £70 first-class fare, from London to Baghdad inclusive. Arrangements were made with Thomas Cook & Son for widespread advertisement of the Nairn Company; and the "Overseas Bureau of Travel" furnished them with a temporary London office.

Very eulogistic press comments celebrated the first anniversary of the inauguration of the Overland Mail Service, which had so undeniably justified its existence. *The Times Weekly Edition*, for example, pointed out that the Nairn Transport Company had carried 1476 passengers and 35,000 lb. of mail during its first twelve months of life, "without a single accident"; and that not once had a steamer connection been missed. Several records were set up. One convoy made the trip from Damascus to Baghdad in exactly twenty-four hours; another, travelling in the reverse direction, actually crossed in a total of twenty-one hours. The record trip, which has never since been equalled (so far as is known), was made by Norman Nairn himself for a wager. In March 1924 he drove Sir Arnold Wilson all the way from Baghdad to Beyrout in sixteen hours and fifty-three minutes—and thus won his wager on a seventeen-hour time limit! Aside from record runs, however, the normal schedules of the Nairn Transport Company had brought Baghdad within nine days of London, and within forty-eight hours' journey of Port Said. That meant a saving of more than three weeks' time as compared with the Suez–Bombay steamship route.

In 1925 the press continued warm in its praises of the achievements of the Nairn Transport Company. The "fascinations" of the "new way" home from India to England, including its sightseeing possibilities, were also enlarged upon by *The Times* newspapers of London, of India and of Baghdad; the new westward orientation of Irak, and the fact that the Lebanons were fast becoming the most accessible "hill station" for its inhabitants. The saving in expense via the new overland route was frequently commented upon: whereby the cost of steamship tickets was reduced, as well as the "enormous wine bill" which was considered one of the inevitable drawbacks of the long sea voyage! The administration and personnel of the Overland Desert Service was continually praised, especially the punctuality and efficiency of the Nairn drivers. Norman Nairn, personally, was lauded by the *Near East Magazine* for having done so much "to unite the Arab kingdoms of Syria and Irak". Perhaps the most significant comment on the Nairn service was made in *The Times Weekly Edition* of 29th January 1925:

"The members of the Irak Frontier Commission have arrived in Baghdad after a comfortable and uneventful journey across the Syrian Desert." The news does not convey any particular idea of achievement, and only those who have made the long trek across the desert from Damascus to the Euphrates realize how the men who carry the mails have turned a remarkable feat of skill, courage and endurance into a matter of weekly routine. "Comfortable and uneventful" the journey may be, but it is so only owing to the organization of the service and the loyalty of the men who serve.

In 1926 the Nairn brothers took an important step. They enlarged and reorganized their Company; and then—for both financial and political reasons—they sold it to a group of Anglo-

French financiers. Norman Nairn arranged, nevertheless, to keep administrative control of the business; he became managing director of "The Nairn Eastern Transport Company Ltd." In order to understand the composition of the new Company, some account must be given of another, a rival motor Company which was bought and amalgamated with the Nairn Transport Company at the time of its reorganization.

Less than five months after the inauguration of the Nairn service, Mr Francis Kettaneh, a Syrian gentleman of Palestinian origin, had founded a rival desert service called "The Eastern Transport Company". He (and his father, who was the Beyrout representative of Thomas Cook & Son) had accompanied Norman Nairn and Ted Lovell when Nairn made his first trial crossing of the desert in May 1923. All that summer, while the Nairns were experimenting with the southern route, Kettaneh explored the desert a little further north. He searched for the Roman road which had once connected Palmyra with Hit; a track that the Beduin still remembered as existing, and which they referred to as the *Darb el-Kufri*—the "Road of the Unbelievers"—on account of its legendary Roman origin. Kettaneh did eventually find traces of the *Darb el-Kufri*, with the help of Arab guides lent by the French Camel Corps; but the whole length of this Roman road was not found until R. P. Poidebard made his aerial reconnaissances several years later.

Norman Nairn, after one tentative excursion north of the Melossa hills, was convinced that the Nairn track should run south of both Jebel Tenf and Jebel Melossa; so he definitely chose the route which skirts the *Hamad*. Francis Kettaneh did not want to compete with the Nairn Transport Company on its own track; and he hoped that, in spite of the occasional roughness of the more northerly route, the attractions of Palmyra would have an irresistible appeal for most desert travellers. So, when the Eastern Transport Company opened its service to the public, their cars took the plains road from Damascus to Palmyra, and then followed the *Darb el-Kufri*, the desert track to Kubaisa and Hit; and thence to Ramadi, Felluja and Baghdad. Before long Hit was cut out of the itinerary, so that cars could follow a more convenient (and shorter) track from Kubaisa to Ramadi.

Beginning in March 1924, Kettaneh's Eastern Transport Company ran two services a week. One of these, a two-and-a-half-day schedule, was planned to show tourists Palmyra and the desert by day; so, instead of crossing the desert during the night (as on the fast service), passengers were put up overnight at rest-houses in Palmyra and Kubaisa. Dodge cars were used exclusively, and their drivers were recruited from six different nationalities. Only one class was catered to; and the £30 single fare (or £50 round-trip fare) was identical with the first-class fares charged by the Nairn Transport Company. The Eastern Transport Company paid no subsidies to the Beduin—fearing them less than the riverain Arabs, whom it is impossible to subsidize. Instead, their guides were chosen from among the Suluba, who are immune from *ghrazzu* and are never molested by other Beduin.

From the beginning, the Eastern Transport Company was not a paying proposition. Even government patronage was of little avail; neither franchises, nor the granting of immunity from duties on tyres and cars, nor the substantial subsidy that was paid to the Company, could keep it from falling into debt. Mr Kettaneh was finally induced to sell his concern to a Lebanese Company (nine months after its inauguration); and the route was thereafter lengthened to include a Baghdad–Teheran branch service. The reorganized Company, under the name of "The Eastern Transport Company Limited" (or "The Beyrout–Baghdad–Teheran Automobiles"), earned £100 a month by carrying the British diplomatic mails between Irak and Iran. But still there was an annual deficit. The Company was overstaffed, for one thing; and from £20,000 to £22,000 a year was expended in running expenses. But probably the most fundamental reason for the eventual failure of the Company was the fact that, in spite of a reduction in the fare, the Nairn Transport Company attracted the majority of trans-desert travellers. Their route was more direct, and its road surface promised a more comfortable journey; also, there was only one wadi to cross instead of three. Furthermore, Nairn drivers

were more careful as well as more punctual than many of the men who drove for the Eastern Transport Company. Travelling with Nairn, one could always count upon the staff living up to a uniform standard of efficiency; but in every other Company that has operated on the desert, the efficiency and reliability of the service has varied with the individual employed.

Two years after the opening of its route, the Eastern Transport Company Ltd. went into the hands of receivers; and the bankrupt Company was bought and amalgamated with its more successful rival. The Nairn Eastern Transport Company Ltd. (under a British chairman resident in London) was registered on 20th September 1926 at the Ottoman Bank of Nicosia, Cyprus. The new Company was also registered at the *Haut-Commissariat*, Beyrout; its head office was established at Damascus, and a branch office at Beyrout. The French authorities undertook to protect that part of the route which lay within Syrian territory. To all intents and purposes the Nairn service carried on as usual, under the management of Norman Nairn. The Nairn track was used exclusively from thenceforward, and the Palmyra–Kubaisa Route was abandoned. Only the Iranian service—though it was operating at a loss—was temporarily maintained. At the end of a year, however, after a further loss of about £1200, the Baghdad–Teheran branch was definitely given up. There was not enough European traffic between Irak and Iran to warrant the maintaining of a regular service; and native motor-car companies were entirely capable of handling the traffic—which was heaviest at the pilgrim season. At Baghdad, Lumsden & Greene continued to act as agents for Nairn for another twelve months; and then a branch office was opened there under the management of Gerald Nairn. At Haifa, C. V. Boutagy (proprietor of the Windsor Hotel) continued to represent the Nairns.

Eight different firms and fourteen individuals constituted the Anglo-French interests in control of the Nairn Eastern Transport Company. The Anglo-Persian Oil Company, La Banque de Paris et des Pays-Bas, the Ottoman Bank, La Banque Ottomane, the Imperial Bank of Persia, Le Crédit Foncier d'Algérie, Stern

Brothers of London, and the Messageries Maritimes Ltd., were the principal shareholders; and of these the Anglo-Persian Oil Company alone held ten thousand of the £53,000 worth of shares. Individual shareholders included the Nairns and Edward Lovell; and of them, Norman Nairn held almost half the total number of privately owned shares. Brigadier-General H. O. Mance, C.B., C.M.G., D.S.O. (also a shareholder), was elected chairman of the Company.

The year following the amalgamation of the Nairn and the Eastern Transport Companies was marked by two events of great interest in the history of the route. The Irak Government built a fort at Rutba Wells, near Wadi Hauran; and the "Six-Wheelers" began to operate on the desert.

Close by Rutba the Nairn track and the Royal Air Force air-furrow meet; so, even aside from the fact that a constant supply of water is available in that part of Wadi Hauran, Rutba was the strategic point for the erection of a fort and petrol depot. As Rutba is in Irak territory, a wireless station was also installed at the fort, for the use of the R.A.F. and Imperial Airways; and a landing-ground which adjoins the building. A rest-house was built within the fort, which has been turned over to Norman Nairn to run for the joint use of Imperial Airways and the Overland Desert Mail. It is equipped with electric light and fans, and with an ice plant. Convoys plan their schedules to arrive at the fort in time for dinner; and as it stands practically half-way between Damascus and Baghdad, this is equally easy to arrange from either terminus. Passengers never fail to be impressed with the quality of this hotel service in mid-desert; and if anyone desires to break the twenty-four-hour trip, comfortable bedrooms are available until the passage of the next convoy. Since 1928 a regular bi-weekly service has been maintained in both directions.

In May 1927 six-wheel "Safeway" saloon coaches were introduced into the regular desert service. The Cadillac and Buick touring cars had proved successful in every way, but their seating capacities were too limited. So Norman Nairn, completely satisfied with the way these General Motors cars had stood up under

the strain of desert work, had visited the United States twice to
order some specially designed autobuses. The "Six-Wheel Company" of Philadelphia collaborated with Mr Nairn on the design,
and built four of them for the Nairn Eastern Transport Company.
The seating capacity of each coach allowed for two drivers and
for fifteen passengers; the latter are accommodated with large
Pullman type armchairs. There are spacious parcel racks, and the
roof was designed to carry one and a quarter tons of luggage.
The petrol capacity is 140 gallons; and petrol consumption is at
the average rate of 4·3–4·4 miles to the gallon. Ice water and
paper-bag sandwich lunches and teas are also carried for the
passengers. Since the six-wheelers began to be used, nights are
no longer spent on the desert. Passengers can sleep in their pullman chairs with relative comfort; and two British drivers go on
every coach, so that one man does not have the strain of driving
all night as well as all day. These large cars run so smoothly that
it is even possible to read while *en route*.

So great an innovation were these six-wheelers that there was
a special christening ceremony in Baghdad for the first of them.
King Feisal of Irak, in the presence of his own suite, his British
"advisers" and His Excellency the High Commissioner, named
the new coach the "Babylon".

The performance of the six-wheelers was all that had been
hoped for. Take for example 1929; during that year alone they
covered more than 95,000 miles and made 187 trans-desert trips.
But Norman Nairn was never the man to stop experimenting.
Improvements could still be made; and there was no certain limit
to the potential increase in desert traffic. Touring cars were still
used by the Company for their second-class passengers and
lorries for the third-class. An aerocar, though it could accommodate only eight people, was tried and gave satisfaction; a new
type of four-wheeler (made by an American Company) was
also experimented with. Between 1927 and 1932 the numbers of
first-, second- and third-class passengers who made use of the
Nairn service increased, roughly, from 2000 to 3000 a year.

The latest experiment of all is a stainless-steel bus-train efficiently streamlined. The desert train is an eighteen-wheeler, an articulated aerocar, with a five-speed gear-box and exceptionally low-pressure balloon tyres measuring 18·40 by 10·50. This bus-train is being used on the desert at the time of writing, though it is undergoing certain modifications. Adjustments can be made under the expert supervision of Ted Lovell at Damascus, where the Company has a fully equipped modern garage.

Certain technical difficulties on the track itself, caused by intense heat, dust (which clogs the machinery and abrades all exposed surfaces) and mud (which, west of Ramadi, is often eighteen inches deep in winter-time), can never be entirely eliminated; but continuous readjustments minimize their ill-effects.

In passing over numerous random statistics, it might be mentioned that the operating expenses of the Nairn Eastern Transport Company averaged more than £31,000 a year for the four years 1927–30 inclusive. The cost of insuring both cars and passengers is included in this figure. Petrol, tyres and tubes accounted for about a fifth of the total; and the generous margin allowed for depreciation accounted for another fifth. It speaks more than well for the business ability of Norman Nairn, and for the efficiency of the staff, that the Nairn Eastern Transport Company's gross profits during this same four-year period averaged more than £11,000—almost £12,000 a year. In spite of these substantial returns, however, the fares are far from excessive, considering the unique quality of the service given. In 1927 the first-class fare, which included a seat in a six-wheeler, hotels at Damascus and Rutba, food on the desert, plus a 100-pound free luggage allowance, was reduced to £20. Four years later there was a further reduction of the first-class (inclusive) fare to £16, without the least diminution in the quality of the service. Second-class touring-car fares were finally reduced to £13, with an 80-pound free luggage allowance; and the third-class lorry fare was reduced to £4.

In the beginning, the Nairns had hoped to develop the freight-carrying side of the business; there was a constant demand for various kinds of machinery in Irak, for example, and a steady export from Iran and Irak of hides and skins. For the first year or two the Company carried freight at a profit, for £25 a ton; but the time came when native Companies and individual (native) lorry-drivers began to compete for this trade; they undercut the Nairns, and then they began undercutting each other to a fantastic extent. Syrians and Irakis take no care of their machines, and they never make allowances for depreciation. The Nairns have only to bide their time; then when the natives fail, as they are bound to do in the long run, the Nairn service will be able to step in and take over the greater part of this freight-carrying in new and improved lorries.

At the end of 1928 the Irak mail contract expired. Meanwhile it had become the new policy of the Irak Government to encourage Irakis; so it was natural, though regrettable, that the Nairn Eastern Transport Company did not have their contract renewed. A native of Baghdad, Nathaniel Haim by name, solicited and obtained the new Irak mail contract. Nevertheless, compensation came to the Company through the French. The Syrian Government awarded them the contract for carrying the Syrian mails to and from Irak. The terms of the contract called for a weekly postal service, with a 36-hour time limit between Damascus and Baghdad. A fine of twelve and a half Syrian pounds (at that time about £2 : 3s.) was payable for every three hours that the mails might be delayed, except for a reason of *force majeure*. The rate of remuneration was fixed at £32 per ton.

One of the more stirring episodes in the history of the Nairn Eastern Transport Company was the Druze Rebellion. The western end of the motor track crosses a region that was infested with Druze Arabs, at the time when they were bitterly hostile to the French. Any service backed by the Syrian Government would, inevitably, have incurred their enmity; and their enmity was no passive thing. In August and September 1925 several drivers and one passenger were injured in raids; a convoy leader was mortally wounded; and a gold consignment (valued at about £9000) was stolen. Even when the French provided an armed escort, a convoy of eleven cars was attacked by the Druzes and their allies. On one occasion the Beduin, well mounted on camels, kept up a running fight for over twenty miles; and one of the Nairns' British drivers captured three Beduin single-handed. Unfortunately space does not permit a description of these various encounters. A third Druze attack caused the Nairns to organize a rapid change of route, in order to carry on the service without any danger to their passengers. Norman Nairn himself, accompanied by Wing-Commander Primrose, had re-connoitred the Amman track with two Cadillac cars, earlier in that same year. So he decided that the wisest course would be to use this "All-Red Route", which would be under the protection of British aeroplane and armoured-car patrols all the way. Ac-cordingly, convoys were sent regularly to and from Baghdad by way of Haifa, Jerusalem, the Amman–Rutba air-furrow, Ramadi and Felluja. The *Near East Magazine* (for 3rd December 1925) commented on the fact that, in spite of the Rebellion, Nairn bookings were "very heavy"; and that sometimes more ap-plications for seats were received by the Company than could be met.

The Amman route, difficult though it is, was in use for almost six months; but it was too great a strain on both the Company and its staff for it to be used any longer than was absolutely necessary. The drivers dubbed the lava country east of Amman the "Bay of Biscay", where the cars, threading their way through basaltic boulders and over soft sand, could only average between five and ten miles per hour. To add to their difficulties, from December to February the wadis between Amman and Rutba were deep in mud. New sets of tyres were required every second trip; ten chassis were fractured; ten radiators were damaged by excessive vibration; and seventy-five springs were broken. It is not surprising that, as soon as the French could guarantee them adequate protection, the Nairn Eastern Transport Company shifted the route northwards again. In the spring of 1926, though the whole of the disturbed Damascus area had still to be avoided, Nairn convoys began to operate on the Tripoli–Homs route to

Palmyra, whence they followed along the track which had been marked out by Kettaneh for the Eastern Transport Company. Until May 1927 the French maintained a motor machine-gun patrol on the Homs–Palmyra–Kubaisa track; until, that is, the Druze uprising was put down, and the High Commissioner was able to sanction the reopening of the direct Damascus–Rutba route.

Not only during the Druze Rebellion were Nairn drivers given the opportunity of displaying their courage and resourcefulness. From time to time there were accidents, and there was one other fatal incident. Once a car broke down, with axle trouble, and was towed for 400 miles across the desert. Another time six cars were bogged, in various positions, on a mud-flat about 350 miles from Damascus. Their drivers worked for most of one night to free the cars; and Gerald Nairn himself walked a total of nine miles, in pouring rain, in order to distribute food and drink to the occupants of all six cars. The worst delay Nairn passengers ever experienced was during the winter when the Amman route was in use. A convoy took ten days to make the crossing from Jerusalem to Baghdad; the cars were stuck for thirty-four hours between Amman and Rutba; and then again, for five whole days, on a mud-flat west of Ramadi. The Royal Air Force sent out a plane to bring in the mails and to take extra food to the convoy, and the aeroplane got mired in its turn. Four days' continuous rain —almost unprecedented in the desert—had turned the mud-flat into a morass. Armoured cars, in this case Fords, rescued both the aeroplane and the convoy. The only occasion upon which a Nairn convoy was attacked, except during the Druze troubles, was in Irak territory. In 1928, only ten miles west of Wadi Hauran, a six-wheeler and a touring car (which was carrying the outgoing Irak mails) were set upon by armed bandits. Two of Nairns' men were wounded and one man was killed; but the driver of the six-wheeler contrived to get his passengers safely back into the fort at Rutba. The mail car was stolen with all it contained; a party of Rutba police gave chase, but no trace was ever found of either the bandits or the stolen car. It is amazing really, when one comes to think of it, that there have not been many more incidents of this kind.

As the above numerous references to mud-flats show, they constitute one of the greatest problems of the three winter months; and the flooding of the Euphrates makes an acute spring problem every two years on an average. For these reasons the Nairns have been thinking about changing the eastern part of their route; they intend eventually to make a new track which will branch southwards (from the present track) about seventy miles east of Rutba, cut out Ramadi entirely, and go directly to Felluja around the southern end of Lake Habbania. One wadi would have to be crossed on the proposed route, and mud-flats could not be entirely eliminated; but it is thought that a good track might be "ironed out" by slowly moving, low-pressure tyres, which would be sufficiently smooth after it had been allowed to harden.

In 1932 and 1933 Norman Nairn made a determined effort to expand the activities of the Company still further. The desert is peculiarly well suited for the establishment of air services; so that a Nairn air line was quite logically projected to supplement the bus service. A passenger-carrying machine was actually imported from the United States, and the services of a Canadian pilot, Alan Fraser Grant, were engaged. But certain high officials of the French Government in Syria refused, at the last moment, to give the requisite sanction. Accordingly, the civil authorities at Beyrout were forced to withdraw the verbal permission which they had previously granted to Mr Nairn for the inauguration of his Damascus–Baghdad air service.

Perhaps the most eloquent comment one could make upon the pioneering achievements of the Nairn Eastern Transport Company is to mention that Norman Nairn has been decorated by two governments for his work in the Near East. He was the first —possibly he is the only—Englishman to have received "La Médaille du Mérite Libanais"; and five years after the opening of the Nairn track, the O.B.E. was bestowed upon him. As the London *Times* had previously said, the desert route had been so

much developed as to have become an economic necessity to
Syria; and it had "developed commercial relations between
Syria, Irak and Persia to an extent undreamed of by the pioneers".
The credit for all this development was specifically given to Mr
Nairn in the presidential address which accompanied the bestowal
of his "Médaille du Mérite Libanais".

There is another motor transport Company which began life
as a rival, but is now what might be called supplementary to the
Nairn Eastern Transport Company. A Syrian, Kawatli Tawil,
founded a small private Company in 1926, and he attempted to
compete with the Nairns on their own track. Within two years,
however, he went bankrupt; and then the Baron André de
Neufville bought and reorganized Tawil's Company, and changed
its route. In January 1928, under the name of the Compagnie
Auto-Routière du Levant, daily coastal services were inaugurated
as well as an eastern service which crosses (four times a week) the
northern frontier of the Syrian Desert. The coastal routes of the
Auto-Routière link Haifa with Beyrout; Beyrout with Aleppo
via Tripoli and Latakia; and Aleppo with Alexandretta. On the
east, the motor route connects Aleppo with Meskineh, and then
follows the right bank of the Euphrates as far as Deir ez-Zor.
From Deir, where cars can cross the river by a modern bridge,
there is an extension of the motor service to Mosul. The Compagnie Auto-Routière du Levant carries the mails as well as
passengers; and it is similar in organization to the Auto-Routière
of Northern Africa. Since 1931 it has been controlled by the
Régie Générale, which also controls the Syrian railways; without,
however, losing its identity or ceasing to be an independent
Company.

The last on the list of Syrian Desert motor routes is the most
unique; three-quarters of its track passes through Arabia. The
Eastern Pilgrim Route, the famous *Darb es-Sitt Zubayda*, which
connects Kerbela and Najaf (or Meshed Ali) with Hayil, Medina
and Mecca, has just been opened to motor traffic. In 1932 a first
trial trip was made by the Public Works Department of Irak,
from Kerbela to Hayil; and two years later a mixed commission

A CAMEL CORPS OF THE 7TH CENTURY, B.C.

Arabian archers on single-humped camels withstand the infantry of Assurbanipal

From an Assyrian relief: British Museum

MOTOR TRANSPORT OF THE 20TH CENTURY

A Nairn autobus on the Damascus-Baghdad route

Photograph by Nairn Transport Co.

of Irakis and Hejazis arrived at Najaf, after having completed a motor trip all the way from Mecca. On 13th January 1935 the Mecca Route was officially opened. The north-eastern end of the track provides a good surface for motor vehicles; but it will be some time yet before it will be smooth and good going from end to end. Nevertheless, it seems likely that all the eastern pilgrim traffic will eventually be re-diverted to its original channel—as in early Saracen times; and that pilgrims will require only five or six days to go from Irak to the Holy Cities of the Hejaz, instead of the two or three weeks which it has taken them to go by Syria and the Mediterranean, or else all the way around Arabia.

4

THE AIR SERVICES

The most modern of all desert services are the air lines. A British line, spanning the *Great Desert*, was the first of these; and it was established for military purposes, before even the Overland Desert Mail service was inaugurated. At the Cairo Conference of 1921 it was decided that the Royal Air Force should open a regular service between Cairo and Baghdad; and Major A. L. Holt, R.E., was commissioned to make the first ground survey for the laying out of a practicable air route across the Syrian Desert. The work which Major Holt did towards the railway was actually a by-product of the preliminary work that he did for the Royal Air Force. On one occasion he and his party were lost in the *Great Desert*, and it took seven Air Force machines two days to find them. The difficulty which was experienced by the pilots of these aeroplanes in finding the wheel-tracks of his Ford cars resulted in the suggestion of ploughing a furrow that would be easy to pick up from the air. A second survey was made by Royal Air Force cars and aeroplanes under the command of Wing-Commander Fellowes. One convoy of cars started from Amman, another set out from Ramadi, and they arranged to meet in mid-desert. The aeroplanes kept in touch with the ground

19

parties and reconnoitred ahead. After the completion of the surveys, a double furrow was ploughed by a Fordson tractor and an ordinary plough, across the Ramadi–Rutba section of the route; and wherever the track turned, an arrow was also ploughed to point the fresh angle. Across the difficult lava country, on the Amman–Rutba section, single furrows were ploughed about a hundred yards in length, and alternate hundred-yard stretches of desert were left unmarked; but the ploughed stretches looked almost like a continuous furrow from the air. Landing-grounds were marked, at intervals of from fifteen to thirty miles, by ploughing a circle about thirty yards in diameter; each of these was lettered. At the end of 1922 the track was re-marked, and then re-fuelling points were installed with sunken tanks. Their petrol pumps were kept locked (against the Beduin), and all pilots using the route were supplied with keys.

The Cairo–Baghdad air route was opened in the summer of 1921; and in October a special arrangement was made for the carrying of civil air mails. Royal Air Force machines, operating in pairs, maintained a fortnightly mail service between Egypt and Irak; and so popular was this air mail route that it was soon expanded to a weekly service in each direction. For the first month the mails were carried by "D.H.9" planes, and after that by Vickers Vernon troop-carriers, which transported Service passengers in addition to the mails. Just before handing over to Imperial Airways, Vickers Victorias were put on the route, and the service was consequently speeded up. The original fee charged for mail was one shilling per ounce; this was later reduced to sixpence per ounce; and after the Overland Desert Mail began carrying the Irak mails for only threepence, the Royal Air Force lowered their rate again, so that their air mail surcharge would correspond to that of the Nairn Service.

At the end of March 1929, Imperial Airways Ltd. opened their Anglo-Indian mail and passenger service with an inaugural flight from Croydon to Karachi. They had taken over the desert air mail from the Royal Air Force, as a going concern; and the desert route automatically became a link in their imperial chain. Of the service as a whole, of the various changes and experiments which have been made in either the Continental or the Mediterranean sections of their route, there is no occasion to speak here. Only the desert section is relevant; and since that had already been organized in the most efficient way possible, no experimenting was necessary —except in the matter of civil air-ports. Tiberias, for instance, was one of Imperial Airways' temporary bases. Flying-boats used the Lake of Galilee, and "Hercules" and "Hannibal" land machines used the Samakh aerodrome adjoining; it was a convenient locality for the Mediterranean and desert services to connect. But they had not reckoned on atmospheric conditions peculiar to the Jordan Valley. Suddenly variable winds, of astonishing velocity, made the place exceedingly unpopular with pilots. Finally, one night one of the "Hannibals" was literally blown to bits at its moorings—all except the fuselage. The huge air-liner was moored so firmly to concrete ground blocks that when there was a sudden change in the direction of the wind, succeeded by an eighty-mile-an-hour gale, something had to give: the wings broke into countless pieces, and the fabric blew into ribbons. After that, Imperial Airways changed their base permanently to Gaza; and there they have built themselves an up-to-date air port and a comfortable rest-house. Their desert route now connects Gaza with Rutba, Ramadi, Baghdad and Basra. In a sense, the desert section continues the length of the Persian Gulf, because the three stations which Imperial Airways have established at Kuwait, Bahrein and Sharja are all on the Arabian side. Originally, the Anglo-Indian service had used Iranian stations (Bushire and Jask) on the eastern side of the Persian Gulf; but they later changed over to the western side for political reasons connected with the resurgence of Iran as a power in the Gulf.

The most serious difficulties with which pilots have to cope, while flying over this particular desert, arise out of occasional violent dust-storms. These occur most frequently in Irak, and sometimes they last for three days at a time; but they do not usually start until after midday. So Imperial Airways have arranged their schedules accordingly. Airways machines fly the desert in the early morning, only after receiving a favourable weather report from Ramadi; and their first experiments with regular night flying were made between Baghdad and Basra. Imperial Airways have had no accidents on the desert, and only very minor ones in Irak. The fatal accident that happened to the air-liner "City of Jerusalem", when it caught fire from wing-tip flares, occurred at Jask, which is east of the Persian Gulf, on the Gulf of Oman.

In April 1929 the Junkers Company started a weekly air service between Teheran and Baghdad, in co-operation with Imperial Airways. But a regular Iranian service, whether motor or aeroplane, was not a paying proposition. After several years' trial it was withdrawn.

This same year (1929) saw the beginning of another Far Eastern air-line; a French Company, *Air Orient*, began its development. First a weekly seaplane service was opened between Marseilles and Beyrout. The next year, the Damascus–Baghdad air mail was inaugurated. At length, in 1931, the France–Indo-China service, a regular weekly air mail, was established, connecting Marseilles with Saigon. With this through line, *Air Orient* incorporated the existing desert air-mail, using the same Damascus–Rutba–Baghdad route. Before its completion many trial trips had been made, and various record flights to French Indo-China—including a five-and-a-half-day flight from Marseilles to Saigon. Not that the French made all the records. Imperial Airways refused to undertake competitive flights, having established itself on as sound a basis as possible from the point of view of general utility, comfort (for its passengers) and safety; but certain individuals did compete. Wing-Commander Kingsford Smith made a five-day flight from England to Karachi in 1930, and he flew from Aleppo to Baghdad. Miss Amy Johnson also made a similar flight (in six days), and she likewise flew from Aleppo to Baghdad.

Late in 1931 the Royal Dutch Air Service—more commonly known as the K.L.M.—inaugurated still another weekly air mail and passenger service between the Netherlands and Java. Like Imperial Airways, the Dutch go via Egypt (instead of Syria); and after flying from Cairo (or rather, the Heliopolis civil aerodrome) to Gaza, they cross the *Great Desert* by the Amman–Rutba–Baghdad route. Elsewhere, the K.L.M. have made a reciprocal agreement with *Air Orient* for the mutual use of repair facilities and air-ports.

It is thanks to aviation that we have today so complete a picture of the Syrian Desert. Long-distance imperial services, whether British, French or Dutch, have not contributed materially to this knowledge—since the desert is but an incidental part of their schedules. The Near and Middle-Eastern military air services, however, have had occasion to fill in the gaps in our conception of the desert. Royal Air Force patrols of the *Great Desert*, and aerial researches in the *Little Desert*, have surveyed the outlines of this vast *Badia* in its entirety. All the hitherto miscellaneous information concerning its various sections; the unco-ordinated maps, charts and archaeological material of the different regions, have been drawn together into a coherent outline. The French Army Air Force, in particular, has been motivated by an antiquarian impulse; and its specific contribution—under the direction of the Reverend Fathers Poidebard and Mouterde—is an exhaustive survey of the *limes* of Roman Syria. The results of their work have been referred to previously; the manner of it was painstakingly thorough. As a general rule, the aerial surveys were made from an altitude of about 1000 feet; but whenever the observer happened to need a closer view of the terrain, the pilot was willing to cruise at a height of from 80 to 100 feet. They were conscientious in the matter of seeking for verification on the ground of whatever discoveries they had made from the air. Sometimes a fragment of a column or an inscription would reward their searching; or again, the unquestionable traces of some sort of building or fortification. When every kind of tangible proof was lacking, trial pits would be dug or rubble cleared away in order to find what might lie hidden beneath the surface. Occasionally, when all marks of a Roman road had disappeared and no faintest shadow of it was traceable from the air, a clue was sought by another method. A string of camels would be given their head, and their uncanny instinct for treading in ancient tracks would often lead an observer to the next discernible trace of the obliterated route.

5

THE DESERT PIPE-LINES OF THE IRAQ PETROLEUM COMPANY

The most recent of all desert enterprises is the laying of the oil pipe-lines across the *Great* and the *Little* Deserts, by the Iraq Petroleum Company. A concession was obtained from the Irak Government by this international concern, which contained (originally) British, French, American and Dutch interests, to exploit 32,000 square miles of oil-fields east of the Tigris. After preliminary surveys and various preparations for the establishing of adequate supply depots, the pipes were laid from Kirkuk to the Mediterranean. Fleets of lorries and ten-wheeled Scammell tractors carried pneumatic drills and explosives back and forth across the desert, as well as the thousands of tons of pipes. Trenches for these pipes were dug straight across the desert, along a line drawn on a map, and with little regard to easy natural gradients. A double line of piping now runs to Haditha on the Euphrates, and there the French and the British lines separate. The French pipe-line, after passing by Palmyra and Homs, terminates at Tripoli; the British line passes close to Rutba, crosses the lava country to Mafrak, and terminates at Haifa. Nine pumping-stations have been built in the Syrian Desert section—four on the Tripoli branch and five on the Haifa branch of the line—to regulate the flow of the 4,000,000 tons of crude oil which are annually to be pumped through the pipes. The stations are large enough to include comfortable living quarters for the staff, with rooms for guests of the Company, and separate cottages for married members of the higher staff. Wherever desert wells or springs are lacking, in the near neighbourhood of each station, the Company has sunk artesian wells. The pumping stations are connected by telegraph lines with each other and with the principal depots and termini of the pipe-line. In addition, a wireless system has been installed, in case the Beduin or violent storms should ever interfere with the working of the telegraph service; at all times direct communication is thus assured with the Iraki police, the desert patrols of

Trans-Jordan, the Royal Air Force, or the French military authorities at Palmyra.

In January 1935, after almost three years of desert work and the spending of £10,000,000, the twin pipe-lines were officially opened, and oil began to flow from Irak to the Mediterranean.

This last great undertaking, projected and completed within the brief span of five years, has set a seal on pioneering enterprises in the Syrian Desert. Perhaps a railway will one day be built across the *Great Desert*; if so, it will follow the carefully made survey of 1932. Possibly a new motor track will be laid instead; and if so, it will be likely to link Mafrak with Thumail and Felluja. But the pioneering element will be lacking in either case, because the ground to be covered has already been surveyed. Similarly any transport scheme which the French might initiate in Palmyrena would be bound to traverse ground that has already been surveyed both by aeroplane and motor car.

The significant fact today is the ease with which the Syrian Desert can be traversed. The comparative safety and brevity of the desert crossing makes the modern traveller feel as though the legendary "flying carpet" had miraculously materialized. Mesopotamia is now within a day's journey of the Mediterranean, instead of being separated by several weeks of caravan travel.

In time, perhaps, a History of the Syrian Desert will be written; the wealth and picturesqueness of all its details be fully exposed. Palmyrene, Byzantine and Arab ruins stand today, mute yet eloquent signposts, pointing into the past. Where Rome marched by, may still be found her roads, her wells, her wayside fortresses. But of the merchants and of the explorers there remains no trace. Beneath the drifting dust and sand of the Syrian Desert their trails lie hidden—clean erased—as are the sea-ways of contemporary wayfarers who sailed the oceans of the then known world. Save only a few travellers, whose works endure as desert classics, these multitudes have passed, and left their tale untold. As has been said:

And of these is a story written: but Allah Alone knoweth all!

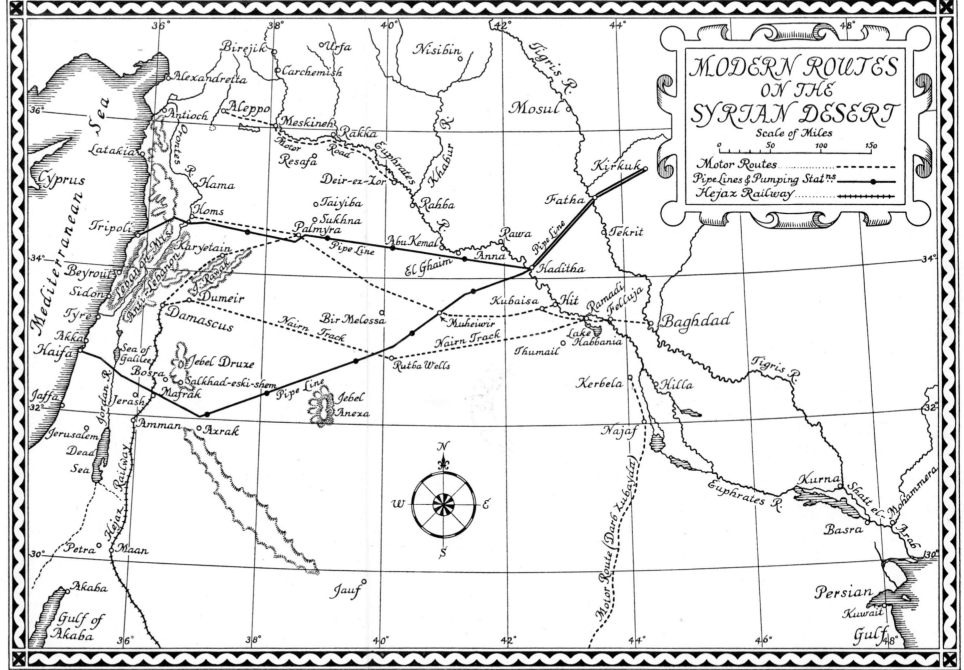

MODERN ROUTES
ON THE
SYRIAN DESERT

Scale of Miles

0   50   100   150

Motor Routes ....
Pipe Lines & Pumping Stat^{ns} _____
Hejaz Railway +++++++++++

C.P. Grant: The Syrian Desert

Emery Walker Ltd., del. et sc.

APPENDIX I

ARABIC TRANSLITERATION [1]

THE transliteration of even the few Arabic words that are essential to a survey of this character presents several difficulties, to writer and reader alike. In describing desert life and customs, only colloquial Arabic is relevant and of use. Unfortunately, colloquial Arabic has never been reduced to any form of writing; and this means that a multitude of Arab dialects, of great variety and flexibility, have never been standardized. Classical or written Arabic has been rigidly systematized; but classical and colloquial Arabic are two entirely distinct languages which have developed separately along parallel lines. They are both in use today, but the written language of the Koran, of the theologians and the schoolmen, has no more in common with any one of the modern spoken Arab dialects than Latin has with modern Italian—even less, because, unlike colloquial Arabic, one can only conceive of Italian as both a written and a spoken language.

Classical Arabic, as defined by *The Encyclopaedia of Islam*, "denotes that form of the Arabic language which since the commencement of Arabic Literature has been used by the Arabic writing nations for all their literary productions". The earliest inscriptions found in the central Syrian Desert, called Safaitic, are a "by-form" of the southern Arabian alphabet. They pre-date the earliest Arabic script which, in the third century A.D., grew directly out of the Nabataean "cursive script" of north-western Arabia. The oldest specimens of classical Arabic, on the other hand, are found in pre-Islamic poems; and this form of the language is thought to have originated in eastern central Arabia. Before the seventh century, this classical poetic language had become the common written language of Arabia; it had lost flexibility, and its rules were defined, with more or less artificiality, by the Arab grammarians. After the Mohammedans adopted the classical language for the transcribing of the Koran, it ceased to undergo any genuine development.

[1] Paragraphs 1-3 (inclusive), CLASSICAL ARABIC: *The Encyclopaedia of Islam*, article (signed by Brockelmann) "Arabia", section on Arabic language and literature. Paragraph 4 to end of Appendix I: written with the advice and suggestions of Mr A. S. Fulton, Assistant Keeper of the Department of Oriental Printed Books and MSS. of the British Museum.

Throughout Moslem lands the language of the Koran was considered a
sacred language, to be preserved intact so far as was possible. Slight
modifications were countenanced, and a variety of scripts took form,
of which *Kufic* (widely used in the Saracen period) and *Nashki* (the
most popular script in Arab countries since the fourteenth century) are
the best known. From the time of the first Mohammedan conquests,
this written language has remained virtually unchanged; and today
the Egyptian and Syrian newspapers are written in the "grammatical
skeleton" of classical Arabic.

The colloquial language, on the other hand, blossomed into a profusion of dialects. Their spontaneous development, shaped by the inter-
mixture of Arab tribes, has been influenced by intercourse with Iranian
and Mongol peoples, and by Christian invaders from Western Europe.
The original dialects have become differentiated, and they have altered
in the process of developing. Modern colloquial Arabic is still adaptable;
and because it has remained unwritten, it is infinitely difficult to trans-
literate.

The problem, then, resolves itself into one of phonetics; and here one
is confronted by another kind of difficulty. There are as many "systems"
of Arabic phonetics as there have been travellers to the lands where
Arabic is spoken. Frenchmen, Englishmen, Americans, Germans,
Hungarians, Slavs and Scandinavians, travelling in or near the Syrian
Desert, have all elaborated glossaries of colloquial Arabic for their own
use; but no uniform international system of phonetics has as yet been
evolved. Arabic place-names have been partially standardized by the
creation of three separate systems of transliteration for the use of map-
makers. But there is no single and inclusive system of English phonetics
in current use, if one excepts those which are in process of development
—along different lines—in the English universities and in the American
University of Beyrout. Consequently, anyone writing about the Near
and Middle East is confronted with the task of compiling a special
glossary for the purpose.

It is not easy to make a glossary, however informal and incomplete.
Recent formal systems for the transliteration of classical Arabic have all
been worked out on a single basic principle: to enable any Arabic
scholar to turn a literal written translation back into the correct Arabic
equivalent. That is, not to be dependent upon the relatively correct
rendering of aural phonetics, but to be able to rely upon a sound-proof
system which—when written—might become standardized. The transcribing of colloquial Arabic, on the other hand, can be based upon no
such guiding principles. One's only guide is the spoken word—a most
elusive quantity, that makes the formulation of any unified phonetic

system very difficult of attainment. The problem, a dual one, is briefly this. A writer must, at first hand, reconcile the differing pronunciations of the various districts where Arabic is spoken. The result must then be compared and reconciled in its turn with the several phonetic systems of a variety of studiously inclined medieval and modern travellers. In the present instance, still more was required in the matter of simplification. A rough-and-ready system has had to be evolved which should satisfy two conditions. First, words and place-names had to be rendered in such a form that the word transcribed might symbolize, phonetically, its equivalent in Syrian Arabic. Secondly, the rendition had, of necessity, to be as easily legible and pronounceable as was compatible with the Arabic words—that is to say, that a genuinely accurate and scholarly method of transcription (involving the use of dashes above and dots below letters, and of apostrophes between them) would be too confusing for this present purpose.

One or two characteristic difficulties may be mentioned by way of example. To indicate them may be illuminating, especially when one considers that each traveller in turn had to face these same problems independently. In the first place, pronunciations vary slightly from village to village, even when the villages in question are close together. The variation is marked among different nomad tribes, and in villages that are far apart geographically. This of course is the principal reason why travellers (who have explored different parts of the Near and Middle East) have worked out such differing phonetic systems. To complicate matters still further, many things have a variety of names. Whatever is of great importance in Arab life is multitudinously denoted; the camel, for instance, is known by some 200 Arabic names. The Arabic spoken in Irak is often unintelligible in Syria. The dialects of Syria and Trans-Jordan are more closely akin, but discrepancies are still to be observed. Arabic as spoken in Arabia is the purest of all the forms of that language; and it is, for obvious reasons, most closely related to the dialects of the nomad tribes that range the Syrian Desert. The Arabic used in Egypt offers the greatest contrast of all, since it is permeated with words derived from English, French and Italian roots. Furthermore, the soft *j* of Syria is transmuted, in Egypt, into a hard *g*.

Over and above these geographical differences, and more important than them all, there are the difficulties inherent in the language itself. For one thing, vowel sounds are, for the most part, interchangeable. This is because only three English vowel combinations (ā, ī (ee) and ū (ou)) are used to represent twenty-five Arabic vowel sounds. The most convenient illustrations of this statement are geographical. For example, the Arabic name of Palmyra has been spelled Tudmor, Tadmor

Tadmur and Tudmur; *ei* has been used in place of *ai* (or *vice versa*), as in Dumeir for Dumair, or Kasr el-Hair for Kasr el-Heir; and the indefinite article may be spelled *el, il* or *al*, indifferently; or modified for euphony to *er, ar, es* or *esh*—depending usually upon the first letter of the noun which it precedes. Also, the final *a* or *e* of a place-name can be lengthened or not, according to choice: as in Rutbah for Rutba, or Meskineh for Meskine. French phonetics (widely used in Syria) have further complicated spelling for the English reader, by substituting such combinations as *ou* for *u*, and *dj* for *j* or for a double *j*. For example, Sukhna (or Sukhne) is spelled Soukhne in French transcriptions, and jebel (meaning mountain) is spelled djebel; similarly, Hajj becomes Hadj, and the Hejaz (more modernly spelled Hijaz in English) becomes the Hedjaz. Lastly, the French have always used a *q* for the guttural sound which the English render as a *k*, like Iraq for Irak. Another complication results from the confusion between the medieval and modern pronunciations of certain place-names, on maps and in travel diaries. For instance, Basra used to be spelt Basrah, Busserah, Bassorah, Bussora and (in the seventeenth century) Balsara, Balsera and Balsora; Beyrout, even today, is alternatively spelled Beirut, Bairut and Beyrouth; Akka, or Acre, was the St. Jean d'Acre of the Crusades; Babylon used often to be confused with Baghdad; Meshed (as in Meshed Ali or Meshed Rahba) was known originally as Mexat, and later as Meched; Rahba was equally often spelled Rhaba or Rahaba; and Tayma has been spelled Teima, Teyma, Tejma and Taima.

Another typical difficulty is that of finding any combination of English letters which will express certain guttural sounds in the Arabic. *Ghr*, more often but less effectively rendered simply as *gh*, indicates one of the most difficult of these—as in the word *ghrazzu*, meaning raiding party or raid; whilst another guttural vowel, inadequately represented by the sound *aye'n* (*'ain*), is not reproducible in English at all.

There is no end to the permutations and combinations which have been used. And if this is true of place-names, it is doubly true of the words of a vocabulary for which there has been no previous need for standardization. To take a single example, the word shaykh has been spelled sheik, shaikh and (less recently) sheick. Famous travellers in Arabic lands, such as the Blunts, Doughty and Burton—not to mention others of non-British nationality, whose phonetics are based upon some foreign language (notably Musil)—have all found different ways of expressing phonetically the same sounds. But no English dictionary of phonetic uniformity has been compiled as a result of their efforts.

To sum up, for the shortcomings of the following system of transliteration, geographical and otherwise, the writer assumes full responsibility. Consistent simplicity has been the one aim, and is the sole excuse for this attempted simplification of the phonetics of an ancient and complex language. The example of T. E. Lawrence might more logically have been followed: by recognizing that almost any Arabic word may be rendered correctly in several different ways, and transcribing it accordingly. Jedda might, after the precedent set by Lawrence, be spelled Jeddah, Jidda or even Jiddah; and the Rualla tribe, Ruwalla (with or without the double *l*). This lack of system could well be imitated, in all its analogous implications, by any aspiring writer on Near Eastern matters. But in a survey of this character, which aims to simplify a picture of certain aspects of desert life over the space of 2000 years, such faithful inconsistencies would—although more in keeping with the vagaries of colloquial Arabic—only be misleading. Such picturesque triplications might detract from the story as a whole; a story which would suffer from any unnecessarily confusing details. Besides, the indexing would also suffer from such diversities.

In the bibliography, and wherever else classical Arabic is needed for the transcribing of proper names, the writer has relied entirely upon the system which has been evolved by the staff of the Arabic Department of the British Museum.

Note.—For the sake of clarity and intelligibility, the plurals of Arabic words have been consistently formed by adding an "s" to the singular of the Arabic word (regardless of any changes of form in the Arabic). Also, in most cases, for the sake of brevity, the Arabic article has been omitted in place names ; *e.g.*, *el*-Irak has been rendered simply as Irak, *the* Jebel *ed*-Druze as Jebel Druze, etc.

GLOSSARY OF ARABIC WORDS AND NAMES

For the sake of clarity, the plurals of Arabic words have been consistently formed by adding an "s" to the singular of the Arabic word.

aba	woollen cloak
Abbas the Great, Shah	.
Abbasid	dynasty of Baghdad
Abd el-Aziz ibn Sa'ud I	first Wahhabi ruler of Nejd
Abd el-Aziz ibn Sa'ud II	King Ibn Sa'ud of Arabia
Abd el-Malik	
Abu Bakr, Caliph .	first successor of Mohammed
Abu l'Abbas Ahmed el-Kalkashandi	
Abulfeda	
aga, el-	captain (usually of the Janissaries)
Agail	an Arab tribe (originally of Nejd)
'ain	natural spring
akhwan, el- . . .	the brotherhood
Akhwan, el- (and el-Ikhwan)	The Brotherhood, founded by King Ibn Sa'ud
Ali	son-in-law of Mohammed
Aneza	principal nomad tribe of the Syrian Desert
Arab	"the people"
Arabia	the "island of the Arabs"
Assurbanipal	
Assyrians	ancient inhabitants of Mesopotamia
Ateiba	a tribe of the Hejaz
Ayyubid	dynasty of Baghdad
Babylonians . . .	ancient inhabitants of Mesopotamia
Badia, el-	the waste, or untilled spaces of land; the wilderness
Badiet el-Irak . .	the Badia of Irak
Badiet esh-Shem . .	the Badia of Syria

barkaness . . . . small company (of camel-men)
Barmecide . . . a Baghdad family, of the palace
                                     nobility
basheer . . . . messenger of good news
bashi (of a caravan) . . leader
Baybars, Sultan ez-Zahir
  Baybars . . . of the Mamluk dynasty of Cairo
bayrakdar . . . standard-bearer
Bedawi . . . . occupants of the Badia; nomads
                                     (plural)
Bedu . . . . singular of Bedawi
Bedui (become Beduin) . dual or collective of Bedawi
Beit Allah, el- . . . The House of God at Mecca
Bekri, el- (el-Bekri)
Beladhori
Beni Sakhr . . . nomad tribe of the south-western Badia
Berid, el- . . . . the post; a courier; post stages
beridi . . . . courier
beridedem . . . applied to mules with tails cut (*i.e.* of
                                     the post)
bir . . . . . dug out spring
birket . . . . reservoir
Buyid . . . . dynasty of Baghdad

Caliph (anglicized form of
  Khalifah) . . . Spiritual Ruler of Islam
caravanserai . . . hostel or rest-house
Chosroes I, the Iranian King

daleel . . . . guide; "pilot" (scout)
Darb el-Hajj . . . Pilgrim Road
Darb el-Kufri . . . Road of the Unbelievers
Darb es-Sa'i . . . Road of the Courier
Darb es-Sitt Zubayda . Road of the Lady Zubayda
Darb es-Sultan . . . Royal Road
Delees . . . . Dervishes: religious (Moslem) fanatics
dhalul . . . . female dromedary
dira . . . . . tribal district, or orbit
diwan . . . . governmental department
diwan el-insha, sahib . . postmaster-general, also chancellor
Dulaim . . . . Arab tribe of the eastern Syrian
                                     Desert, and of central Mesopotamia

el-   .   .   .   .   .   the
emir   .   .   .   .   prince
Emir el-berid (and, later:
    el-Emir-akhor)   .   .   Director of the Post
Emir el-Hajj   .   .   .   Commander of the Hajj

Fatimid (Fatimites)   .   .   dynasty of Egypt
Feisal, late King of Irak
fellaheen .   .   .   .   peasants
felucca   .   .   .   .   sail-boat
firman   .   .   .   .   edict of an Ottoman sultan
Frangi (Arabic form of the
    term *Frank*)   .   .   .   European. Any European, or "out-
                                        lander," from the Arab point of
                                        view (cf. Rauwolff, in Ray's *Travels*
                                        (1693), vol. i, p. 138)

Ghassanid   .   .   .   an Arab dynasty and kingdom; vassals
                                        of the Byzantine emperor
Ghazali, el-
ghrazzu (more accurately:
    ghazw)   .   .   .   raiding; the act of campaigning
guffa   .   .   .   .   round boat, or coracle, cemented with
                                        pitch

Hadar   .   .   .   .   settled Arabs (collective)
Hadari   .   .   .   .   „   „   (singular)
Hadariyeen   .   .   .   „   „   (plural)
hadarah   .   .   .   .   culture, civilization
hader   .   .   .   .   present; ready (adv.)
hadi   .   .   .   .   homing pigeon, best variety
Hajj, el- .   .   .   .   the Pilgrimage
Hajji   .   .   .   .   one who has made the Pilgrimage to
                                        Mecca. *Hajji* is the commonest
                                        (Turkish) form of the word

Hajji Khalifa
Hajji Mohammed el-
    Bassam
hakim   .   .   .   .   physician
Hamad, el-   .   .   .   the hard, barren, stony (type of)
                                        desert
hamam   .   .   .   .   homing pigeon, generic name
Harb   .   .   .   .   Beduin tribe of western Arabia

Harra, el- .   .   .   .   the lava country
Harun er-Rashid, Caliph
Hejira, el-   .   .   .   the Flight, and therefore also the year
                                          of the Flight of Mohammed

Hittites
Howeitat .   .   .   .   nomad tribe of the south-western Badia
Hulagu, the Tatar

Ibn Battuta
Ibn Haukal
Ibn Jubair
Ibn Khordadbeh
Ibn er-Rashid
Ibn Sa'ud (see Abd el-Aziz II)
Idrisi (Edrisi)
Ihram, el-   .   .   .   pilgrim dress
Ilkhan   .   .   .   .   ruler of the Tatar Khanate of Persia
Inglesi   .   .   .   .   Arabic form of the term "the English"
Islam   .   .   .   .   literally means: "Resignation to the
                                          Will of God". A word that is gener-
                                          ally used by Mohammedans to
                                          denote their religion. The observance
                                          of "the five duties" is implied: (1)
                                          bearing witness that there is but one
                                          God; (2) reciting the daily prayers;
                                          (3) giving the legal alms; (4) ob-
                                          serving Ramadan (the month-of-
                                          fasting); (5) making the Pilgrimage
                                          to Mecca once in a lifetime

janissary .   .   .   .   Turkish regular infantryman
jawaiz   .   .   .   .   levy; duties
jebel   .   .   .   .   mountain: upland, mountainous region
jehad   .   .   .   .   holy war: against unbelievers, and against
                                          evils of the flesh
jerboa   .   .   .   .   desert rat

Ka'aba, the   .   .   .   the Black Stone
kadi, el- .   .   .   .   judge (cadi in Turkish transcriptions)
kafar   .   .   .   .   toll
kafila   .   .   .   .   caravan; townspeople's word for kufi
kahweji   .   .   .   .   coffee-maker

20

kal'a (kal'at) . . .	fort
Kalkashandi, el-	
kasr	fort, castle
Katib es-Sirr . . .	Secretary of State (*i.e.* "Secretary of the Secret Chancellery")
keffiya	cloth turban (Beduin)
kelek	raft—the kind used on the Euphrates and Tigris rivers
Khan	supreme ruler (Tatar); deputy governor (Persian or Iranian)
khan	rest-house; *see* caravanserai
khawaja . . .	Mr (mister); also head of a house
khifara . . .	money payments; tribute or subsidy exacted for protection
Khitat, el- . .	a work of el-Makrizi
khlas	finish; the end
khuwa (or el-ukhuwa) .	the bond of brotherhood
kirba . . .	small leather water-skin
Kudama	
kufi	convoy; a Beduin word
Kufic	an early Arabic script, named after the city of Kufa
Lakhmid . . .	an Arab dynasty and kingdom; vassals of the Sasanian Iranians
leben . . .	sour-milk drink
Lihyanites . .	predecessors of the Nabataeans in northern Arabia and Arabia Petraea
Mahdi, Caliph el-	
mahmal, el- . .	sacred litter of the *Hajj*: named from the two girths which support the palanquin
Makrizi, el-	
Malik, Abd el-	
Mamluk . . .	dynasty of Egyptian sultans
Mansur, Caliph	
manzel . . .	Turkish imperial order, authorizing one to accompany the government post
"Masalik el-Absar" .	a work of el-Omari
Mas'udi, el-	

matarea	large leather water-skin
maurid	water-hole
merkab, el– . . .	tribal palanquin, covered with ostrich feathers
Midhat Pasha	
Minaeans	primitive Arabians
Moali	tribe of the north-western Badia
Mo'awia, Caliph	
mohaffa	camel-panniers, for carrying passengers
Mohammed, the Prophet	
Mohammed Ali	
Mongols	peoples of Central Asia
Montefik	semi-nomad tribe of the south-eastern Badia
Moslem	anyone who professes the religion of Islam
muezzin	one who calls to prayer
mugubrines . . .	Turkish infantry on desert duty
Mukaddasi, el–	
mukowam . . .	camel master, or driver
Musta'sim, Caliph	
Nabataeans . .	Arabs of Arabia Petraea. An ancient designation
nadeer	messenger of bad news
na'ib	governor; viceroy, or vice-sultan
Naskhi	an Arabic script, the most popular since the fourteenth century
niyaba, el– . . .	the governorship or the lieutenancy
Nuri Shaalan	
Omar, Caliph . . .	second successor to Mohammed
Omari, el–	
Omayyad . . .	Saracen dynasty of Damascus
otfa, el–	variety of tribal palanquin; different type from *el-merkab*
Othman, Caliph . .	third successor to Mohammed
Ottoman Turks . .	a Mongolian people
Parthians	Middle Easterners; the rulers of Iran from third century B.C. to third century A.D.

pasha	governor-general of a *pashalik*
pashalik	Turkish province
Phoenicians . . .	ancient inhabitants of Palestine
piastre	Turkish, Syrian and Spanish coins of different values (see Table of Moneys and Exchange, Appendix 4)
Ptolemies. . . .	Hellenes of Egypt
rafeek	a "human passport" or tribal representative (see pp. 172 and 212)
Ramadan	the Mohammedan lunar month that is dedicated to fasting—*i.e.* total abstinence between sunrise and sunset
Rashids	a ruling family of Jauf
rotl (rotola) . . .	standard of weight: about 5 lb.
Rualla	nomad tribe of the Badia; a principal section of the Aneza
Sabaeans	primitive Arabians
Safaitic	primitive Arabic inscriptions in the Syrian Desert
Sahib el-Berid . . .	postmaster-general
Sahib diwan el-insha . .	postmaster-general, also chancellor
saiyid	principal tribal shaykh
Samawa, as- . . .	the central and southern regions of the Syrian Desert
sanjak	subdivision of a *pashalik*
Sasanians	later Iranians, successors to the Parthians (after third century A.D.)
segmans (segmenes) . .	foot-soldiers
Seleucids	Hellenes of Asia Minor, Syria and the Middle East
Selim Sawwaf	
Seljuk (as distinguished from Ottoman) Turks	
Shah	the ruler of Iran
Shammar	nomad tribe of Nejd
shaous (shaoush) . .	captain of the guard; sometimes aide-de-camp
Shatt el-Arab . . .	the Tigris-Euphrates rivers, after their junction

Shawwal	a lunar month in the Arabic calendar
shaykh . . .	tribal leader, senior, or man of authority
Shaykh es-Sa'a . . .	the shaykh in charge of a municipal postal organization
Sherarat	nomad tribe of the south-western Badia and of the Wadi Sirhan
Shi'a	an Iranian Islamic sect: the "Followers" —i.e. Followers of Ali, cousin and son-in-law of Mohammed
shik	camel-thorn
sikka, el-	distance between postal stations
simoom	"poison wind" of the Badia
sitt	lady; madame
Sitt Zubayda . . .	wife of Harun er-Rashid
souk	bazaar
spahis	Turkish cavalrymen
Subh el-A'sha . . .	a work of el-Kalkashandi
Suleiman the Magnificent .	a Sultan of Turkey (1520–66)
Suluba	the "Gypsy" tribe of the Badia (see note, p. 22)
Sunna, el- . . .	body of Islamic law, based upon the Koran and its interpreted dogma
Sunni	"orthodox" Mohammedans; self-styled "Traditionists", who acknowledge the first four Caliphs (Khalifahs) to have been the rightful successors of Mohammed
surra	tribute
tarboosh	Turkish headgear
"Ta'rif bil Mustalalah esh-Sharif", et- . . .	a work of el-Omari
tarjuman	interpreter, or dragoman
tatar	Turkish dispatch-bearer; courier
Tatars	Mongolian people of Central Asia
Tawaf, el- . . .	the rite of "Circumambulation"
tell	hill
thurrm	grass forage
Timur the Mongol	
ukhuwa, el- . . .	the bond of brotherhood

wadi	dry river-bed, or watercourse
Wadian, el-	the eastern section of the "Great Desert", or as-Samawa
Wahhab, Mohammed ibn Abd el-	
Wahhabis	a Puritan Islamic sect of Nejd; followers of el-Wahhab
Walid, el-	
Yahya	
Yakut	
Zair	one who has "visited" the tomb of the Prophet Mohammed
Zengid	dynasty of Baghdad
Ziyarat	"Visitation"
Zubayda, Sitt	wife of Harun er-Rashid

APPENDIX 3

GEOGRAPHICAL GLOSSARY

Abadan
Abu Kemal
Abu Kir
Achera, Kasr
Aden
Aelana (*see* Akaba)
Ain el-Kom (Ayun al-Kûm)
Akaba
Akaba, Gulf of
Akka (St. Jean d'Acre)
Aleppo (Haleb; formerly Beroea)
Alexandretta (Iskanderun)
Alexandria
Algiers
Amej, Kasr
Amman
Ampelone (*see* Leuce Come)
Anatolia
Anbar
Aneza, Jebel
Aneza, Kal'at
Anna
Anti-Lebanon Mountains
Antioch
Arabia Felix
Arabia Petraea
Aradus
Arak (Erek)
Armenia, the Kingdom of Little
Arnab, Kasr
Assyria
Azrak
Azrak, Kasr

Baalbek
Babylon
Babylonia
Bactria
Badia, el- (the Wilderness)
Badiet el-Irak
Badiet esh-Shem
Baghdad
Bahrein, the Islands of
Bali (also Balkis; formerly
    Zeugma-Apamea)
Bandar Abbas
Basra (formerly Bassora and also
    Bussorah)
Beida
Beilan Pass, the
Belka, Kal'at el-
Bengal
Beriara (the Little Desert:
    Bavera?)
Beroea (*see* Aleppo)
Beyrout (Beirut)
Bir Melossa
Birejik (formerly Birtha and Bir,
    originally Macedonopolis)
Bishri, Jebel (Jebel Busheer)
Bombay
Bosra eski-Shem
Burka
Bushire
Byblus

Cairo (el-Misr)

Calcutta
Calicut
Cambodia
Carchemish (*see* Jerablus)
Ceylon
Chalcis
Champa
Charax (*see* Mohammera)
China
Circesium (Kirkisiya)
Constantinople (Stamboul)
Crimea, the
Croydon
Ctesiphon
Cyprus

Dahana, the
Damascus (Damask esh-Shem)
Deir ez-Zor
Delhi
Diarbekr
Druze, Jebel
Dumeir
Dura-Europos (*see* Salahiya)

Egypt
England
Ephesus
Erzi, Jebel
Euphrates, River (el-Frat)

Famagusta
Felluja
Fez
Forat
Forklus
Frat, el- (river Euphrates)

Gabaji
Galilee
Gaza

Gerrha
Ghaim, el-
Graine

Habbania, Lake
Haditha
Hadramaut
Haifa
Hair, Kasr el-
Haleb (*see* Aleppo)
Halebiya (originally Zenobia)
Hama
Hamad, the
Hamadan
Hamdh, Wadi
Harra, the
Hasa, the
Hasa, Kal'at el-
Hass, Jebel el-
Hauran, the
Hauran, Wadi
Hayil
Hejaz, the
Hikla (Hagla)
Hilla
Hindostan
Hira (Lakhmid: formerly Lakh-
    mid capital)
Hit (Is or Id)
Homs

Iathrib (*see* Medina)
India
Indo-China
Indus, river
Irak
Iran (*see* Persia)
Isa, Nahr (canal)
Iskanderun (formerly Scandaroon:
    see Alexandretta)
Ispahan

Jaber Castle
Jafar
Jaffa
Jask
Jauf (originally Adumu, and
 Dumat el-Jandel)
Java
Jerablus
Jerash
Jericho
Jerusalem
Jidd, el-
Jedda (Jidda)
Jordan, river
Jubba
Jubb el-Ghanam (Jub al-Gannam)
Jumeima

Kara
Karachi
Karun, river
Karyetain
Kashan
Kasim, the
Kasr el-Hair (see Hair, el-Kasr)
Katif, el-
Katrani, Kal'at el-
Kawatil
Kebbaz, Kasr
Kenghavar
Kerak, el- (see Trans-Jordan)
Kerbela
Khabur, river
Khan Muktar
Khorasan
Khotan
Kirkisiya (formerly Circesium)
Kirkuk
Kubaisa
Kubakib
Kufa (see Meshed Ali)
Kurna

Kut el-Amara
Kuwait
Kuwebda

Latakia
Lebanon Mountains
Leghorn
Leuce Come
London

Maan
Macedonopolis (see Birejik)
Madagascar
Madras
Mafrak
Mahra, el-
Maldive Islands
Maneh, Wadi
Mardin
Marseille
Mayadin
Mecca
Medain Saleh
Medina
Medinat es-Salam (see Baghdad)
Mediterranean
Melossa, Bir (Bir Melossa)
Melossa, Jebel
Membij (formerly Hierapolis)
Meshed Ali (also Najaf: suburb
 of Kufa)
Meshed Rahba (see Mayadin)
Meskineh (formerly Thapsacus)
Mesopotamia
Messina
Mezerib
Misr, el- (see Cairo)
Mocha
Mohammera
Mongolia
Morocco
Mosul

Mudik, Kal'at el-
Mudowwara
Muheiwir
Muslimiya

Najaf (*see* Meshed Ali)
Nefud, the
Nejd
Nicosia
Nineveh (ruins on the Tigris,
    opposite Mosul)
Nisibin
Nushki

Obolla, el- (ancient suburb of
    Basra)
Obolla, Nahr el- (canal)
Oman
Ormuz
Ostend

Palestine
Palmyra (Tadmor)
Palmyrena
Paris
Patras
Persia (*see* Iran) [1]
Persian Gulf
Petra
Petraea
Philippine Islands, the
Port Said
Port William

Quetta

Rahba (*see* Meshed Rahba)
Rahhaliya
Rakka (formerly Nicephorium)

Ramadi
Ramleh
Rawa (on the Euphrates, opposite
    Anna)
Rawak, Jebel
Red Sea
Resafa
Riyadh
Rub el-Khali, the
Rumma, Wadi er-
Russia
Rutba Wells

Safad (*see* Tiberias)
Saigon
Sakaka
Salahiya (*see* Dura-Europos)
Salkhad
Samakh
Samarra
Samava (Samawa)
Samawa, as- (the Great Desert)
Samsat
Sardis
Sa'udi Arabia
Scandaroon (*see* Alexandretta)
Scio
Sebkha Jebbul
Seleucia
Sergiopolis (*see* Resafa)
Sfira
Shammar, Jebel
Sharja
Sharmley
Shatt el-Arab (Tigris–Euphrates)
Shem, esh- (Syria)
Shiraz
Shittat
Shubait, Jebel

[1] Throughout this book *Iran* and *Iranian* have been consistently substituted
for *Persia* and *Persian*, in accordance with a recent fiat of the Shah of Iran—
except when referring to the Persian Gulf.

Sidon (Sa'ıda)
Sinai
Sirhan, Wadi
Sivas
Smyrna
Somaliland
Spasinou Charax (see Charax)
Stamboul
Suab, Wadi
Suedia
Suez
Sukhna
Sultaniya
Surat
Susa
Syria (esh-Shem)

Tadmor (Palmyra)
Taif
Taiyiba
Tangier
Tartus
Taurus Mountains
Tayma
Tebuk
Tehama, the (coastal plain of
western Arabia)
Teheran
Tell Ahmar (formerly Til-
Barsib)
Tenf, Jebel
Terablus (see Tripoli)

Thapsacus (see Meskineh)
Thumail (Tammel)
Tiberias
Tigris, river
Trans-Jordan
Trebizond
Tripoli (formerly Terablus)
Tunis
Turkestan
Tyre

Ukhaidir (Al Kadder)
Umm el-Jemal
Umm el-Kurun
Urfa
Urr

Venice
Vienna
Vologesia

Wadian, the
Wasit

Yemen
Yenbo

Zebeir (formerly spelled Xebire,
Zebeer and Zobair)
Zerka, Kal'at ez-
Zeugma-Apamea (see Bali) (also
Zeugma-Seleucia)

APPENDIX 4

TABLE OF MONEYS AND EXCHANGE [1]

Approximate Exchange Values in English Shillings

Byzant (or *solidus*) . . . . Ten shillings
(Second to sixth centuries A.D.)

Dinar . . . . . . Ten shillings
(Seventh to eleventh centuries A.D.)

Denarius, silver coin of Palmyra . . One shilling
(Second to third centuries A.D.)

EIGHTEENTH-CENTURY COINS CURRENT IN THE LEVANT

Approximate values in English shillings

Dollars
  The Levant dollar . . . . One crown (five shillings)
  Maria Theresa thaler, of 1780 . .   ,,   ,,
  (Still current in Arabia)
  Spanish real (or rumi) . . .   ,,   ,,

Ducat . . . . . . Ten shillings

Larin, silver coin of Basra . . . Tenpence
  ($\frac{2}{5}$ of the standard rupee)

Livre, the French gold pound . . Eighteen shillings
  (Not very stable)

Piastres
  Spanish silver coin . . . . One crown (five shillings)
  Turkish silver coin . . . .   ,,   ,,

[1] For the following information on money and exchange values, the writer is indebted to the Department of Coins and Medals at the British Museum.

Reales, of the East India Company

One real	Sixpence
Four reales	Two shillings and sixpence
Eight reales	One crown (five shillings)

Rupee, standard of the East India Co. . Two shillings

Basra rupee . . . . . One shilling and sixpence
(¾ of standard rupee)

Sequin (secchino, zecchino, also Chequin) Seven shillings and sixpence

———

Turkish gold pound in the nineteenth century—after 1844 it was quoted at   Eighteen shillings and two-pence

APPENDIX 5

SELECTED BIBLIOGRAPHY

I.—Useful General Bibliographies and Encyclopaedias

Bibliography of the Bibliothèque Archéologique et Historique du Service Des Antiquités et Des Beaux-Arts. Haut-Commissariat de la République Française en Syrie et au Liban.

Catalogue of the York Gate Library. Second edition. London (1886).

Carruthers, Douglas. *The Desert Route to India.* London (1929). Bibliography, pp. 180-189.

Gazetteer of the Persian Gulf: see Lorimer, J. G.

Gazetteer of the World, A. Dictionary of Geographical Knowledge. London (1856).

Hughes, T. P. *Dictionary of Islam.*

Iraq Report, The. "On the Progress of Iraq during the Period 1920-1931." (Colonial No. 58.) London (1931).

Longrigg, S. H. *Four Centuries of Modern Irak.* London (1925).

Lorimer, J. G. *Gazetteer of the Persian Gulf.* Especially vol. i—Historical; and i, Appendix K: "Mail Communications and The Indian Post Office in the Persian Gulf". 2 vols. London (1915).

Masson, Paul. *Éléments d'une bibliographie française de la Syrie.* Marseille (1919).

Syria, A Handbook of. Prepared by the Geographical Section of the Naval Intelligence Division, Naval Staff. Admiralty. I.D. 1215. (London (1920).

Syria: Revue d'art oriental et d'archéologie, Tomes 1 to 16, 1920 to date. Paris (1920-35).

The Cambridge Histories, especially *The Cambridge Ancient History.*

The Encyclopaedia of Islam. "A Dictionary of the Geography, Ethnography and Biography of the Muhammadan Peoples." Originally edited by M. Th. Houtsma.

II.—Histories of Exploration and Travel Collections

Baker, J. N. L. *History of Geographical Discovery and Exploration.* Maps. London (1931).

Beazley, C. Raymond. *The Dawn of Modern Geography.* 3 vols. London (1897–1906).

Cary, M., and Warmington, E. H. *The Ancient Explorers.* London (1929).

Goeje, M. J. de. *Bibliotheca Geographorum Arabicorum.* 3 vols. Paris (1879–89).

Hakluyt Society Publications. First and Second Series of Works issued by the Society. Cambridge University Press.

Hakluytus Posthumus or Purchas His Pilgrimes. "Contayning a History of the World in Sea Voyages and Lande Travells by Englishmen and others . . ." By Samuel Purchas, B.D., 1625. 20 vols. Mac-Lehose edition. Glasgow (1905).

Heawood, Edward. *A History of Geographical Discovery in the Seventeenth and Eighteenth Centuries.* Cambridge Geographical Series. (1912.)

Harleian Collection, The. Voyages and Travels. 2 vols. London (1745).

Hogarth, D. G. *The Penetration of Arabia.* London (1904).

Mélanges d'histoire et de géographie orientale. Henri Cordier. 4 vols. Paris (1914).

Miscellanea Curiosa. Vol. iii. Containing a Collection of Curious Travels, Voyages, etc. London (1708).

Moore, J. H. *A New and Complete Collection of Voyages and Travels . . .* 2 vols. London (1780).

Murray, Hugh. *Asia.—Historical Account of Discoveries and Travels in Asia.* 3 vols. London (1820).

Newton, A. P., and others. *Travel and Travellers of the Middle Ages.* A Comparative Study. Series: The History of Civilization. London (1926).

Ray, John. *Collection of Curious Travels and Voyages.* 2 vols. London (1693 and 1738).

Sykes, Sir Percy. *A History of Exploration.* With Maps. Chapters 31, 32 and 33 on Arabia. London (1934).

Venetian Calendar of State Papers. Especially from 1592 to 1635.

Wilson, Sir Arnold T. *Early Spanish and Portuguese Travellers in Persia.* London (1927).

III.—MAPS

Arrowsmith, A. *Outlines of the Countries between Delhi and Constantinople.* 1814. Additions to, 1816.

Cambridge Ancient History. Maps in vol. i, p. 224; vol. iii, p. 1; vol. viii, pp. 155 and 658; vol. vi, pp. 1 and 357; vol. vii, p. 1.

Cambridge Medieval History. Atlas, illustrating medieval commerce.

Carruthers, Douglas. Map in the *Geographical Journal*, vol. lii, 3 (Sept. 1918), p. 204, accompanying an article on "The Great Desert Caravan Route, Aleppo to Basra" (*Ibid.* pp. 157-184).

"Carte Internationale du Monde au 1,000,000."

Chesney, F. R. Maps appended to *The Expedition for the Survey of* . . . *the Euphrates and the Tigris* . . . *1835–1837*.

Dussaud, R. Maps in the *Topographie historique de la Syrie antique et médiévale*. Paris (1927).

Garrett, Robert, *Northern Syria*: III. New York (1903).
   Corrected version of Kiepert's *Syria*. London (1907).

Kiepert, F. O. A. Map of Syrian Desert. Berlin (1910).

Kiepert, Dr. Heinrich. *Atlas Antiquus*. Twelve maps of the Ancient World. 5th edition. Berlin (1869).

Kiepert, Dr. Richard. Map of Syrian Desert. Berlin 1893).

Musil, Alois. Portfolio of maps accompanying the set of works published by the American Geographical Society of New York. Oriental Explorations and Studies. New York (1927–28).

Oestrup, J. E. Map appended to *Historisk-topografiske Bidrag til der syriske order*. (1895.)

Olivier, G. A. Atlas appended to *Voyage dans l'empire othoman*. Paris (1807).

Oppenheim, Max von. Map accompanying *Vom Mittelmeer zum Persischen Golf durch den Hauran, die syrische Wüste und Mesopotamien*. Berlin (1899).

Petermann, A. von. *Klein-Asien*. Berlin (1875).

Philips' Historical Atlas. Ramsay Muir and George Philip. London (1911–27).

Poidebard, A. Map of Roman routes in *Palmyrena*, accompanying *La Trace de Rome dans le désert de Syrie*. Paris (1934).

Rennell, Major James. Map of the Syrian Desert, No. 7, dated 1809, in the Atlas folio accompanying his book, *Treatise on the Comparative Geography of Western Asia*. London (1831).

Sachau, Eduard. Maps accompanying *Am Euphrat und Tigris*. Leipzig (1900).

Ritter, Carl. Map of Arabia. Berlin (1852).
   Map of the *Badiet e' Schâm*. Berlin (1854).
   Bearbeitet von H. Kiepert.

Royal Atlas of Modern Geography, The. London (1904).

Sarre-Herzfeld. *Routenkarte im Euphrat und Tigris*. Printed in *Archäologische Reise*, Tome I. (1911.)

Valle, Pietro della. Map of the Syrian Desert. Compiled by Du Val. British Museum's Catalogue of Printed Maps, No. 46900(5).

Walker, John. Sketch Map of Routes, Constantinople to India. 1867.

IV.—Primary Sources

Abulfeda, Ismail ibn Ali (Imad al-Din Abu al-Fida). *La Géographie d'Aboulfeda traduite de l'Arabe* . . . (par M. S. Guyard). 2 vols. Paris (1848).

Ainsworth, William F. *A Personal Narrative of the Euphrates Expedition.* 2 vols. London (1888).

Andrew, Sir William P. *Memoir on the Euphrates Valley Route to India.* With official correspondence and maps. London (1857).

   Letter to . . . Palmerston on the . . . importance of the Euphrates Valley Railway. London (1857).

   The Euphrates Valley Route to India. Paper read before the British Association at Brighton. (1873.)

Anonymous Letters of an Englishman, 1858–1862. "Rambles in the Deserts of Syria and among the Turkomans and Bedaweens." London (1864).

Arabian Nights' Entertainments, The. New revised edition by Townsend, Rev. G. Fyler. London (?): later than 1839.

Arvieux, Chevalier Laurent d'. Mémoires du, Contenant ses Voyages, 1679. 6 vols. Paris (1735).

   Travels in Arabia the Desert. Published by Mr de la Roque. London (1718).

Asher, A. *The Itinerary of Rabbi Benjamin of Tudela.* 2 vols. New York (1840).

Balbi, Gasparo. *Viaggio dell' Indie Orientali.* Venice (1590).

Barker, John, Consul-General at Aleppo. *Syria and Egypt under the last five Sultans of Turkey* . . . Edited by E. B. B. Barker. 2 vols. London (1876).

Beawes, William. *A Journey from Aleppo to Basra in 1745.* Printed in Hakluyt, Second Series, No. LXIII. (Edited by Douglas Carruthers.) Chap. i, pp. 1-40.

Bell, Gertrude L. *Amurath to Amurath.* London (1911).

   Letters. 2 vols. London (1927).

Bell, Richard, The Travels of . . . (and John Campbell) *in the East Indies, Persia, and Palestine,* 1654–1670.

Birdwood, Sir George. *Report on the Old Records of the India Office.* London (1891).

Birdwood, Sir G., and Foster, W. *The Register of Letters, etc., of the Governour and Company of Merchants of London trading into the East Indies,* 1600–19. London (1893).

Bischoff, Dr. Theodor. "A Journey from Palmyra through the Desert to Aleppo." Article in *Globus,* 1881, vol. xl, No. 23, pp. 363-366.

Black, C. E. Drummond. "A Railway from the Mediterranean to India", address delivered 17th February 1909, published in *Proceedings of the Central Asian Society*. London (1909).

Blunt, Lady Anne. *Bedouin Tribes of the Euphrates*. 2 vols. London (1879). *A Pilgrimage to Nejd: The Cradle of the Arab Race*. 2 vols. London (1881).

Breasted, James H. Article on "Salihiya", in *Syria*, vol. iii (1922).

British Consulate at Beyrout, Syria. *Archives*. Register Nos. 2003 and 2663; File No. 26. 17th December 1931.

Figures (furnished by the Irak Police) on trans-desert traffic.

Browne, W. G. *Travels in Africa, Egypt and Syria—from the year 1792–1798*. London (1799).

Bugnon, M. Géographe ordinaire de S. A. Royale de Lorraine. *Relation Exacte Concernant les Caravanes ou Cortèges de Marchands d'Asie*. Nancy (1707).

Burckhardt, J. L. *Travels in Syria and the Holy Land*. London (1822). *Notes on the Bedouins and Wahabys*. Collected during his travels in the East, by the late J. L. Burckhardt. 2 vols. London (1831).

Burton, Captain Sir Richard F. *Personal Narrative of a Pilgrimage to Al-Madinah and Meccah*. 2 vols. London (1893).

Burton, Richard F., and Drake, Chas. F. T. *Unexplored Syria*. 2 vols. London (1872).

Butler, H. C. *Publications of an American Archaeological Expedition to Syria*. New York (1903).

Butler, H. C., Norrio, F. A., and Stoever, E. R. *Geography and Itinerary*. With map of Syria. Princeton (1930). (*Ibid.* in *Geog. Review*, 1920, vol. ix, No. 2.)

Butler, Captain S. S. "Baghdad to Damascus Via El Jauf." Article in the *Geographical Journal*, vol. xxxiii, No. 5, pp. 517-535. (May 1909.)

Callier, Le Capitaine Camille. "Les Couriers de Turquie et la caravane de Bagdad." Fragment de la relation inédite du voyage du Capitaine Callier. Article in the *Bulletin de la Société de Géographie*. 11me Ser., No. 8 (1837), pp. 288-302.

Cameron, V. L., Commander R.N. *Our Future Highway*. 2 vols. London (1880).

Capper, James, Esq., Colonel in the Service of the Honourable East India Company. *Observations on the Passage to India, through Egypt, and across the Great Desert . . . with . . . remarks . . .* London (1783).

Carmelite Chronicle. See Gollancz, Sir Hermann.

Carmichael, J. *A Journey from Aleppo to Basra in 1751*. Printed in Hakluyt, Second Series, No. LXIII. (Edited by Douglas Carruthers.) Chap. iv, pp. 131-179.

Carré, Monsieur. *Voyages des Indes Orientales*. Paris (1699).

Carruthers, Douglas. *Arabian Adventure: To the Great Nafud in Quest of the Oryx*. London (1935).

"The Arabian Ostrich." *The Ibis*, July 1922, pp. 471-474. London (1922).

The Desert Route to India. "Being the Journals of Four Travellers by the Great Desert Caravan Route between Aleppo and Basra, 1745-1751." Published by the Hakluyt Society, Second Series, No. LXIII. London (1929).

"A Journey in North-Western Arabia" (1909). Published in the *Geographical Journal*, vol. xxxv, p. 225 *et seq.* (March 1910.)

Cartwright, John. *The Preacher's Travels Through Syria, Persia*, etc. London (1611).

Castiau, Marcel. "En Syrie: Le long du chemin des pèlerins de la Mecque." Published in *Le Bulletin de la Société Royale de Géographie d'Anvers*. Tome 27, pp. 19-66. (1903.)

Černik, Josef. *Technische Studien-Expedition durch die Gebiete des Euphrats und Tigris nebst Ein- und Ausgangs-Routen durch Nord-Syrien*. 2 vols. and maps. (1875-1876.)

Chabot, J.-B. *Choix d'inscriptions de Palmyre*. Traduites et commentées. Paris (1922).

Chesney, General F. R. *Narrative of the Euphrates Expedition*. "Carried on by Order of the British Government—during the Years 1835, 1836 and 1837." London (1868).

The Expedition for the Survey of . . . the Euphrates and the Tigris . . . 1835-1837 . . . with maps and geographical notices. 2 vols. London (1850).

Coote, General Sir Eyre. *Diary*, 1771. Printed from the original MS. in the *Geographical Journal* (i.e. *Journal of the Royal Geographical Society*), vol. xxx, pp. 198-211. (1860.)

Coryate, Thomas. *Coryat's Crudities*. Reprinted from the edition of 1611, with his letters from India. 3 vols. London (1776).

Cumont, Franz. *Études syriennes*. Paris (1917). Also articles in *Syria*, vols. iii and iv (1922 and 1923).

Dallam, Master Thomas, Diary of, 1599-1600. Published by the Hakluyt Society, lxxxvii. (1893.)

Dalrymple, G. Elphinstone. *The Syrian Great Eastern Railway to India. By an extremely new route*. Pamphlet, London (1878).

Damoiseau, Louis. *Voyage . . . dans le désert*. 2 vols. Paris (1839).

Doughty, Charles M. *Travels in Arabia Deserta*. Introduction by T. E. Lawrence. London (1933). Also an earlier edition of 1921.

Dumreicher, André Von. *Trackers and Smugglers in the Deserts of Egypt*. New York (1931).

Dundas, H., and Wellesley, R. C. *Opinions of . . . Melville . . . and Wellesley upon an open trade to India.* London (1813).

Dussaud, René. *Topographie historique de la Syrie antique et médiévale.* With 16 maps. Chapter V is on desert routes. Paris (1927).

East India Company. *Further Papers respecting the Trade between India and Europe.* London (1802).

Letters, etc., of the E.I.C. See Sir William Foster.

Edrisi, see Idrisi.

Foster, Sir William. *Early Travels in India,* 1583–1619. Oxford (1921). *The English Factories in India,* 1634–36. A continuation of the Letters of the East India Company. Oxford (1911).

Foster, William, and Danvers, F. C. *Letters of the East India Company.* Vols. i–vi inclusive. (1909.)

For other papers and records relating to the East India Company see entries under Birdwood, Foster, Manesty and Sainsbury.

Fowle, Captain T. C. W. *Travels in the Middle East.* London (1916).

Fridolin, M. le Major. Article on the *Hajj* stations of the Western Pilgrim Route in the *Revue des Deux Mondes,* vol. vi, p. 97. (1854.)

Gabriel, Albert. Articles on *Kasr el-Heir* in *Syria,* vols. viii, pp. 304–322 (1927), and xiii, pp. 317-320 (1932).

Garrett, Robert. Publications of an American Archaeological Expedition to Syria, 1899–1900. *Topography and Itinerary.* Part I. New York (1903).

Gaudefroy-Demombynes. *La Syrie à l'époque des Mamelouks.* D'après les auteurs arabes. Description géographique, économique et administrative. Paris (1923).

Gautier, E. F. *Une Excursion à Palmyre.* Article published separately by the *Mémorial Henri Basset.* Tome xvii, pp. 281-291. Paris (1928).

Gedoyn "Le Turc" (Louis). *Journal et Correspondance.* (1625.) Paris (1909). Published by A. Boppe.

Gibb, H. A. R. *The Damascus Chronicle of the Crusades.* London (1932).

Godinho, Manual. *Relaçao do novo caminho . . . vindo da India para Portugal.* Lisbon (1665).

Gollancz, Sir Hermann. *The Settlement of the Order of Carmelites in Mesopotamia.* (Bassora.) Chronicle of Events between 1623 and 1733. London (1927).

Graham, Cyril C. "Explorations in the Desert East of the Hauran." Article in the *Journal of the Royal Geographical Society,* vol. xxviii, pp. 226-263. (1858.)

Griffiths, Julius (M.D.). *Travels in Europe, Asia Minor and Arabia.* London (1805).

Haifa–Baghdad Railway Survey of 1932. Traffic Estimate.

Halifax, Dr. Wm. "Relation of a Voyage to Tadmor in 1691." Edinburgh (1695).

"A Relation of a voyage from Aleppo to Palmyra in Syria." Also an "Extract of the Journals of two several voyages of the English Merchants of the Factory of Aleppo to Tadmor, anciently call'd Palmyra". (Both papers appear in *Miscellanea Curiosa.*) London (1708).

Hamy, Dr. E.-T. *Voyage d'André Michaux en Syrie et en Perse* (1782–1785). D'après journal et correspondance. Published in *Le Congrès International de Géographie*, IXe Congrès, vol. cxlv, p. 366. (1908.)

Hansard. Parliamentary Debates. Debates in the House of Commons, 9th June 1834; 14th July 1834. "Report on Steam Navigation to India."

Hedin, Sven A. *Bagdad, Babylon, Nineve.* Paris (1917).

Helfer, J. W. *Travels of Dr. and Madame Helfer.* 2 vols. Map. London (1878).

Heude, Lieutenant William, of the Madras Military Establishment. *A Voyage up the Persian Gulf, and a Journey Overland from India to England, in 1817.* London (1819).

Holt, Major A. L. "The Future of the North Arabian Desert." Article in the *Geographical Journal*, vol. lxii, 4, pp. 259-271. (October 1923.)

Howel, Thomas. *A Journal of the Passage from India.* London (1789) (1791).

"*Voyage en retour de l'Inde*, par terre, et par une route en partie inconnue jusqu'ici. Suivi d'Observations sur le passage dans l'Inde par l'Égypte et le Grand Désert, par James Capper." Traduit . . . par Théophile Mandar. Paris (1797).

Huber, Charles. *Journal d'un voyage en Arabie*, 1883–1884. Paris (1891).

Ibn Battuta, Muhammad ibn Abd Allah. *Travels.* Translated by S. Lee. London (1829).

Travels in Asia and Africa, 1325–1354. Translated and selected by H. A. R. Gibb. London (1929). ("The Broadway Travellers" Series.)

Ibn Gubayr (*i.e.* Jubair, Muhammad ibn Ahmad). *Viaggio in Ispagna . . . Siria . . . Mesopotamia. . . .* Translated by C. Schiaparelli. Rome (1906). (Also, edition by W. Wright, Leyden (1852).)

Ibn Haukal, Ibrahim ibn Muhammad, Abu Ishak. *Mesalek u Memalek. Oriental Geography of Ebn Haukal.* Translated by Sir W. Ouseley. London (1800).

Descriptio Iracae Persicae . . . Translated by P. J. Uylenbroek. (1822.)

Ibn Khordadbeh, Ubaid Allah ibn Abd Allah. "Le Livre des routes et provinces." Trad. by C. Barbier de Meynard (in the *Journal Asiatique*, Jan.–June 1865). Paris (1865).

Idrisi, Muhammad ibn Muhammad, al-. *La Géographie d'Édrisi* . . . 2 vols. Trad. by Amédée Jaubert. Paris (1836).

India Office. Home Series. Misc. 470. *Letter Book*, 1799–1800, pp. 195–218 (*re* the British Dromedary Post).

Indian Antiquary, The, xxxvi. (1907.)

Irwin, Eyles. *A Series of Adventures in the Course of a Voyage up the Red Sea, on the Coasts of Arabia and Egypt; and of a Route through the Deserts of Thebais, hitherto Unknown to the European Traveller. In the year MDCCLXXVII*. London (1780).
   Epistles . . . from London to Busrah . . . London (1783).

Itineraria Romana. "Itineraria Antonini Augusti et Burdigalense", ed. Otto Cuntz. (1929.)

Itinerarium, Antonini Placentini. Ed. Dr. J. Gildemeister. Berlin (1889).

Ives, Edward. *A Voyage from England to India, in the year MDCCLIV*. London (1773).

Journal of a Deputation Sent to the East. "By the Committee of the Malta Protestant College, in 1849." 2 vols. London (1855).

The Koran, translated from the Arabic by Rev. J. M. Rodwell. No. 380 of Everyman's Library. London (1929).

Laborde, Léon de. *Journey through Arabia Petraea to Mount Sinai and the Excavated City of Petra—the Edom of the Prophecies*. London (1838).

La Boullaye-le-Gouz, Fr. de. *Voyages et Observations . . . en Syrie et en Perse*, 1647–48. Paris (1653).

Lawrence, T. E. *Revolt in the Desert*. New York and London (1927).
   Seven Pillars of Wisdom: A Triumph. Oxford (1926); London (1935).

Layard, Right Hon. Sir A. H. *Discoveries in the Ruins of Nineveh and Babylon, with Travels in . . . the Desert*. London (1853).

Leachman, G. E. "A Journey Through Central Arabia." Article published in the *Geographical Journal*, vol. xliii, 5 (1914), pp. 500–520.
   "A Journey in North-Eastern Arabia." Article published in the *Geographical Journal*, vol. xxxvii, 3 (1911), pp. 265–274.

Le Blanc, Vincent. *Les Voyages fameux du Sieur Vincent Le Blanc*. Paris (1648).

Le Strange, Guy. *Palestine Under the Moslems. A Description of Syria and the Holy Land from* A.D. 650–1500—translated from the works of the Mediaeval Arab Geographers. (Palestine Exploration Fund.) London (1890).

Levant Company, The. At the Public Record Office, London. Miscellaneous Correspondance: *S.P.* 110/10-72; Supplementary Lists, Indexes and Foreign Office Records: *F.O.* 78, 147-195, and 250-290.

Linschoten, J. H. Van. *The Voyage of . . . to the East Indies.* From the old English translation of 1598. Hakluyt Society. 2 vols. Nos. LXX and LXXI. London (1885).

Manesty. *Bombay Factory Records.* At the India Office. Persia and Persian Gulf. No. 20, 1799-1811.

Manrique, Fray Sebastien. *Travels,* 1629-1643. 2 vols. Hakluyt Society, Nos. LXI, LXII. London (1927).

Martin, Robert M. *The Despatches of . . . the Marquess Wellesley . . . in India.* 5 vols. London (1836).

Massignon, Louis. *Mission à Mésopotamie* (1907-8). 2 Tom. (1910-12.)

Masudi, Ali ibn Husain, el-. Historical Encyclopaedia entitled *Meadows of Gold and Mines of Gems.* Translated from the Arabic by Aloys Sprenger. London (1841).

Maundrell, Henry. Chaplain to the English Factory at Aleppo. *A Compendium of a Journey from Aleppo to Jerusalem; also the Travels of Dr. Thos. Shaw, and a Journey to Palmyra.* London (1699).
Travells to Beer and Mesopotamia. London (1714).

McCallum, Major D. "The Discovery and Development of the New Land Route to the East." Article published in the *Journal of the Central Asian Society,* vol. xii, Part I (1925), pp. 44-67.

Mizrahi, T. *Le Commerce du Levant.* Beyrout, Syria. 18th March (1932).

Moritz, Dr. "Reise in Syrien." In *Verhandl. Gesell. für Erdkunde,* Bd. XIII (1886), p. 163. Berlin (1886).

Mukaddasi, Muhammad ibn Ahmad, al-. "A Description of the Moslem Empire." Translated from the Arabic by G. S. A. Ranking . . . London (1897).
Description of Syria. Including Palestine (about A.D. 985). Translated and annotated by Guy Le Strange for the Palestine Pilgrims Text Society. London (1892).

Müller, Ct. Victor. *En Syrie avec les Bédouins. Les Tribus du désert.* Paris (1931).

Musil, Alois. *Arabia Petraea.* (Untranslated from German.) Vienna (1907). The following, published by the American Geographical Society Oriental Explorations and Studies:
The Northern Heǧâz. New York (1926).
Arabia Deserta. New York (1927).

The Middle Euphrates. New York (1927).

Palmyrena. New York (1928).

Northern Neğd. New York (1928).

The Manners and Customs of the Rwala Bedouins. New York (1928).

Nairn Eastern Transport Company. Books of the Company. (1926–1933.)

Niebuhr, C. *Voyage en Arabie et en d'autres Pays circonvoisins.* Amsterdam (1780).

Notitia dignitatum et admin. . . . in partibus Orientis. Ed. Böcking. Bonn (1839).

Oestrup, Joannes E. *Historisk-topografiske Bidrag til der syriske orker.* With map. (1895.)

Olivier, G. A. *Voyage dans l'Empire Othoman, l'Égypte et la Perse.* Fait par ordre du Gouvernement, pendant les six premières années de la République. 3 vols. with Atlas. Paris (1801–7).

Oppenheim, Baron Max von. *Bericht über seine Reise durch die syrische Wüste nach Mosul . . . mit einer Tafel.* Berlin (1894).

Vom Mittelmeer zum Persischen Golf durch den Hauran, die syrische Wüste und Mesopotamien. 2 vols. Berlin (1899).

Ormsby, Lieutenant H. A., I.N. His travels in 1831 are told in Wellsted's *Travels to the City of the Caliphs.*

Parliamentary Papers. "Report of a Select Committee of the House of Commons." (Railway Project to India. The Euphrates Valley Railway Project.) P.P. No. 322. London (22nd July 1872).

Parsons, Abraham. *Travels in Asia and Africa,* etc. Edited by John Paine Berjew. London (1808).

Pegolotti, Balducci. *Pratica della Mercatura.* Leipzig (1886).

Peters, J. P. *Nippur or Explorations and Adventures on the Euphrates.* 2 vols. New York and London (1898).

Peutinger Table. *Tabula Itineraria Peutingeriana,* ed. of Scheyb. (1753); re-ed. Leipzig (1824 and 1844).

Philby, H. St. J. B. *Arabia.* Published in the "Modern World Series". London (1930).

The Heart of Arabia. 2 vols. London (1922).

"Jauf and the North Arabian Desert." Article in the *Geographical Journal,* vol. lxii, No. 4, pp. 241–259. London (October 1923).

Philosophical Transactions of the Royal Society. Original ed. Edinburgh, 1695–7. "Relation of a Voyage from Aleppo to Palmyra in Syria." Vol. xix, pp. 83–110, 129–160.

Pinto, Fernão Mendez. *Peregrinaçiones.* 4 vols. Lisbon (1725). (1829.)

Plaisted, B. *A Journey from Basra to Aleppo in 1750.* Printed in Hakluyt,

Second Series, No. LXIII (edited by Douglas Carruthers), chap. iii, pp. 51-128.

Poidebard, A., and Mouterde. Inscription on the broken column: found on the Palmyra–Hit route. Original Greek text, with French translation and commentary, printed in *Syria*, vol. xii, pp. 105-115. (1931.)

Poidebard, R. P. Antoine. *La Trace de Rome dans le Désert de Syrie.*
"Le Limes de Trajan à la Conquête Arabe." *Recherches Aériennes* (1925–32). Introduction de Franz Cumont. Paris (1934).

Poujoulat, B. *Voyage dans l'Asie Mineure, en Mésopotamie, à Palmyre, en Syrie, en Palestine et en Egypte.* . . . 2 vols. Paris (1840–41).

Purchas, Samuel. *His Pilgrimes.* 20 vols. Glasgow (1905–7).

Quatremère, E. M. *Histoire des Sultans Mamlouks de l'Égypte.* Translation of el-Makrizi. 2 vols. Paris (1842).

Raswan, Carl R. *Black Tents of Arabia (My Life amongst the Bedouins).* Boston (1935).

Rauwolff, Dr. Leonhart. *Itinerary*, 1573–74. Published in *Ray's Travels*, I. (1693.)
Journey into the Eastern Countries. Printed in John Ray's *Travels*: (1693) vol. ii, pp. 61-88; (1738) vol. ii, pp. 1-150 (pp. 1-338).

Rawlinson, Sir Alfred, Bart. *Adventures in the Near East*, 1918–22. London (1923).

Rennell, Major James. *A Treatise on the Comparative Geography of Western Asia.* 2 vols. London (1831). Map dated 1809.
Illustrations . . . of the Expedition of Cyrus . . . to Babylonia. London (1816).

Roberts, G. *A Journey from Basra to Aleppo in 1748.* Printed in Hakluyt, Second Series, No. LXIII (edited by Douglas Carruthers), chap. ii, pp. 43-47.

Rostovtzeff, Michael I. *Caravan Cities.* Translated by D. and T. Talbot Rice. Oxford (1932).
Out of the Past of Greece and Rome. New Haven (1932).

Rousseau, J. B. L. J. *Voyage de Bagdad à Alep* (1808). Published from his MS. Journal, Louis Poinssot. Paris (1899).

Rubruquis, Gulielmus de. *Journey of . . . to the Eastern Parts of the World*—1253–1255. Hakluyt Society. London (1900).

Russell, Alex. *The Natural History of Aleppo and Parts Adjacent.* 2 vols. London (1756). (1794.)

Rutter, Eldon. "Damascus to Hail.". Article in *Journal of the Central Asian Society*, vol. xviii, pp. 61-73. London (1931).
The Holy Cities of Arabia. London (1930).

Ryley, J. Horton. *Ralph Fitch England's Pioneer to India and Burma.* (With verbatim narrative.) London (1899).

Sachau, Dr. Carl Eduard. *Am Euphrat und Tigris . . . dem Winter 1897–98.* (With 5 maps.) Leipzig (1900).

　Reise in Syrien und Mesopotamien. Maps. Leipzig (1883).

Sainsbury, Ethel B., and Foster, Wm. *A Calendar of the Court Minutes, etc., of the East India Company, 1635–1639.* Oxford (1907).

Saldanha, J. A. Selections from *State Papers, Bombay,* regarding the East India Company's connection with the Persian Gulf, with a summary of events, 1600–1800. London (1905).

Sanderson, John, English Merchant Adventurer. *The Travels of . . . in the Levant,* 1584–1602. Hakluyt Society, Second Series, No. LXVII. London (1931).

Sandys, George. *A Relation of a Journey.* London (1615).

Sanson, Nicolas (Le Sieur Sanson d'Abbeville). *L'Asie,* "En plusieurs Cartes Nouvelles, et exactes; et en Divers Traictes de Géographie, et d'Histoire". Paris (1652).

Schiaparelli, C. *Ibn Gubayr.* (Translated from the original Arabic.) Rome (1906).

Schiltberger, Johann, a native of Bavaria. *The Bondage and Travels of . . . in Europe, Asia and Africa,* 1396–1427. Translated and annotated by Telfer and Brunn. Hakluyt Society, No. LVIII. London (1879).

Seyrig, Henri. "Kasr el-Heir." Article published in *Syria,* vol. xii, pp. 316–318. (1931.)

Sprenger. *Die Post- und Reisrouten des Orients.* Leipzig (1864).

Sykes, Mark. "Narrative of a Journey East of Jebel ed-Druse, March 1898." Published in the *Palestine Exploration Fund Quarterly Statement for 1899,* pp. 47–57.

Tavernier, John Baptiste, Baron of Aubonne. *Through Turky and Persia to the Indies.* Made English by J. P. Part II: Travels in India. London (1684).

Tavernier, Bernier (*i.e.* J. B.). "The Travels of, and other Great Men." Printed in *Collections of Travels.* London (1684). (Same as preceding.)

　Les Six Voyages de J. B. Tavernier . . . en Turquie, en Perse et aux Indes. 2 vols. Paris (1676).

　Voyages . . . avec atlas, 7 vols. Paris (1810).

Taylor, Major John. Of the Bombay Establishment. *Travels from England to India in the year 1789, by way of the Tyrol, Venice, Scandaroon, Aleppo, and over the Great Desert to Bussora; with instructions for Travellers; and an account of the expence of travelling.* 2 vols. London (1799).

　Considerations on the practicability and advantages of a more speedy communication between Great Britain and her Possessions in India:—With an Outline of a Plan for the more Ready Conveyance of Intelligence overland by the way of Suez. London (1795).

Teixeira, Pedro, *The Travels of.* " Narrative of Journey from India to Italy; and the History of the Kings of Persia and of Harmuz." Published at Antwerp, 1609. Translated and annotated by Wm. F. Sinclair, with notes and introduction by Donald Ferguson, for the Hakluyt Society, Second Series, No. IX. London (1902).

Tenreiro, Antonio. *Itinerario.* Lisbon (1560). (1565.)

Teonge, *Rev'd Henry, Diary of.* (1676.) London (1825).

Thévenot, Monsieur Jean de. *Relation d'un Voyage fait au Levant.* 2 vols. Paris (1674).

Thielmann, Lieutenant Baron Max von. *Journey in the Caucasus, Persia and Turkey in Asia.* Translated by Chas. Heneage, F.R.G.S. 2 vols. London (1875).

Thomas, Bertram. *Arabia Felix: Across the Empty Quarter of Arabia.* With a Foreword by T. E. Lawrence. London (1932).

Thompson, *Charles, The Travels of.* 2 vols. London (1767).

Valle, *Pietro della, The Travels of . . . in India.* From the old English translation of 1664, by G. Havers. Hakluyt Society Publications, No. LXXXIV. 2 vols. London (1892).

Valle, *Pietro della, The Travels of . . . into East-India and Arabia Deserta, in familiar letters . . . to Signor Mario Schipano.* London (1664 and 1665).

Varthema, *Lodovico di, The Travels of, in Egypt, Syria, Arabia Deserta . . . India. . . .* A.D. 1503–1508. Translated from the original Italian edition of 1510, for the Hakluyt Society. With map. London (1863).

Venetian Calendar of State Papers. Especially from 1592 to 1635.

Vidal, Honoré. Copy of a lost letter (of 1820) to M. Barbié du Bocage (26 Mars, 1824), re Vidal's voyages, 1807–14. Published in *Le Bulletin de la Société de Géographie,* vol. ii, pp. 100-102. Paris (1824). *Ibid.* Second Series, vol. vi, pp. 5-9. (1836.)

Wallin, G. A. *Notes taken during a Journey through Part of Northern Arabia, in 1848.* London (185?).

Wellesley, Marquis. *Despatches.* London (1836).

Wellsted, J. R. *Travels to the City of the Caliphs.* 2 vols. London (1840). *Travels in Arabia.* 2 vols. London (1838).

Yakut, ibn Abd-Allah. *Dictionnaire des Lieux,* ed. Uylenbrock. (1822.)

Young, Major Sir Hubert. *The Independent Arab.* London (1933).

Zenon Papyri, I.

    Columbia Papyri. (1934.)

"Business Papers of the Third Century B.C. dealing with Palestine and Egypt." W. L. Westermann and E. S. Hasenoehrl. New York (1934).

Zwemer, S. M. and A. E. *Zigzag Journeys in the Camel Country*. New York (1911).

V.—Secondary Sources

Ali, Emir Abdul Aziz el-Hassani. *Economic History of Syria*. An Arabic work, untranslated. Damascus (1923).

Ambrose, Gwilym. "English Traders at Aleppo (1658–1756)." Pamphlet reprinted from the *Economic History Review*. London (1931).

Armstrong, H. C. *"Lord of Arabia": Ibn Sa'ud*. London (1934).

Belfield, Squadron-Leader A. G. N. "The Overland Mail to Baghdad." Article in the *English Review*. (January 1925.)

Belloc, Hilaire. *The Battleground: Syria and Palestine*. London (1936).

Bouchier, E. S. *Syria as a Roman Province*. Oxford (1916).

Carruthers, Douglas. "The Great Desert Caravan Route, Aleppo to Basra." Article in the *Geographical Journal*, vol. lii, 3, pp. 157-184; map, p. 204. (September 1918.)

Chapot, V. *La Frontière de l'Euphrate—de Pompée à la conquête arabe*. Paris (1907).

Charles-Roux, Fr. *Les Échelles de Syrie et de Palestine—au XVIIIe siècle*. Paris (1928).

Charlesworth, M. P. *Trade-Routes and Commerce of the Roman Empire*. Cambridge (1924).

Cook, S. A. Article on the Beduin in the *Cambridge Ancient History*, vol. i—V.

Dehèrain, H. Articles in *Syria*, vols. iii, p. 339 (1922), and vi, p. 187 (1925).

Dhorme, P. Article on Aleppo in *Syria*, vol. viii, p. 41. (1927.)

Dussaud, René. Articles in *Syria*: on the researches of Group-Captain Rees, vol. x, pp. 144-163 (1929); and review of Musil's work, *ibid.* pp. 52-62, in vol. x (1929).

Earle, E. M. *Turkey, the Great Powers and the Baghdad Railway*. New York (1923).

Ephemerides: The Royal Air Force and British Empire Air Services Diary, 1928–1932.

Epstein, Mordecai. *The Early History of the Levant Company*. London (1908).

Gaudefroy-Demombynes. *Le Pèlerinage à la Mekke*. Paris (1923).

General Motors Export Company. Pamphlet entitled *The Desert Mail: Across Syria from Beirut to Bagdad.* With map and illustrations. New York (1925).

Glanville, S. R. K. Article on camels in the *Journal of Egyptian Archaeology*, xii (1926), p. 58 and notes 3 and 4.

Gray, G. B. Article on Persia in the *Cambridge Ancient History*. iii–VII, p. 193 . . . and iv–IV.

Harford, F. D. "Old Caravan Roads and Overland Routes in Syria, Arabia, and Mesopotamia." Article in the *Nineteenth Century*, pp. 97-113. (July 1918.)

Harper, Harry. *The Romance of a Modern Airway*, etc. London (1930).

Heeren, A. H. L. *Historical Researches into the Politics and Intercourse of the Nations of Antiquity.* 3 vols. London (1833).

Heyd, Wilhelm von. *Histoire du commerce du Levant au Moyen Âge.* 3 vols. Leipzig (1885–86).

Hill, Roderic. *The Baghdad Air Mail.* London (1929).

Hogarth, D. G. *The Life of Charles M. Doughty.* London (1928).
The Nearer East. London (1915).
Article (obituary) *re* Colonel G. E. Leachman in the *Geographical Journal*, vol. lvi, pp. 326–327. (October 1920.)

Hogben, S. J. *The Muhammedan Emirates of Nigeria.* London (1930).

Hoskins, H. L. *British Routes to India.* London (1928).

Hudson, G. F. *Europe and China.* London (1931).

Huntington, Ellsworth. *Palestine and its Transformation.* New York (1911).

Keane, John. *The Evolution of Geography.* London (1899).

Kremer, A. von. *Kulturgeschichte des Orients unter den Chalifen.* Vienna (1875).

Lammens, Henri (le Père). *Islam: Beliefs and Institutions.* London (1929).
La Mecque à la veille de l'Hégire. Mélanges de l'Université St. Joseph Beyrouth. (T. IX.) Beyrout (1924).
La Syrie, précis historique. 2 vols. Paris and Beyrout (1921).
Le Berceau de l'Islam. Scripta Pontificii. Rome (1914).

Legacy of Islam, The. A co-operative study edited by Sir Thomas Arnold and Alfred Guillaume. Oxford (1931).

Le Strange, Guy. *Baghdad During the Abbasid Caliphate.* From Contemporary Arabic and Iranian sources. Oxford (1924).
Lands of the Eastern Caliphate. 2 vols. London (1905).

Loeper, M. "A History of the British Indian Overland Mail." Article in *L'Union Postale* (the International Postal Journal). (1883.)

Lorimer, J. G. (I.C.S.). *Gazetteer of the Persian Gulf, Oman and Central Arabia*, vol. i (historical). Calcutta (1915).

MacDonald, Sir George. Article, "Rome in the Middle East", in *Antiquity*, pp. 373-380. (December 1934.)

Margoliouth, D. S. *Mohammedanism*. London (1928).

Musil, Alois. Article on one of his expeditions, in the *Geographical Journal*, vol. xlii, pp. 194-196. (August 1913.)

Oertel, F., in the *Cambridge Ancient History*, vol. x, chap. xiii.
"The Economic Unification of the Mediterranean Region: Industry, Trade and Commerce", in the *Cambridge Ancient History*, vol. x, chap. xiii, pp. 382-424.

O'Shea, F. B. *Memorandum on the British Indian Post Offices in the Persian Gulf and Turkish Arabia*. Revised edition by F. Whymper (1905). London (1888).

Pearson, J. B. *A Biographical Sketch of the Chaplains of the Levant (Aleppo) Co.* Cambridge (1883).

Rawlinson, Hugh George. *British Beginnings in Western India, 1579–1657: An Account of the early days of the British Factory of Surat.* London (1920).
Intercourse between India and the Western World, from the Earliest Times to the Fall of Rome. Cambridge (1926).

Roberts, Paul E. *India under Wellesley*. London (1929).

Roederer, Dr. C. et Paul. *La Syrie et la France*. (Serie: Les Grands Problèmes colonieux.) Paris (1917).

Rostovtzeff, M. Articles in *Cambridge Ancient History*, vol. vii, chap. v, and vol. viii, chap. xx.

Royal Air Force and British Empire Air Services Diary (1919, 1929–1932). See *Ephemerides*.

Smith, George Adam. *The Historical Geography of the Holy Land*. London (1906).

Smith, Sidney. Vol. iii, chaps. i, ii, iii and v of the *Cambridge Ancient History*.

Tarn, W. W. "Ptolemy II and Arabia." Article in the *Journal of Egyptian Archaeology*, vol. xv, pp. 9-25. With notes by Sidney Smith. (1929.)
Vol. vi, chaps. xii, xiii and xv in the *Cambridge Ancient History*.

Thompson, R. Campbell. *Tavernier's Travels in Mesopotamia*. London (1910).

Thureau-Dangin, François. Articles in *Syria*, vols. v (1924) and x (1929).

Trautz, M. Article on G. A. Wallin in the *Journal of the Central Asian Society*, vol. xix (1932), pp. 131-150.

West, L. C. "Commercial Syria under the Roman Empire." *Trans·
  Amer. Phil. Assoc.*, vol. lv (1924), p. 159.
Whiteway, R. S. *Rise of Portuguese Power in India*. London (1899).
Wilson, Sir A. T. *Mesopotamia, 1917–1920*. London (1931).
  The Persian Gulf. Oxford (1928).
  Early Spanish and Portuguese Travellers in Persia. London (1927).

VI.—PERIODICAL MATERIAL

(A): MAGAZINES AND JOURNALS

Aeroplane. Special number to commemorate 21 years of the Flying
  Services. Article called "The Years Between", by C. M. McAlery.
  (10th May 1933.)
American Journal of Numismatics. Washington (1917).
Antiquity. London.
Asiatic Register. London.
Bulletin de la Société de Géographie. Paris (1822–37).
Bulletin de la Société Royale de Géographie d'Anvers. Antwerp.
Bulletin Economique Trimestriel. Le Moniteur Officiel du Commerce et
  de l'Industrie. Paris and Beyrouth.
English Review.
General Motors Export Co. "The Desert Mail Across Syria from Beirut
  to Baghdad." New York (1925).
Geographical Journal. Formerly *Journal of the Royal Geographical Society*.
  London.
  Proceedings of the Royal Geographical Society.
Graphic (weekly). London.
Illustrated London News.
L'Illustration. Paris.
Journal Asiatique. Paris.
Journal of Egyptian Archaeology. London.
Journal of Roman Studies. London.
Journal of the Royal Central Asian Society. London.
Modern Transport. Article "Motor Transport across the Syrian Desert—
  Regular Passenger and Goods Services from Haifa to Baghdad."
  London (10th December 1927).
Motor. London.
Near East Magazine. London.
Nineteenth Century. London.
Revue des Deux Mondes. Paris.
Revue Mondiale. Paris.

Sphere. London.
Syria. Revue d'Art Oriental et d'Archéologie. Paris (1920–35).
Traveller's Gazette. London.

(B): NEWSPAPERS

La Bourse Égyptienne.
Egyptian Gazette.
Manchester Guardian.
Morning Post.
The (London) *Times*, Daily and Weekly Editions.
The Observer.
The Times of Baghdad.
The Times of India.
The Times of Mesopotamia.

APPENDIX 6

NOTES ON SOURCES

CHAPTER I

Part 2

Pages 6-8. GEOGRAPHY OF THE SYRIAN DESERT:
Personal observation of the writer.
Also: *The Encyclopaedia of Islam*, article on Arabia.
Carruthers, D., article in the *Geographical Journal*, "The Great Desert Caravan Route, Aleppo to Basra", lxxii (1928), p. 278.
Lawrence, T. E., *Seven Pillars of Wisdom* (1935), pp. 33-35.
Leachman, G. E., article in the *Geographical Journal*, xliii (1914), p. 508, "A Journey through Central Arabia".
And conversation with Mr Douglas Carruthers.
Further information on the *Nefud*—
Bell, G. L., *Letters* (1927), i, pp. 337-339.
Carruthers, D., *Arabian Adventure* (1935), chap. v, pp. 114-130.
Leachman, G. E., article in the *Geographical Journal*, xxxvii (1911), p. 273, "A Journey in North-Eastern Arabia".
Raswan, Carl, *Black Tents of Arabia* (1935), chap. ix, pp. 43-46.

Pages 8-9. THE CHANGING COURSES OF THE TIGRIS-EUPHRATES:
Le Strange, G., *Baghdad during the Abbasid Caliphate* (1924), pp. 7-9 (including note).
Le Strange, G., *Lands of the Eastern Caliphate* (1905), i, p. 29 and map.

Pages 9-10. THE SYRIAN DESERT PLATEAU:
Holt, A. L., article in the *Geographical Journal*, lxii (1923), p. 262, "The Future of the North Arabian Desert"; also map.

Contour maps of the Syrian Desert (*e.g.* Bartholomew and Stanford's).

Sebkha or Salt Marshes—

Bell, G. L. (1927), *op. cit.* i, p. 280.

Musil, A. (1927), *Arabia Deserta*, p. 48.

Teixeira, Pedro, *The Travels of*, Antwerp (1609),
London (1902), p. 102.

Earthquakes and the Volcanic Zone—

Doughty, C. M., *Travels in Arabia Deserta* (1933),
map at end of volume.

The Encyclopaedia of Islam, article "Arabia", p. 368.

Musil, A., *Palmyrena* (1928), pp. 270-271.

Pages 10-12. HISTORICAL GEOGRAPHY OF THE SYRIAN DESERT:

Keane, J., *The Evolution of Geography* (1899), repro-
ductions of the maps of Herodotus, Strabo and
Ptolemy, pp. 10, 20 and 30; medieval maps (12th-
16th centuries), pp. 48, 70, 79, 82, 130 and 148.

Beazley, C. R., *The Dawn of Modern Geography*
(1897–1906), iii, 385.

Burckhardt, J. L., *Notes on the Bedouins and Wahabys*
(1831), i, map of Arabia and the Syrian Desert.

Cary and Warmington, *The Ancient Explorers* (1929),
chap. ix, pp. 184-193.

Ritter, C., map of Arabia (1852), printed by
Kiepert.

Musil, A., *Arabia Deserta*, appendix III, pp. 497-508.

Sanson, N., *L'Asie* . . . (1652), pp. 4, 8, 10, 16, 32,
and maps.

Philips' *Historical Atlas* (1927), maps 2, 32, 40 and 82.

Smith, G. A., *The Historical Geography of the Holy
Land* (1906), p. 5.

Also conversation with Professor J. S. Crawford,
of the American University of Beyrout.

Legacy of Islam, Essay 3, "Geography and Commerce"
(1931), by J. H. Kramers, pp. 79-107.

Syria, x (1929), p. 54 and map (article by Dussaud).

(Page 14). For an account of hunting in the Desert in
modern times, see Raswan, C. (1935), chap. 27
(on "Anaga, the Falcon").

Page 12.   THE *GREAT DESERT*, OR *AS-SAMAWA:*

Bell, G. L. (1927), *op. cit.* i, pp. 273-274.

Butler, S. S., article in the *Geographical Journal*,

xxxiii (1909), p. 522, "Baghdad to Damascus via El Jauf".

Leachman, G. E., in the *Geographical Journal, op. cit.* p. 503.

Musil, A., *Arabia Deserta*, appendix IV, pp. 508-511.

Rutter, Eldon, article in the *Journal of the Central Asian Society*, xviii (1931), p. 64, "Damascus to Hail".

Also: Article by E. H. Keeling in the *Geographical Journal*, lxiii, 2 (1924), p. 153.

The Near East, 4th June 1925.

The Times, London, 30th May 1925.

Re the Wadi Sirhan—

Lawrence, T. E., *Revolt in the Desert* (1927), p. 59.

Musil, A., *Arabia Deserta*, p. 483.

Rutter, Eldon (1931), *op. cit.* pp. 72, 73.

Pages 12-14. THE LITTLE DESERT, OR PALMYRENA:

Personal observation of the writer.

Also: Teixeira, Pedro (1902), *op. cit.* pp. 97-100 and 104.

Capper, J., *Observations on the Passage to India, through Egypt, and across the Great Desert . . .* (1783), pp. 68-80.

Taylor, J., *Travels from England to India in the Year 1789 . . .* (1799), i, pp. 228-256; and 289.

Chesney, F. R., *Narrative of the Euphrates Expedition* (1868), pp. 52-63.

Thielmann, M. von, *Journey in the Caucasus, Persia, and Turkey in Asia* (1875), ii, pp. 199-210.

Geographical Journal, lxiii, 2 (1924).

Syria, xiii (1932), p. 217.

The Times, London, 3rd May 1926; 9th, 15th and 28th May 1929; and 22nd Dec. 1930.

Cf. Travellers' statements in Hakluyt, lxiii (1929), pp. 17, 78, 83.

N.B.—Many other travellers have also described the *Great* and the *Little Deserts*; *i.e.* many more references might be given.

Pages 14-15. WILD ANIMAL LIFE:

Teixeira, Pedro (1902), *op. cit.* pp. 36-43, 99, 101, and 104.

Tavernier, J. B., *Through Turky and Persia to the Indies* (1684), i, p. 65.

Carré, M., *Voyages des Indes Orientales* (1699), p. 255.

Taylor, J. (1799), i, *op. cit.* pp. 227, 228, 235, 238, 253, 269, 295, 296 and 298.

Griffiths, J., *Travels in Europe, Asia Minor and Arabia* (1805), p. 354.

Olivier, G. A., *Voyage dans l'Empire Othoman, l'Égypte et la Perse* (1807), p. 464.

Lawrence, T. E. (1927), *op. cit.* p. 59.

Blunt, Lady Anne, *Bedouin Tribes of the Euphrates* (1879), i, pp. 89 and 92-93 (account of the maneless lions killed by Arabs at Deir-ez-Zor—as recently as 1878).

Capper (1783), pp. 61, 66, 68, 80.

Statements of travellers in Hakluyt, *op. cit.* pp. 9, 12, 15, 81-83, 92, 139.

Carruthers, D., information obtained in person.

Also *Arabian Adventure* (1935), pp. 142-150, 190-191.

Raswan, C. (1935), *Black Tents of Arabia. Passim*, especially the last two chapters (27 and 28) in the book.

Pages 15-16. DOMESTICATED ANIMALS:

Re Camels:

Musil, A., *Palmyrena*, p. 261.

Musil, A., *The Rwala Bedouins* (1928), pp. 338, 348 and 357.

The *Journal of Egyptian Archaeology*, xii (1926), p. 58 and note 3, article by S. R. K. Glanville.

Raswan, C. (1935), pp. 30 and 55.

Also: Teixeira (1902), pp. 45 and 108 (note 1).

Tavernier, J. B. (1684), *op. cit.* p. 50.

Taylor, J. (1799), i, pp. 244 and 291.

Thielmann, M. von (1875), ii, pp. 176-177 and 201-204.

Bell, G. L. (1927), *op. cit.* i, pp. 271 and 277.

Beawes and Plaisted, in Hakluyt, lxiii (1929), pp. 30 and 96.

Re Horses:

Musil, A., *The Rwala, op. cit.* pp. 349, 356, 379 and 382.

Also: Teixeira, P. (1902), pp. 43 and 73.

Taylor, J. (1799), i, p. 259.

Raswan, C. (1935), pp. 28-30 and illustration opposite p. 113.

Part 3

Page 16. ARAB MIGRATIONS:

The Encyclopaedia of Islam, article on Arabia.

Cook, S. A., article in the Cambridge Ancient History, i, chap. v, pp. 181-237, especially pp. 181-183.

Lawrence, T. E., Seven Pillars of Wisdom (1935), pp. 35-37.

Smith, G. A. (1906), op. cit. p. 5.

Professor J. S. Crawford, op. cit.

Pages 16-17. THE WAHHABIS:

The Encyclopaedia of Islam, article on Arabia.

Philby, H. St. J. B., Arabia (1930), pp. 8-25, 44, 54, 55, 72, 81-103, 226 and 364.

Sykes, Sir Percy, A History of Exploration (1934), p. 279.

Armstrong, H. C., "Lord of Arabia": Ibn Sa'ud (1934), pp. 10-16, and maps on pp. 236 and 251.

Margoliouth, D. S., Mohammedanism (1928), pp. 176-180.

Pages 17-23. BEDUIN TRIBES OF THE SYRIAN DESERT:

The Encyclopaedia of Islam, article on Arabia, and article on the Saracens.

Blunt, Lady Anne (1879), op. cit. ii, pp. 187-205. Also ii, p. 110.

Burckhardt, J. L. (1831), op. cit. i, pp. 1-32, and ii, pp. 1-50.

Cameron, V. L., Our Future Highway (1880), ii, pp. 1, 2 and 160-167.

Coote, Sir Eyre, diary published in the Journal of the R.G.S., xxx (1860), pp. 201, 204 and 208.

Doughty, C. M., Index to Arabia Deserta.

G.-Demombynes, La Syrie . . . des Mamelouks (1923), p. 183 (B), and note 3.

Heude, Wm., A Voyage up the Persian Gulf, and a Journey Overland from India to England, in 1817 (1819), pp. 63-66 and 86.

Lawrence, T. E. (1927), pp. 58 and 59.

Leachman, G. E., in the *Geographical Journal*, xxxvii (1911), p. 266.

Rousseau, J. B. L. J., *Voyage de Bagdad à Alep* (1808), pp. 118 and 121.

Raswan, C. (1935), p. 67.

Pages 23-24. CHARACTERISTICS AND HABITS OF THE BEDUIN:

The Encyclopaedia of Islam, article on Arabia.

Lammens, H., *La Mecque à la veille de l'Hégire* (1924), pp. 7-12.

Lawrence, T. E., in the *Introduction* to Doughty (1933), pp. xxi-xxv.

Lawrence, T. E. (1935), *op. cit.* chap. iii, pp. 38-43.

Professor J. S. Crawford, of the American University of Beyrout.

Hajji Selim Sawwaf of Damascus.

Beawes, Wm., in Hakluyt, lxiii (1929), p. 30.

The seasonal migrations of the Rualla:

Raswan, C. (1935), pp. 64-82, and p. 107.

Pages 24-25. COMMERCIAL ADAPTABILITY OF THE BEDUIN:

Mr Douglas Carruthers.

Professor J. S. Crawford.

Lawrence, T. E., in Doughty (1933), *op. cit.* p. xxiv.

For the use of cars by the Rualla see Raswan, Carl, *Black Tents of Arabia* (1935), pp. 81, 83 and 85. For their use of armed cars to protect their migrations, *ibid.* p. 78; and "modern raiding" with "battle-cars", *ibid.* pp. 29, 93-98, 131 and illustration opposite p. 90.

Pages 25-26. NON-COMMERCIAL TENDENCIES OF THE BEDUIN:

The Encyclopaedia of Islam, article on Arabia.

For references to the Agails see Chapter IV, part 2, pp. 137-139.

Pages 26-27. DISTINCTION BETWEEN THE SETTLED AND THE NOMAD ARABS:

Taylor, J. (1799), i, pp. 260, 278, 279 and 280.

Musil, A., *Arabia Deserta*, pp. 483 and 494.

Bell, G. L., *Amurath to Amurath* (1911), pp. 93, 117 and 131.

Professor J. S. Crawford, *op. cit.*

Page 27. THE "DESERTICOLAE":

Valle, Pietro della, *The Travels of . . . into East India and Arabia Deserta* (1665), pp. 260 and 261.

Pages 27-28. CHANGED CONDITIONS SINCE THE GREAT WAR:
>> Hogarth, D. G., article in the *Geographical Journal*, lxii (1923), pp. 269-270.
>> Also: Conversations with Mr Douglas Carruthers and Professor J. S. Crawford.

Page 28. For information concerning the death of Colonel Leachman the writer is indebted to Major C. G. Lynam.

Pages 29-30. TRAVELLERS' OPINIONS OF THE BEDUIN IN THE EIGHTEENTH CENTURY:
>> Plaisted, B., in Hakluyt, lxiii (1929), pp. 73 and 75, 94 and 98.
>> Carmichael, J., in Hakluyt, lxiii (1929), p. 177.
>> Beawes, Wm., in Hakluyt, lxiii (1929), p. 37.
>> Capper, J., *Observations on the Passage to India, through Egypt, and across the Great Desert* ... (1783), pp. 58, 59, 65 and 77.
>>> Cf., especially, Colonel Capper's remarks: "Many travellers give the Arabs an exceeding bad character ... faithless and rapacious, in whom no confidence can be reposed. *I confess they do not appear to me in that light*; they certainly like most men endeavour to make the best bargain they can for themselves; but for my own part I never found them inclined to ask for more than was justly their due" (p. 58).
>> Griffiths, J. (1805), *op. cit.* pp. 318, 320, 386, 388 and 389.
>> Heude, Wm. (1819), *op. cit.* pp. 51, 84 and 89.

Pages 30-31. See the works of Doughty, the Blunts, G. L. Bell, Musil, etc.—as listed in the Bibliography—for confirmation of their attitude to the Beduin. Also conversations with Mr Douglas Carruthers and Colonel T. E. Lawrence.
> *Re* the murder of Huber see Hogarth, D. G. (1904), p. 281.
> Ralli, A., *Christians at Mecca*, London (1909), pp. 237-243.

CHAPTER II

Part I

Pages 33-45. (A) EARLIEST TRADE ROUTES ACROSS THE SYRIAN DESERT:
1. General:
>> Maps in the *Cambridge Ancient History*, especially

those in i, p. 224; iii, p. 1; vi, pp. 1 and 357; and
vii, p. 1.

Heeren, A. H. L., *Historical Researches into the
Politics and Intercourse of the Nations of Antiquity*
(1833), especially iii, appendix C, and pp. 470,
487 and 490, quoting the Old Testament, Agathar-
chides, Marinus of Tyre, Ptolemy and Strabo.

Hogarth, D. G., *The Nearer East* (1915), map on p. 223.

Kiepert, Dr. H., *Atlas Antiquus* (1869). Twelve maps
of the Ancient World, especially maps Nos. II,
III and XII.

Musil, Alois, *Arabia Deserta* (1927), appendix V,
pp. 514-516.

  Also portfolio of maps accompanying his
works (1926).

(Pages 35-36). *Syria*, x (1929), pp. 144-163 (Dussaud
re Rees' explorations).

2. The Ancient Northern Route:

(Pages 40-41). Thureau-Dangin, F., and R. P. Dhorme,
articles in *Syria*, v (1924), p. 265; x (1929), pp.
186-188.

Bell, G., *Amurath to Amurath* (1911), map and p. 99.

3. (*a*) Roman Routes:

Bell, G., *Letters* (1927), i, pp. 76-79 and 94.

Burckhardt, J. L., *Travels in Syria and the Holy Land*
(1822), p. 366.

Butler, H. C., and Norrio and Stoever, *Geography
and Itinerary* (1930): *passim*, and especially the map
of Syria (1920).

Cameron, V. L., *Our Future Highway* (1880), i, pp.
112, 136 and 141.

Cumont, F., *Études syriennes* (1917), pp. 1 and 17.

Dalrymple, G. E., *The Syrian Great Eastern Railway
to India* (1878), pp. 8 and 12.

Dussaud, R., *Topographie historique de la Syrie
antique et médiévale* (1927), chap. v, especially pp.
263-267 and 348; also maps, especially No. XIV,
opposite to p. 472.

Graham, Cyril C., article in the *Journal of the R.G.S.*,
xxviii (1858), pp. 226-263, and map.

Heeren, A. H. L., *Historical Researches* (1833), iii,
pp. 491-502.

Musil, A., *Palmyrena* (1928), pp. 237-243. Citing Ptolemy, the *Peutinger Table*, the *Itinerarium Antonini* (corrected to A.D. 336) and Miller's *Itineraria romana* (1916).

Poidebard, R. P. Antoine, *La Trace de Rome dans le Désert de Syrie* (1934). *Passim.*

Also: Conversations with le Père Poidebard, with Professor J. S. Crawford, and with Mr Francis Kettaneh.

(*b*) Palmyrene Routes:

Dussaud (1927), *op. cit.* chap. v.

Dussaud, R., article in *Syria*, x (1929), pp. 59 and 128 (citing the *Notitia dignitatum*).

Heeren (1833), *op. cit.* ii, pp. 450-456 (citing Appian, Pliny and certain Palmyrene inscriptions).

Huntington, E. (1911), pp. 369-370.

MacDonald, Sir Geo., article, "Rome in the Middle East", in *Antiquity* (1934, Dec.), pp. 373-380. (Review of Poidebard's *Trace de Rome*, etc.)

Syria, xii (1931), pp. 100-115, article by the Rev. Fathers Mouterde and Poidebard.

(B) VARIOUS CROSSINGS OF THE EUPHRATES THAT WERE POPULAR IN DIFFERENT HISTORICAL PERIODS:

(Pages 41-42). Bell, G. (1911), p. 97.

Cumont, Franz, *Études syriennes* (1917), pp. 42, 120-126, 250.

The Encyclopaedia of Islam, article "Birejik".

Musil, A., *Palmyrena*, *op. cit.* pp. 260-262.

Olivier, G. A., *Voyage dans l'Empire Othoman, l'Egypte et la Perse* (1807), pp. 448-449.

Teixeira, P. (1902), *op. cit.* p. 86.

Syria, articles and editorials in iii (1922), p. 207 (Cumont); x (1929), pp. 186-8 (Thureau-Dangin); xi (1930), pp. 105 and 130-132 (Dussaud).

Carruthers, D., Hakluyt, Second Series, lxiii (1929), p. 156, note 1.

Military Crossings of the Euphrates:

Both Cyrus and Alexander crossed the river at Thapsacus (now Meskineh)—

See the *Cambridge Ancient History*, vi, maps on pp. 1 and 357.

But the Emperor Julian crossed at Tell Ahmar—

See Thureau-Dangin in *Syria*, x (1929), p. 188.

Cumont, F. (1917), p. 14.

(C) MEDIEVAL SARACEN AND MAMLUK DESERT ROUTES:

Butler, S. S., in the *Geographical Journal*, xxxiii, 5 (1909), p. 534.

Dussaud, R. (1927), pp. 262, 267, 283 and 300. Also the references already given under (A), 3 (*a*): Roman Routes; and map on p. 472.

Dussaud, R., article in *Syria*, x (1929), pp. 54 and 55 (with map).

Idrisi, M. ibn M., el-, *La Géographie d'Edrisi* . . . (1836), ii, pp. 145-146.

Musil, A., *Arabia Deserta* (1927), App. VI, pp. 516-528.

Le Strange, G., *Lands of the Eastern Caliphate* (1905), i, pp. 10 and 11.

Also: Gaudefroy-Demombynes, *La Syrie à l'époque des Mamelouks* (1923), pp. 244 and 245 (note 9).

Le Strange, G., *Palestine Under the Moslems* (1890), pp. 240, 530 and 545.

Quatremère's *el-Makrizi* (1842), p. 92.

(D) CARAVAN ROUTES FROM THE MAMLUK PERIOD TO THE TWENTIETH CENTURY:

The references cited are the same as those for the preceding section, (C).

Also, in addition:

Burton and Drake, *Unexplored Syria* (1872), map at the beginning of vol. i.

Huntington, Ellsworth, *Palestine and its Transformation* (1911), p. 368.

Itinerarium, Antonini Placentini (1889), pp. 33 and 34.

Musil, A., *Arabia Deserta*, pp. 527 and 529 (citing the *Constantinople Codex*, Pietro della Valle, Tavernier and Wallin (1854)).

Tavernier, J. B., *Les Six Voyages de J. B. Tavernier . . . en Turquie, en Perse et aux Indes* (1676), i, p. 286.

Tavernier, J. B., *Through Turky and Persia to the Indies* (1684), i, p. 60; and iii, pp. 109-110.

(E) THE PROBLEM OF THE EARLY TRADE CONNECTIONS BETWEEN JAUF AND IRAK:

(Pages 37-38). Smith, Sidney, article in the *Cambridge Ancient History*, iii, chap. i, part 5.

Also: Conversation with Mr Sidney Smith, Keeper of the Department of Egyptian and Assyrian Antiquities of the British Museum.

N.B.—Professor W. A. Albright, Director of the American School of Oriental Research (Jerusalem), disagrees with Mr Smith's conclusions on the subject.

Musil, A., *Arabia Deserta*, App. VIII, pp. 484-487 and 553-570.

(F) NECESSITY OF LEVEL DESERT TRACKS FOR THE TRADE ROUTES OF MERCHANT CARAVANS:

(Pages 42-43). Tavernier, J. B. (1684), *op. cit.* iii, p. 107.
Musil, A., *Palmyrena*, pp. 260-264.

Also: Conversations with Professor J. S. Crawford, and with Hajji Selim Sawwaf.

(G) THE HAJJ OR PILGRIM ROUTES:

(Pages 43-44). (1) The Western *Darb el-Hajj*: see the references given in the notes for Chapter VII, pp. 223-224.

(2) The Eastern Pilgrim Route; see the references given in the notes for Chapter VII, pp. 222-223.

(H) THE ALTERNATING, PROSPEROUS PERIODS OF THE NORTH-SOUTH, EAST-WEST DESERT ROUTES:

(Pages 44-45). Conversation with Mr Sidney Smith, of the British Museum.

(I) THE GREAT AND LITTLE DESERT ROUTES:

Note on page 40 and page 44.
See reference notes for Chapter VI, Part 2.

Also: Carruthers, D., Hakluyt, lxiii (1929), *passim*.

Maps: Major James Rennell (1809).

Ritter and Kiepert (1854).

Carruthers, D., in Hakluyt, lxiii (1929), p. 196, and in the *Geographical Journal*, lii, 3 (1918), p. 204.

(J) For the geographical material used on pages 36-37 and 38-39, see reference notes for Chapter I, part 3.

Part 2

THE HISTORICAL BACKGROUND:

Pages 45-50 and the diagram which illustrates the periods of maximum and minimum usage of the trans-desert routes serve as an introduction to the expanded text which follows (Chapter II, Part 2, inclusive). The reference notes are therefore identical for pages 45-50 and 50-78.

N.B.—For most of the historical data that are made use of in part 2, the usual histories and manuals of history (e.g. Ploetz) may be consulted. The following references are given only for material which is not conveniently accessible in standard outlines of history.

Pages 50-51. ANCIENT EMPIRES, AND THE ORIGINS OF TRADE AND COMMERCE:

Rostovtzeff, M., *Caravan Cities* (1932), chap. i, "Caravan Trade. An Historical Survey", pp. 1-37; especially pp. 8-16.

Pages 51-52. CONCERNING THE RISE OF TADMOR:

Rostovtzeff (1932), *op. cit.* p. 17.

Syria, v (1924), p. 74. Review of P. Dhorme's *Palmyre dans les textes assyriens.*

First use of camels on the Syrian Desert—

Glanville, S. R. K., in the *Journal of Egyptian Archaeology*, xii (1926), p. 58 and notes 3 and 4.

Conversation with Mr Sidney Smith.

Also: Sidney Smith in the *Rev. d'Ass.* xii, p. 87.

Pages 52-53. THE POSSIBLE CHANGE OF CLIMATE IN THE SYRIAN DESERT:

Capper, J., *Observations on the Passage to India, through Egypt, and across the Great Desert* ... (1783), pp. 109-110.

Huntington, E. (1911), *op. cit.* pp. 270-272, 362, 370 and 380.

Musil, A., *Palmyrena*, pp. 77 and 81.

Philby, H. St. J. B., *Arabia* (1930), p. xv.

Also: Philby and Major A. L. Holt in the *Geographical Journal*, lxii, 4 (1923), pp. 242 and 261.

Syria, xiii (1932), pp. 217-218, review of Victor Müller's *En Syrie avec les Bédouins. Les Tribus du désert.*

Conversation with Professor Assad Rustum, of the American University of Beyrout.

Pages 53-54. COMMERCIAL DEVELOPMENT OF THE ASSYRIAN AND IRANIAN EMPIRES:

Rostovtzeff (1932), pp. 16-23.

Pages 54-55. THE NEAR EAST HELLENIZED:

The *Cambridge Ancient History*, chapters by M. Rostovtzeff in vols. vii and viii; especially vii, chap. v, pp. 157, 158, 173-176, 184-185, 190-191 and 196 (for statement concerning Chinese art of the Han period); and viii, chap. xx, pp. 619-630, 651-654 and 658-666.

Also: Rostovtzeff (1932), pp. 23-28.

Page 55. PRE-ROMAN TRADE ROUTES:

See reference notes for Chapter II, part 1 (A).

Also: Heeren, A. H. L. (1833), ii, pp. 101-106 and 450-456.

Laborde, L. de, *Journey through Arabia Petraea to Mount Sinai* (1838), pp. 306-307.

Musil, A., *Arabia Deserta*, pp. 467, 480-481 and 515.

Tarn, W. W., maps in the *Cambridge Ancient History*, vi, pp. 1 and 357.

Page 56. TRADE CONNECTIONS OF JAUF:

See Part 1 (E) (reference notes for paragraph 8, part 1, of this same chapter).

Also: Musil, *Arabia Deserta*, App. I, pp. 477-493, and App. VII, pp. 531-552.

Pages 56-58 (and footnote, p. 58). THE CARAVAN EMPIRE OF PETRA:

Rostovtzeff (1932), chap. ii, "Petra", pp. 37-53.

Tarn, W. W., article in the *Journal of Egyptian Archaeology*, xv (1929), pp. 9-25, "Ptolemy II and Arabia".

Pages 58-59. BOSRA AND THE CARAVAN CITIES OF TRANS-JORDAN:

Rostovtzeff (1932), pp. 33-34; and chap. iii, "Jerash", pp. 54-90.

Pages 59-61. THE CARAVAN EMPIRE OF PALMYRA:

Rostovtzeff (1932), chap. iv, "Palmyra and Dura", pp. 91, 119; and chap. v, "The Ruins of Palmyra", pp. 120-152.

Also: Map showing the Parthian Empire in 51 B.C., in the *Cambridge Ancient History*, x, p. 47.

Gautier, E. F., *Une Excursion à Palmyre* (1928), p. 290.

Huntington, E. (1911), *op. cit.* pp. 362 and 370.

Syria, xii (1931), pp. 107-115, *re* the columnar inscription on the Palmyra-Hit route (article by Poidebard and Mouterde).

Conversation with Monsieur Daniel Schlumberger.

Pages 61-62. The Fiscal Laws of Palmyra:

Chabot, J. B., *Choix d'inscriptions de Palmyre* (1922), pp. 25-37.

Pages 62-65. General Trade Conditions in the Roman Period (in the Near East):

Oertel, F., in the *Cambridge Ancient History*, x, chap. xiii, pp. 382-424, "The Economic Unification of the Mediterranean Region: Industry, Trade and Commerce". Especially Part 6, "The Range and Methods of Commerce" (*i.e.* in the Augustan Empire).

Rostovtzeff (1932), pp. 101-119.

Rawlinson, H. G., *Intercourse between India and the Western World* (1926), chaps. vi, vii and viii, pp. 101-181.

West, L. C., "Commercial Syria under the Roman Empire", *Trans. Amer. Phil. Ass.* lv (1924), p. 159.

Charlesworth, M. P., *Trade Routes and Commerce of the Roman Empire* (1924). *Passim.*

(Pages 62-63). For detailed references *re* Roman Roads and Trade Routes in Syria and Palmyrena, see notes under part 1 (A), 3 (*a* and *b*), of this same chapter: especially the references to Dussaud, Musil and Poidebard.

(Page 63). The information concerning the walls of Palmyra was obtained from Monsieur D. Schlumberger.

Footnote on page 64 is based upon Rostovtzeff (1932), pp. 92-99, and chap. vi, "The Ruins of Dura", pp. 152-219.

Page 65 *et seq.* Syria and Mesopotamia until 1258:

Lammens, H., *La Syrie, précis historique* (1921).

Le Strange, G., *Baghdad during the Abbasid Caliphate* (1924).

Should be consulted for general conditions.

Also: Le Strange, G., *Lands of the Eastern Caliphate* (1905).

(Pages 65-66). The above, and Carruthers, D., in the *Geographical Journal*, lii, 3 (1918), p. 158.

Page 66.   Activities of Jewish Merchants:

Asher, A., *The Itinerary of Rabbi Benjamin of Tudela* (1840). *Passim.*

N.B.—In vol. i, p. 87, Benjamin of Tudela remarks that "Thadmor in the desert [*i.e.* Palmyra] contains 2000 warlike Jews".

Heyd, W., *Histoire du commerce du Levant au Moyen
Âge* (1885–1886), i, pp. 125-128.

Ibn Khordadbeh, trans. by Barbier de Meynard in
the *Journal Asiatique* (May-June 1865), pp. 512-515.

Page 66 *et seq.* GENERAL CONDITIONS CONCERNING TRADE AND COM-
MERCE:

See Heyd, W. (1885–1886), *op. cit.*, especially
vol. ii.

Page 67, Footnote. THE MOSLEM INHERITANCE FROM THE SASANIAN
IRANIANS:

Le Strange, G. (1905), i, pp. 1-6, 57, and map.

Abulfeda, *La Géographie d'Aboulfeda* . . . (1848), ii,
pp. 66-68.

Page 67. SYRIAN (ARAB) PRINCES IN CONFLICT WITH THE FATIMIDS
OF EGYPT:

Gibb, H. A. R. (1932), Introduction to *The Damascus
Chronicle of the Crusades.*

Pages 67-68. THE CENTURY OF TATAR RULE IN ASIA:

Newton and Others, *Travel and Travellers of the
Middle Ages* (1926), chap. vii, pp. 124-258, by
Professor Eileen Power: "The Opening of the
Land Routes to Cathay", especially pp. 125-128,
132-136, 142 and 152. Also map opposite page 128.

Heyd, W. (1886), ii, *op. cit.*

Pages 68-71. TRADE AND COMMERCE UNTIL THE COMING OF THE OTTO-
MAN TURKS:

Heyd, W. (1886), ii, *op. cit.*, especially pp. 4-11 and
456-466.

Ibn Battuta (1929), *op. cit.* pp. 20-21 and 303-306.

Also for general information:

Gaudefroy-Demombynes, *La Syrie à l'époque des
Mamelouks* (1923). *Passim.*

Pages 71-73. LEVANT TRADE IN THE FIFTEENTH AND SIXTEENTH CEN-
TURIES:

Heyd, W. (1886), ii, *op. cit.* p. 467 *et seq.*, *Mélanges
d'histoire et de géographie orientale*, "Relations de
l'Europe et de l'Asie avant et après le voyage de
Vasco de Gama", H. Cordier (1914).

Carruthers, D., in the *Geographical Journal*, lii, 3,
op. cit. pp. 158-160.

Pages 73-74. ENGLAND IN THE NEAR EAST:

Epstein, M., *The Early History of the Levant Company*

(1908). *Passim.* Especially chap. v, pp. 52-73, 90-100 and 214-216.

Harford, F. D., article in the *Nineteenth Century* (July 1918), pp. 97-113, "Old Caravan Roads and Overland Routes in Syria, Arabia, and Mesopotamia". Especially pp. 98-110.

Letters of the East India Company, i, pp. 273-274; ii, p. 261; and vi, p. 43.

Also: Reference notes for page 151, part 3 of Chapter IV.

Pages 74-75. For the Testimony of Early Travellers see the next Chapter (III), reference notes for parts 1 and 2, and Chapter IV, part 3.

Pages 75-76. GENERAL CONDITIONS, 1600-1745:

Venetian Calendar of State Papers, for the years 1592-1635 (information indexed under "Aleppo").

Taylor, J. (1799), i, pp. 220-221 (for the banyan-tree simile).

Carruthers, D., in Hakluyt (1929), *op. cit.* pp. xxiii and xxvi.

Pages 76-77. CONDITIONS IN THE SECOND HALF OF THE EIGHTEENTH CENTURY:

Diaries of Plaisted and Carmichael (printed in Hakluyt, lxiii (1929), *op. cit.* pp. 49-179); Capper (1783), and Taylor (1799), i and ii.

Carruthers, D., in the *Geographical Journal,* lii, 3, pp. 160-184.

For the Revival of the Desert Post see reference notes for VIII, parts 2 and 3.

Pages 77-78. DEVELOPMENTS OF THE NINETEENTH AND TWENTIETH CENTURIES:

Carruthers, in the *Geographical Journal,* lii, 3, *op. cit.*

Harford, in the *Nineteenth Century* (1918), *op. cit.*

Also: Reference notes for Chapters VIII and IX.

CHAPTER III

Part 1

Pages 79-80. PRE-MOHAMMEDAN TRAVELLERS:

Itineraria Romana (1929).

Itinerarium, Antonini Placentini (1889).

Cary and Warmington (1929), chap. vii, especially
pp. 130-136, 138-151, 155-162, and maps opposite
pp. 140, 148 and 164.
Newton and Others (1926), chaps. (pp. 1-70)—
I (by Prof. A. P. Newton);
II (by M. L. W. Laistner); and
III (by the Rev. Claude Jenkins).

Pages 80-81. TRAVEL IN THE WORLD OF ISLAM:
Newton and Others (1926), chap. v, *op. cit.*
Gibb, H. A. R. (1929), *Ibn Battuta*, pp. 15-40.

Pages 81-82. MOHAMMEDAN TRAVELLERS:
See the prefaces to the works of the individual
Moslems mentioned; *i.e.*
el-Mukaddasi (1892) and (1897),
Ibn Haukal (1822),
Ibn Jubair (1852) and (1906),
Yakut (1822),
Idrisi (1836),
Abulfeda (1848),
as cited in the Bibliography.
For general remarks about the same, see:
The Legacy of Islam (1931), chap. iii, essay on
"Geography and Commerce" (by J. H.
Kramers), pp. 79-107.
Newton and Others (1926), chap. v (by Sir
T. W. Arnold), pp. 88-104.

Page 82. IBN BATTUTA:
Travels (1929), pp. 72-74, 78-85 and 303-5.
Also: Preface to the edition of 1929, by H. A. R.
Gibb, pp. 1-15, and Sykes, Sir Percy (1934), pp.
84-96.

Pages 82-83. JEWISH TRAVELLERS IN THE MIDDLE AGES:
Benjamin of Tudela, editions of A. Asher (1840),
M. N. Adler (1907).
Whiteway, R. S., *Rise of Portuguese Power in India*
(1899), pp. 53-54.
Wilson, Sir A. T., *Early Spanish and Portuguese
Travellers in Persia* (1927), pp. 2-7.
Refusal of Jews to travel on Sunday:
Teixeira (1902), p. 44.
Beawes, in Hakluyt, lxiii (1929), p. 13.
Carmichael, in Hakluyt, lxiii (1929), p. 172.

Page 83.   PORTUGUESE TRAVELLERS:

        Carruthers, D., in the *Geographical Journal*, lii, 3 (1918), p. 160.

        Carruthers, D., in Hakluyt, lxiii (1929), p. xvi.

        Taylor, J., *Travels from England to India in the Year 1789* . . . (1799), i, pp. 17 and 18.

        Wilson, Sir A. T., *Early Spanish and Portuguese Travellers in Persia* (1927), pp. 19-21 (*re* Antonio Tenreiro).

Pages 83-84. VENETIAN TRAVELLERS:

        Carruthers, D. (1918), *op. cit.* pp. 160-162.

        Carruthers, D., in Hakluyt, *op. cit.* pp. xvii, xviii.

        Purchas, S., *Hakluytus Posthumus or Purchas His Pilgrimes* (1625); (1905), x, p. 139.

Page 84.   USE OF THE EUPHRATES ROUTE:

        Carruthers, D. (1918).

        Carruthers, D. (1929), pp. xvii-xix.

        Ray's *Travels* (1738), ii, pp. 1-139 (*re* Rauwolff's Voyage down the Euphrates).

Pages 84-85. PIONEERS OF THE EAST INDIA COMPANY:

        Purchas, S. (1625), *op. cit.* ii, p. 288.

        Sanderson, J., *The Travels of* . . . *in the Levant, 1584-1602*. Hakluyt Society. Second Series, lxvii (1931), p. xi.

        Taylor, J. (1799), i, p. 19.

        Ryley, J. H., *Ralph Fitch, England's Pioneer to India and Burma* (1899), pp. 47 and 48.

        N.B.—The narrative of Ralph Fitch's trip from Tripoli to Ormuz is probably based upon the account of this same trip which was given by Caesar Frederick. Frederick's narrative had been translated before the return of Fitch in 1591.

Page 85.   EARLY SEVENTEENTH CENTURY TRAVELLERS:

        Purchas, S. (1625), ii, p. 297.

        Letters of the East India Company, ii, pp. 98, 105.

        Carruthers, D. (1929), *op. cit.* pp. xix-xxi.

        Longrigg, S. H., *Four Centuries of Modern Irak* (1925), pp. 330-332.

Pages 85-86. PEDRO TEIXEIRA:

        The Travels of (1902), Introduction and pp. 33-132.

        Also: Wilson, Sir A. T. (1927), *op. cit.* p. 23.

Baker, J. N. L., *History of Geographical Discovery and Exploration* (1931), p. 132.

Pages 86-87. PIETRO DELLA VALLE:

The Travels of, in Hakluyt, lxxxiv (1892), Introduction and pp. 262-280.

Page 87.   TAVERNIER:

Tavernier, J. B., *Les Six Voyages de* . . . (1676).

Tavernier, Bernier, *The Travels of* . . . and other great men (1684), i, pp. 1-84; ii, pp. 53-95; iii, pp. 99-113.

Also: Thompson, R. C., *Tavernier's Travels in Mesopotamia* (1910).

Articles in the *Encyclopaedia Britannica* and in Michaud's *Biographie Universelle*.

Pages 87-88. MANRIQUE:

Manrique, Fray Sebastien, *Travels*, 1629–1643, in Hakluyt, lxi (1927), pp. 368-375.

Re Godinho's Travels: Murray's *Asia* (1820), i, pp. 405-409.

Re General Conditions of the Period: Carruthers, D., in Hakluyt (1929), *op. cit.* pp. xxi, xxiii and xxvi.

Page 88.   JOHN CAMPBELL:

Indian Antiquary, xxxvi (1907), pp. 130-133.

Pages 88-89. M. CARRÉ:

Voyage des Indes (1699), i, pp. 216-277, 402; and ii, p. 129.

Pages 89-90. *RE* DE THÉVENOT:

Voyage . . . au Levant (1674), ii, pp. 41-117.

Page 90.   *RE* NIEBUHR:

Voyage . . . (1780), pp. 322-336.

Page 90.   *RE* THE PERIOD 1673–1745:

Carruthers, D., in Hakluyt (1929), *op. cit.* pp. xxiii and xxvi.

Longrigg, S. H. (1925), *op. cit.* p. 333.

Part 2

Pages 90–92. *RE* DAMASCUS:

Ibn Haukal, *Mesalek u Memalek.* Translation (1800), pp. 41 and 42.

el-Mukaddasi, *Description of Syria.* Translation (1892), pp. 16, 17, 23 and 24.

Idrisi, *La Géographie d'Edrisi* . . . Translation (1836), i, p. 349.

Ibn Battuta, *Travels in Asia and Africa*, 1325–1354. Translation by H. A. R. Gibb (1929), p. 65.

Journal of a Deputation to the East (1855), ii, p. 480.

The Encyclopaedia of Islam, article on "Damascus".

Pages 92-95. *Re* ALEPPO:

ALEPPO TO THE TWELFTH CENTURY:

Coryate, T., *Coryat's Crudities* (1776), iii, chap. i.

Fitch, R., printed in Ryley, J. H. (1899), *op. cit.* pp. 48 and 49 and notes.

Rauwolff, L., printed in Ray's *Travels* (1738), ii, pp. 61-65.

Cumont, Franz, *Études syriennes* (1917), p. 13.

The Encyclopaedia of Islam, article "Haleb" (Aleppo).

Syria, viii (1927), p. 41, article on Aleppo by P. Dhorme.

ALEPPO, TWELFTH TO EIGHTEENTH CENTURIES:

Idrisi (1836), *op. cit.* ii, p. 156.

Teixeira, P. (1902), pp. 113 and 114.

Tavernier, J. B. (1684), i, p. 58.

Thévenot, J. de, *Relation d'un voyage fait au Levant* (1674), ii, pp. 58 and 73.

Taylor, J. (1799), i, pp. 211, 213, 217, 220 and 224.

Olivier, G. A., *Voyage dans l'Empire Othoman l'Égypte et la Perse* (1804), p. 301.

THE GOVERNMENT OF ALEPPO:

Teixeira, P. (1902), pp. 115-118.

Tavernier, J. B. (1684), i, p. 59.

Venetian Calendar of State Papers, 8th July 1623 (p. 57), and 22nd June 1624 (p. 358).

Griffiths, J., *Travels in Europe, Asia Minor and Arabia* (1805), pp. 311, 334, 336 and 343.

THE EUROPEAN "NATIONS" OF ALEPPO—"FACTORIES" OF THE FLEMISH, VENETIANS, FRENCH AND ENGLISH MERCHANTS:

Teixeira, P. (1902), pp. 118-121.

Griffiths, J. (1805), p. 342.

Letters of the East India Company, v, p. 290.

Olivier, G. A. (1804), p. 301.

Dehérain, H., in *Syria*, iii (1922), p. 339.

Coote, Sir E., in the *Journal of the R.G.S.* xxx (1860), p. 211.

Teonge, Rev. H., *Diary of* (1676) (1825), pp. 160-178.

Publications of the Hakluyt Society, lxxxvii, pp. ix and xxxvi-xxxix.

Heyd, W. von, *Histoire du commerce du Levant au Moyen Âge* (1886), ii, pp. 462-465.

Page 95. POPULATION OF ALEPPO:

Dr. Russel, printed in Moore, J. H., *A New and Complete Collection of Voyages and Travels* (1780), ii, pp. 723-725.

Arvieux, Le Chevalier L. d', *Mémoires du* (1735), vi, p. 411.

DIPLOMATIC AND SOCIAL IMPORTANCE OF ALEPPO:

Biddulph, Wm., in Purchas, viii, pp. 248-278.

Coote, Sir E., *op. cit.* p. 211.

Ives, Edw., *A Voyage from England to India in the Year MDCCLIV* (1773), ii, pp. 371-372.

Capper, J. (1783), p. 53.

Taylor, J. (1799), i, pp. 219-220.

Arvieux, L. de (1735), vi, *op. cit.* pp. 1-60 and 521-587.

Charles-Roux, Fr., *Les Échelles de Syrie et de Palestine —au XVIIIe siècle* (1928), "Annexe vii", pp. 200-204.

Carruthers, D., in Hakluyt, *op. cit.* pp. xxiv and xxv.

Page 95. DECLINE OF ALEPPO:

Syria, iii (1922), p. 339.

Syria, x (1929), p. 77.

Bell, G. L. (1911), p. 16.

Pages 95-97. RE BAGHDAD:

Teixeira (1902), pp. 61-72.

Thevenot, J. de (1674), ii, p. 117.

Olivier (1804), p. 388.

Heude, Wm. (1819), pp. 181-187.

Thielmann, M. von (1875), ii, p. 154.

Le Strange, G., *Baghdad during the Abbasid Caliphate* (1924). *Passim.*

The Encyclopaedia of Islam, article "Baghdad".

Idrisi (1836), i, p. 365.

Pages 97-100. RE BASRA: GENERAL HISTORY OF BASRA, AND IMPORTANCE OF THE CITY:

The Encyclopaedia of Islam, articles "Basra" and "Kufa".

Ibn Battuta (1929), pp. 86-88.

Howel, T., *Voyage en retour de l'Inde* (1797), pp. 23 and 24.

Ryley, J. H. (1899), p. 54.

Page 97.   CANALS OF MEDIEVAL BASRA:

Ibn Haukal (1800), pp. 63 and 64.

Idrisi (1836), i, p. 368.

Le Strange, G., *Lands of the Eastern Caliphate*, pp. 46 and 47.

Abulfeda (1848), ii, pp. 67 and 71-73.

Page 98.   DEPOPULATION OF BASRA:

The *Carmelite Chronicle* (1623; 1927), p. 495.

Capper, J. (1783), p. 86.

Taylor, J. (1799), i, pp. 267 and 269.

Page 98.   THE CARMELITES AT BASRA:

The *Carmelite Chronicle* (1927), pp. 448-450, 476 and 477.

La Boullaye-le-Gouz, *Voyages et observations en Syrie et en Perse* (1653), pp. 264 and 272-276.

Thévenot, J. de (1674), ii, p. 312.

Page 99.   TRAVELLERS' COMMENTS UPON BASRA:

Teixeira (1902), pp. 17 and 27-31.

Joseph Salbancke, in Purchas (1609), iii, p. 87.

Valle, P. della (1665), pp. 245-247.

Thévenot, J. de (1674), ii, pp. 308 and 309.

Tavernier (1684), ii, pp. 88-91.

Taylor, J. (1799), i, pp. 265, 267 and 269.

Heude, Wm. (1819), pp. 48-50 and 134.

Pages 99-100.   THE BUSY SEASON AT BASRA:

Thévenot, J. de (1674), ii, pp. 312-323.

Tavernier (1684), ii, p. 89.

Griffiths, J. (1805), p. 389.

Heude, Wm. (1819), pp. 47 and 48.

The *Carmelite Chronicle* (1927), p. 508.

Page 100.   THE EAST INDIA COMPANY AT BASRA:

Foster, Wm., *The English Factories in India* (1634-1636), pp. 185 and 243.

Taylor, J. (1799), i, p. 270.

Griffiths, J. (1805), pp. 384 and 390.

Page 100.   THE PERSIAN GULF, MUSCAT, BUSHIRE, ETC.:

Taylor, J. (1799), i, p. 350.

Heude, Wm. (1819), pp. 22, 32, 36, 38, 41-44.
Tavernier, J. B. (1684), iii, pp. 245-247 (*re* the
Persian Gulf and Bandar Abbas).
Thévenot, J. de (1674), ii, pp. 311-312, 329-330.
Wilson, Sir Arnold (1928), *The Persian Gulf.*
Passim.
Re Ormuz: Heude, *op. cit.* p. 35.
Ryley, J. H. (1899), pp. 53-55.
The Venetian Calendar of State Papers, 23rd July
1622 and 27th Jan. 1623 (pp. 376 and 555).

Pages 100-101. SYRIAN PORTS:
Teixeira (1902), pp. 120-121 and 130-134.
Taylor, J. (1799), i, pp. 159-163.

Part 3

Pages 101-103. REOPENING OF THE GREAT DESERT ROUTE, AND MID-
EIGHTEENTH CENTURY TRAVELLERS:
Maundrell, H. (1714), "A Compendium of a
Journey to Jerusalem . . ."
Moore, J. H., *A New and Complete Collection of*
Travels and Voyages (1780), ii, pp. 681-708.
Carruthers, D., Hakluyt, lxiii (1929), containing
the narratives of: Beawes, Roberts, Plaisted and
Carmichael.   Also Introduction, pp. xxv-xxx.
Carruthers, D., and Harford, F. D., article *re*
Carmichael in the *Geographical Journal,* li (1918),
pp. 323-325.
Longrigg, S. H., *Four Centuries of Modern Irak*
(1925), pp. 333-335.
Ives, Edw., *A Voyage from England to India* (1773),
ii, especially pp. 379-389.
Howel, T. (1797), *op. cit.,* especially pp. 22-112.
The *Geographical Journal,* lxxii, 3 (1928), pp. 275-
278, article on Claudius Rich, signed by M. K.

Pages 103-104. FOUR NOTABLE ENGLISH TRAVELLERS, 1771-1790:
Coote, General Sir Eyre, Diary, printed in the
Journal of the R.G.S. xxx. (1860), pp. 198-
211.
Capper, Colonel James (1783), Journal, published
in *Observations on a Passage to India,* pp. 40-108
and 109. With map.

Griffiths, Dr. Julius, *Travels in Europe, Asia Minor and Arabia* (1805), pp. 348-384; and map.

Taylor, Major John, *Travels from England to India in the Year 1789* (1799). Especially i, pp. 226-260, and map.

Taylor, Major John, *Considerations on the Practicability and Advantages of a More Speedy Communication between Great Britain and her Possessions in India* (1795), p. 46.

Pages 104-105. LATER EIGHTEENTH CENTURY TRAVELLERS:

Carruthers (1918), *op. cit.*

Longrigg (1925), *op. cit.*

Re M. de Bourg see Capper (1783), pp. 100-103.

Re Michaux see Hamy, Dr. E. T., in *Publications of the IXe Congrès International de Géographie*, cxlv (1908), p. 366.

Olivier, G. A., *Voyage dans l'Empire Othoman, l'Egypte et la Perse* (1801-7). Especially map, in vol. for 1806; and vol. for 1807, pp. 439-470.

Pages 105-106. EARLY NINETEENTH CENTURY TRAVELLERS:

Rousseau, J. B. L. J., *Voyage de Bagdad à Alep* (1808; 1899), pp. 1-150.

Also, *re* Rousseau, note by M. Barbié du Bocage, in the *Bulletin de la Société de Géographie* for 1822-3, i, pp. 250-251; and article by M. Henri Dehérain in *Syria*, vi (1925), p. 187.

Re Honoré Vidal, letters and notes in the *Bulletin de la Société de Géographie*, i, pp. 101 and 110; ii, pp. 100-102; and vi, pp. 5-10.

Page 106.

Rennell, Major James, *A Treatise on the Comparative Geography of Western Asia* (1831), especially Major Rennell's Introduction.

N.B.—Major Rennell's maps are to be found in the British Museum.

Also: Carruthers, D., in Hakluyt (1929), *op. cit.* pp. 132-134.

Baker, J. N. L. (1931), p. 246.

Heude, Wm., *A Voyage up the Persian Gulf, and a Journey Overland from India to England, in 1817* (1819). Especially pp. 52-80.

Pages 106-107. Chesney, General F. R., *Narrative of the Euphrates Expedition* (1868), pp. 50-95 and 333-345.

Also: Baker, J. N. L. (1931), p. 246.

Longrigg, S. H. (1925), p. 337.

Pages 107-108. THE TRAVELS OF ORMSBY AND OF WELLSTED:

Wellsted, J. R., *Travels to the City of the Caliphs* (1840), pp. 327-334.

Also: Carruthers, D., *Arabian Adventure* (1935), pp. 151-152. Also the private notes of Mr Carruthers.

Page 108.   Callier, Captain C. Fragment of the narrative of Callier, published in the *Bulletin de la Société de Géographie*, Onziéme Série, No. 8 (1837), pp. 288-302.

Also: article by M. Dehérain in *Syria*, vi (1925), p. 291.

Pages 108-109. SYRO-ARABIAN EXPLORERS:

General: Baker, J. N. L., *History of Geographical Discovery and Exploration* (1931), pp. 247-255.

Butler, S. S., article in the *Geographical Journal*, xxxiii, 5 (1909), p. 517.

Hogarth, D. G., *The Penetration of Arabia* (1904). *Passim.*

Sykes, Sir Percy (1934), *op. cit.* chaps. 31, 32 and 33; and map, p. 280.

Particular: Burckhardt, J. L., *Travels in Syria and the Holy Land* (1822). *Passim.*

Re Wallin, G. A., article by M. Trautz in the *Journal of the Central Asian Society*, xix (1932), pp. 131-150.

Wallin, G. A., "Narrative of a Journey from Cairo to Medina and Mecca, etc., in 1845", *Journal of the Royal Geographical Society*, xxiv (1854), pp. 115-207.

Wallin, G. A., "Notes taken During a Journey through Part of Northern Arabia", in 1848, are in the *Geographical Journal*, xx (1850).

Pages 109-110. Doughty, C. M., *Travels in Arabia Deserta* (1933). *Passim.*

Also: Baker, J. N. L. (1931), pp. 252-253.

Hogarth, D. G., *The Life of C. M. Doughty* (1928).

Page 110.   HUBER AND EUTING:

Huber, Chas., *Journal d'un voyage en Arabie* (1891).

Especially pp. 40-51; map, p. 44; and the introduction to same.

Huber, C., "Voyage dans l'Arabie Centrale", in *Bull. Soc. de Géog.*, VIIme série, vol. vi, pp. 92-148.

Also: Hogarth, D. G. (1904), *op. cit.* p. 281.

Baker, J. N. L., *op. cit.* (1931), p. 252.

Page 110.　　TRAVELS OF THE BLUNTS:

Blunt, Lady Anne, *Bedouin Tribes of the Euphrates* (1879). Especially vol i, *passim*.

A Pilgrimage to Nejd (1881).

Also: Longrigg, S. H. (1925), *op. cit.* p. 339.

Pages 110-111. ADDITIONAL NINETEENTH CENTURY TRAVELLERS:

Thielmann, Max von, *Journey in the Caucasus, Persia, and Turkey in Asia* (1875). Especially ii, pp. 198-239.

Bischoff, Dr. T., "A Journey from Palmyra through the Desert to Aleppo", article in *Globus* (1881), xl, No. 23, pp. 363-366.

Černik, J., *Technische Studien-Expedition durch die Gebiete des Euphrats und Tigris nebst Ein- und Ausgangs-Routen durch Nord-Syrien* (1875-6). *Passim*.

Anonymous Letters of an Englishman, Rambles in the Deserts of Syria, etc. (1864). Especially pp. 239-250 and 274-282.

Pages 111-112. MAPS OF THE SYRIAN DESERT:

Ritter, Carl (1852) and (1854).

Kiepert, Dr. R. (1893).

Oppenheim, Max von (1894).

Oppenheim, Max von, *Vom Mittelmeer zum Persischen Golf durch den Hauran, die syrische Wüste und Mesopotamien* (1899).

Oestrup, J. E., *Historisk-topografiske Bidrag til der syriske orker* (1895). With map.

Sachau, Eduard, *Am Euphrat und Tigris* (1900). With maps.

Also: Baker, J. N. L. (1931), pp. 246 and 255.

Syria, viii (1927), p. 303.

Pages 112-113. PERIOD OF EXPLORATION, 1908-1914:

Butler, S. S., article in the *Geographical Journal*, xxxiii, 5 (1909), pp. 517-535.

Carruthers, D., conversation with, and article in the *Geographical Journal*, xxxv, 3 (1910), pp. 225-248.

Also: Baker, J. N. L. (1931), pp. 254-255.

Carruthers, D., article in the *Geographical Journal*, lix (1922), pp. 321-334, and pp. 401-418, *re* Shakespear.

Pages 113-115. Alois Musil: his works, as cited in the Bibliography.

Also: articles and notes in the *Geographical Journal*, xlii (1913), pp. 194-195; and lxxii (1928), pp. 278-280.

Also: article in *Syria*, x (1929), pp. 52-63.

Pages 115-117. GERTRUDE BELL: *Amurath to Amurath* (1911). *Passim* *Letters* (1927), especially i, pp. 267-270 and 311, 355.

Also: Obituary in the *Geographical Journal*, lxviii (1926), pp. 366-367; and conversation with R. P. Antoine Poidebard.

Hogarth, D. G., on G. Bell's "Journey to Hayil", the *Geographical Journal*, lxx (1927).

Pages 117-118. COLONEL LEACHMAN:

Articles in the *Geographical Journal*, xxxvii, 3 (1911), pp. 265-274, and xliii, 5 (1914), pp. 500-520.

Obituary, signed by D. G. Hogarth, in the *Geographical Journal*, lvi, 4 (1920), pp. 325-326.

Also: a conversation with Major C. G. Lynam.

Pages 118-119. COLONEL LAWRENCE:

Revolt in the Desert (1927). *Passim.*

Introduction to C. M. Doughty's *Arabia Deserta* (1933).

Also: a conversation with Col. Lawrence.

Pages 119-120. Captain Fowle: *Travels in the Middle East* (1916), especially the introduction, and pp. 55-63.

Pages 120-121. ARCHAEOLOGICAL WORK IN PALMYRENA:

General: Poidebard, A., *La Trace de Rome dans le Désert de Syrie* (1934). Especially the introduction.

Syria, v (1924), p. 121; and x, p. 274.

Re Salahiya: *Syria*, iii (1922), p. 178; and iv (1923), pp. 206-207.

Re Kasr el-Hair: *Syria*, viii (1927), pp. 304-307 and

322; xii (1931), pp. 316-318; xiii (1932), pp. 317-320.

Dussaud *re* Müller: *Syria*, xiii (1932), p. 217.

Also: Dussaud, Poidebard and Müller as cited in text.

Pages 121-122. EXPLORATION OF THE GREAT DESERT:

General: Baker, J. N. L. (1931), p. 255.

Syria, xii (1931), p. 189.

The *Geographical Review*, ix (1920), No. 2, *re* Butler, Norrio and Stoever.

The discovery by Group-Captain Rees: article by René Dussaud in *Syria*, x (1929), pp. 144-163.

Page 122. THE HOLT-PHILBY EXPEDITION OF 1922:

Holt, Major A. L., article in the *Geographical Journal*, lxii, 4 (1923), pp. 259-271.

Philby, H. St. J. B., article in the *Geographical Journal*, lxii, 4 (1923), pp. 241-259.

Pages 122-123. ELDON RUTTER:

Journal Central Asian Soc., xviii (1931), pp. 61-73.

Also: Sykes, Sir Percy (1934), pp. 292-293.

Page 123. CARL RASWAN: his book, *Black Tents of Arabia* (1935).

CHAPTER IV

Part 1

Part 1 is entirely based on Lammens, H., *La Mecque à la veille de l'Hégire* (1924)

Pages 126-127. CARAVAN ORGANIZATION: pp. 232, 233, 282-285, 248, 262, 303.

Pages 127-128. THE OFFICIAL CARAVANS: pp. 236, 281, 303.

Page 128. ANNUAL EXPENSES OF THESE: p. 274.

Pages 128-129. RE THE CARAVAN LEADER: pp. 275-277, 303.

Page 129. (Quotation) Comparison with Palmyrene caravans: p. 277. The columnar inscription is printed in *Syria*, xii (1931), pp. 105-107.

Pages 129-130. RE DALEELS: p. 277.

Page 130. RE THE COURIERS: p. 272.

Page 130. RE THE CAMEL DRIVERS: p. 262.

Pages 130-131. TRADE WITH THE BEDUIN: p. 303.

Part 2

Pages 131-132. THE GREAT ANNUAL CARAVANS:
     Van Linschoten, J. H., *The Voyage of . . . to the
     East Indies*, in Hakluyt, lxx and lxxi (1885), i,
     pp. 48-50; ii, p. 152.
     Tavernier, J. B., *Travels* (1684), ii, p. 60.
     Taylor, Major J., *Travels from England to India in
     the Year 1789* (1799), i, p. 299.
     (Footnote) Olivier, G. A., *Voyage dans l'Empire
     Othoman . . .* (1807), p. 433.

Page 132.   ORIGIN OF THE NAME *KAFILA*:
     Teixeira, Pedro (1902), p. 33.
     Van Linschoten (1885), *op. cit.* ii, p. 152.

Pages 132-133. DESCRIPTION OF *KAFILAS*:
     Van Linschoten (1885), i, 49-50.
     Valle, Pietro della (1665), p. 257.

Page 133.   THE GREAT DESERT ROUTE:
     Van Linschoten (1885), i, p. 48.
     F. Kettaneh and reference notes for Chapter VI,
     part 2.

Pages 133-134. HOMING PIGEONS AS CARAVAN COURIERS:
     Carruthers, D., in Hakluyt, lxiii (1929), p. xx (cf.
     Gaspar de Bernardino).

Page 134.   PRELIMINARY PREPARATIONS FOR THE ORGANIZING OF
    THE GREAT CARAVANS:
     Callier, C., article, "Les Couriers de Turquie et
     la caravane de Bagdad", in the *Bulletin de la
     Société de Géographie*, 11me Ser., No. 8 (1837),
     pp. 295-296.
     Rousseau, J. B. L. J., *Voyage de Bagdad à Alep*
     (1808), pp. 41 and 42.
     Olivier, G. A. (1807), *op. cit.* pp. 455-457.
     Tavernier (1684), *op. cit.* i, p. 45.

Pages 134-135. THE CARAVAN *BASHI* AND THE BARKANESS
     Olivier, G. (1807), pp. 455-457.
     Rousseau (1808), p. 40.
     Callier, C. (1837), p. 296

Page 135.   OFFICERS OF THE CARAVANS:
     Rousseau (1808), pp. 40-44.

Page 135.   THE CARAVAN ON THE MARCH:
     Olivier (1807), p. 457.

Rousseau (1808), p. 44.

Callier (1837), p. 297.

Page 136.   HALTS AND ENCAMPMENTS:

Rauwolff, Dr. L., "Itinerary", published in *Ray's Travels* (1693), i, p. 124.

Taylor (1799), i, p. 253.

Olivier (1807), pp. 456 and 457.

Callier (1837), pp. 297-298.

Page 137.   *GHRAZZU* EN ROUTE:

Olivier (1807), p. 456.

Callier (1837), p. 300.

Pages 137-138. *RE* THE AGAILS:

Taylor (1799), i, pp. 263, 276 and 278.

Burckhardt, J. L., *Notes on the Bedouins and Wahabys* (1831), ii, pp. 28 and 29.

Rousseau (1808), pp. 5 and 40-42.

Callier (1837), pp. 295 and 296.

Thielmann, Max von, *Journey in the Caucasus, Persia and Turkey in Asia* (1875), ii, pp. 154 and 176.

Pages 138-139. CARAVANS AND THE BEDUIN:

The Encyclopaedia of Islam, article on Arabia.

Taylor (1799), i, pp. 276 and 277.

Pages 139-142. *RE* THE GENERAL SAFETY OF THE GREAT DESERT ROUTE:

Van Linschoten (1885), i, p. 49.

Teixeira (1902), pp. 43, 105.

Valle, Pietro della (1665), pp. 254, 262, 274.

Tavernier (1684), pp. 61-64.

Beawes, quoted in Hakluyt, lxiii (1929), pp. 33 and 34.

Olivier (1807), pp. 456 and 457.

Pages 142-143. THE BASRA MERCHANT CARAVANS:

Plaisted, in Hakluyt, lxiii (1929), pp. 63, 98, 100, 103.

Eliot,   ,,   ,,   ,,   p. 119.

Beawes,   ,,   ,,   ,,   pp. 7 and 34.

Roberts,   ,,   ,,   ,,   p. 45.

Pages 143-144. THE CAMEL CARAVANS:

Plaisted, in Hakluyt, *ibid.* pp. 62 and 93.

Beawes,   ,,   ,,   pp. 34 and 38.

Eliot,   ,,   ,,   p. 119.

Page 144.   AVERAGE SIZES OF THE ANNUAL CARAVANS:
             Cf. the sizes of all the caravans specified in the
             diaries of trans-desert travellers.

Pages 144-145. Also, in particular:
             Beawes, in Hakluyt, *ibid.* p. 11.
             Plaisted,   „   „   pp. 68 and 80.
             Carmichael, „   „   p. 138.
             Olivier (1807), p. 439.
             Rousseau, J. B. L. J. (1808), p. 111.
             Also: See Carruthers, D., Introduction to Hakluyt,
             lxiii (1929), p. xxxiii.

Pages 145-146. SUPPLY CAMELS OF A CARAVAN:
             Teixeira (1902), p. 73.
             Tavernier (1684), i, pp. 47, 61.
             Beawes, in Hakluyt, *ibid.* p. 11.
             Carmichael, „   „   p. 138.

Pages 146-148. RATES OF CAMELS AND LENGTH OF CARAVAN JOURNEYS:
             Averages based on the diaries of trans-desert
             travellers; also upon conversations with desert
             travellers.
             Also: special studies as to the average rate of camel
             travel.
             Rennell, Major James, *A Treatise on the Com-
             parative Geography of Western Asia* (1831), i, pp.
             xlix, li and 1.
             Howel, Thos., *Voyage en retour de l'Inde* ... (1797),
             p. 112 and note.
             Taylor (1799), ii, pp. 317 and 318.

Part 3

Pages 148-149. SYRIAN TRADE WITH SOUTH ARABIA AND WITH MECCA:
             Lammens, H. (1924), pp. 269-301.

Pages 149-150. ARTICLES IN THE ALEPPO BAZAARS:
             Rauwolff, Dr. L., in *Ray's Travels*, (ed. of 1693)
             i, pp. 85 and 86, (ed. of 1738) ii, chap. viii (en-
             titled "Of the Great Trading and Dealing of
             the City of Aleppo . . ."), pp. 61-65.
             Teixeira (1902), pp. 118 and 119.
             Heyd, W., *Histoire du commerce du Levant au
             Moyen Âge* (1886), ii, p. 457.

Page 150.   ADDITIONAL IMPORTS INTO ALEPPO AND DAMASCUS IN
                   THE EIGHTEENTH CENTURY:
        Journal of a Deputation to the East (1855), p. 480.
        Browne, W. G. (1799), p. 386.
        Taylor (1799), i, pp. 268-270.

Page 150.   SYRIAN EXPORTS, SEVENTH TO SEVENTEENTH CENTURIES:
        el-Mukaddasi, *Description of Syria* (1892), pp. 69-
          70.
        Lammens, *op. cit., ibid.*
        Browne, W. G., *Travels in Africa, Egypt and Syria*
          (1799), p. 398.
        Heyd, W. (1886), ii, pp. 458 and 459.

Pages 150-151. SYRIAN EXPORTS IN THE SEVENTEENTH CENTURY:
        Letters of the East India Company, i, pp. 68, 71.
        Tavernier (1684), ii, p. 56.

Page 151.   EUROPEAN TRADING IN ALEPPO AND IN BASRA:
        The Venetian Calendar of State Papers, 6th July and
          19th Dec. 1613; 13th June 1615.
        Taylor (1799), i, p. 345.
        Letters of the East India Company, iv, pp. 248, 249,
          27th Nov. 1616, 27th June 1617; v, p. 316; vi,
          p. 280.
        Foster, Wm., *The English Factories in India*
          (1634–1636), pp. 153, 159, 168, 185, 194,
          255, 313.
        Van Linschoten (1885), ii, p. 159.
        Tavernier (1684), iii, p. 230.
        Harford, F. D., in *The Nineteenth Century*
          (1918), p. 109 (note 25): quoting a MS. of
          1583.

Page 151.   R*E* NEGOTIATIONS FOR THE PERSIAN SILK TRADE:
        Lammens, H. (1924), p. 301.
        Letters of the East India Company—
          II, pp. 98, 99 (19th August 1614).
          IV, pp. 246, 248, 249 (27th Nov. 1616).
          V, pp. 189, 278-283 (2nd April and 2nd June
            1617).
          VI, pp. 32-39 and 293 (note) (4th August 1617)
            (July-Aug. 1629).
        Venetian Calendar of State Papers—
          30th Sept. 1617 (p. 14).
          9th June 1619 (pp. 558-559)

16th Sept. 1619 (p. 11).
30th April 1622 (p. 311).
8th March 1624 (p. 234).
10th August 1626 (pp. 456, 502-503).
21st July 1628 (p. 181).
18th Feb. 1631 (p. 474).
6th Sept. 1632 (p. 3).
14th Feb. 1633 (p. 75).

Pages 151-152. THE INDIGO AND GALL-NUT TRADE:
Teixeira (1902), pp. 86, 118, 119.
Letters of the East India Company—
II, p. 214.
I, pp. 273-274.
III, p. 305.
V, pp. 81 (note), 280-281 and 288.
Foster, Wm., *The English Factories in India* (1634–1636), pp. 163-166 and 174-187.
de Thévenot (1674), ii, pp. 311-312, 329-330.

Pages 151-152. CARAVAN STATISTICS:
Venetian Calendar of State Papers—
10th May 1618 (p. 213).
15th April 1628 (p. 54).

Page 152.   EUROPEAN IMPORTS INTO THE NEAR EAST:
Venetian Calendar of State Papers—
5th Oct. 1635 (pp. 460, 461).
Letters of the East India Company, v, pp. 280, 281, 283 (note) and 288.
Teixeira, Pedro (1902), pp. 118 and 120.
Taylor (1799), i, pp. 268, 270, 345.
de Thévenot (1674), ii, pp. 311-312, 329-330.

Pages 152-153. TRADE WITH THE BEDUIN :
Lammens, H. (1924), *ibid.*
Tavernier (1684), p. 61.
Taylor (1799), i, pp. 275-276.
Callier (1837), p. 296.

Part 4

Pages 153-154. TOLLS AND CUSTOMS DUES ON THE NORTHERN ROUTE:
Teixeira (1902), pp. 54 and 55.
Tavernier (1684), p. 71.
Plaisted, in Hakluyt, lxiii (1929), p. 124.

24

Page 154.   TOLLS AT ALEPPO, BASRA, BIREJIK AND ANNA:
                 Letters of the East India Company, vi, p. 293
                   (note).
                 Tavernier (1684), ii, pp. 67 and 71.
                 Teixeira (1902), p. 85.
                 Valle, P. della (1665), pp. 266-269.
                 Plaisted, in Hakluyt, *op. cit.* pp. 89 and 128.

Pages 154-155.   TRIBUTE-TOLLS ALONG THE GREAT DESERT ROUTE:
                 Valle, P. della (1665), pp. 257, 258, 266, 267, 269-
                   271.
                 Teixeira (1902), p. 103.
                 Tavernier (1684), p. 111.

Pages 155-156.   TRIBUTES EXACTED BY BEDUIN:
                 Valle, P. della (1665), pp. 257, 258.
                 Tavernier (1684), i, pp. 61-64, ii, p. 1.

Page 156.   TRIBUTES EXACTED BY BEDUIN IN THE EIGHTEENTH
                 CENTURY:
                 Capper, J., *Observations on the Passage to India*
                   (1783), p. 63.
                 Taylor (1799), i, pp. 257, 258.

                              Part 5

Pages 156-158.   MODERN MERCHANT CARAVANS:
                 Based upon conversations with *Hajji* Selim
                   Sawwaf, of Damascus, and Professor Crawford,
                   of the American University of Beyrout, and
                   Mr Francis Kettaneh, of Beyrout.
                 Also: *The Encyclopaedia of Islam*, article "Arabia".
                 Reference for the footnote *re* the *Akhwan* (or
                   Ikhwan).
                 Philby, H. St. J. B. (1930), p. 226.

Page 158.   MODERN USE OF THE *AKHWAN* AND THE AGAILS:
                 Messrs Norman Nairn and Francis Kettaneh.

                            CHAPTER V

                              Part 1

Pages 159-161.   THE FOUR PRINCIPAL ROUTES:
                 Beawes, in Hakluyt, lxiii (1929), pp. 5-6.
                 Plaisted,   „   „   „   p. 102.

Tavernier (1684), i, pp. 2 and 60; ii, pp. 43 and
66-77.

Howel, T. (1797), pp. 121-128.

Taylor, Major J., i, pp. 1 and 6, ii, pp. 314-316 and
319.

See also: Reference notes for Chapter II, part 2,
pages 76-77; reference notes for Chapter VIII,
part 3, pages 249-250.

(Page 160, footnote). Taylor (1799), ii, p. 335.

Eliot, in Hakluyt, lxiii (1929), p. 126.

Pages 161-163. THE NORTHERN ROUTE:

Beawes, in Hakluyt, *ibid.* p. 17.

Eliot, ,, ,, pp. 122-126.

Carmichael, ,, ,, p. 177.

La Boullaye-le-Gouz, *Voyages et observations en
Syrie et en Perse* (1653), p. 264.

Tavernier (1684), ii, p. 67; iii, pp. 103 and 108.

Thévenot, J. de (1674), ii, p. 74.

Taylor (1799), ii, pp. 313, 322, 323 and 328-333.

(Page 161, footnote). Tavernier (1676), i, p. 162
(*re* the country between Aleppo and Birejik).

Mosul to Baghdad:

Thompson, R. C., *Tavernier's Travels in Mesopotamia* (1910), p. 147.

Young, Sir H., *The Independent Arab* (1933), pp.
25 and 23-32.

Pages 163-164. THE EUPHRATES-FELLUJA RIVER TRIP: THE PIONEERS OF
THE EAST INDIA COMPANY:

Gazetteer of the Persian Gulf, i, pp. 1616-1620.

Also: reference notes for Par. 17, Chapter III, part 1.

Pages 164-166. RE BIREJIK AND RIVER CRAFT:

The Encyclopaedia of Islam, article "Birejik".

Cumont, F., *Études syriennes* (1917), pp. 120, 130-
132 and 250.

La Boullaye-le-Gouz (1653), pp. 333-334.

Chesney, F. R., *Narrative of the Euphrates Expedition* (1868), pp. 181-182 and 416.

Also *ibid.* p. 77, *re* boat-building at Hit.

Cameron, V. L., *Our Future Highway* (1880), ii,
pp. 45 and 49-51.

Pages 166-167. DIFFICULTIES AND DANGERS OF RIVER TRAVEL:

Rauwolff, Dr. L., account of his river journey

printed in *Mr. Ray's Travels* (1738), ii, pp. 70-
138.

Thévenot, J. de (1674), ii, p. 76.

Tavernier (1684), ii, p. 59.

Griffiths, J., *Travels in Europe, Asia Minor and Arabia* (1805), p. 383.

Chesney, Col. F. R. (1868), pp. 63, 81, 93 and 226.

Also: see the diary of—

Howel, Dr. T. (1797), pp. 22-112.

Heude, Wm., *A Voyage up the Persian Gulf . . .* (1819), pp. 52-80, especially p. 69.

Pages 167-168. RIVER ROUTES FROM BAGHDAD TO BASRA:

Purchas, iii, voyage of Joseph Salbancke and Robert Covert (in 1609).

Teixeira (1902), pp. 32-33.

Beawes, Plaisted and Eliot in Hakluyt, lxiii (1929), pp. 25, 64, 120-121, and 127-128.

Taylor (1799), ii, pp. 324, 325, 336, 340 and (especially) p. 337.

Howel (1797), pp. 25, 26 and 35.

Page 168.   FURTHER DANGERS OF RIVER TRAVEL:

See references given for pages 166-167, for the journeys of Howel and Heude.

Also: Taylor (1799), i, pp. 299-314.

The Times, London, 7th March 1934.

Pages 168-169. THE LITTLE DESERT ROUTE:

Eliot, in Hakluyt, lxiii (1929), p. 120.

Tavernier (1684), iii, pp. 109-110.

Callier, C., article in the *Bulletin de la Société de Géographie*, 11me Sér., No. 8 (1837), p. 294.

Pages 170-171. SHORTER VARIATION OF THE LITTLE DESERT ROUTE:

See reference notes for the *Darb-es-Sa'i*, in para. 14, part 3, Chapter VIII.

Also: Manrique, Fray S., *Travels* (1629-1643) (1927), pp. 368-381.

Pages 171-172. THE GREAT DESERT ROUTE:

Beawes, in Hakluyt, lxiii (1929), pp. 25-26 and 29.

Teixeira (1902), p. 33.

Howel, T. (1797), p. 24.

Capper, J., *Observations on the Passage to India* (1783), pp. xix and xx.

Also: *Re* the mileage of the Route see Carruthers, D.,

Beawes, and Plaisted in Hakluyt, lxiii (1929),
pp. xxx, 32, 33 and 96.
Also: Reference notes for Chapter VI.

Page 172. THE *RAFEEK* SYSTEM:
Capper, J. (1783), p. 58.
Beawes, in Hakluyt, *ibid.* p. 13.
Taylor, J. (1799), i, p. 277.
Griffiths, J. (1805), pp. 349 and 351.
Bell, G. L., *Letters* (1927), i, p. 346.
Carruthers, D., *Arabian Adventure* (1937), p. 47.

Pages 173-174. ADVANTAGES OF THE OPEN DESERT:
Tavernier (1676), i, p. 286; (1684), iii, pp.
109-110.
Teixeira (1902), p. 56.
Venetian Calendar of State Papers, No. 690,
p. 503.

Part 2

Pages 174-175. VARIOUS WAYS OF MAKING THE DESERT CROSSING:
Tenreiro, see Wilson, Sir A. T., *Early Spanish
and Portuguese Travellers in Persia* (1927), pp.
19-21.
Teixeira (1902), p. 33.
Tavernier (1684), iii, p. 110.
Travel with a dispatch-bearer:
Taylor (1799), ii, pp. 293 and 325-326.
Heude (1819), p. 189.
Eliot, in Hakluyt, lxiii (1929), p. 126.

Pages 175-176. THE HIRING OF A PRIVATE CARAVAN:
Taylor (1799), i, pp. 226, 293, 295, and ii, p. 67,
ii, 119 (*re* Taylor's personal expenses).

Page 176. THE NECESSITY OF MAKING A CONTRACT WITH EVERY
CARAVAN *BASHI*:
Beawes, in Hakluyt, *ibid.* p. 7.
Plaisted,   „   „   p. 93.
Capper (1783), p. 58.

Pages 176-179. CONTRACT BETWEEN COLONEL CAPPER AND SHAYKH
SULEIMAN, OCTOBER 1778:
(Original text) extracted from Capper (1783), pp.
55-58.
Also: *ibid.* pp. 58, 80 and 85.

Page 179.   BARON THIELMANN'S CONTRACT:
                  Thielmann, M. von, *Journey in the Caucasus, Persia,
                       and Turkey in Asia* (1875), ii, pp. 173 and 175.

Pages 180-181. NECESSITY OF A FIRST-RATE CARAVAN *BASHI*:
                  Beawes, in Hakluyt, *ibid.* pp. 7 and 13.
                  Griffiths (1805), pp. 320 and 386-388.
                  Also: See reference notes for Chapter VI, part 3,
                       B (1).

Pages 181-182. EXPENSES AND SUPPLIES:
                  Teixeira (1902), p. 33.
                  Roberts, in Hakluyt, lxiii (1929), p. 46.
                  Beawes,   „   „   „   pp. 8 and 9.
                  Plaisted,   „   „   „   pp. 63, 65-67
                                                          and 117-118.

                  Carmichael, „   „   „   p. 176.
                  Eliot,   „   „   „   pp. 127-128.
                  Capper (1783), p. 67.
                  Taylor (1799), i, pp. 226, 241-242 and 250; ii, pp.
                       67, 70, 119-120, 322-323, 325 and 328.
                  Griffiths (1805), p. 352.

Pages 182-184. MOHAFFAS:
                  Teixeira (1902), p. 73.
                  Beawes, in Hakluyt, *ibid.* p. 12, also pp. 7, 9 (note)
                                                          and 10.
                  Roberts,   „   „   pp. 46 and 47.
                  Plaisted,   „   „   pp. 67 and 119.
                  Taylor (1799), i, pp. 226 and 250.
                  Griffiths (1805), p. 352.

Page 184.   RELATIVE COSTS OF CAMELS AND HORSES:
                  Beawes, in Hakluyt, *ibid.* pp. 8 and 11.
                  Carmichael, „   „   p. 176.
                  Thielmann (1875), ii, pp. 175-176.

Pages 184-186. COSTUME AND WEAPONS:
                  Plaisted, in Hakluyt, *ibid.* pp. 63 and 118.
                  Capper (1783), p. 2.
                  Taylor (1799), i, pp. 316 and 317.
                  (Page 186). The incident happened to M. Borel de
                       Bourg. See Capper (1783), p. 102.

Page 187.   THE BLUNTS AS TRAVELLERS:
                  Blunt, Lady Anne (1879), i, pp. 39, 40, 57-66 and
                       72-88.

CHAPTER VI

Part 1

Page 189.   AN IMAGINARY PRIVATE CARAVAN:
             Taylor (1799), i, pp. 226 and 293.
Pages 189-190. POWERS OF THE CARAVAN *BASHI*:
             Beawes, in Hakluyt, lxiii (1929), pp. 7 and 13.
             Also: Reference notes for Chapter IV, part 1, para.
             4; Chapter IV, part 2, para. 8.
Pages 190-191: DAILY ROUTINE OF TRAVEL:
             Beawes, in Hakluyt, *ibid.* pp. 10, 19 and 27.
             Plaisted,   „   „   pp. 69 and 94-96.
             Carmichael, „   „   pp. 138-139.
             Griffiths (1805), p. 356-357.
Pages 191-192. FOOD ON THE DESERT:
             Teixeira (1902), pp. 40 and 44.
             Valle, Pietro della (1665), pp. 269-270.
             Tavernier (1684), i, p. 62.
             Capper (1783), pp. 67-68.
             Taylor (1799), i, pp. 237, 244, 286 and 287.
             Griffiths (1805), p. 367.
             Chesney, F. R. (1868), p. 59.
Page 192.   HUNTING ON THE DESERT:
             Beawes, in Hakluyt, *ibid.* p. 15.
             Plaisted,   „   „   p. 92.
             Taylor (1799), i, p. 248.
             Description of a Sword Dance—
             Taylor (1799), i, pp. 241 and 242.

                         Part 2

Pages 193-205. LANDMARKS AND ITINERARY:
             Maps of the Great Desert Route—
             Major James Rennell (1809).
             Ritter and Kiepert (1854).
             Carruthers, D., printed in the *Geographical Journal*,
             lii, 3 (1918), p. 204, and in Hakluyt, lxiii (1929),
             p. 196.
             SEBKHA JEBBUL:
             References in Hakluyt, lxiii (1929), in the Journals

of Four Travellers, 1745–51 (edited by D. Carruthers), pp. 9 n., 135 n. and 136 n.

SFIRA and HIKLA:

Hakluyt, lxiii, *ibid.* pp. 9, 89 n., 135 n., 136 n. and 142 n.

Jebel Shubait,

Jebel el-Hass, and

Jebel Bishri: pp. 137 n.-139, 89 n., 145 n. and 84 n.

TAIYIBA:

Tavernier (1684), p. 110.

Teixeira (1902), pp. 102–103.

Valle, della (1665), p. 269.

Coote, Sir E., in the *Journal of the R.G.S.*, xxx (1860), p. 208.

Capper (1783), pp. 64 and 65 (seen only in the distance, but not visited).

Carré (1699), pp. 248–252.

Olivier (1807), pp. 466–467.

Rousseau (1808), pp. 155–156.

Musil, *Palmyrena*, pp. 76–77.

Also: References in Hakluyt, lxiii, pp. xx, xxi, xxvi, xxviii, xxx, 6, 13-14, 90, 91, 97, 85-88, 140 and 142-143.

SUKHNA:

Ibn Battuta (1929), p. 304.

Teixeira (1902), pp. 100 and 101.

References in Hakluyt, lxiii, pp. xxxiv, 14, 141 n. and 142.

Shrine of a Moslem *Hajji*:

Coote, Sir E., *op. cit.* p. 208.

AIN EL-KOM:

Coote, Sir E., *ibid.* p. 209.

References in Hakluyt, lxiii, pp. 15, 17, 32, 86 n., 133, 138 n., 139 n., 140-141.

KASR EL-HAIR:

Coote, Sir E., *ibid.* p. 207.

MM. Gabriel and Seyrig in *Syria*, viii (1927), pp. 304-322; xii (1931), pp. 316-318; xiii (1932), pp. 317-320.

References in Hakluyt, lxiii, pp. 15 n., 86-87 (notes), 133, 140 n., 143-145.

JUBB EL-GHANAM (and the neighbouring region):
  References in Hakluyt, lxiii, pp. 16 n., 83 n., 84 n.,
    148, and especially p. 146 n.
  Rennell, Major J., map of 1809.
  Teixeira (1902), pp. 92-94.
WADI HAURAN:
  References in Hakluyt, lxiii, pp. 91 and 152 (notes).
ANNA:
  Idrisi (1836), ii, p. 145.
  Ibn Battuta (1929), p. 304.
  Teixeira (1902), pp. 81, 85 and 87.
  Olivier (1807), p. 448.
  Journal of a Deputation to the East (1855), ii, p. 666.
  Bell, G. (1911), pp. 92-95.
  References in Hakluyt, lxiii, pp. 6, 120 and 156 n.
  The Encyclopaedia of Islam, article on Anna.
HIT:
  Teixeira (1902), p. 55.
  Olivier (1807), p. 448.
  References in Hakluyt, lxiii, pp. 6, 19, 20 and 156 n.
  Idrisi (1836), ii, p. 144.
  The Encyclopaedia of Islam, article on Hit.
KUBAISA and AIN EL-ARNAB:
  Taylor (1799), i, pp. 235-236.
  References in Hakluyt, lxiii, pp. 7, 19, 20, 25, 29,
    32, 79, 102, 103, 120, 126, 155-156.
ABU KIR and THUMAIL:
  References in Hakluyt, lxiii, pp. 91 and 157 n.
RAHHALIYA and SHITTAT:
  Capper (1783), pp. 72, 73 and 77.
  Taylor (1799), i, p. 240.
  Bell, G. L. (1911), p. 139.
  References in Hakluyt, xxxi, lxiii, 21 n., 78 n. and
    158 n.
UKHAIDIR:
  Tavernier (1684), i, p. 62.
  Bell, G. L. (1911), pp. 140 and 144.
  Carmichael, in Hakluyt, lxiii, pp. 133 and 158-164.
  See also in Hakluyt, *ibid.* pp. 21 n., 44, 76-77.
UMM EL-KURUN and the *Darb es-Sitt Zubayda*:
  References in Hakluyt, lxiii, notes on pp. 28, 75
    and 169.

MESHED ALI:

Teixeira (1902), pp. 46 and 48.

Taylor (1799), i, p. 247.

Griffiths (1805), p. 371.

The Encyclopaedia of Islam, article on Kufa.

References in Hakluyt, lxiii, pp. xix, xxi, 46, 75-76, 99, 165 and 167.

Also, for Beawes' visit, *ibid.* pp. 21-24 and 27.

ZEBEIR:

References in Hakluyt, lxiii, notes on pp. 32 and 174.

Beawes, in Hakluyt, *ibid.* p. 32: remark that the "passage" from Meshed Ali to Zebeir was "in all respects the worst part of all the journey".

Pages 203-205. NATURE OF THE PASSAGE OVER THE "GREAT SYRIAN DESERT":

Plaisted, in Hakluyt, lxiii, pp. 90-92 and 100-102.

See also references of Beawes and Carmichael, Hakluyt, *ibid.* pp. 11-12, 26, 139, 145 and 148.

Part 3

Pages 205-209. (A) TRIALS OF THE DESERT JOURNEY:

Beawes, in Hakluyt, lxiii, p. 7 (quotation).

Plaisted,   „   „   p. 62.

Teixeira (1902), p. 36.

Valle, della (1665), p. 260.

Desert Winds:

P. della Valle (1665), p. 260.

Griffiths (1805), p. 364.

Statements of Travellers in Hakluyt, lxiii, pp. 28 and 67.

Intense Heat:

Teixeira (1902), p. 36.

Griffiths (1805), pp. 366-384.

Extreme Cold, Snow and Rain:

Teixeira (1902), p. 108.

Taylor (1799), i. pp. 243 and 292-293.

Bell, G. L. (1927), i. p. 266.

Carmichael, in Hakluyt, lxiii, pp. 168-169 and 136.

Water Problems:

Griffiths (1805), pp. 360 and 370-378.

Taylor (1799), ii, pp. 337-338.

Bell, G. L. (1927), i, pp. 274-275.

Statements of Travellers in Hakluyt, lxiii, pp. 10 (note 2), 77, 85, 90, 91, 119 and 128.

Tavernier (1684), iii, p. 112.

Pages 209-217. (B) DANGERS FROM THE ARABS:

    (1) Dishonest Caravan *Bashis* and Cameleers [1]—

        Teixeira (1902), pp. 39, 80, 107-108.

        Valle, della (1665), pp. 259, 264 and 267.

        Plaisted, in Hakluyt, *ibid.* pp. 70-73 and 98-100.

      A Contrary Opinion—

        Capper (1783), p. 85.

      Also: Plaisted, in Hakluyt, *ibid.* pp. 98 and 99, *re* "Seid Talub".

    (2) Dangers to Caravans: arguments for and against the safety of the desert routes [1]—

        Teixeira (1902), pp. 43, 89 and 111.

        Valle, della (1665), pp. 265 and 267-268.

        Tavernier (1684), iii, p. 110.

        Plaisted, in Hakluyt, *ibid.* p. 88.

        Taylor (1799), i, pp. 254-256 and 277.

        Griffiths (1805), pp. 349 and 364.

        Rousseau (1808), p. 93.

        Huntington (1911), pp. 354 and 356.

        Fowle, T. C. (1916), p. 58.

  (Page 212). The Safe Journey of a Small Caravan—

    Teixeira (1902), p. 90.

  (Pages 214-215). Modern Incident in Trans-Jordan: told to the writer by Major Smith, O.C. of the Trans-Jordan Police Force.

  (Page 215). Anecdote report by Baron Thielmann (1875), ii, p. 173.

  (Page 216). Incident: Capper (1783), pp. 63-64 (encounter with Shaykh Fadil's tribe).

Pages 217-218. (C) ADVICE TO TRAVELLERS:

    Teixeira (1902), p. 101.

    Taylor (1799), i, pp. 315-316, 293; ii, p. 343.

    Plaisted, in Hakluyt, *ibid.* pp. 63, 70, 102 and 118.

---

[1] See also preceding reference notes on the *Rafeek* System, page 172, Chapter V, part 1.

CHAPTER VII

Part 1

Page 219. *Re* The Founding of the Islamic Pilgrimage:

The Encyclopaedia of Islam, article on the Ha'j ("el-Hadjdj").

G.-Demombynes, Le Pèlerinage à la Mekke (1923), pp. 313, 323, 324.

Pages 219-220. Mecca and Medina, "Pilgrimage" and "Visitation":

The Koran (Rodwell's Translation, 1929), p. 395.

Burton, R. F., Personal Narrative of a Pilgrimage to Al-Madinah and Meccah (1893), appendix on the Hajj Ceremonies (passim), and especially ii, pp. 286, 304, 305. Also: ii, appendices I and II, pp. 279-326 passim.

Pages 220-221. Obligation of the Hajj defined:

The Encyclopaedia of Islam, "el-Hadjdj".

G.-Demombynes, Le Pèlerinage à la Mekke, op. cit. pp. 312, 314, 316, 318.

Ibn Gubayr (1906), p. 171.

Page 221. Preparations for the Pilgrimage and its Results:

The Encyclopaedia of Islam, op. cit.

G.-Demombynes, Le Pèlerinage à la Mekke, pp. 155-156.

Ibn Battuta, Travels (1929).

The Arabian Nights' Entertainments, pp. 435-437.

Page 222. The Four Hajj Centres and the Annual Pilgrimages:

Teixeira (1902), p. 122.

Varthema, L., The Travels of . . . (1863), p. 36.

Sanderson, J., The Travels of . . . in the Levant (1931), pp. 45 and 46.

de Thévenot (1674), ii, pp. 321 and 322.

Doughty (1921), p. 57.

Lammens, H., Le Berceau de l'Islam (1914), p. 169.

Castiau, M., En Syrie: Le long du chemin des Pèlerins . . . (1902), p. 21.

Margoliouth, D. S., Mohammedanism (1928), pp. 119 and 122.

Pages 222-223. THE EASTERN *HAJJ* ROUTE:

> Ibn Gúbayr (1906), pp. 167-193.
> Abulfeda (1848), ii, p. 131.
> Ibn Battuta (1929), pp. 78-85.
> Coote, Sir Eyre (1860), in the *Journal of the R.G.S.*, xxx (1860), p. 206.
> Leachman, G. E., in the *Geographical Journal*, xxxvii (1911), p. 267.
> Le Strange (1905), p. 11.
>> (*N.B.*—Formerly Fayd was the principal pilgrim centre and station in Nejd.)
> de Thévenot (1674), ii, p. 322.

Pages 223-224. THE WESTERN *HAJJ* ROUTE:

> Abulfeda (1848), ii, pp. 118-128.
> Idrisi (1836), i, p. 359.
> Ibn Battuta (1929), pp. 72-75.
> Varthema (1863), p. 18.
> Burckhardt, J. L., *Travels in Syria and the Holy Land* (1822), appendix III, pp. 656-661.
> Fridolin, in *Revue des Deux Mondes*, vi (1854), p. 97.
> Castiau (1902), pp. 32-59.
> Doughty (1933), i, pp. 1-95.
> Musil, *Arabia Deserta*, p. 518.
> Dussaud, R., *Topographie Historique de la Syrie antique et médiévale* (1927), p. 340.
> And conversation with *Hajji* Selim Sawwaf.

Page 225.   THE *DARB EL-HAJJ*—ITS APPEARANCE:

> Castiau (1902), p. 38.
> Doughty (1933), i, pp. 56-57.
> Bell, G. (1927), i, p. 71.
> Personal observation of the writer.

Page 225.   For Ibn Jubair's description of the Eastern *Hajj* see Ibn Gúbayr (1906), pp. 167-193.

Part 2

Pages 225-226. OFFICERS OF THE *HAJJ*:

> Doughty (1933), i, pp. 9 and 69.
> *Hajji* Selim Sawwaf.

Page 226.   A PARTICULAR *HAJJ* CARAVAN:

> Maundrell, H., "A Compendium of a Journey

from Aleppo to Jerusalem and a Journey to
Palmyra" (1699), pp. 116 and 117.

Pages 226-227. THE MAHMAL:

Maundrell (1699), *op. cit.* p. 117.

Doughty (1933), i, pp. 61 and 62.

G.-Demombynes (1923) (*Pèlerinage à la Mekke*),
pp. 158-161.

Hughes' *Dictionary of Islam*, article on the "Mahmal".

The Rualla captured and have possessed,
since 1793, the sole remaining Beduin *Markab*,
the *Ark* or tribal palanquin decorated with
black ostrich feathers. See Raswan, C. (1935),
pp. 75-78 and 110, and illustration opposite
p. 82.

Pages 227-228. THE *HAJJ* FUND:

Doughty (1933), i, pp. 4 and 10.

Hajji Selim Sawwaf.

Page 228.   PROTECTION AGAINST THE BEDUIN:

Varthema (1863), pp. 19-21 and 35.

Burckhardt, J. L., *Notes on the Bedouins and
Wahabys* (1831), i, p. 5, and ii, p. 3.

G.-Demombynes (1923), p. 313 (note 1) *op. cit.*

Lammens, H., *La Mecque à la veille de l'Hégire*
(1924), p. 276.

Doughty (1933), i, pp. 10 and 11.

Pages 228–229. MINIMUM FARE TO MECCA:

Hajji Selim Sawwaf.

Camel Coaches:

Ibid.

Doughty (1933), i, p. 65.

Page 229.   *RE* THE MUKOWAMS:

Hajji Selim Sawwaf.

de Thevenot (1674), ii, pp. 321 and 322.

Doughty (1933), i, p. 3.

Pages 229-230. SIZE OF THE *HAJJ* CARAVANS:

Varthema (1863), p. 16.

Manrique, Fray S., *Travels*, 1629-1643, in Hakluyt,
lxi, lxii (1927), pp. 379 and 380.

Journal of a Deputation to the East (1855), p. 480.

Castiau (1902), p. 20.

Doughty (1933), i, pp. 7, 57 and 58.

Pages 230–231. LENGTH OF THE PILGRIMAGE ROUND TRIP:
Hajji Selim Sawwaf.
Varthema (1863), p. 18.
Doughty (1933), i, p. 57.
Koran (1929), p. 359.
Burton (1893), ii, pp. 289–292.

Pages 231–232. THE HAJJ EN ROUTE:
Hajji Selim Sawwaf.
Doughty (1933), pp. 60–62, 65 and 72.
Burton (1893), ii, p. 65.
Rennell, J., A Treatise on the Comparative Geography
of Western Asia (1831), i, pp. xlix, li
Varthema (1863), p. 18.

Pages 232–233. HALTS OF THE HAJJ CARAVANS:
Hajji Selim Sawwaf.
Doughty (1933), i, pp. 19, 71 and 86.
The Koran (1929), p. 359 (note 2).

Page 233. EUROPEAN HAJJIS:
Varthema (1863), p. xxvii.
Burton (1893), ii, appendices IV, V and VI, pp.
333–402, on Ludovicus Vertomannus, Joseph
Pitts and Giovanni Finati.

Pages 233–234. THE HAJJ IN THE TWENTIETH CENTURY:
Leachman, G. E., in the Geographical Journal,
xxxvii (March 1911), p. 272.
The Iraq Report (1920–1931), pp. 73, 74.
Laborde, L. de, Journey through Arabia Petraea to
Mount Sinai (1838), p. xxviii, and map.
Hajji Selim Sawwaf.

Page 234. SPIRITUAL CHARACTER OF THE HAJJ:
Hajji Selim Sawwaf.
Burton (1893), ii, appendix I on the Hajj, p. 279.
The Encyclopaedia of Islam, article on the Hajj.

CHAPTER VIII

Part 1

Pages 235–236. ANTECEDENTS OF THE SARACEN POSTAL SYSTEMS:
Gray, G. B., article in the Cambridge Ancient
History, iv, chap. vii, especially p. 193.

Rostovtzeff, M., article in the *Cambridge Ancient History*, vii, chap. V, pp. 173-176; and viii, chap. XX, p. 663.

The Encyclopaedia of Islam, article on the *Barid*.

Gaudefroy-Demombynes, *La Syrie à l'époque des Mamelouks* (1923), p. 241 (notes 1, 2); and xx.

Pages 236-237. PERPETUATION OF THE BYZANTINE AND SASANIAN POSTAL SYSTEMS:

    el-Mukaddasi, *Description of Syria* (1892), p. 75.

    Le Strange, G., *Lands of the Eastern Caliphate* (1905), i, p. 11.

    G.-Demombynes', *La Syrie . . . des Mamelouks*, p. 239 (and note 4).

        N.B.—G.-Demombynes' *La Syrie . . . des Mamelouks* supplements Le Strange's work on Syria and Palestine. Le Strange's latest contemporary sources were Abulfeda and Ibn Battuta; G.-Demombynes used el-Omari and el-Kalkashandi as well.

    The Encyclopaedia of Islam, op. cit.

Page 237.   THE *BERID* IN THE NINTH CENTURY:

    Ibn Khordadbeh, "Le Livre des Routes et Provinces", translated by C. B. de Meynard, in *Le Journal Asiatique* (1865), i, pp. 11, 12 and 501-512.

Page 238.   POST ROADS OF THE ABBASID PERIOD:

    Le Strange (1905), pp. 9 and 11.

Pages 238-239. THE *BERID*, ELEVENTH–THIRTEENTH CENTURIES:

    Quatremère's *el-Makrizi* (1842), ii, pp. 88 and 89.

    The Encyclopaedia of Islam, article on the *Barid*.

Pages 239-240. THE *BERID* OF THE MAMLUK SULTANS:

    G.-Demombynes, *La Syrie . . . des Mamelouks*, pp. xxi, 239, 240, 241 and notes.

    Quatremère's *el-Makrizi* (1842), ii, pp. 87-93, especially pp. 89 and 90.

    The Encyclopaedia of Islam, article on the *Barid*.

Page 240.   POSTAL ROUTES, AND THE IMPERIAL POSTAL SCHEDULES OF THE MAMLUK PERIOD:

    G.-Demombynes, *La Syrie . . . des Mamelouks*, pp. 141, 183, 241 (note), 244 and 245 (note 9).

    Quatremère's *el-Makrizi* (1842), ii, pp. 91 and 92.

    Le Strange, G., *Palestine under the Moslems* (1890), p. 545. Cf. the Diary of Ibn Jubair.

Pages 240-241. IMPORTANCE OF THE *BERID*:
Quatremère's *el-Makrizi* (1842), ii, pp. 87 and 88.
The Encyclopaedia of Islam, op. cit.

Part 2

Page 241.   THE END OF THE MAMLUK *BERID*:
Quatremère's *el-Makrizi* (1842), ii, p. 89.

Pages 241-242. THE LOCAL COURIER SYSTEM UNDER THE OTTOMANS:
Callier, C., *Les Couriers de Turquie et la caravane de Bagdad* (1837), pp. 290-293.

Pages 242-244. THE TATARS OF THE OTTOMAN EMPIRE:
Howel, Thos., *Voyage en retour de l'Inde* (1797), pp. 43 and 115.
Callier, C. (1837), *op. cit.* pp. 289 and 290.

Page 244.   ORIGIN OF THE PIGEON POST:
G-Demombynes, *La Syrie . . . des Mamelouks*, p. 183, and Appendix III, pp. 250 and 251.

Pages 244-245. THE PIGEON POST IN THE OTTOMAN PERIOD:
Ibn Battuta, *Travels in Asia and Africa*, 1325–1354, translated by H. A. R. Gibb (1929), p. 63.
Van Linschoten, J. H., *The Voyage of . . . to the East Indies* (1885), i, pp. 50 and 51.
Diary of Thomas Dallam, in Hakluyt, lxxxvii, (1893), p. 32.
Tavernier (1684), ii, p. 55.
Carruthers (1929), Hakluyt, lxiii, pp. xx-xxi.
Harford, F. D., article in *The Nineteenth Century*, July (1918), p. 112.

Page 245.   THE END OF THE PIGEON POST:
Teonge, Rev. Henry, *Diary of* (1676; 1825), p. 113 (note).
Callier, C. (1837), p. 294.

Part 3

Pages 245-246. EUROPEAN TRANS-DESERT COMMUNICATIONS:
Teixeira (1902), p. 32 (and note).
Harford, F. D. (1918), *op. cit.* pp. 109-110—quoting the Finch MSS.

Pages 246-247. COURIERS OF THE EAST INDIA COMPANY. INAUGURATION OF A TRANS-DESERT SERVICE:
Foster and Danvers, *Letters of the East India Com-*

pany, iv, p. 291 (10th March 1615); v, pp. 50,
53 (17th Jan. and 26th Nov. 1616); v, pp. 188,
278, 284-286 (1st, 2nd and 27th June 1617); vi,
p. 43, letter No. 520.

Foster and Sainsbury, *Court Minutes of the E.I.C.*,
p. 148 (27th Jan. 1636), p. 260 (26th April 1637).

Pages 247-248. (A) REGULAR DESPATCHING OF THE "DOUBLE CON-
VEYANCE":

Foster and Danvers, *Letters of the East India Company*, vi, pp. 31, 37, 45, 158 (and note), 169 and
171 (1617 and 1618).

English Factories in India, pp. 176, 179 and 279
(1634–1636).

Venetian Calendar of State Papers, 21st Jan. 1632
(p. 64).

(B) TROUBLE CAUSED BY PORTUGUESE AGENTS, AND
RESULTING CHANGE OF ROUTE:

Foster and Danvers, *Letters of the East India Company*, v, pp. 278, 279 (2nd April and 2nd June
1617).

English Factories in India, op. cit. pp. 185 and 186.

(C) COMPLAINTS *Re* DELAYS IN THE COURIER SERVICE:

Letters of the East India Company, v, pp. 188, 285;
vi, pp. 31, 45, 158 (note), 169, 171.

Foster, *English Factories in India*, p. 245.

Cf. despatches sent from Ispahan on 2nd June and
4th August, 1617, received at the same time in
London: on 13th May 1618.

Page 248.   UNSETTLED CONDITION OF THE OTTOMAN EMPIRE,
DANGER TO TRAVELLERS:

Venetian Calendar of State Papers, 17th Sept. 1607
(p. 33); 2nd Oct. 1627 (p. 400).

Foster and Danvers, *Letters of the East India Company*, i, pp. 274-276, 286, 298, 302, 308 (3rd
August, 28th Oct. and 9th Nov. 1613).

Tavernier (1684), iii, p. 112.

Pages 248-249. RELATIVE SAFETY OF THE DESERT ROUTES:

Venetian Calendar of State Papers, 10th August
1626, p. 503.

Carruthers, Hakluyt, lxiii (1929), p. xxxii.

Pages 249-250. ROUTES TO INDIA VIA SUEZ AND BASRA—COM-
PARISONS:

Irwin, E., *A Series of Adventures in the Course of a Voyage up the Red Sea* . . . (1780), pp. 349, 352.

Capper (1783), pp. vii, viii and xii.

Taylor (1795), pp. 12, 46-48.

Taylor (1799), ii, pp. 6, 7 and 16.

Page 250, Footnote. Record Sailing Ship Voyages:

Taylor (1799), ii, pp. 10 and 11.

Pages 250-251. COLONEL CAPPER'S SUGGESTIONS:

Capper (1783), pp. xi, xix and xx, 41 and 42.

Pages 251-252. MAJOR TAYLOR'S PLAN:

Taylor (1795), *passim*; and especially pp. 2, 41, 44, 45.

Taylor (1799), ii, pp. 1-62, and especially pp. 16, 20-22 and 31-40.

Insistence upon native Couriers:

Taylor (1799), i, p. 294.

Pages 252-253. ADOPTION OF THE MARQUIS WELLESLEY'S PLAN:

Wellesley's Despatches (1836), ii, pp. 248, 394, 581; iv, p. 131.

Chesney (1868), pp. 330, 358.

Gazetteer of the Persian Gulf, i, p. 2439.

Pages 253-254. RECOMMENDATIONS (REPORT) OF SAMUEL MANESTY:

India Office (Home Series), Miscellaneous, 470.

Letter Book, 1799-1800, pp. 211-216.

Re John Barker (p. 214)—

"John Barker Esq., H.M.'s present proconsul at Aleppo, whose zeal and ability in the performance of his official duties are really worthy of the highest praise." He was the first to succeed in deterring the *tatars* in his employ from taking charge of merchandise, when they were carrying British Government dispatches to Constantinople.

Page 254. RECOMMENDATIONS (REPORT) OF HARFORD JONES:

I.O. (H.S.), Misc., 470, *op. cit.* pp. 199-206.

Pages 254-255. INAUGURATION OF THE OVERLAND DESERT MAIL:

I.O. (H.S.), Misc., 470, pp. 217, 218.

Minutes of the Council on the dispatch of packets overland. No. 9 official.

From the Governor of Bombay, 18th Feb. 1800.

From the Governor of Bombay, 12th March 1800.

Also: *The Gazetteer of the Persian Gulf*, i, p. 2439.

Pages 255–257. THE BRITISH DROMEDARY POST, 1800–1862:

Chesney (1868), pp. 4, 5, 21, 148, 330, 331, 354 and 358.

Individuals cited by Colonel Chesney who were instrumental in the reorganizing of the overland mail route—after 1833: Consul-General Farren, Mr Peacock ("late principal Examiner of the India House"), and Mr Cabell, of the India Board.

The Gazetteer of the Persian Gulf, i, pp. 226, 227, 1837, 2439, 2440, 2462.

Professor Crawford of the American University of Beyrout.

Page 257.   INDEPENDENT STATUS OF THE SYRIAN DESERT P.O., AND THE INTERRUPTION OF COMMUNICATION BETWEEN INDIA AND BASRA, 1844–62:

The Gazetteer of the Persian Gulf, i, p. 2440.

Pages 257–258. THE BRITISH DROMEDARY POST FROM 1862–1886:

The Gazetteer of the Persian Gulf, i, pp. 226, 227, 2445, 2462.

Thielmann (1875), ii, p. 162.

Pages 258–259. THE *TATAR* POST TO 1914:

The Gazetteer of the Persian Gulf, i, pp. 2462, 2463.

Bell (1911), pp. 118, 131.

Bell (1927), i, pp. 266, 267.

Professor Crawford, *op. cit.*

Page 259.   The references for all post-War, trans-desert postal services are given in Chapter IX, parts 3 and 4.

CHAPTER IX

Part 1

Pages 261–262. THE ORGANIZING OF THE EUPHRATES EXPEDITION:

Chesney, General F. R., *Narrative of the Euphrates Expedition* (1868), pp. 148, 149; and lists of officers and men, App. 12, pp. 542–558; and pp. 220–222.

Bulletin de la Société de Géographie, vii (1837), pp. 120 and 391–393. Letters of M. Fontanier and of Honoré Vidal.

The Gazetteer of the Persian Gulf, i, p. 226.

Page 262. Mohammed Ali's (or Ibrahim Pasha's) Opposition to the Landing of the Expedition:
> Chesney (1868), pp. 199, 205, 451, 453 and 455.

Page 262. Transport of the Steamers to Port William:
> Chesney (1868), pp. 188-206; and Appendices VII-X, pp. 446-491, *i.e.* the Reports of Major-General J. B. Estcourt, Commander R. F. Cleveland, Captain E. P. Charlewood, and Captain James Fitzjames.

Page 262. The Slip-Ways at Port William:
> Chesney (1868), pp. 202, 203 and 469.

Page 262. Launching of the *Euphrates* and the Trip to Birejik:
> Chesney (1868), pp. 203, 222-223.

Page 262. Beginning of the Survey of the Euphrates River:
> Chesney (1868), pp. 200, 201 and 224-228.

Page 262. Work of the Euphrates Expedition:
> Chesney (1868), pp. 224-325 and pp. 352-354 for "summary of operations".

Page 262. Treaty with the Aneza: and Friendliness of the Arabs of the *Little Desert*:
> Chesney (1868), p. 240, App. V, pp. 432-438: Report of Captain H. B. Lynch; especially pp. 434 and 437.

Pages 262-263. Results of the Euphrates Expedition:
> Chesney (1868), pp. 354-360.
> *Gazetteer of the Persian Gulf*, i, p. 226.

Part 2

Pages 263-264. The Euphrates Valley Railway Project:
> *Gazetteer of the Persian Gulf*, i, pp. 227, 239.
> Andrew, W. P., *Memoir on the Euphrates Valley Route to India* (1857), pp. xvi, 6, 176-178 and 197.
> Andrew, W. P., *The Euphrates Valley Route to India* (1873), pp. 20, 31 and 62.

Page 264. Arguments for a Railway Short-cut to the East:
> Andrew, W. P., *Memoir* ... (1857), pp. vii, xi, xvi and 180.
> Cameron, V. L., *Our Future Highway* (1880), i, pp. 1-3; and ii, p. 337.

Pages 264-265. FIRST RAILWAY PROJECTS AFTER 1872:

> Dalrymple, G. E., *The Syrian Great Eastern Railway to India* (1878). *Passim.*
>
> Cameron, V. L. (1880), i, pp. 108, 112; ii, pp. 292, 301, 302 and 306.

Page 265. MESOPOTAMIAN RAILWAYS:

> Earle, E. M., *Turkey, the Great Powers and the Baghdad Railway* (1923). *Passim.*
>
> Wilson, Sir A. T., *Mesopotamia* (1931), i, pp. 33 and 34.
>
> *L'Illustration*, No. 4546 (19th April 1930).

Pages 265-266. PROPOSED *LITTLE DESERT* RAILWAYS:

> Thielmann (1875), ii, p. 175.
>
> *The Times*, London, 17th Sept. 1930.

Pages 266-267. PROPOSED *GREAT DESERT* RAILWAYS:

> Black, C. E. Drummond, Address, " A Railway from the Mediterranean to India", and debate reported in the *Proceedings of the Central Asian Society.*
>
> *Journal of the Royal Central Asian Society*, xviii-xxx (1908–1910).
>
> Butler, Capt. S. S., in the *Geographical Journal*, xxxiii, 5 (1909), p. 535.
>
> Cameron, V. L. (1880), ii, pp. 300, 301.
>
> Dalrymple, G. E. (1878), pp. 3, 6.

Pages 267-268. THE BEDUIN PROBLEM; ADVANTAGES AND DISADVANTAGES OF A *GREAT DESERT* RAILWAY ROUTE:

> Cameron, V. L. (1880), ii, pp. 292, 302, 337. (See also pp. 289-321 inclusive.)
>
> *The Iraq Report* (1931), p. 58.
>
> Conversation with Mr R. V. Vernon, of the Colonial Office (London).

Page 269. THE DAMASCUS-ANNA PROPOSED RAILWAY:

> Cameron, V. L. (1880), ii, pp. 292-293.
>
> N.B.—This was one of the ten railway schemes itemized in pp. 289-321 (*i.e.* Chapter XIV).

Pages 269-270. POST-WAR PROPOSED RAILWAYS AND SURVEYS:

> *The Times*, London, 17th Sept. 1930.
>
> *The Haifa-Baghdad Railway Survey*, 1932, unpublished.
>
> Mizrahi, T., *Le Commerce du Levant* (1932).

British Consulate at Beyrout, *Archives*, Reg. No. 2003, 2663, 17th Dec. 1931.

Conversation with Mr Francis A. Kettaneh.

Part 3

NOTE.—Much of the information in part 3 is based upon the writer's personal, first-hand knowledge of conditions in Syria and of the desert routes; and most of the detailed information was gleaned from conversations with Mr Norman Nairn and others who were associated, directly or indirectly, with the Nairn Eastern Transport Company.

Pages 270-271. FIRST THOUGHT OF THE *LITTLE DESERT* AS A MOTOR HIGHWAY:

The *Times of India*, 22nd March 1925.

Harford, in *The Nineteenth Century* (1918), p. 113.

Page 271. THE FIRST MOTOR CROSSING FROM SYRIA TO IRAK:

McCallum, Major D., article in the *Journal of the Central Asian Society*, xii (1925), pp. 44-49 and 53.

Modern Transport, 10th Dec. 1927.

The Sphere, 20th Oct. 1923, article by Dorothy Mackay.

The Motor, 14th Oct. 1924.

The Times, London, 31st May 1923.

The Baghdad Times, 11th May 1923.

Also: Conversations with Messrs F. A. Kettaneh and Edward Lovell.

Page 272. ORIGIN OF THE NAIRN TRANSPORT COMPANY:

Conversations with the Nairn Brothers.

The Marlborough Express (N.Z.), 24th Jan. 1925.

The Auckland Star, 3 Dec. 1929.

Page 272. EXTENSION OF THE NAIRN SERVICE TO IRAK, ACROSS THE DESERT:

McCallum (1925), *op. cit.* pp. 49 and 50.

The Times, London, 31st May 1923.

N.B.—Many newspaper accounts of the early "pioneer" activities of the Nairn Transport Co. are necessarily somewhat inaccurate.

Pages 272-274. THE OVERLAND DESERT ROUTE, AND THE NAIRN
TRACK,

> McCallum (1925), *op. cit.* pp. 51 and 52.
> Keeling, E. H., article in the *Geographical Journal*:
> lxiii, 2 (1924), pp. 152 and 153.
> *The Times*, London, 31st May 1923.
> *The Motor*, 14th Oct. 1924.
> Books of the Nairn Eastern Transport Company.

Page 274.　　THE IRAK MAIL CONTRACT:

> *The Baghdad Times*, 28th Aug. 1923.
> *The Sphere*, 20th Oct. 1923.
> Books of the Nairn Transport Company.

Pages 274-275. RELATIONS OF THE NAIRN TRANSPORT COMPANY WITH
THE BEDUIN:

> Information from Mr Norman Nairn.
> Also: McCallum (1925), *op. cit.* pp. 50 and 54.

Pages 275-276. SPECIAL REGULATIONS FOR THE DESERT CROSSING:

> McCallum (1925), *op. cit.* pp. 55-56.
> Keeling, E. H. (1924), *op. cit.* pp. 151 and 153.
> *The Times of Mesopotamia*, 6th Oct. 1923, "Mail
> Edition".
> *The Times of India*, 25th Feb. 1925.

Page 276.　　FRIENDLINESS OF THE SYRIAN GOVERNMENT TO THE
NAIRN TRANSPORT COMPANY:

> Information from Mr Norman Nairn.
> Also: McCallum (1925), *op. cit.* p. 50.

Page 276.　　Messageries Maritimes' Advertisement in *The Near
East*, 1st Nov. 1923.

> The London Office and Advertising Arrangements
> of the Nairn Transport Company.
> Books of the Company.
> *The Sphere*, 20th Oct. 1923.

Pages 276-277. PRESS COMMENTS ON THE ACHIEVEMENTS OF THE
NAIRN TRANSPORT COMPANY:

> *The Times*, London, 31st May and 15th Nov.
> 1923; 19th Aug. and 15th Nov. 1924.
> *The Times, Weekly Edition*, 29th Jan. 1925, article
> "On the Baghdad Mail".
> *The Near East*: 1st, 22nd, 29th Nov. 1923; 20th
> Nov., 13th March and 5th June 1924.
> *The Times of Baghdad*, 11th May 1923 and 14th
> Nov. 1923.

The Times of India, 25th Feb. 1925, article, "The
Desert Mail. Organization of the Nairn Company."

The Times of India, Illustrated Weekly, 22nd
March 1925, article, "The New Way Home:
Four Hundred Miles of Desert".

The Morning Post, London, 4th March 1924,
article ,"The Desert Mail".

The Egyptian Gazette, 26th Nov. 1924, article,
"London to Baghdad in Nine Days. The Syrian
Desert Route."

The Traveller's Gazette, Dec. 1923.

The English Review, Jan. 1925, pp. 96 and 97,
article by Squadron Leader A. G. N. Belfield,
"The Overland Mail to Baghdad".

McCallum (1925), *op. cit.* p. 54.

The Graphic, 30th Aug. and 29th Nov. 1924,
articles, "To India by Motor Car" and "The
New Carpet of Baghdad".

Pages 277-278. REORGANIZATION OF THE NAIRN TRANSPORT COMPANY
IN 1926:
Books of the Company.
Modern Transport, 10th Dec. 1927.

Pages 278-280. RE THE EASTERN TRANSPORT COMPANY:
Books of the Eastern Transport Company, Ltd.
Modern Transport, 10th Dec. 1927.
Conversations with Mr Francis A. Kettaneh.

Pages 280-281. AMALGAMATION OF THE NAIRN AND THE EASTERN
TRANSPORT COMPANIES:
Books of the Nairn Eastern Transport Company.
Modern Transport, 10th Dec. 1927.

Pages 281-282. RUTBA WELLS AND THE INAUGURATION OF THE SIX-
WHEELERS:
Books of the Nairn Eastern Transport Company.
General Motors Export Company (1925). Pamph-
let on *The Desert Mail*.
Modern Transport, 10th Dec. 1927.
The Motor, 17th July 1928.

Page 282. CHRISTENING CEREMONY OF THE FIRST SIX-WHEELER,
AND DESCRIPTION OF THE SIX-WHEELERS:
The Times of Baghdad, 27th May 1927 and 17th
Feb. 1928.

The Times, London, 3rd July 1926.
The Sphere, 6th Oct. 1928.

Pages 282–284. OPERATING STATISTICS AND TECHNICAL PROBLEMS
OF THE NAIRN EASTERN TRANSPORT COMPANY:
Books of the Company.
Conversations with Mr Norman Nairn.
Modern Transport, 10th Dec. 1927.

Page 284. THE MAIL CONTRACTS, 1929:
Books of the Nairn Eastern Transport Company.

Pages 284–286. PRESS COMMENTS DURING THE DRUZE REBELLION:
The Times, London, 28th and 31st August 1925;
5th, 10th and 14th Sept. 1925; 3rd May and 3rd
July 1926.
The Daily Mail, 28th Aug. 1925.
The Times of Baghdad, 29th May 1925.
Modern Transport, 10th Dec. 1927.
The Near East, 3rd Dec. 1925.
La Bourse égyptienne, 7th Jan. 1926, article, "Les
Conquistadores de la Route".

Pages 286–287. PRESS COMMENTS *RE* THE NAIRN SERVICE IN TIMES OF
PEACE:
The Times, London, 6th Feb. and 3rd May 1926;
13th Aug. 1928.
The Times, Weekly Edition, 29th Jan. 1925.
The Times of Baghdad, 8th Feb. 1926.
The Times of India, 25th Feb. 1925.
Also, McCallum (1925), *op. cit.* pp. 58–59.

Page 287. PROJECTED CHANGES OR IMPROVEMENTS IN THE NAIRN
SERVICE:
Mr Norman Nairn.
Mr Alan Fraser Grant.

Pages 287–288. PRESS COMMENTS ON THE ACHIEVEMENTS OF THE
NAIRNS:
The Times, London, 3rd May 1926.
Le National, Beyrout, 30th Aug. 1927.

Page 288. LA COMPAGNIE AUTO-ROUTIÈRE DU LEVANT:
Notes received from a Manager of the Company; and conversation with Mr F. A.
Kettaneh.

Pages 288–289. THE NEWEST DESERT MOTOR ROUTE (*i.e.* THE EASTERN
PILGRIM ROUTE):
Information from Mr Francis A. Kettaneh.
Also: *The Times*, London, 31st Dec. 1934.
The Observer, London, 13th Jan. 1935.

Part 4

Pages 289–290. THE ROYAL AIR FORCE DESERT AIR MAIL:
The Aeroplane, 10th May 1933, article, "The Years
Between", by C. M. McAlery, pp. 829 and 832.
Ephemerides (1919–30).
The Iraq Report (1931), pp. 143 and 147.
The Near East, 6th Sept. 1923.

Pages 290–292. IMPERIAL AIRWAYS:
Hill, Roderic, *The Baghdad Air Mail* (1929). *Passim.*
Conversations with Mr Brenard and officials and
pilots of Imperial Airways, Ltd.
Also: *The Times*, London, 5th, 28th and 30th March,
1st, 5th and 15th April, 1st May, 8th July, 9th,
17th and 30th Sept., 28th Oct., and 14th Nov.
1929. 14th Jan., 18th Feb., 18th June and 30th
Sept. 1930. 25th March and 1st Sept. 1931.

Page 292.   THE JUNKERS TEHERAN SERVICE:
The Times, London, 19th April and 16th Sept.
1929. Also 1st Jan. 1930.

Page 292.   AIR-ORIENT:
Information as to organization and schedules from
the Beyrout Office of *La Compagnie Air-Orient.*
Also: *The Times*, London, 20th, 22nd, 26th and 28th
Feb., 16th March and 19th June 1929. 3rd April
1930. 17th and 29th Jan., 9th and 26th June 1931.
Record flights: *The Times*, London, 14th Oct. and
8th Dec. 1930.

Pages 292–293. THE ROYAL DUTCH AIR SERVICE:
The Times, London, 21st Feb. and 13th Oct. 1931.

Page 293.   (A) ROYAL AIR FORCE PATROLS AND SURVEYS:
Syria, x (1929), pp. 144-163.
The Times, London, 4th July 1929.

(B) AERIAL SURVEYS OF THE FRENCH ARMY AIR FORCE:
Poidebard (1934), Author's Introduction.
Antiquity, Dec. 1934, pp. 373-374.

Part 5

Pages 294-295. PIPE LINES OF THE IRAQ PETROLEUM COMPANY:
    Information from officials of the Iraq Petroleum
    Company.
        Also: *The Times*, London, 15th and 22nd Jan. 1935.
        The Observer, London, 13th and 20th Jan. 1935.
Page 295.   POSSIBLE MOTOR TRACK ACROSS THE *GREAT DESERT*:
    Information from Mr Francis A. Kettaneh.

INDEX